BRITISH AND AMERICAN LETTER MANUALS, 1680–1810

BRITISH AND AMERICAN LETTER MANUALS, 1680–1810

Volume 3:
Complete Letter-Writers, 1740–1795

EDITED BY
Eve Tavor Bannet

Routledge
Taylor & Francis Group

LONDON AND NEW YORK

First published 2008 by Pickering & Chatto (Publishers) Limited

2 Park Square, Milton Park, Abingdon, Oxon OX14 4RN
711 Third Avenue, New York, NY 10017, USA

Routledge is an imprint of the Taylor & Francis Group, an informa business

First issued in paperback 2017

BRITISH LIBRARY CATALOGUING IN PUBLICATION DATA
British and American letter manuals, 1680–1810
1. Letter writing – Early works to 1800
I. Bannet, Eve Tavor, 1947–
808.6'0941'09033

ISBN-13: 978-1-85196-918-0 (set)
ISBN-13: 978-1-1387-5066-1 (hbk)
ISBN-13: 978-1-138-11162-2 (pbk)

Typeset by Pickering & Chatto (Publishers) Limited

CONTENTS

Introduction   vii

On Epistolary Style
    A Gentleman of Fortune, *The New Art of Letter Writing, Divided into
    Two Parts*, 2nd edn (1762)   1
Some London Styles   15
    Samuel Richardson, *Letters Written to and for Particular Friends, on
    the Most Important Occasions* (1741)   19
    Charles Hallifax, *Familiar Letters on Various Subjects of Business and
    Amusement* (1755)   23
    George Fisher, *The Instructor: Or, Young Man's Best Companion* (1767) 42
Manuals Published in London, Edinburgh, Boston, New York, Philadelphia,
    Hartford and Salem
    [Anon.], *The Complete Letter-Writer; or Polite English Secretary*. 12th
    edn (1768)   47
Manuals Published in Glasgow, New York and New Haven   175
    H. W. Dilworth, *The Complete Letter Writer; or Young Secretary's
    Instructor* (1783)   177
    H. W. Dilworth, *The Complete Letter Writer, or Young Secretary's
    Instructor* (1793)   273
Manuals Published in Aberdeen and London
    David Fordyce, *The New and Complete British Letter-Writer; or Young
    Secretary's Instructor in Polite Modern Letter-Writing* [1790]   295
Manuals Published in Philadelphia
    [Anon.], *The American Letter-Writer: Containing a Variety of Letters
    on the Most Common Occasions in Life* (1793)   353

Editorial Notes   463

INTRODUCTION

Since the proper contents of letter classes throughout the century remained stable, and the polite repeated and varied the same commonplaces on the same occasions, it was style which primarily distinguished one letter and one letter-writer from another. The style made the man. Style was as important in a letter as regional and class accents have been in speech, and in many of the same ways. Style showed whether the writer was a gentleman, an upstart or a provincial, whether he or she was polite, educated, or *à la mode,* affected or old fashioned, and just how skilled a letter writer he or she was. One could easily write the right things in the wrong manner. Not surprisingly therefore, at mid-century, volumes of letters designed exclusively 'for the Improvement of Style' began to proliferate. More general manuals also distinguished themselves from one another by their style, touting their letter collections as stylistically more correct and up to date than other letter manuals on the market, and offering themselves as authoritative guides to style.

As the first entry below explains, there were two dimensions of epistolary style. The first was the style proper to each class of letter. This depended on the letter's contents, on the relative rank and status of writer and addressee, and on the degree of familiarity between them: 'We are obliged to suit our Expressions to the Nature of the Subject and the Rank of Persons'. For instance, a letter of condolence could not be written in a witty or joking style; it must use expressions borrowed from the heart rather than the head and deploy the grave and serious style to give religious or philosophical consolation. The letter of condolence must also be written differently – with more deference, in more elevated language, with fewer *sententiae* – to a superior than to an equal or inferior. Style in these regards was absolutely conventional.

The second dimension of epistolary style bears on what features were taken to constitute that 'beautiful Simplicity' and 'natural' conversational style which had always been viewed as proper to letters. By mid-century, long exordiums, bombastic complemental figures, fables, histories, and proverbs, once very popular features of letters, were regarded as outdated. According to the Gentleman of Fortune in the first extract below (pp. 1–13), the polite style of the day in

1762 was perspicuous and clear, 'close in reasoning', 'natural' in its connections and transitions, not too familiar even to equals, and restrained in its flattery and deference to superiors. To achieve this effect, the words must flow smoothly in such a manner as to please the ear; the length and cadences of sentences ('periods') must be suitably diversified to add variety; copiousness must be avoided, and letters must be short. Style in this regard was equally conventional, but differed according to the tastes of different times and places. As the Gentleman of Fortune points out, what is perceived as natural in style changes over time, and we should therefore 'consult the Taste of our Age and Nation' in determining the proper style in which to write.

In fact, in the world of manuals and of letter collections, there were several styles about. Four of these are illustrated in the second entry below. These various styles circulated widely because during the second half of the eighteenth century, the *Complete Letter-Writers* which dominated the English or Scottish markets and which were regularly culled in America, were compilations. These offered a variety of styles for the reader to choose from. They also corrected at least some of the letters they had culled from elsewhere to suit modern tastes by eliminating long periodic sentences and laboured turns of phrase, simplifying prose, and conveying meaning more clearly and concisely. This could also be described as switching down to approximate more closely what had been known (and practised) as 'the simple style'.

Just as eighteenth-century *Academies of Complement* increasingly took account of the *Secretary* phenomenon, and *Secretaries* either rewrote letters culled from *Academies* or appropriated elements of their complemental style, so the *Complete Letter-Writers* which dominated the second half of the eighteenth century reacted dynamically to both. Early editions of *The Complete Letter-Writer; or Polite English Secretary* (1755), for instance, contained a section of complemental letters, which was only dropped from the manual in 1759. *Letter-Writers* generally dealt with *Secretaries* by swallowing them up. They confined the household, family, business and beyond-the-sea letters that *Secretaries* typically offered to one or two sections within their collections, and expanded the scope of letter manuals to include other things – letters of courtship and marriage, moral and philosophical letters, aristocratic letters, letters of news or travel, and/ or letters 'for the improvement of style'. The latter were usually authentic letters by eminent people or distinguished writers. Not all *Letter-Writers* included all of the above, but at a minimum they did include letters of courtship and marriage to show that they had taken over and modernized both the household-family functions of *Secretaries* and the wooing functions of *Academies*.

Letter-Writers also began to conceive of the letter manual as 'a portable library', and to decorate their title pages with a list of the various moral, practical, philosophical or worldly subjects addressed by the letters within. Some of these lists became quite elaborate and detailed.

Letter-Writers, in other words, sought to be more 'complete' than *Secretaries*, both by extending the range of subjects and occasions addressed in their letter collections, and by seeking to appeal to an even wider range of buyers. As the *Complete Letter-Writer; or Polite English Secretary* put it in its Preface to the Reader: 'It is from this great Variety of Examples for *Stile* and *Manner* ... that we presume to call this Performance by the Name of *The Complete Letter-Writer*; such a Number of Letters being inserted as to answer the Purpose of almost every Individual, from the Boy at School to the Secretary of State'. The compiler also emphasized that the reader 'will here meet with many Epistles of the lower Class' because 'these could not be omitted without deviating from the grand Point in View, namely, *General Utility*'.[1]

Notes:

1. [Anon.], *The Complete Letter-Writer, or Polite English Secretary* (London: Printed for S. Crowder and H. Woodgate, 1755), preface.

A Gentleman of Fortune, *The New Art of Letter Writing, Divided into Two Parts. The First, Containing Rules and Directions for Writing Letters on All Sorts of Subjects ... The Second, a Collection of Letters on the Most Interesting Occasions of Life*, 2nd edn (London: T. Osbourne, 1762), pp. 1–11. Bodleian Library, Oxford University, shelfmark Vet. A5 e.5869.

The New Art of Letter Writing was designed, its title page claimed, to inculcate 'the true Style and Manner of polite Epistolary intercourse'. Despite the manual's title (*The New Art*), the Introduction repeats long-standing commonplaces about epistolography – but with added urgency, since at mid-century everyone agreed that 'the Necessities of Life oblige almost all Manner of Persons to have Recourse to an Epistolary Correspondence', including 'the Ignorant' (below, p. 3). Among these commonplaces is the Ciceronian identification of letters with speech, and of correspondence with conversation. This identification had become problematical for the eighteenth century, since it was widely recognized that there were also significant differences between writing and speaking, especially when a person's ordinary speech was less than polite or correct. The author indicates several of these differences. For instance, he rewords Locke's point in *Thoughts on Education* that: 'No Gentleman can avoid shewing himself in this Kind of Writing ... [A man's letters] lay him open to severer Examination of his Breeding, Sense and Abilities than Oral discourse, whose transient Faults, dying for the most part with the Sound that gives them Life, and so not subject to strict Review more easily escape Observation and Censure'.[1] The author also points out that letter-writing is an art, with conventions borrowed from classical orations, which have to be learned. He therefore struggles to reconcile the traditional injunction that 'the first rule is to write as we speak', with injunctions for following the elaborate rules of the epistolary art.

This manual describes itself as a second edition which is entirely different from the first, which does not appear to have survived. There was also a third edition which reproduces the second and appeared the following year.

Notes:

1   John Locke, *Some Thoughts Concerning Education*, ed. John W. and Jean S. Yolton (Oxford: Clarendon, 1989), p. 243 (no. 189).

THE
A R T
OF
LETTER-WRITING.

PART I.

CHAP. I.
Of the Neceſſity *of writing* LETTERS, *and of the* Style *they ought to be written in.*

Othing is ſo common as to write Letters : But it is not a common Thing to indite them well. The Neceſſities of Life oblige almoſt all Manner of Perſons to have Recourſe to an Epiſtolary Correſpondence : For the Ignorant as well as the Learned have often an Occaſion to correſpond by Letter with their abſent Friends. To ſucceed in this Kind of Compoſition is not ſo eaſy as generally
B　　　　　　　　thought.

The Art of Letter-Writing.

thought. To learn it, good Precepts for pointing out an accurate Method, and the best Examples for imitation, are equally requisite.'

Nothing, in regard to the Commerce of Life, is more necessary than a Work of this Sort. We must, however, except the Arts and Graces of Conversation; because we have greater and more frequent Occasions for Speaking than Writing. Entertaining one another constantly is a Kind of Study, as by it we are insensibly accustomed to express ourselves with Ease and Propriety; whereas, writing but rarely and with some Reluctance, most People are embarrassed when obliged to take up their Pen: And thus it happens that the proper Style for Letter-writing is not attained without considerable Difficulty. Of this, Experience daily convinces us. Out of a hundred Persons that speak well, scarce ten will be found that write in the same Degree of Perfection, though it should seem nothing more was wanting than to commit to Paper what we have a Mind to express.

Let none flatter themselves; much more Exactness is required for Writing than Speaking. We ought to consider, that the Eyes are more faithful than the Ears. What we see on Paper, remains subject to our Criticism; and the most Part of the Things said to us, fly off from our Reflexions. Add to this, that the Discourse we hear, is supported by Succours, which, whatever may be presented us to read, is deficient in. A passionate Tone of Voice makes a deep Impression, and the Air that accompanies Words, often steals to the Heart.

It has been observed in all Times, that the most famous Orators were never fond of publishing their Speeches, being, with good Reason, persuaded that but half the Orator is found in writing. *Demosthenes,* named by Excellence 'The *Eloquent,*' would never let any of his Discourses appear till a good While after they were pronounced.

A Speech

The Art of Letter-Writing. 3

A Speech is in some Measure indebted, for the agreeable Emotions it produces, to the Advantages of Pronunciation, such as the Sweetness and Clearness of the Voice, accompanied with a due Emphasis, or the good Presence of him that speaks; but a Piece of Writing can please only by essential Graces: So that we cannot be too exact in revising our Letters, in order to send them without Fear of regretting what we have done: For we are well assured by the Masters of the Art, that they must be incorrect or ill polished, when they come out of our Hands immediately; because Faults are both less excusable, and appear greater in them, than in Works of some length: The only Means therefore for avoiding these Inconveniencies, is not to write with Precipitation; but to order our Thoughts and Words in such regular Justness and Perspicuity, as that the one may not seem Enigmatical, nor the other want an Interpreter.

We have several Books of Letters abounding with Instructions for writing them, and yet we write not the better. The little Benefit we receive from all these Directions, is an incontestable Proof, that, instead of helping us to write a Letter well, the far greater Part of them only serve to cramp the Genius and detain the flow of Thought in a Circle of Confusion. The surest Rule is to write as we speak. Think well, speak well, and you will write well. Nature, it is said, forms Poets, and Art Orators. If this same Nature has not, as it were, laboured to make us good Writers, by granting us happy Dispositions, we shall meet with great Difficulty in becoming Masters of the Epistolary Style. When it is our Lot not to be born with this rich Talent, we must read much, and transcribe often such Collections of Letters as are most in Request for their Beauty of Thought and Elegance of Diction: And thus we shall form ourselves by Degrees, and Art and Study will supply the Defects of Nature.

B 2 Three

Three Things, in my Opinion, need only be obferved in Letters. 1. To take care not to be haughty
in writing to Supèriors. 2. Not to demean yourfelf
in addreffing an Inferior. 3. To hold an equal Rank
with Equals. Afterwards, having reflected a Moment
on the Subject of your Letter, to enter immediately
upon it without any long Preamble, as formerly, and
withal to fancy that you are fpeaking to the Perfon
you write to.

Let nothing be affected in your Letters, nor any
Thing foreign to what you intend to treat of.
Write as you fpeak; that is, without Art, without
Study, and without making a Shew of your Wit.
Guard againft a Rock, which Pedants and the Unju-
dicious generally fplit upon : This is, by either feek-
ing after great and founding Words, or a Swell of
pompous Thought, and both very often on frivolous
Occafions. Such a Style and Manner will never pafs
for natural; at léaft, they will meet with the Ap-
probation of none but thofe who have fet afide the
Decorum of common Senfe. It is true, the Method
of writing as we fpeak, which is undoubtedly the
better, becaufe more natural, was not formerly in
Vogue; but now, few chufe to put their Mind on the
Rack to difcover the falfe Luftre of a Thought: We
are pleafed to fee every Thing difplayed in natural
Colours; and, when thefe Colours neither ftrike the
Eye nor Mind, we are difgufted at the Difficulties the
Writer puts us to, as if he defigned not to be un-
derftood.

If a Stranger was to write from the Extremities of
the Earth, we fhould judge whether he was a Perfon
of Genius, Knowledge, and Politenefs, by obferving
in his Letters an eafy, fimple, and natural Turn, and
at the fame Time an Elegance and Delicacy of Expreffion, fo much the more charming, as proceeding
from Nature alone. If, on the contrary, his Thoughts
are confufed; if his Phrafes are unnatural and deftitute

tute of that beautiful Simplicity, the diſtinguiſhing Characteriſtic of the Epiſtolary Style; we may, with good Reaſon, conclude, that he is a Man of ſcanty Knowledge and of a very ill Taſte.

But, if every Thing ought to appear natural in a Letter, and if Art ought to be abſolutely concealed in it, let not, however, a familiar Eaſe be confounded with a graceleſs Simplicity. Let it be remembered, that a Character of Politeneſs ſhould always diſtinguiſh the Letters of well-bred Perſons. And, as all Sorts of Subjects are treated of in Letters, there is no confining ourſelves to one particular Style. We are obliged to ſuit our Expreſſions to the Nature of Subjects and the Rank of Perſons. We muſt riſe nobly, when we write to Perſons of great Conſideration by their Condition of Life; and, on the other Hand, deſcend to more familiar Ways of Speaking, when we communicate our Thoughts and Opinions to intimate Friends.

We ſhould uſe all the good Senſe we are capable of, in giving an Account of an important Negociation; and nothing but Terms of Tenderneſs in teſtifying to Parents the Share we bear in their Affliction or Joy. Here, more Sentiments than Thoughts are required; the Mind is to ſpeak leſs than the Heart. If our Imagination ſports in wanton Airs amidſt Compliments of Conſolation, it will be believed that we are not in the leaſt affected, and that we are leſs attentive to the Intereſts of others, than our own Reputation. And indeed, it is not the way to merit Applauſe, to be ſo ſtudious of being witty on ſuch Occaſions. Humour and Pleaſantry are better reſerved for facetious Topics. Judgment requires this Variety: It would have us diverſify our Style according to the Nature of the Subjects to be treated of. There is not a ſurer Rule than to be directed by ſo good a Guide: It leads us where we ought to go.

It is not difficult to ſee what Sort of Style may ſuit

B 3　　　　　　　　　　　　beſt.

6   *The Art of Letter-Writing.*

best a Letter; but I know not whether it be very eafy
to fupport the Character that has been made Choice
of. Our moft famous Authors are not fo exact in
this Particular, as not to be fometimes wanting to it.
Let Uniformity therefore be maintained : Without it,
we fhall never attain to the Good and the True in
Writing.

To what has been already hinted, concerning the
Difagreeablenefs of the bombaftic Style, it will not be
amifs to add, that no figurative Thoughts and Expreffions, which are either too ftrong or too brilliant,
fhould be ufed in Letter-writing, efpecially if the
Subject-matter could recommend itfelf fufficiently by
an eafy and familiar Air. It is true, that in a well-
grounded Charge againft a Perfon, and which is made
only on preffing Occafions, it may be allowable to
ufe a bold and even vehement Manner of Speaking.
The fureft Maxim is to be judicious and referved in
the ufe of Figures. A Style flags, when intirely deftitute of them; and, on the contrary, when they
croud in upon one another, it degenerates into Fuf-
tian.

Let us not forget to examine exactly the Matter we
are to treat of: It may have different Faces, it may
appear in different Lights ; all fhould be carefully in-
fpected, and that which fuits beft our Defign muft
be chiefly attended to.

Let us avoid Comparifons in Writing; fuch Beauties prefent a Sort of a too vulgar Air: I know not
even whether they can be efteemed Beauties. At
leaft, let it be an inviolable Law to us, to confult the
Tafte of our Age and Nation. Polite Perfons will
fcarce ever now infert in their Letters, Fables, Hiftory, Proverbs or Sentences ; fo that we may fafely
renounce thefe pretended Ornaments, which were
formerly fo ftudioufly fought after. Add to this, the
Affectation fo common to fine Wits, of writing frequently without Neceffity and without Matter : In
fuch,

The Art of Letter-Writing.   **9**

fuch Cafe we often defert Reafon and Truth to devote ourfelves to our Ideas, and to follow Conjectures: The Sallies of Imagination may, indeed, feem to amufe us; but it is not worth our While to lay ourfelves under fuch continual perplexing Reftraints for the fake of fhining agreeably for nothing.

Though, generally fpeaking, all Letters ought to be fhort, as thofe of Bufinefs, Society, and mere Compliment; together with thofe written to Perfons, who by their Employment are little at Leifure; yet, the Fear of their being long, fhould not contract the Style, fo as to make it obfcure, or that Circumftances fhould be omitted, which are effential to our Subject. If we require an Eclairciffement, or give an Account of an Affair of Moment, muft we treat this Matter as that of a Compliment, inftead of fhewing it with all the Particulars that may contribute to a fuller Inftruction? We are not prohibited to enlarge on thefe Occafions, provided we fall not into Repetitions. However, a Letter of this Sort fhould not, by its Length, fwell into the Form and Dimenfions of a Differtation or Treatife.

Cuftom teaches us, that the Style ufed in a literary Commerce ought to be always equal; deftitute of fublime Figures; clofe in Reafoning; natural in the Chain and Connexion of Matter; diverfified in the Conftruction and Extent of Periods; exact in Order; and efpecially noble without Pride, and without being abrupt or impetuous: It feems alfo that each Period ought to contain a particular Thought; becaufe a Difcourfe, not aided by the Voice or Prefence, cannot be fupported without continual Strokes of Genius, in which, notwithftanding, all pointed Wit fhould be carefully guarded againft.

It were ftill to be wifhed, that, in Letters of Refpect, the Submiffions made were kept within certain Bounds, exceffive Flattery and fervile Complaifance being banifhed from our Thoughts: When we grovel fo

     bafely,

bafely, far from acquiring the Efteem, we draw upon ourfelves the Contempt, of thofe we pretend to in-gratiate ourfelves with. The oppofite Extreme, of treating too familiarly thofe above us, muft be equally avoided. In point of Praife, how fhall we deem agree-able and furprizing an Eulogium made without Deli-cacy, and quite fulfome? Praife, 'tis true, is a com-mon Ingredient in Writing and Speaking; but the Queftion is, how to make a decent Offering of that Kind of Incenfe. Few follow the Counfel of *Horace*, who would have us exprefs common Things and Sub-jects as if they were not. This Manner, which is not common, is a Turn that makes what we fay our own, and heightens it with the Graces of Novelty, though a Thoufand others have faid the fame before us.

In the Placing of Words we muft confult the Ear, and judge whether its Satisfaction be compleat. How-ever, the Care of pleafing the Ear fhould be no Bar to the Gratifications of the Mind. It is not enough that Words fhould be noble according to the Subject, or flow fmoothly in harmonic Numbers; rather let us examine if they give a perfect Idea of the Things we defign to exprefs. Let us alfo confider, that, writ-ing only with a View of making ourfelves underftood, none but fuch Terms as are moft in Ufe ought to be made Choice of: The antiquated may be well fet afide, and thofe newly coined adopted with Precau-tion. In like Manner, it will not be amifs to be as referved as poffible in the Ufe of Epithets and Ad-verbs. 'Tis certain, a Style not embarraffed with them will appear more agreeable.

The Affectation of having Periods of the fame Length is another Fault: Their Extent and Cadence ought therefore to be diverfified in as great a Degree as can be, avoiding, at the fame Time, all Rnimes and Confonance.

Our Style need not be too copious, unlefs we are willing it fhould firft fatigue, and afterwards become

insup-

infupportable: Notwithftanding, let it not be fo clofe as to fall into Obfcurity. Concifenefs is undoubtedly one of the greateft Beauties of Difcourfe ; but it borders fo nearly upon Obfcurity, that it is very difficult, in following the one, not to fall into the other ; and it will be always more advifable to pay a due Attention to Perfpicuity, the Chief of all Perfections in Writing, without which, all others muft be ufelefs : In fhort, we write and fpeak only to be underftood.

C H A P. II.

What a Letter *is ; and of the Parts of a* Letter.

WHAT we call commonly 'Letter,' the *Romans* called ' Epiftle :' They borrowed this Word from the *Greek*, to exprefs a Thing which was to be fent ; fo that Epiftle anfwers pretty exactly to ' Miffive,' which our Anceftors derived from the *Latin* Word, and which fome ufe to this Day. In reftraining the Signification, we fpecify, by Epiftles, the Letters we have from the Ancients, whether the Authors of them were prophane, or that we find them in the *New Teftament* and elfewhere : Thus we always fay, ' The Epiftles of *Cicero*, and of *Pliny* ; the Epiftles of St. *Paul*, and of St. *Jerom*.' The Dedications that appear at the Head of Books, have likewife retained the Name of Epiftles, as well as thofe written in Verfe for Praifing fome illuftrious Perfon, or Satyrizing the Vices of the Age. To give, in fine, an exact Definition of a Letter, it may be faid, ' That it is a Piece of Writing which we fend to an abfent Perfon, to let him know what we would fay, if we were in a Condition to fpeak to him.' To make this Piece of Writing agreeable, clear, and intelligible, we

B 5   muft

muſt baniſh from it all Common Places; all unneceſſary and ſuperfluous Ways of Speaking; all Equivo-
cations; and, laſtly, all falſe Thoughts.

The greater Part of Letters form a Kind of Converſation among thoſe who cannot entertain one another in a different Manner: They ought therefore to
retain in their Expreſſion that eaſy and natural Air
we obſerve in Dialogues. The Ancients imitated in
their Epiſtles the Manner Friends are accuſtomed to
ſpeak to each other in: They began by a Kind of
Compliment in regard to Health, as it is uſual with
Perſons accoſting one another. " If you are in good
Health, ſaid they, it will be a ſenſible Pleaſure to
me; for my Part, I am in very good Health." They
concluded by a " Farewell," as is cuſtomary with Perſons that ſeparate and take Leave. The Middle of
the Epiſtle contained the Subject, and the Reaſons
that might ſupport it. We obſerve nearly in our Letters a like Method: We have firſt Recourſe to Civilities, whether we are obliged to thank the Perſon we
write to, or to excuſe ourſelves; or that we have
ſome Favour to aſk, or ſome Affair to recommend to
him. Theſe firſt Civilities may be deemed what is
called the Exordium in an Harangue: They ſerve to
inſinuate us into his Mind, and to diſpoſe him to
receive favourably what we have to ſay to him. When
we enter upon our Matter, we make appear to him,
according to the Difference of Subjects, either the
Juſtice of our Pretenſions, or the Share we take in
whatever affects him. It is afterwards cuſtomary to
finiſh by a Proteſtation of Service.

But why do we not find, in moſt Letters, the four
Parts which Maſters of Eloquence make in ſome Meaſure eſſential to the Compoſition of Harangues?
We have taken Notice of an Exordium; and it will
be eaſy to comprehend that the Expoſition of the Subject ſerves as a Narration, and that the Reaſons for
juſtifying our Requeſt, holds the Place of a Proof or
Confirma-

The Art of Letter-Writing.   11

Confirmation. If we conclude by Proteſtations of a perfect Submiſſion, or eternal Gratitude, it is in order to touch the Heart, and to perſuade. Such is the Intent of the Peroration of a Diſcourſe, wherein the moſt vehement Figures are uſed for gaining a powerful Aſcendant over the Minds of the Auditory.

Now, tho' this Order may be obſerved, yet it will be better to diſregard, than to endeavour to make it appear. Nothing muſt ſhew Reſtraint or Affectation in a Letter ; every Particular in it ought to breathe the Liberty that reigns in common Converſation. *Cicero*, the moſt accurate Perſon we find in this Kind of Writing, ſeems often at a Loſs how to proceed : He heſitates, as it were, to ſeek after more proper Terms : He checks himſelf, and intermingles Things which ſeem as if they ſhould have been ſeparate : It is eaſily perceived that he took but little Care or Pains in writing them, and perhaps ſometimes deſignedly, according to what he ſays himſelf to his Friend *Atticus*, " Epiſtolas debere interdum hallucinari," ' Letters ſhould ſometimes commit Blunders.'

SOME LONDON STYLES

Samuel Richardson, *Letters Written to and for Particular Friends, on the Most Important Occasions* (London: C. Rivington, J. Osborn and J. Leake, 1741), pp. 39–42. Glasgow University Library, shelfmark gow Sp Coll Bk2-k.3.

Charles Hallifax, *Familiar Letters on Various Subjects of Business and Amusement: Written in a Natural, Easy Manner; And Publish'd, Principally, for the Service of the Younger Part of Both Sexes* (London: R. Baldwin. 1755), pp. 15–25, 97–104. Cambridge University Library, shelfmark 7240.d.54.

George Fisher, *The Instructor: Or, Young Man's Best Companion. Containing Spelling, Reading, Writing, and Arithmetic, in an Easier Way than Any yet Published*, 19th edn (London: H. Woodfall, J. Fuller, W. Strahan, J. Rivington, R. Baldwin et al, 1767), pp. 46–50. Robinson Library, Newcastle University, shelfmark Bradshaw 374.1 FIS.

The following extracts are offered as examples of different styles prevalent at mid-century. Letters were frequently culled from Samuel Richardson's *Letters Written to and for Particular Friends, on the Most Important Occasions* (1741) and from Charles Hallifax's *Familiar Letters on Various Subjects of Business and Amusement* (1754) by a variety of other, far more popular regional and transatlantic manuals. Their styles would therefore be widely familiar across the Atlantic world. Fisher's *Instructor* was reprinted innumerable times on both sides of the Atlantic in different English, Scottish and American editions; its letter writing style would therefore be widely familiar too. Letters were also frequently culled from Eliza Haywood's *Epistles for the Ladies* (London: T. Gardner, 1749), which is available from Pickering & Chatto and therefore not reproduced here.

Samuel Richardson (bap. 1689–1761) was the author of several hugely popular epistolary novels: *Pamela* (1740), *Clarissa* (1747–8) and *Sir Charles Grandison* (1753–4). He was also one of several well known eighteenth-century writers who composed letter manuals. His *Letters Written to and for Particular Friends* are now often known as *Familiar Letters*, after the title given to them by their modern editor.

Like all letter manuals, Richardson's *Letters Written to and from Particular Friends* was designed to provide 'Rules to Think and Act by, as well as Forms to Write after';[1] in other words, this was both a conduct book and a set of letter-writing models. Richardson's Preface concentrates on the duties and principles of conduct he hopes to inculcate, perhaps assuming that these might be less obvious to contemporaries than the manual's letter-writing function. Richardson's letter-writer went through five London editions between 1741 and 1752, a respectable but not stunning achievement. Many of Richardson's letters did, however, live on in other manuals. Later manuals usually drew upon Richardson for models of writing and conduct for people in the lower and lower-middle ranks; they also culled some of the letters of advice in which his collection abounds.

Charles Hallifax's *Familiar Letters* announces in its introduction that it is designed 'chiefly to form the Style'; but also to 'form the judgement' by conveying knowledge of the world ('what you may depend upon from your Equals, and what you are to expect from your Superiors; or rather, what you are not to expect from them').[2] Nothing is known about Hallifax, and this too may have been a pseudonym. But appropriately for a name borrowed from earls, Hallifax's manual was overall more upmarket than Richardson's, offering many 'Letters written to the greatest Person, and from those in different Stations' as well as many 'Letters of Politeness and Ceremony' situated primarily among the gentry. The style of Hallifax's letters to superiors is exemplified in the second extract from this manual (below, pp. 34–41). However, the letters most frequently culled from Hallifax, besides some of his letters of advice, were letters between elder and younger brothers, and letters between parents and children written in the sentimental style (as in the first extract, below, pp. 23–33). This manual is described in its Introduction as a compilation of manuscript letters by different hands, to which the compiler had added letters of his own. Though describing the letters as 'Written in a Natural Easy Manner' on its title page, it therefore contained different styles. There were five London editions of Hallifax's manual between sometime before 1754 (described as the second edition) and 1765, some of which spell his name with a single L.

George Fisher's *The Instructor: Or Young Man's Best Companion* was a *vade mecum*. Besides instruction on grammar, spelling, making ink, and letter writing, it contained sections on arithmetic ('both vulgar and decimal'), on double-entry book-keeping, geography, astronomy and gardening, together with forms of bills of lading, invoices, receipts and bills of exchange and all the standard legal forms. *The Instructor* was emphatically designed 'to form the young Man's Mind for Business', (though it did have instructions for women on how to make pickles and wine) *The Instructor* offered relatively few model letters, but began its collection with a mixed letter 'of business and love'. This was an extremely common type of letter at a time when people often preferred to do business (especially transatlantic business) with family, friends and acquaintance, and it suggests that the models from different letter classes which follow could also be combined. The style of Fisher's letters is simpler, tauter and closer to ordinary conversation than Richardson's or Hallifax's, and even non-business letters are short and functional, and get straight to the point.

Fisher's *Instructor* was a huge transatlantic best-seller. There were twenty-eight London editions between *c.* 1735 and 1798, plus multiple London printings outside this series which describe themselves as 'a new edition' or 'for the booksellers'. Multiple editions were also printed in Edinburgh between 1762 (or earlier) and 1799. The edition of 1773 describes itself as the twenty-second. Glasgow produced five runs between 1786 and 1796, and Dublin and Belfast one printing each, in 1736 and 1754 respectively. Fisher's *Instructor* was also printed multiple times in America in slightly different forms, and under three different titles: *The American Instructor*, *The Instructor or American Young Man's Best Companion* and *The Instructor or Young Man's Best Companion*. Franklin & Hall were one of its American printers.

These were not the only styles in circulation. The styles seen in Volumes 1 and 2 were still around. Complemental letters, letters translated from the French or Latin, and letters borrowed from John Hill's *Young Secretary's Guide* continued to be reprinted. Older manuals also survived in peoples' homes and libraries; indeed, judging by inscriptions and marginalia, manuals on both sides of the Atlantic were handed down in families and were often still in use a century or more after their publication date.

Notes:

1   Samuel Richardson, *Letters Written to and for Particular Friends, on the Most Important Occasions* (London: C. Rivington, J. Osborn and J. Leake, 1741), preface. p. 2.

2   Charles Hallifax, *Familiar Letters on Various Subjects of Business and Amusement: Written in a Natural, Easy Manner; And Publish'd, Principally, for the Service of the Younger Part of Both Sexes* (London: R. Baldwin. 1755), p. v.

LETTER XXVI.

From a Country Chapman beginning Trade, to a City Dealer, offering his Correspondence.

S I R,   *Manchester, Oct. 20.*

THE Time of my Apprenticeship, with Mr. *Dobbins* of this Town, being expired, I am just going to begin for myself in *Chesterfield,* having taken a Shop there for that Purpose. And as I know the Satisfaction you always gave to my Master in your Dealings; I make an Offer to you of my Correspondence, in Expectation that you will use me as well as you have done him, in whatever I may write to you for. And this I the rather expect, as you cannot disoblige Mr. *Dobbins* by it, because of the Distance I shall be from him; and I shall endeavour to give you equal Content with regard to my Payments, &c. Your speedy Answer, whether or no you are disposed to accept of my Offer, will oblige,   *Your humble Servant.*

L E T-

LETTER XXVII.

In Anſwer to the foregoing.

SIR,

I HAVE received yours of *October* 20. and very chearfully accept the Favour you offer me. I will take Care to ſerve you in the beſt manner I am able, and on the ſame foot with Mr. *Dobbins*; not doubting you will make as punctual Returns as he does; which intitles him to a more favourable Uſage, than could otherwiſe be afforded. I wiſh you Succeſs with all my Heart, and am

Your obliged Servant.

LETTER XXVIII.

From a Maid-ſervant in Town, acquainting her Father and Mother in the Country, with a Propoſal of Marriage, and aſking their Conſents.

Honoured Father and Mother,

I Think it my Duty to acquaint you, that I am addreſſed to for a Change of Condition, by one Mr. *John Tanner*, who is a Glazier, and lives in the Neighbourhood by us. He is a young Man of a ſober Character, and has been ſet up about two Years, has good Buſineſs for his Time, and is well beloved and ſpoken of by every one. My Friends here think well of it, particularly my Maſter and Miſtreſs; and, he ſays, he doubts not, by God's Bleſſing on his Induſtry, to maintain a Family very prettily: And I have fairly told him, how little he has to expect with me.

But

But I would not conclude on any thing, however, till I had acquainted you with his Proposals, and asked your Blessings and Consents. For I am, and ever will be,

Your dutiful Daughter.

LETTER XXIX.

From the Parents, in Answer to the preceding.

Dear Nanny,

WE have received your dutiful Letter. We can only pray to God to direct and bless you in all your Engagements. Our Distance from you, must make us leave every thing to your own Discretion ; and as you are so well satisfied in Mr. *Tanner*'s Character, as well as all Friends, and your Master and Mistress, we give our Blessings and Consents with all our Hearts : We are only sorry we can do no more for you. But let us know when it is done, and we will do some little Matters, as far as we are able, towards Housekeeping. Our Respects to Mr. *Tanner*. Every body joins with us in Wishes for your Happiness ; and may God bless you, is all that can be said, by

Your truly loving Father and Mother.

LETTER XXX.

From the same, acquainting her Parents with her Marriage.

Honoured Father and Mother,

I Write to acquaint you, that last *Thursday* I was married to Mr. *Tanner*, and am to go home to him in a Fortnight. My Master and
Mistress

Miftrefs have been very kind, and have made me a Prefent towards Houfekeeping of Three Guineas. I had faved Twenty Pounds in Service, and that is all. I told him the naked Truth of every thing. And indeed did not intend to marry fo foon ; but when I had your Letter, and fhew'd it him, he would not let me reft till it was done. Pray don't ftraiten your felves out of Love to me. He joins with me in faying fo, and bids me prefent his Duty to you, and tell you, that he fears not to maintain me very well. I have no Reafon to doubt of being very happy. And your Prayers for a Bleffing on both our Induftry, will, I hope, be a Means to make us more fo. We are, and ever fhall be, with Refpects to all Friends,

Your moft dutiful Son and Daughter,

LETTER XXXI.

Recommending a Superior Man-Servant.

SIR,

THE Bearer of this is Mr. *John Andrews,* whom I mentioned to you laft time I faw you ; and for whofe Integrity and Ability to ferve you in the Way you talked of, I dare be anfwerable. I take the greater Pleafure in this Recommendation, as I doubt not it will be of Service to you both. And am, Sir,

Your moft obedient Servant.

LETTER V.

To a Mother, to thank her for her Care and Tenderness.

Honoured Madam,

I HAVE written twice to my Brother, and not doubting but that he would inform you of my being well, I have taken the Liberty to omit writing to you. I beg you will be pleased to hear the Reasons that weighed with me against a very earnest Inclination, that whether you tell me I was right, or not, you may acquit me of the Charge of Disobedience, or Want of Respect as well as Gratitude.

The

[16]

The Pain with which I faw you parted from me on the Road, has made an Impreffion on my Heart which Time will never wear out; and I hope as it will always keep in my Remembrance your Ten-dernefs as well as Care for me, that befide the na-tural Right all your Commands have to Obedience from me, I fhall on another Principle avoid every Thing that is wrong, left it fhould give you Dif-quiet.

I fhould be unnatural and unpardonable not to have the moft fincere Regard for the Peace of your Mind, and for its Compofure: God prevent that I fhould do any Thing that might affect the firft, and I fhall hope my true Concern will guard me againft every Thing that might difturb the latter. Indeed, Madam, the Care of this prevented my writing; I feared that a Letter from me, be the Contents ever fo indifferent, might recall my Re-membrance too fully before you, and that the fame Pain might attend it, as did your parting with me. This was the only Reafon of my not writing before; and in the moft fincere Truth I have done Violence to myfelf in omitting that Teftimony of my Duty and Refpect.

As to Occafions of writing, I have yet none, more than to tell you that I do not forget to whom I owe my Attention; and to fay how great an Happinefs it will be to me to receive your farther Thoughts as to Things that are about me. I have yet entered into no Acquaintance with them, be-ing determined, fo far as my Youth and fcanty Judgment may allow of it, to confider them before I mix myfelf among them: For this Purpofe I have hitherto kept within the Houfe, where partly from the Converfation of my Relations, and partly from that of Perfons of their Acquaintance who vifit them, and fome of whom are Perfons of very refpectable

[17]

spectable Talents, I settle in myself some Character
of the several Persons I am likely to meet with,
and of the Occurrences which may fall in my
Way; but of all this, having not yet established
within myself any firm Opinion, I shall take the
Freedom to write to you.

The greatest Subjects of my Consideration, Madam, are the Instructions and the Cautions you gave
me; these will never be out of my Remembrance;
and although perhaps the Tenderness of the Parent,
or the Fears of the Mother, may have represented
some of these in stronger Lights than they are ordinarily seen, yet when I compare them with the Observations I have yet had Opportunities of making,
I find them all most perfectly just, and all very
necessary.

No Person I am sure ever had the Happiness of a
more affectionate Mother; and I am fully persuaded
that the great Experience you have had of the World,
will render you, more than most People, able to judge
of the Course of Things: I think it a great Happiness
that so excellent an Adviser is so much concerned in
my Welfare; and I do promise you, Madam, in the
most sincere Manner, that I will always prefer to all
other Considerations in the World, the Admonitions
which you shall be pleased to give me. I shall also
look upon myself as accountable for the least Articles
of my Conduct to you, as well as to God and my
own Heart; and it will scarce be a greater Obligation
upon me to do in every Thing as I ought, that the
Eye of that all-seeing Judge is upon me, than that
any wrong Step in my Behaviour will, beside throwing myself into Difficulties, make you unhappy.

You cannot know, Madam, how much and how
gratefully I think of your Care in placing me where
I now am; where, under the Eye of a good and
prudent Person, I have an Opportunity to consider of
my

[18]

my future Conduct, and to fee Things before I am placed among them, and to confider this great World before I may be faid to make a Part of it. I fee it as a terrible as well as a profitable Scene of Action,: I have already fet down many Things which I fhall avoid like Death, and which I fhould elfe perhaps have fallen into heedlefly : I hope my future Experience will fhew me many more. Indeed on the little that I fee at prefent, I cannot wonder that of the Youths, who at my unthinking and rafh Time of Life, are let loofe into the Danger, and never confider it till they are in the midft of it, if they ever confider it at all, the greater Part are ruined. I hope I fhall profit even by their Misfortunes ; but whatfoever Advantages I have over the reft of the young Men I meet withal, I fhall always remember with a due Gratitude that I owe them to you.

I pray daily that you may continue in all Refpects happy. You'll let my Brother know, Madam, that I fhall endeavour to think of all Things as he would have me: He has taught me to write long Letters ; but if it be not tedious to you, I cannot think the Time it has taken me could be more worthily employed ; nor can I account that a Trouble which, befide that it is a Duty and a Satisfaction to myfelf, will give you Pleafure.

I am, Honoured Madam,

     with all Duty and Affection,

         Your obedient Son.

L E T-

[19]

LETTER VI.

From a Mother to her Son.   In answer to the former.

Dear Child,

I Have this Moment read your Letter, and I am
set down to write to you. Where corresponding
is a Trouble, People may defer it to the latest Hour;
but why should I deny myself a Moment the Pleasure
of conversing with you. My Dear, continue in the
Thoughts you have at present, and you will add all
that can be now thrown into the Portion of my Happiness. I interrupt myself by casting my Eye over
and over upon your Letter, and the Fulness of my
Heart prevents my informing you of its Sensations.
If you should see more Blots than this which is just
now made in my Writing, do not wonder, or be
uneasy: I will not dissemble to you that they are
made by Tears; but, dearest Son, these are Tears
that flow from Transport, which has no other Expression. Sure no Mother was ever happier in her
Children. Your Brother is esteemed, nay, he is almost adored by every body: Your Sister is settled to
an Advantage that was beyond my utmost Expectation: And yet she is so good a Woman, that her
Husband thinks himself under everlasting Obligations. You, my dear *Jack*, were my only Care;
and I had more Fear for you than all: As the
youngest, that is, Child, as the latest Remembrance of your honoured Father, you had a larger
Share of my Tenderness than either; and you was
destined to a Scene of the greatest Danger: Heaven
alone can tell what have been my Anxieties and
Fears about you, and how continual my Prayers
for your Security; they are all granted; and instead of being, as I feared you would, an Occasion
of

[20]

of continual Alarm to me, you are adding more than any of them to my Contentment. I know your good Heart, and I can fee what a Joy it is to you to perceive you make me happy : In fuch a Mind as yours there can be wanting no other Motive to be good befide the Excellence of Virtue ; but I am fure that if this were not fufficient, the very Thought that your Mother's Peace depended upon your Conduct would keep you in the Way of Goodnefs.

My dear Child, regard your Brother : No Perfon is fo able to advife you, and he loves you with more than the common Affection of the Relation ; he admires your good Senfe, and he efteems your Principles. Dear Son, think what an Honour it is to have the Efteem of fo excellent a Man ; think what a Happinefs it is to have fo fine a Character at fo tender an Age as yours ; and as you fhew me how much my Satisfaction is an Object of your Concern, remember what a Tranfport it muft be to me to hear of you fo favourably.

I fhall not repeat to you, my dear, the Cautions which I gave you, for I fee you will not need to be put again in Remembrance : Only, reverence Truth, be acquainted with no one till you know that he deferves it, and avoid bad Women.

If it can give you Satisfaction, and I am fure it will do fo, to hear that every Thought of your Heart has my perfect Approbation, you hear it truly ; but although there is not any the leaft Part of your Conduct that does not give me Pleafure, there is, although you will be furprifed to hear it, fomething in your Brother's with refpect to you that gives me Pain. He told me of your asking his Advice upon an inconfiderable Subject, and his giving it to you rather honeftly than elegantly. Dear Child, take Care of your Heart, and you may be lefs uneafy about your
Expreffion :

[21]

Expreffion : Let your Thoughts be good, and never be uneafy about the Words you put them in. The Books recommended to you may be good for nothing, but you have no Occafion for any ; nor is it a Pin matter in the Affairs of Life whether you put every Word where it fhould be. But this is all a Trifle ; nor fhall I pretend to enter into the Matter ; if it be worth any Confideration, he is the beft Judge, fo pray mind him ; but what I fpeak of is the Manner in which he fays he wrote of your Coufin.

My dear, always refpect your Elders, and do not let any little School-boy's Leffon put you above them in your own Opinion, becaufe they have for gotten it : Nor becaufe your Coufin is a plain Man, do you fuppofe he is lefs capable to advife you. He is a Perfon of undoubted Probity and Uprightnefs of Heart, and that is worth all the *Greek* and *Latin* of *Weftminfter* and *Eton :* He has made his Way to a plentiful Fortune, and he has the Refpect and Efteem of all that ever he was concerned with. Would you wifh for a better Character or better Fortune ? God fend you may conduct yourfelf through the World juft as he has done : I that would weary Heaven with Prayers for you, wifh you no-thing better. I do not pretend to fay your Brother is wrong in his Judgment about this Matter, for I do not underftand the Nature of it ; all that I know is, you will never write a Letter that will pleafe me more than this you have fent already, and I think had I been in his Place, I would not have put any thing into your Mind upon an Occafion of fuch little Confequence that fhould have abated your Regard for a Perfon whofe Advice will be of Service to you. But I know you will not let it do fo. Pre-ferve, I defire you, that Refpect for him which his Years, and his Integrity, and his Succefs in the World require ; and whatfoever you may think

about

[22]

about this Trifle, do not let it leſſen your Eſteem for
one whom your Mother recommends to you.

My Dear, I have ſaid the more upon this Subject, becauſe it ſeems the only one on which you
are in Danger to err; and I have thought it the
more neceſſary to ſay ſo, becauſe the Regard I
deſired you to pay to your Brother might have rendered it a Kind of Duty, to go into this Error: I
have ſpoke to him about it, and he deſires me to ſay
that he is perfectly of my Opinion!

Farewell, my deareſt Boy; you have a very eaſy
Task before you; ſeeing ou are already ſo good,
that you need only go on in the ſame Path, to make
all that love you happy.

Your affectionate Mother.

LETTER VII.

To an elder Brother, concerning a Lady.

Dear Brother,

WHEN I wrote laſt to my Mother, for I
underſtand the Letters directed to her or to
you, to be no Secret to either, I had no Thought
of ſending another ſo ſoon. I had reſolved, in my
own Opinion, and had been confirmed in it by the
Commands of the moſt prudent and beſt of Parents,
to ſee more of the great World before I mixed
myſelf among thoſe who compoſe it. And conſequently thought till after the Time of that Conſideration I ſhould have nothing to write to you: For
that I ſhould not preſume to ſend you my Imagi-
nations

[23]

nations concerning Things with which I had not
been acquainted, as Thoughts that could at all deferve your Attention. But I have been taken abroad
'before I was aware of it, and perhaps I can never
have a greater Occafion of writing to you.

My Coufin, to whom my Mother has commanded me to pay an abfolute Obedience, had a
Curiofity, or elfe he had been prevailed upon by
the Curiofity of his Family, to fee a Perfon who
performs fome Feats of Dexterity upon a Wire. I
would rather have omitted it, but it was their Pleafure I fhould go with them ; and I wifh I could tell
you that I found no Satisfaction in the Expedition :
As to the Man we went to fee I fhall fay little of
him ; for although the Things he does are furprifing,
the Danger of his falling, and his own Fear of
it, prevented a good-natured Perfon from feeing
them.

If I was not entertained with the Exploits, I was
much lefs fatisfied with the Behaviour of the Company : Indeed, Brother it is a Place of fo much
Indecency and Wickednefs, that I wonder fome
Regulations are not made in it. I never faw fuch a
Mixture of the better and meaner Sort of People ;
and I cannot think that the latter will be improved
by feeing the Debauchery of the former ; or that
the lower Sort will not be taught bad Cuftoms by
the Vicioufnefs and Extravagance of the higher.
It feemed ftrange to me to fee a Perfon, feemingly,
of great Diftinction liftening to the Ribaldry of a
Porter over his Liquor ; and I was grieved to obferve, that feveral of low Rank, and mean Intel-
lects, had Opportunities of feeing unbecoming Freedoms among thofe who ought to fet them better
Examples ; but there was only a little Part of the
Time in which I could attend to fuch Things.
There are a 'Number of upper Places prepared for
the

[24]

the better Sort of People who come there, and we
had one of thefe: In the next but one there was
another Family, feemingly of grave and reputable
Perfons; and among them a young Gentlewoman,
as nearly as I can guefs, of my own Age. I do
not know whether the Comparifon with the bold
Perfons who were in the other Place made this
Lady's Behaviour appear more amiable to me; or
whether fhe has not a Modefty that is fuperior to
the reft of her Sex; but certainly her Perfon, her
Looks, and her Behaviour, commanded Refpect and
Admiration.

I do not know whether it might be Fancy, but
I once thought fhe looked favourably upon me: I
muft confefs it would have been Infenfibility had I
looked otherwife than with Approbation upon her;
and indeed I could not think any thing befide
worthy the looking at: There was a Modefty in
her Countenance that quite engaged me; and if
at any Time I faw her Eyes, they had a Sweet-
nefs fuch as I have never feen in thofe of any one
before.

I am afraid to confefs to you what I have done
in confequence of this little Interview: I have
written a Letter, not to herfelf, but to her Father. You fee, tho' afraid to confefs, I am more
afraid to conceal any thing from you: I tell you
that I have written this Letter; but be pleafed to
underftand me rightly; I have not fent it; nor
fhall I take fuch a Step without your Approbation,
and the Permiffion of my Mother. On the contrary, I enclofe it to you, that if you think favourably of my Intentions, you may give me the
Support of Reafon, and the Sanction of a Parent's
Authority to what I am doing: I beg you to fhew
it to my Mother; but prepare her for it firft: I
need not indeed ask you to do that, for I know
you

[25]

you will read this Letter to her; that will tell her my true Thoughts. If fhe will countenance my Defigns, and you approve of them, I fhall proceed. You know I have fomething independently of my intended Profeffion; and probably the Lady alfo has fome Fortune; but of this I have made no Enquiry. Pray tell my Mother, that if I could prevail with fo agreeable, and I doubt not, fo worthy a Perfon, to accept my Offer, I am certain I could be more happy with her upon a little, than without her with a larger Fortune: I know this will be of fome Weight both with you and her; for I know you both wifh my Happinefs: If it be of enough to make you overlook all other Intentions, as it makes me difregard them, I fhall think it a happy Omen of my Fortune: if otherwife, and it fhould be your Opinion that this is a wrong Meafure, I will, tho' it be very difficult to think I can do it, yet I will conquer my Inclinations, and endeavour never to think of it farther. You know I fhall be impatient for an Anfwer; pray let me receive it foon.

Your moft affectionate Brother.

[97]

LETTER LXII.

*To a Person of Quality, requesting his Interest for
a Place.*

My Lord,

WHEN I recollect the many Kindnesses I
have had the Honour to receive from you,
and the Place your Lordship has been pleased to grant
me in your Friendship, I have the Boldness to suppose, a Letter, which brings a Petition to you, will
neither surprise your Lordship, nor be disagreeable.

It cannot be unknown to your Lordship, that
my Affairs are very little to my Satisfaction ; or
that my Circumstances make it often necessary for
me to decline those Parties to your Lordship's
Country Seat, in which you do me the great Honour to name me as one of the Company. I have
no Ambition but to be in your Lordship's Favour ;
but I cannot make the Opportunities of waiting on
you so frequent as I could wish, and, as your Lordship is pleased to say, it would be agreeable to you
that they should be.

My Lord, this is the immediate Occasion of an
Application which my Friends would have had me
made some Time since to your Friendship ; but I was
backward to do it, thinking it but a bad Return for
many Favours already conferred, to ask more : However, at present, I am rather pressed by the Strait-
ness of my Circumstances, than prevailed upon by
their Sollicitations, to make this Application, in
which the great Indulgence with which your Lordship has been pleased to honour me, assures me that
I shall be considered otherwise than as a common
Supplicant.

F   When

[98]

When I have mentioned my Requests to your Lordship, it is incumbent upon me to set them within their true Limits: I beg Leave to observe to your Lordship, that I neither have the Confidence to place my Expectations high; nor the Ambition to desire any Thing that is considerable. Your Lordship will smile to be informed, that a Person, who has had the Honour of a Place at your Table, and has continued to appear not so meanly as to be remark'd at it, has done this upon less than Thirty Pounds a Year. A Person, from whose Indulgence I received a Part of this, is lately dead, my Lord; and his Appointments dying with him, that Portion of my Income is lost; and it is no little Affliction to me, that I am not able to go into Mourning for one, whom the World knew to be so kind to me, and for whom, beside Gratitude, I had the most true Affection.

But I trespass too much upon your Lordship's Time, and upon your Compassion. I have only mentioned so much to countenance what I shall add, when in limiting my Petition to your Lordship's Interest for any Place of forty Pounds a Year, I do most certainly assure your Lordship, that it will make me compleatly happy, being more than I have ever enjoyed: If I may have Leave to add any Thing to the Request, it is, that I should be happy if the Post which brought me in this little Salary did not so perfectly engross my Time as to prevent my sometimes doing myself the Honour of waiting on your Lordship, and expressing my Gratitude for the conferring on me so great a Benefit.

I am, my Lord,

with the greatest Respect,

Your Lordship's most obedient,

and most humble Servant.

LET-

[99]

LETTER LXIII.

The Nobleman's Anfwer.

S I R,

I AM very forry to hear of your Misfortune, and, upon my Honour, do not want Inclination to ferve you; but it is not in my Power. I have the Children of all the leading People in the Borough to provide for, and they all expect the Sort of Places you mention: Befide that, I have an Intereft to keep up in two Counties; fo that I would not have you place the leaft Dependance upon me. As to the Lofs of your Relation, I am very forry, if it adds to the Inconvenience of your Affairs; but for the Matter of Mourning, I fhould never think it worth while to wear it for thofe that did not leave enough to pay for it. I heartily wifh I could do any Thing to ferve you; but as I cannot, the next Service is to prevent your fruitlefs Expectations.

I am, Sir, yours, &c.

LETTER LXIV.

From a Perfon of Credit, to a Duke, to requeft his Favour and Intereft.

My Lord Duke,

W HEN I had the Honour to wait on your Grace with the Model of the Machine I had contrived for conveying the Water more ef-
F 2 fectually

[100]

fectually out of Mines, your Grace was pleafed to
fay, that I deferved Encouragement.   This has
emboldened me to lay before your Grace the prefent State of my Affairs; which is, that being fol-
licited to come up to *London* by fome who thought
well of the Undertaking, in Hopes of being, in
fome Degree, recompenfed for the Pains it has
coft me, I left a Family ill provided for in *Dur-
ham*, and flattered myfelf to have made them fome
Remittances; but it has not been my good Fortune to be received with that Heartinefs I had
hoped.   For more than outward Civility I have
not experienced from any : Moreover, I have very
fcanty Means of fupplying my own Neceffities at
prefent.

In this Situation, my Lord Duke, I have been
prompted by my Neceffities, and encouraged by
your Grace's Goodnefs to me, to moft humbly
follicit of your Grace, your Intereft in fome little
Appointment, of which I know there are very
many continually becoming vacant.   Upon fomething of this Kind, the leaft of which would be
fufficient, I could fend up for my Family, and here
profecute my Labours under many Advantages,
which are altogether wanting in the Country, in
fuch Manner, that they might become ufeful to the
Public.

I do moft humbly entreat your Grace's Pardon
for my great Prefumption in this Application; and
if I could farther obtain from your Grace's Bounty
fome little Matter to provide me with the Necef-
faries of Life, until this happened to fall, I fhould
be at all Times proud to fpeak to the World my
great Obligations to your Grace's Humanity and
Generofity; and to fay, that in *England* there was,
at leaft, one Nobleman, who countenanced and
protected Induftry; however little there might be

of

[101]

of Advantage yet accruing from the Profecution of
the Point in View.

> *I am, with all Submiffion,*
> *and with the greateft Gratitude,*
> *my Lord,*
> *Your Grace's moft obedient,*
> *and moft humble Servant.*

LETTER LXV.

From a Man of Quality; in anfwer to a Petition
from a Perfon of Merit.

S I R,

I Have received your Letter, and fhall be glad to
ferve you; for I think there is a great Merit in
your Difcovery, and the Public ought to fupport you
in the Profecution, and bringing of it to Perfection. I
am forry I am at prefent with-held from doing you
the Service you require; for my Hands are tied up
by a mutual Obligation among a great Number of
us, never to give more than the Price of a Ticket
for a Benefit Play; never to pay an Author more
than the felling Price of his Book; and many other
Things of a like Nature; among which is the not
giving abfolute Money to thofe who apply to us. I
am forry, Sir, this prevents my ferving you in this
Refpect; but in your Requeft of a Place, you fhall
have my beft Intereft, and I hope it will be brought
about foon. I have written this Letter to you with
my own Hand, to convince you how much I am inclined to ferve you, and am,

> *S I R,*
> *Yours, &c.*

F 3 L E T-

[102]

LETTER LXVI.

From a Perſon who had depended a long Time upon the promiſed Services of a Nobleman.

May it pleaſe your Grace,

IT is now between three and four Years, in which I have been on your Grace's Recommendation, labouring at the compleating my Machine for public Service, which is much nearer to Perfection than it has at any Time been; and I verily believe, hath only been prevented from being abſolutely perfected by the Narrowneſs of my Circumſtances, which obliging me to many Ways of getting my Bread, the moſt of which took up nearly all my Time, hath prevented my Opportunities of labouring upon it in that conſtant Way I could have wiſhed. In all this Time, during which I have from Space to Space troubled your Grace with Letters, to many of which you have been pleaſed to return me moſt favourable Anſwers, either by your own Hand, or that of ſome principal Servant, I have been kept in Hopes by the Expectation of ſome Place under the Government, or ſome Reward from it, the which ſhould have enabled me to have ſent for my Family, at this Time a Burthen to the Pariſh from which I came; at leaſt, to have diſcharged thoſe ſmall Debts I had contracted here; and giving up all farther Hopes to have gone to them. But I am, at length, ſenſible how very many there are who apply, and are recommended: And how difficult it is for a Perſon, even of your Grace's high Rank, and with your great Humanity, to procure any Thing for thoſe whom you favour.

However,

[103]

However, at this Time, my Lord Duke, I beg Permiſſion to mention to your Grace, that I am under greater Misfortunes than ever, being in the Priſon of the Marſhalſea for a ſmall Debt of two Pound eight Shillings, and my Models, and other Effects, ſeized upon by the Perſon where I lodged, and, as I am told, about to be purchaſed for a Trifle, by a Perſon in *London*, who, knowing the Nature of them, will compleat my Diſcovery, and reap the Advantage of it. I am very deſirous that a Thing ſo uſeful to the Public ſhould be brought to Perfection; but I would have ſome Reward for the Pains I have taken in it, whoſoever has the Honour. The whole Amount of the Due for Rent being one Pound eighteen Shillings, I do moſt humbly beg of your Grace, having no other Friend in the World, that you will be pleaſed to order ſome one of your Grace's Servants to take the Models out of thoſe Perſons Hands, that I may have an Opportunity, if it is to go from me, at leaſt, to ſell it on ſome more proper Terms.

I make no Doubt, but your Grace will be pleaſed to order this little Favour to be ſhewn to me; and I will inſtantly on the Sale return the Money to the Perſon who disburſed it; after which, preſuming once more to wait upon your Grace, to take my Leave, I will return to my Family, heartily praying the great Author of all Things to bleſs your Grace with every earthly Felicity; and, for the Sake of others, who may deſign any Thing for the Good of the Public, that Perſons of your Grace's Humanity and Goodneſs may hereafter have Opportunities of more readily obtaining thoſe Rewards for

F 4

the

[104]

the deferving, which they are pleafed to follicit for
them.

I am, with the greateft Gratitude,

and moft profound Refpect,

my Lord,

Your Grace's moft obedient,

and moft humble Servant.

LETTER LXVII.

The Nobleman's Anfwer.

Mr. Moody,

YOU have fent me a very long Letter which
I ordered my Secretary to read, and tell me
the Contents of it. It feems you expect fome Affiftance in regard to your Goods; you will remember that you came an entire Stranger to me,
and without any Recommendation. I am forry for
your Misfortune; but I cannot pretend to meddle
in your private Affairs. And I defire you will not
trouble yourfelf to write any more Letters to me.
I wifhed to ferve you; but I cannot provide for all
the World.

Yours, &c.

George Fisher, *The Instructor: Or, Young Man's Best Companion* (1767)

Familiar letters on several occasions, and on divers subjects.

Before we enter upon *Arithmetic,* it may be proper to give some examples of letters on various subjects, and upon divers occasions; which letters frequently read over, and sometimes copied, may be a good introduction to a handsome style, and a commendable manner of writing: besides the help and use they may be of in noting and observing the method of spelling good English, and orthographically placing *great letters,* or *capitals,* where they ought to be; and also in imprinting in the mind the due notion of points, stops &c. and when and where to be made.

Letters are variously worded, and ought properly to express the desires, thoughts, &c. of the writer to the reader, that thereby the receiver of the letter may fully understand, and be justly informed of the occasions, wants, or intentions of the sender.

Letters being writ on several subjects, and on sundry occasions, they may be ranked under these denominations, or several heads following, *viz. letters of proffered assistance, of thanks, of excuse, of reproof, of advice or counsel of recommendation, of remonstrance, of business, and of amusement; letters consolatory, congratulatory, and exhortatory; also familiar and mixed letters, containing various subjects.*

I shall not have room to touch upon every one of these particularly; but I shall give sundry examples promiscuously, as follows, *viz.*

A LETTER *from a son to his father.*

Honoured Father,

As I have not had a letter from you, since your favour on the 8th of October last, which I answered by the next post; I take this opportunity of inquiring after your health, and that of my sister. I have herewith sent you, sir, by Samuel Simple, the Pempsey carrier, a spaniel dog, called *Tray;* who is an excellent good one of his kind, and fit for the sport of your place; is very free for the water; and if he hath any fault, it is being a little too eager; but he is young, and may be brought to what you please to have him. Pray give my love to my sister, and be pleased to accept of my duty to yourself, who am,

London, Dec. 6.
1762.

             Sir, Your most dutiful son,
                 and humble servant
              ANTHONY ADDLEHILL

The ANSWER

Dear Son,   *Pempsey, 28th Xber 1766.*

I Received your letter of the 6th instant, and thank you for enquiring after my health, which, I thank God, I perfectly enjoy at present, as I wish and hope you do yours. – I received your present of the dog; but the poor cur was almost starved, having (as I suppose) had nothing on the road; but he us now in good condition, and hath been tried as to his mettle, which I find to be good. I have sent you by the carrier half a dozen wild ducks, which Tray fetched when I had shot them, Your sister remembers her love to you, and hath send you a turkey and a chine of bacon, to which I wish you and your friends (if you invite any) a good stomach. My prayers to God for your prosperity, temporal and eternal, are constantly offered up by   *Your loving father,*
                                              ANDREW ADDLEHILL.

P.S. We have a great many wild-fowl in our
level, so that you may expect another present of
that kind in a little time.

Note. *The letters P. S. signify* postscript; *which name is given to any thing which is (like the above four lines) wrote below the body of a letter.*

A LETTER *from a young man to his uncle.*

Honoured Uncle,

The many kind and courteous things that you have done for me, oblige me, in point of gratitude, as well as duty, (as an opportunity now offers itself), to make a tender to you of my poor, but real and heart service, in the affair between you and Mr. *A. B.* of this place: And if you will please but to communicate to me your intentions, and give me your directions therein, I will execute them with all punctuality; and will, from time to time, give you an exact account of my proceedings therein, Therefore, in expectation of your commands, I remain,

                               Sir, Your most obliged nephew,
Norwich. Dec. 7.
1766.   *and very humble servant,*
                                              BRIAN BING

The Uncle's ANSWER.

                                    London, Dec. 12. 1766.
Nephew,

I Take the offer of your service in the business between me and Mr. *A. B.* of your city very kindly, and think none fitter to adjust that affair than yourself; but

I am unwilling to go to law, and had rather, much rather, that you would endeav-our to bring him to some reasonable accommodation; for in such a contests the winner is commonly a loser in the end. Therefore if you can bring him to any reasonable terms, I shall be very glad: You understand the affair, and so I shall commit it wholly to your discreet and good management, being persuaded that you will do for me as for yourself; in which opinion I remain

Your loving and affectionate uncle,
BAZIL BING.

A LETTER *from a niece to her aunt.*

Madam,

The trouble I have already given you puts me to the blush, when I think of intruding again on your goodness; but necessity, which frequently obliges us to such actions as are contrary to our inclinations, is the motive that induces me to be thus troublesome now. Pray, dear Madam, excuse me, if I once more beg your assistance, which I do not doubt, but you very well know I stand greatly in need of, at this time; and I shall ever have a grateful remembrance of your goodness to me; and I hope I shall be, one time or other, in a capacity of making some return for the many obligations your goodness hath conferred upon me.

Land. Dec. 7.   *Your most respectful niece,*
1766.   *and very humble servant,* PNNELOPE PINCH.

A LETTER *of profered assistance to a friend.*

Dear Friend,

I should be false to true friendship, if I should neglect or cast off my friend in adversity. I have heard that you are under some misfortune, and at present need my assistance. I therefore send you these lines for you consolation, desiring you to bear up against your ill-luck with as much patience and mind as you can: For assure yourself, I shall suddenly follow this epistle in person, and come, I hope, opportunely enough to your assistance; till which time, take courage, and be assured that you shall not be disappointed of timely help, from, dear friend,

Yours in reality,
TIMOTHY TIMELY

A brother to a sister

Dear Sister,

My great distance and long absence from you (though I have not wanted good company) makes me very solicitous concerning your welfare: Natural affec-tion inclines me strongly to have you in remembrance, rendering your health and welfare in every respect as dear as my own; and there is nothing at my command, but, if you request, it shall be freely yours. Notwithstanding the distance, I purpose (God willing) to make you a visit very shortly; and had done it before now, but an urgent occasion interposed, the particulars of which being too long for a letter, I shall acquaint you with when I see you. Pray give my due respects to all friends, particularly to honest MR. *S. T.* and so in expectation of finding you all well at my arrival, I conclude,

Dear Sister,
Your affectionate brother,
And humble servant,
HENRY HEARTY

A LETTER *from a youth at school to his parents.*

Honoured Father and Mother,

I Received your kind letter of the 4th of November last, and also the several things therein mentioned, by the Chichester carrier, for which I return you my most humble and hearty thanks, they coming very seasonably to the relief of my necessities. – I endeavour to make the best improvement in my learning that I possibly can, (though at the first it seemed a little irksome and hard): and I hope to gain the point at last, for which you sent me hither. Pray, dear parents, accept of my most humble duty to yourselves, and kind love to my brothers and sisters, and to my quondam *playfellows,* particularly to Jacky Jinglebrains, and tell him, I hope by this time he begins to be a little serious – I am,

London. Dec. 6.   *Honoured parents,*
1766.   *Your dutiful son, and humble servant,*
STEPHEN STUDIOUS.

Another.

Honoured Sir,

I Am very much obliged to your for all your favours; all I have to hope is, that the progress I make in my learning will be no disagreeable return from the same: Gratitude, duty, and a view of future advantages, all conspire to make me fully sensible how much I ought to labour for my own improvement, and your satisfaction, in order to shew myself, upon all occasions, to be

Eton-School,   *Your most obedient son,*
May 8. 1766.   DANIEL DILIGENT.

[Anon.], *The Complete Letter-Writer; or Polite English Secretary. Containing, Familiar Letters on the Most Common Occasions in Life. Also A Variety of More Elegant Letters for Examples and Improvement of Style, from the Best Modern Authors, Together with Many Originals*, 12th edn (London: Stanley Crowder, 1768), title page, Preface, Contents, pp. 50–154, 184–92. British Library, shelfmark 1607/4355.

The Complete Letter-Writer was a compilation originating in London which contained four sections. The first section, 'Miscellaneous Letters on the most useful and common Occasions' contains household and business letters after the manner of *Secretaries*. It consists of letters taken without attribution from Hill, Goodman (see Volume 2), Mather, Richardson, Hallifax and Haywood. But several of these culled letters have been rewritten, often inconspicuously, to alter their ideology and modernize their style. The compiler's focus is on matters of politeness, education and letter-writing. The second section consists of 'Letters of Courtship and Marriage', many of which were taken from Richardson and Hallifax. Many of the letters in this section appear with answers, to create little conduct book scenarios of proper and improper courtships.

In early editions of this manual, the third section consisted of *Lettres gallantes* and of letters culled from *Academies of Complement* (see Volume 1); but these were replaced in 1759 by a more improving collection of 'Familiar Letters of Advice and Instruction'. This section and the fourth, called ' Elegant Letters on Various Subjects to Improve the Stile and Entertain the Mind', consist of (often genuine) letters by 'eminent authors', who were variously writers, monarchs, ministers, and well known political or social figures. These two sections are not given in their entirety below.

This manual described itself in its Preface as complete not only with regard to its contents, but also with regard to its intended readership. And indeed, *The Complete Letter-Writer* was found so generally useful that it became a virtually standard transatlantic manual. After 1768, it was both imported into America and reprinted multiple times, with only minor variations, by English, Scottish and American printers. There were at least nineteen London editions before 1800, and twelve Scottish editions between 1768 and 1796. Edinburgh printers dropped the subtitle 'polite, English Secretary' and simply called the manual *The Complete Letter-Writer*. The Scots were, after all, not English. During the 1790s, American printers in Boston, New York, Philadelphia, Hartford and Salem, who printed their own versions of this manual – again with only minor variations – adopted the Scots' truncated title, which also suited Americans better after Independence. The contents of this manual were changed with virtually every London edition from the first in 1755 to the twelfth in 1768, but remained constant after that. Consequently the extracts below are taken from the 1768 London edition. After 1768, when it began to be reprinted in the Scottish and American provinces, *The Complete Letter-Writer* circulated with the bulk of its contents and most of its sequencing more or less intact. This means that for the rest of the century, users of this manual in different parts of Britain and America were exposed to mostly the same letters in the same contexts, despite America's political break with England.

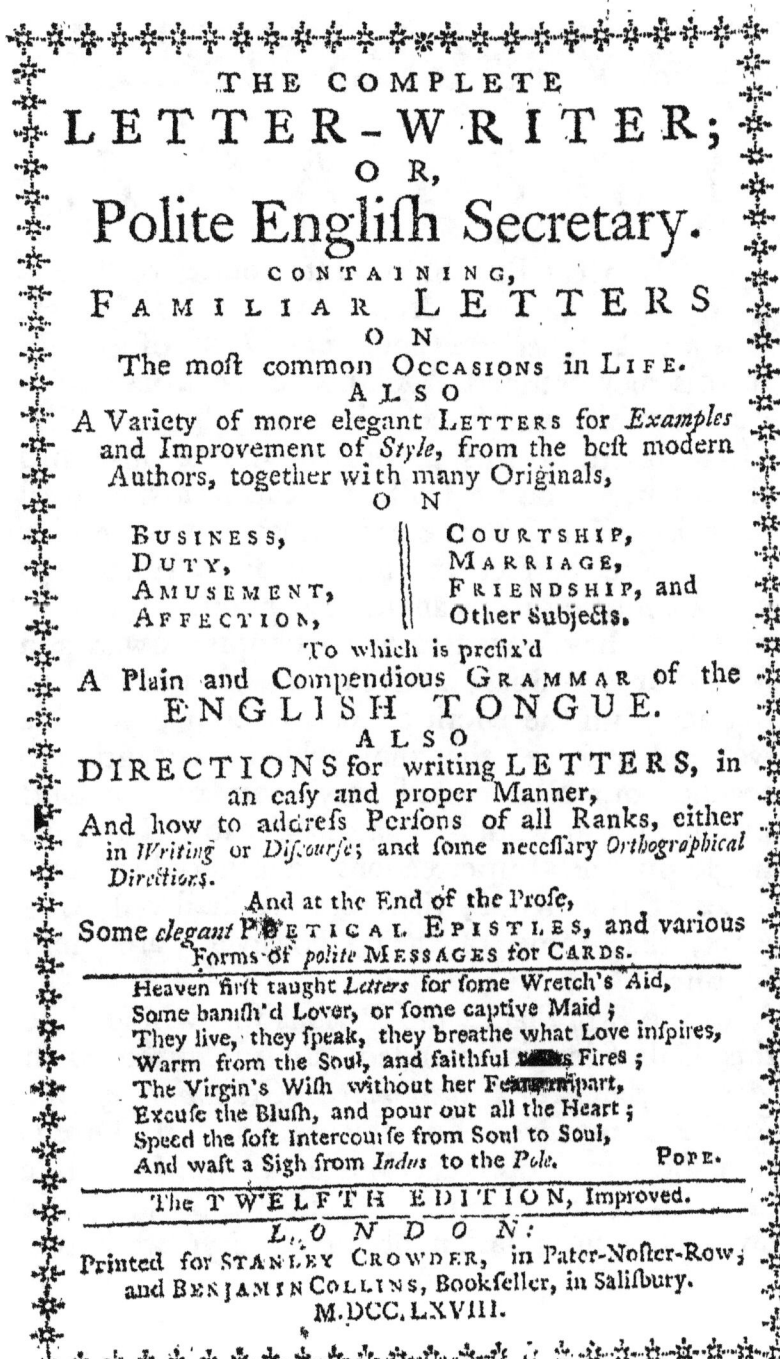

THE COMPLETE
LETTER-WRITER;
OR,
Polite English Secretary.

CONTAINING,
FAMILIAR LETTERS
ON
The moſt common OCCASIONS in LIFE.
ALSO
A Variety of more elegant LETTERS for *Examples* and Improvement of *Style*, from the beſt modern Authors, together with many Originals,
ON

BUSINESS,	COURTSHIP,
DUTY,	MARRIAGE,
AMUSEMENT,	FRIENDSHIP, and
AFFECTION,	Other Subjects.

To which is prefix'd
A Plain and Compendious GRAMMAR of the
ENGLISH TONGUE.
ALSO
DIRECTIONS for writing LETTERS, in
an eaſy and proper Manner,
And how to addreſs Perſons of all Ranks, either in *Writing* or *Diſcourſe*; and ſome neceſſary *Orthographical Directions.*

And at the End of the Proſe,
Some *elegant* POETICAL EPISTLES, and various Forms of *polite* MESSAGES for CARDS.

Heaven firſt taught *Letters* for ſome Wretch's Aid,
Some baniſh'd Lover, or ſome captive Maid ;
They live, they ſpeak, they breathe what Love inſpires,
Warm from the Soul, and faithful to its Fires ;
The Virgin's Wiſh without her Fears impart,
Excuſe the Bluſh, and pour out all the Heart ;
Speed the ſoft Intercourſe from Soul to Soul,
And waft a Sigh from *Indus* to the *Pole*.   POPE.

The TWELFTH EDITION, Improved.
LONDON:
Printed for STANLEY CROWDER, in Pater-Noſter-Row; and BENJAMIN COLLINS, Bookſeller, in Saliſbury.
M.DCC.LXVIII.

PREFACE.

AS a great Part of the Intercourse of Mankind has ever been transacted by Letter, it is a just Reflection upon any Man, especially in this more refined Age, not to be able to acquit himself handsomely in this Respect. The Occasions to do this are so very numerous, and the Shame of doing it ill, so great, in low as well as in high Life, that every Endeavour to render them more perfect in this Accomplishment, is at least intitled to a candid Reception.

There have been many Attempts towards a Work of this Sort; and tho' it were unkind to detract from the Merit of such Labours, yet this we must observe, that those which have hitherto reached our Notice, fall very short of the End proposed. It would be a disagreeable Task, to single out the Imperfections in other Performances of this Kind; therefore we shall only observe, that some of them, however, are here supplied.

In the first Place, the Persons for whose Use this Collection is intended, are presented with *A very plain and compendious Grammar of the English Language:* To which are added, Directions how to address Persons of all Ranks either in Writing or Discourse. This, we presume, is laying the Foundation of our Design well and

as

P R E F A C E.

as it ought to be.   The Rudiments of a Tongue once obtained, we proceed eafy to raife our Superftructure; without this we do nothing.

Next is an Introduction, containing Directions for inditing proper Letters on moft Occafions, and the Sentiments of feveral eminent Authors on Epiftolary Writing.

But the chief Branch of this Defign, and which indeed compofes the main Body of the Work, is a proper Collection of Letters, (with fome Originals) by eminent Authors, upon Subjects very various in their Nature, and therefore not eafily thrown under regular Claffes. *Bufinefs, Duty, Amufement, Affection, Courtfhip, Friendfhip,* and a Multiplicity of other Affairs that may require a *Letter,* are here made the Subject of ours; fo that on moft Occafions no Perfon can be at a Lofs for a Pattern to direct him. And it is from this great Variety of Examples for *Stile* and *Manner,* a *Grammar* for writing true *Englifh,* and other neceffary Directions, that we prefume to call this Performance by the Name of *The Complete Letter-Writer;* fuch a Number of Letters being inferted as to anfwer the Purpofe almoft of every Individual; from the Boy at School to the Secretary of State. Nor let it offend the Delicacy of any Reader, that he will here meet with many Epiftles of the lower Clafs: Thefe could not be omitted without deviating from the grand Point in View, namely, *General Utility.*

CON-

C O N T E N T S.

A Plain and compendious GRAMMAR of the Englifh Tongue   Page 1

The INTRODUCTION, containing fome general Directions for writing Letters, and how to addrefs Perfons of Diftinction, in Writing or Difcourfe, &c.   31

Some farther Directions and Obfervations on Epiftolary Correfpondence, and fubfcribing and directing Letters   37

Some neceffary Orthographical Directions for writing correctly, and when to ûfe Capital Letters and when not   49

P A R T I.

MISCELLANEOUS Letters on the moft ufeful and common Occafions.

LETTER

I. From a Brother at Home, to his Sifter abroad on a Vifit, complaining of her not writing   50

II. His Sifter's Anfwer   51

III. A young Gentleman's Letter to his Papa, written by a School-Fellow   ib.

IV. Another on the fame Subject   52

V. To a Friend againft Wafte of Time   ib.

VI. In Anfwer to a Friend   53

VII. To a young Gentleman   ib.

VIII. From a Young Lady, in Anfwer to a Letter fhe had received from her Mamma, advifing her to perfevere in the Chriftian Duties fhe had been inftructed in   54

IX. From a young Lady to her Mamma, requefting a Favour   56

X. From a young Gentleman to his Papa, defiring that he may learn to dance   57

XI. From a young Lady to her Papa, who lately embarked for the Eaft-Indies, in the Company's Service; but detained at Portfmouth by contrary Winds   58

XII. From a young Woman juft gone to Service, to her Mother at Home   59

XIII. Her Mother's Anfwer   ib.d.

XIV. The Daughter to her Mother   61

XV. The Mother's Anfwer and Advice: 62

A 3   XVI. A.

CONTENTS.

LETTER

XVI. A Son's Letter at School to his Father   65

XVII. A Letter of Excuse to a Father or Mother   ib.

XVIII. To Mr. ———.   ib.

XIX. From a young Apprentice to his Father, to let him know how he likes his Place and goes on   67

XX. From a Daughter to her Mother, by Way of Excuse for having neglected to write to her   68

XXI. From Robin Redbreast in the Garden, to Master Billy Careless abroad at School   ib.

XXII. From one Sister to another   70

XXIII. In Answer to the foregoing   71

XXIV. From Lady Goodford to her Daughter, a Girl of fourteen Years old, then under the Care of her Grandmother in the Country   72

XXV. To a young Lady, cautioning her against keeping Company with a Gentleman of a bad Character   74

XXVI. A Letter of Thanks, &c.   75

XXVII. From an Apprentice to his Friends   76

XXVIII. From an elder Brother to a younger   ib.

XXIX. A Letter from a Nephew to an Uncle, who wrote to him a Letter of Rebuke   77

XXX. Letter from a Niece to her Aunt   ib.

XXXI. Letter from a Youth at School to his Parents   78

XXXII. Letter from an Apprentice in Town, to his Friends in the Country   ib.

XXXIII. From an elder Brother in the Country, to his younger Brother, put an Apprentice in London   79

XXXIV. A Letter of Excuse for Silence, and Assurance that 'twas not out of Disrespect   80

XXXV. A Letter from a Servant in London, to his Master in the Country   ib.

XXXVI. From a Father to his Son just beginning the World   81

XXXVII. To an intimate Acquaintance to borrow Money   83

XXXVIII. To an Acquaintance, to borrow a Sum of Money for a little Time   ib.

XXXIX. An Answer to the foregoing   ib.

XL. Miss J——, in answer to Mrs. ——, making an Apology for not answering her Letter sooner   84

XLI. Miss

CONTENTS.

XLI. Miss J——— to Miss Lovelace, on the present Letter-Writers, and her Opinion of a well-wrote Letter 84

XLII. To Miss L. in Answer to her Description of Windsor 86

XLIII. Miss J. to Miss L. from an Inn on the Road, giving an Account of her Journey 87

XLIV. To Miss L. on the Expressions and Compliments commonly made Use of in Letters 88

XLV. From Miss Jones to Lady ——— 89

XLVI. From a Tradesman to his Correspondent, requesting the Payment of a Sum of Money 90

XLVII. The Answer. 91

XLVIII. To a Lady, inviting her into the Country for the Summer ib.

XLIX. From a young Person in Trade to a Wholesale Dealer, who had suddenly made a Demand on him 92

L The Wholesale Dealer's Answer 93

LI. From a young Person just out of his Apprenticeship, to a Relation, requesting him to lend him a Sum of Money ib.

PART II.

LETTERS of COURTSHIP and MARRIAGE.

I. From a young Person in Business to a Gentleman, desiring Leave to wait on his Daughter 95

II. From a Young Lady to her Father, acquainting him with a Proposal of Marriage made to her 96

III From a Daughter to a Mother upon the same Occasion ib.

IV. The Mother's Answer to the foregoing 97

V. A Young Lady's Answer to a Gentleman's Letter, who professes an Aversion to the tedious Forms of Courtship 98

VI. The Lady's Reply to another Letter from the same Gentleman, wherein he more explicitly avows his Passion 99

VII. From to Aunt to her Nephew, who had complained of ill Success in his Addresses ib.

VIII. From a Daughter to a Father, wherein she dutifully expostulates against a Match he had proposed to her, with a Gentleman much older than herself 100

IX. From

CONTENTS.

IX. From a young Lady to a Gentleman that courted her, whom she could not like, but was forced by her Parents to receive his Visits, and think of none else for her Husband   102

X. From a young Lady to a Gentleman who courts her, and whom she suspects of Infidelity   103

XI. From a Gentleman engaged to a Lady, who had been seen talking to another, in Answer to the foregoing   ib.

XII. From a Gentleman to a Lady, whom he accuses of Inconstancy   104

XIII. From a Lady to her Lover, who suspected her of receiving the Addresses of another. In Answer to the above   105

XIV. From a young Tradesman to a Lady he had seen in Public   106

XV. From a Relation of the Lady, in Answer to the above   107

XVI. From a Lover who had Cause of Displeasure, and determines never to see the Lady again   ib.

XVII. From a young Lady to her Father, acquainting him with the Addresses of a young Tradesman   108

XVIII. Her Father's Answer, on a Supposition that he does not approve of the young Man's Addresses   109

XIX. The Father's Answer, on a Supposition that he does approve of the young Man's Addresses   110

XX. A modest Lover desiring an Aunt's Favour to him for her Niece   ib.

XXI. The Aunt's Answer, supposing the Gentleman deserves Encouragement   111

XXII. From a respectful Lover to his Mistress   112

XXIII. The Answer   113

XXIV. A Gentleman to a Lady, professing an Aversion to the tedious Formality in Courtship   ib,

XXV. The Lady's Answer, encouraging a farther Declaration   114

XXVI. The Gentleman's Reply, more openly declaring his Passion   ib.

XXVII. The Lady's Answer to his Reply, putting the Matter on a sudden Issue   115

XXVIII. A facetious young Lady to her Aunt, ridiculing her serious Lover.   116

XXIX. Her

CONTENTS.

XXIX. Her Aunt's Anſwer, rebuking her ludicrous Turn of Mind   118

XXX. A Sailor to his Sweetheart   119

XXXI Her Anſwer   120

XXXII. Miſs Molly Smith to her Couſin, giving her an Account of a very remarkable Inſtance of Envy, in one of her Acquaintance who lived in the City of York   121

XXXIII. From an unknown Lady to a young Gentleman, on whom ſhe had unfortunately fixed her Affections   123

XXXIV. From the ſame Lady to the ſame Gentleman, on his expoſing and making public the foregoing   124

XXXV. Lydia to Harriot, a Lady newly married   125

XXXVI. Harriot's Anſwer to the above   127

XXXVII. To my Lady Lucy Sidney, upon the Marriage of my Lady Dorothy to my Lord Spencer   128

XXXVIII A Letter from Lady Wortley Montague againſt a Maxim of Monſ. Rochefaucault's, " That Marriages are convenient, but never delightful."   129

PART III.

FAMILIAR LETTERS of ADVICE and INSTRUCTION, &c. in many Concerns in Life.

I. A Letter from Judge Hale, Lord Chief Juſtice of England, to his Children ; on the ſerious Obſervance of the Lord's Day, (commonly called Sunday) when he was on a Journey   136

II. Earl of Strafford to his Son, juſt before his Lordſhip's Execution   137

III. From a Gentleman at Liſbon, immediately after the Earthquake, to his Son in London   139

IV. To Amelia, with a Gold Thimble   140

V. On the Viciſſitudes of human Life   141

VI. From a Father to his Son, on his Admiſſion into the Univerſity   142

VII. To Demetrius, with a Preſent of Fruit, on early riſing   144

VIII. To Lucinda, on the Happineſs of a domeſtic Matrimonial Life   146

IX. To Cleanthes, on Friendſhip, Age, and Death   148

X. A

C O N T E N T S.

X. A Letter from Biſhop Atterbury to his Son Obadiah, at Chriſtchurch College, in Oxford   151

XI. From a young Lady in one of the Canary Iſlands, to her Siſter in England, whom ſhe had never ſeen ; containing a preſſing Invitation to her to come over, and deſcribing the Beauties of the Place in order to prevail on her   152

XII. From Miſs Middleton to Miſs Pemberton, giving her the melancholy Account of her Siſter's Death   154

XIII. Miſs Middleton's Letter to her Siſter, wrote a few Hours before her Death, adviſing her not to defer making the neceſſary Preparations for Futurity   156

XIV. A Letter to Miſs W———, adviſing her to take Care of her Houſe, &c.   157

XV. From a ſenſible Lady, with a never-failing Receipt for a Beauty-Waſh   159

XVI. Domeſtic Rule, the Province of the Wife   161

XVII. From a Lady to her Acquaintance on growing old   163

XVIII. To a Lady who had loſt her Beauty by the Small-Pox   165

PART IV.

ELEGANT LETTERS on various Subjects, to improve the STILE and entertain the MIND, from eminent Authors.

I. From Mr. Gay, giving an Account of two Lovers who were ſtruck dead by the ſame Flaſh of Lightening   167

II. A moſt charming and affectionate Letter, univerſally admired, written by Mr. Pope, to the Biſhop of Rocheſter, about a Month before his Baniſhment   169

III. To Lady ———, from Mr. Pope, on witty and ſerious Letters   171

IV. From Mr. Pope to the Hon. Mrs. H—   172

V. From Mr. Pope, to Mr. Steel, on Sickneſs and dying young   173

VI The Parlour Looking-Glaſs to the beautiful Angelica   175

VII. From Hortenſius to his Friend Palemon, giving him an Account of his Happineſs in Retirement   178

VIII. A Letter of Conſolation on the Death of a Friend   179

IX. From.

CONTENTS.

IX. From a Gentleman to his Son, juft arrived from Paris, againft fervile Complaifance and Talkativenefs; with fome Directions for behaving politely in Company   180

X. A Letter written to the Dean of Waterford by a Widower, the Father of fix Children, under the fictious Name of Elzevir   183

XI. From *** to Cleora, on the Pleafures of Retirement   184

XII. By Mr. Pope in the Stile of a Lady   186

XIII. To Mrs. Rowe, on the Vanity of all fublunary Enjoyments   ib.

XIV. Mr. Locke to Anthony Collins, Efq;   187

XV. Earl of Rochefter to the Honourable Henry Saville   188

XVI. Earl of Rochefter to the fame   189

XVII. To Cleora   190

XVIII. To Colonel R***s, in Spain, from his Lady in England   191

XIX. Laura to Aurelia   192

XX. From Polydore to Alonzo; giving an Account of his accidentally meeting Aurelia, and of her Falfehood to him, &c.   194

XXI. From a Gentleman who died at Conftantinople, to his Friend in England; giving him an Account of the Manner of his Death   198

XXII. From **** to his Sifter; demonftrating the Unreafonablenefs of her Grief, on Account of his fudden Death, fince 'twas an immediate Tranfition to a State of Immortality and endlefs Blifs   200

XXIII. A Letter from Ariftus, giving his Friend a Relation of the fudden Death of his Bride, who was feized in the Chapel while the facred Rites were performing   201

XXIV. From Mr. Pope to Mr. Addifon   203

XXV. Mrs. Penruddock's laft Letter to her Hufband   205

XXVI. Mr. Penruddock's laft Letter to his Lady   207

XXVII. From a Perfon in Town to his Brother in the Country, defcribing a public Execution at Tyburn   ib.

XXVIII. Mifs Paget to Mifs Charlotte Vokes   210

XXIX. Mifs

CONTENTS.

XXIX. Miſs Vokes to Miſs Paget   212

XXX. Miſs Paget to Miſs Vokes, with a Deſcription of the dear Ball. A full and true Account of the Birth, Parentage and Execution, Life, Character and Behaviour of the Dancers   213

XXXI. From Miſs Vokes to Miſs Paget, not quite in the uſual Strain   220

XXXII. Miſs Evelyn to Lady Evelyn, giving her an Account of Mrs. Macnamara's Grandeur   221

XXXIII. The celebrated Mrs. Rowe to the Counteſs of Hertford   223

XXXIV. To Clitander, a melancholy Valetudinarian 224

XXXV. To Ariſtodemus   226

    To the Editor of the Complete Letter-Writer 227

XXXVI. Mr. Pope to Dean Swift   229

XXXVII. To Lord Treaſurer Oxford, on the Death of his Daughter the Marchioneſs of Carmarthen, by D. Swift   232

XXXVIII. From Sir Thomas Fitzoſborne, on the Death of his Father, to his Friend Euphronius   234

XXXIX. From Sir Thomas Fitzoſborne to Philotes, on the Loſs of a Friend   236

XL. From the ſame to Palamedes, againſt Viſitors by Profeſſion.   237

XLI. Lady Jane Douglas to Lady Mary Menzies   238

XLII Miſs Paget to Miſs Vokes, her Counſel to her Friend, upon the Subject of unequal Matrimony 241

XLIII. Miſs Vokes to Miſs Paget   242

POETICAL EPISTLES.

An Epiſtle to Philander, an eminent Tutor in the Capital   244

An Epiſtle from Arthur Grey, the Footman, to the Object of his Deſires, after his Condemnation for attempting a Rape   246

Forms of Meſſages for Cards and Billets, &c.   249

The Complete

LETTER-WRITER.

PART I.

Miscellaneous LETTERS on the moſt useful and common Occaſions.

LETTER I.

From a Brother at Home, to his Siſter Abroad on a Viſit, complaining of her not writing.

Dear Siſter,

I Muſt acquaint you how unkind 'tis taken by every Body here, that we ſo ſeldom hear from you; my Mother, in particular, is not a little diſpleaſed, and ſays, you are a very idle Girl; my Aunt is of the ſame Opinion, and none but myſelf endeavour to find Excuſes for you; but I beg you will give me that Trouble no more, and, for the future, take Care to deſerve no Rebuke, which you may eaſily do by writing ſoon and often. You are very ſenſible how dear you are to us all, think then with yourſelf, whether it be right to omit giving us the only Satisfaction that Abſence affords to real Friends, which is often to hear from one another.

Our beſt Reſpects to Mr. and Mrs. Herbert, and Compliments to all Friends,

From your very affectionate Brother,

T. C.

LET-

The Complete LETTER-WRITER. 51

LETTER II.

The Sister's Answer.

Dear Brother,

I'LL not set about finding Excuses, but own my Fault, and thank you for your kind Reproof; and, in Return, I promise you never to be guilty of the like again. I write this immediately on the Receipt of yours, to beg my Mamma's Pardon, which you, I know, can procure; as also my Aunt's, on this my Promise of Amendment. I hope you will continue to excuse all my little Omissions, and be assured, I am never so forgetful of myself, as to neglect my Duty designedly. I shall certainly write to Mamma by next Post; this is just going, which obliges me to conclude with my Duty to dear Mamma, and sincere Respects to all Friends,

Your ever affectionate Sister, M. C.

LETTER III.

A young Gentleman's Letter to his Pappa, written by a School-Fellow.

Dear Pappa,

ACCORDING to your Commands, when you left me at School, I hereby obey them; and not only inform you that I am well; but also, that I am happy in being placed under the Tuition of so good a Master, who is the best natured Man in the World; and, I am sure, was I inclinable to be an idle Boy, his Goodness to me would prompt me to be diligent at my Study, that I might please him: Besides, I see a great Difference made between those that are idle and those that are diligent; idle Boys being punished as they deserve, and diligent Boys being encouraged: But you know, Pappa, that I always loved my Book; for you have often told me, if I intended ever to be a great Man, I must learn to be a good Scholar, lest, when I am grown up, I should be a Laughing-Stock or Make-Game to others, for my Ignorance: But I am resolved to be a Scholar.

F 2 Pray

Pray give my Duty to my Mamma, and my Love to my Sifter.
      I am, dear Pappa,
       Your moft dutiful Son.

LETTER IV.
Another on the fame Subject.

Dear Pappa,

AS I know you will be glad to hear from your little Boy, I fhould be very naughty if I did not acquaint you that I am in good Health, and that I am very well pleafed with my Mafter; for he is very kind to me, and tells me, that he will always love young Gentlemen that mind their Learning: Therefore, I am fure, he will ftill love me; becaufe you know, Pappa, I always loved my Book: For you have told me, that Boys who do not mind their Learning, will never become Gentlemen, and will be laughed at for their Ignorance, though they have ever fo much Money: And as I am fure you always fpeak Truth, and I would willingly be a Gentleman, like you, I am refolved to be a good Scholar, which, I know, will be a Pleafure to you and my Mamma, and gain me the Love of every Body.

Pray give my Duty to my Mamma, my Uncle, and my Aunt, and my Love to my Sifter and Coufins.
    I am, dear Pappa,
     Your moft dutiful Son.

LETTER V.
To a Friend againft Wafte of Time.

Dear SIR,

CONVERSE often with yourfelf, and neither lavifh your Time, nor fuffer others to rob you of it. Many of our Hours are ftolen from us, and others pafs infenfibly away; but of both thefe Loffes, the moft fhameful is that which happens thro' our own Negleft. If we take the Trouble to obferve, we fhall find that one confiderable Part of our Life is fpent in doing evil, and the other in doing nothing, or in doing what we fhould not do. We don't feem to know the Value of Time, nor how precious a Day is; nor do we confider, that every Moment brings us nearer to our End. Re-
             fleft

The Complete LETTER-WRITER. 53

fleɛt upon this, I entreat you, and keep a ſtriɛt Account of Time. Procraſtination is the moſt dangerous Thing in Life. Nothing is properly ours but the Inſtant we breathe in, and all the Reſt is nothing; it is the only Good we poſſeſs; but then it is fleeting, and the firſt Comer robs us of it. Men are ſo weak, that they think they oblige by giving of Trifles, and yet reckon that Time as nothing, for which the moſt grateful Perſon in the World can never make amends. I am &c.

LETTER VI.

In Anſwer to a Friend.

SIR,

TO tell you in anſwer to yours, what I think of Proſperity, is, that I take it to be more dangerous to our Virtue than Adverſity. It is apt to make us vain and inſolent; regardleſs of others, and forgetful of God, ambitious in our Purſuits, and intemperate in our Enjoyments. Thus it proved to the wiſeſt Man on Earth, I mean Solomon. But I much admire what you ſay of Silence, and wiſh I could praɛtiſe that paſſive Virtue, which is the firſt Step of Wiſdom, the Nurſe of Peace, and the Guardian of Virtue. Words do but ruffle and diſcompoſe the Mind, betraying the Soul to a thouſand Vanities. I hope you will in our next Meeting, find me greatly improved in what you ſo much recommended to me. I remain, Sir, yours, &c.

LETTER VII.

To a young Gentleman.

SIR,

I Dare venture to affirm that Learning, properly cultivated and applied, is what truly makes the Gentleman, and that a wiſe Man is as much ſuperior to an ignorant Perſon, as a Man is above the Level of a Brute. Wherefore you cannot do better than to apply yourſelf ſeriouſly to the Cultivation of your Mind; to which Purpoſe nothing will contribute more, than your preſcribing yourſelf a regular Method of Study. The Morning is undoubtedly more proper for Reading than any other Part of the Day; becauſe the Mind is

then

then free and difengaged, and unclouded by thofe Vapours which we generally find after a full Meal. Nevertbelefs I would not affect to read over a Multitude of Volumes, nor read with Greedinefs; I would rather chufe to read a little and digeft it. Neither would I regard the Number, fo much as the Choice of my Books, &c.

LETTER VIII.

From a young Lady, in Anfwer to a Letter fhe had received from her Mamma, aduifing her to perfevere in the Chriftian Duties fhe had been inftructed in.

Moft honoured Madam,

I AM at a Lofs for Words to exprefs the Joy I felt at the Receipt of your Letter; wherein you are pleafed to acquaint me, that nothing ever gave my dear Mamma greater Pleafure, and Satisfaction, than the Account I have given her in the Conduct I obferve in my Spiritual Affairs; and that I may ftill add to that Comfort (which fhall ever be my Study) when an Opportunity offers itfelf, I prefume to continue the Information.

When I have properly difcharged my Duty to that Divine Being, to whom I am indebted for my Exiftence, I repair to my Toilet; but not with an Intent to cloath my Body (which I know muft fooner or later fall into Corruption) with vain Attire, but with fuch as is decent and innocent; regarding fine Robes as the Badges of Pride and Vanity; keeping thofe Enemies, to our Sex in particular, at too great a Diftance, ever to dare an Attempt upon my Mind

When public Prayers and Breakfaft are over, I apply my Thoughts to the Duties of the School; and divide the Time appointed for them as equal as poffibly I can, between the feveral Branches of Education I am engaged in, both before and after Dinner.

When School is finifhed for the Day, I, accompanied by a young Lady, who is my Bedfellow, and of a like Difpofition, retire to our Room, where we improve ourfelves by Reading. Books of Piety are our moft common Choice: Thefe warm our Wills, and enlighten our Underftandings: They inftruct us in the Caufe of our Mifconduct, and prefcribe to us a Remedy: They neither
flatter

The Complete LETTER-WRITER. 55

flatter a dignified Title, nor infult the Peafant who tills the Ground; but, like painted Buftos, look upon every one alike. In fine, they refresh the Memory, enlarge the Understanding, and inflame the Will; and, in a delightful Manner, cultivate both Virtue and Wifdom.

Having finifhed our Reading, either of Piety or Hiftory, which we prefer next, (efpecially fuch as relates to our own Country) and Supper and Prayers are over, I retire alone to my Room, to take an impartial View of the Actions of the Day. If my Confcience does not accufe me of having committed any Thing criminal, I give Glory to God; and with bended Knees, and an humble Heart, return him unfeigned Thanks for protecting me againft thofe Temptations which the Enemy to Mankind is ready to allure us with: For, I am perfuaded, it was not my Strength of Virtue that withftood the Temptations, but his affifting Grace that enabled me to overcome them; and if I am confcious to have done amifs, I fue for Pardon, and lay not my Body to reft, till I have procured Peace to my Soul.

If at any Time I am permitted to pay a Vifit, (which Liberty your Indulgence has allowed) I take care to time it properly; for there are certain Times when Vifits become rather troublefome, than friendly: Wherefore I avoid it when much Company is expected; or when I am certain that Family Affairs will not admit of fufficient Leifure to receive them: The former on my Account, the latter on my Friends: That is, much Company affembled together, ferves rather to confufe our Ideas, than enliven them. Wherefore, when I am fo unfortunate to ill-time a Vifit, I withdraw as foon as Civility and Ceremony will permit me; for, in my weak Opinion, Madam, long Converfations grow dull, as few of our Sex are furnifhed with a fufficient Fund of Materials for long Difcourfes, unlefs it be to comment upon the Frailties of the Abfent, and turn their Misfortunes into a Subject for our moft cruel Diverfion.

This, Madam, is a Vice you have often cautioned me againft, and I fhall be particularly careful to avoid it; being both an unchriftian and difengenuous Principle, to feaft ourfelves at another's Expence.

This,

56   The Complete LETTER-WRITER.

This is all I have to offer at prefent; and am, with great Humility,   Moft honoured Madam,

Your moft dutiful Daughter.

L E T T E R IX.

From a young Lady to her Mamma, requefting a Favour.

Dear Mamma,

THE many Inftances you have given me of your Affection, leave me no Room to believe that the Favour I prefume to afk will be difpleafing: Was I in the leaft doubtful of it, I hope my dear Mamma has too good an Opinion of my Conduct, to imagine I would ever advance any Thing that might give her the leaft Diffatisfaction.

The Holidays are nigh at Hand, when all of us young Ladies are to pay our feveral perfonal Refpects and Duties to our Parents, except one; whofe Friends (her Parents being dead) refide at too great a Diftance, for her to expect their Indulgence in fending for her: Befides, were they to do fo, the Expence attending her Journey would be placed to her Accompt, and deducted out of the fmall Fortune left her by her Parents.

This young Lady's Affability, Senfe, and good Nature, have gained her the Friendfhip and Efteem of the whole School; each of us contending to render her Retirement (as I may juftly call it) from her native Home and Friends, as comfortable and agreeable as we poffibly can.

How happy fhould I think myfelf above the reft of our young Ladies, if you will give me Leave to engage her to fpend the Holidays with me at Home! And I doubt not but her Addrefs and Behaviour will attract your Efteem, among the reft of thofe fhe has already acquired.

Your Compliance to this Requeft, will greatly add to the Happinefs I already enjoy from the repeated Indulgencies and Favours conferred on her, who will always perfevere to merit the Continuance of them.

I am, with my Duty to Pappa.

Dear Mamma,

Your moft dutiful Daughter.

L E T-

The Complete LETTER-WRITER.   57

LETTER X.

From a young Gentleman to his Pappa, desiring that he may learn to dance.

Dear Pappa,

YOUR affectionate and paternal Behaviour convinces me, that you are absolutely resolved to spare no Cost in any Branch of Education that is essentially necessary in the Employment you purpose I shall hereafter follow: And though I am certain you intend that Dancing shall have a Share in my Studies, nevertheless, permit me to put you in mind of it, and also to desire you will no longer, on Account of the Strength of my Limbs, (which I am sensible is the Motive that retards me from beginning) delay your Orders to my Master; for I am persuaded, from an Instance I am Witness of in our School of a young Master, who is much weaker in his Limbs than ever I was, that Dancing will rather strengthen than weaken my Joints.

It is not my Emulation for dancing a Minuet, that is the Motive that induces me to be thus pressing; for, I presume, there are other Things more necessary belonging to this Qualification than that; such as to walk well; to make a Bow; how to come properly into a Room, and to go out of it; how to salute a Friend or Acquaintance in the Street, whether a Superior, Equal, or Inferior; and several other Points of Behaviour, which are more essential than dancing a Minuet.

These Points of Behaviour I often blush to be ignorant of; and have several Times been the Ridicule of those young Chaps, who are advanced in the Knowledge of this Accomplishment: And as I am persuaded you would not chuse I should be a Make-Game to any of my School-Fellows, doubt not but you will send your immediate Orders for my beginning; which Favour, added to the many others you have already conferred, will greatly oblige,   Dear Pappa,
Your most dutiful Son.

LET-

58. The Complete LETTER-WRITER.

LETTER XI.

From a young Lady to her Pappa, who lately embarked for the East-Indies, *in the Company's Service, but detained at* Portsmouth *by contrary Winds.*

Dear Pappa,

I Flatter myself you are too well convinced of my steady Adherence to my Duty and Affection, ever to imagine I will omit the least Opportunity that offers, to pay you my most humble Duty.

I beg my dear Pappa may not be offended if I say, that it gives me a secret Satisfaction to hear you are still within the Reach of a Post Letter: And though I cannot have the Pleasure of a paternal Embrace, yet I rejoice in the Expectation of receiving the wished for Account of your Health's Continuance; which to me, my dear Mamma, and Brother, is the greatest Blessing that Providence can possibly bestow upon us.

Oh! Sir, though short to some the Interval of Time since I received your Blessing, ere your Departure from us, to me it seems an Age! And when I reflect how many such I am doomed to bear in the Absence of the best of Parents, I am inconsolable! And if it were possible that Nature could subsist on Sleep alone, I could with Pleasure renounce every Amusement whatever, and make the silent Pillow my Retreat.

Oh! may the Divine Being be your Protector against the many Dangers of that boisterous Element you are obliged to traverse! May he direct such gentle and favourable Breezes that may conduct you to your destined Port! May he add to this a happy and successful Voyage! and to crown all my Wishes, grant you a speedy and safe Return.

I have nothing worthy Notice to advise you of, but that we are all (God be praised) in the same good Health you left us, and are in great Expectation of the same comfortable Account in your Answer to this, from

Dear Pappa,
Your most dutiful Daughter.

L E T-

The Complete LETTER-WRITER.   59

LETTER XII.

From a young Woman juft gone to Service, to her Mother at Home.

Dear Mother,

'TIS a Fortnight, this very Day, that I have been at Mr. Johnfon's; and I thank God, I begin to find myfelf a little eafier than I have been: But, indeed, I have fuffered a great deal fince I parted from you, and all the reft of our Friends. At our firft coming hither, I thought every Thing looked fo ftrange about me: And when John got upon his Horfe, and rode out of the Yard, methought every Thing looked ftranger and ftranger; fo I got up to the Window, and looked after him, till he turned into the London Road, (for you know we live a Quarter of a Mile on the farther Side of it) and then I fat down and cried; and that always gives me fome Relief. Many a Time have I cried fince; but I do my beft to dry up my Tears, and to appear as chearful as I can.

Deareft Mother, I return you a thoufand Thanks for all the kind Advice you were fo good as to give me at parting; and I think it over often and often: But yet, methinks, it would be better if I had it in Writing; that would be what I would value above all Things: But I am afraid to afk for what would give you fo much Trouble. So, with my Duty to you and my Father, and kind Love to all Friends, I remain ever

Your moft dutiful Daughter.

LETTER XIII.

Her Mother's Anfwer.

My dear Child,

I AM very forry that you have fuffered fo much fince we parted: But 'tis always fo at firft, and will wear away in Time. I have had my Share too, but I bear it now pretty well; and hope you will endeavour to follow my Example in this, as you ufed to fay you loved to do in every Thing. You muft confider, that we never fhould have parted with you, had it not been for your Good. If you continue virtuous and obliging, all the

Family

Family will love and efteem you. You will get new
Friends there; and I think I can affure you, that you
will lofe no Love here; for we all talk of you every
Evening; and every Body fpeaks of you as fondly or
rather more fondly than ever they did. In the mean
Time, keep yourfelf employed as much as you can,
which is the beft Way of wearing off any Concern.
Do all the Bufinefs of your Place; and be always ready
to affift your Fellow-Servants where you can in their
Bufinefs. This will both fill up your Time, and help
to endear you to them: And then you will foon have as
many Friends about you there, as you ufed to have here.
I don't caution you againft fpeaking ill of any Body
living, for I know you never ufed to do it: But if you
hear a bad Story of any Body, try to foften it all you
can; and never tell it again, but rather let it flip out of
your Mind as foon as poffible. I am in great Hopes
that all the Family are kind to you already, from the
good Character I have heard of them; but I fhould be
glad to fee it confirmed by your next, and the more
particular you are in it the better. If you have any
Time to fpare from your Bufinefs, I hope you will give
a good Share of it to your Devotions: That's an Exercife which gives Comfort and Spirits without tiring one.
My Prayers you have daily. I might have faid hourly:
And there is nothing that I pray for with more Earneftnefs, than that my deareft Child may do well. You did
not mention any Thing of your Health in your laft; but
I had the Pleafure of hearing you was well, by Mr. Cooper's young Man, who faid he called upon you in his
Way from London, and that you looked as frefh as a
Rofe, and as bonny as a Blackbird.——You know James's
Way of talking.————However, I was glad to hear
you was well, and defire you will not forget to mention your Health yourfelf in your next Letter. Your
Father defires his Bleffing, and your Brothers their
kind Love to you. Heaven blefs you my dear Child!
and continue you to be a Comfort to us all, and more
particularly to

Your affectionate Mother.

L E T-

The Complete LETTER-WRITER.   61

LETTER XIV.

The Daughter to the Mother.

Dear Mother,

THO' we begin to have fuch cold Weather, I am
got up into my Chamber to write to you. God
be thanked I am grown almoft quite eafy, which is owing to my following your good Advice, and the Kindnefs that is already fhewn me in the Family. Betty
and I are Bed-fellows; and fhe, and Robin, and Thomas, are all fo kind to me, that I can fcarcely fay which
is the kindeft. My Mafter is fixty-five Years of Age
next April; but by his Looks you would hardly take
him to be fifty. He has always an eafy fmiling Countenance; and is very good to all his Servants. When he has
happened to pafs by me, as I have been dufting out the
Chambers, or in the Paffage, he generally fays fomething to encourage me; and that makes one's Work go
on more pleafantly. My Miftrefs is as thin as my
Mafter is plump: Not much fhort of him in Age;
and more apt to be a little peevifh. Indeed that may
eafily be borne; for I have never heard my Mafter fay
a fingle Word of any of us, but what was kind and
encouraging. My Mafter, they fay, is vaftly rich;
for he is a prudent Man, and laid up a great deal of Money while he was in Bufinefs, with which he purchafed
this Eftate here, and another in Suffex, fome Time before he left off. And they have, I find, a very good
Houfe in London, as well as this here; but my Mafter
and Miftrefs both love the Country beft, and fo they
fometimes ftay here for a whole Winter, and all the
Summer conftantly; of which I am very glad, becaufe I
am fo much the nearer you: And I have heard fo much
of the Wickednefs of London, that I don't at all defire
to go there. As to my Fellow-Servants, 'tis thought
that Betty (who is very good-natured, and as merry
as the Day is long) is to be married to the jovial Landlord over the Way; and, to fay the Truth, I am apt
to believe that they are actually promifed to one another.
Our Coachman, Thomas, feems to be a very good,
worthy Man: You may fee by his Eyes that it does his
Heart good whenever he can do a kind Thing for a iy

G

of the Neighbours. He was born in the Parish, and his Father has a good Farm of his own in it, and rents another. Robin, the Footman, is good-natured too ; he is always merry, and loves to laugh as much as he loves to eat ; and I'm sure he has a good Stomach. But I need not talk of that, for now mine is come again, I eat almost as hearty as he does. With such Fellow Servants, and such a Master, I think, it would be my own Fault if I am not happy. Well in Health, I assure you I am, and begin to be pretty well in Spirits ; only my Heart will heave a little still every Time I look towards the Road that goes to your House. Heaven bless you all there! and make me a deserving Daughter of so good a Mother.

LETTER XV.

The Mother's Answer and Advice.

Dear Child,

THE next Piece of Advice that I gave you, was, " To think often how much a Life of Virtue is " to be preferred to a Life of Pleasure ; and how much " better, and more lasting, a good Name is than " Beauty."

If we call Things by their right Names, there is nothing that deserves the Name of Pleasure so truly as Virtue : But one must talk as People are used to talk ; and, I think, by a Life of Pleasure, they generally mean a Life of Gaiety.

Now our Gaieties, God knows, are at best very trifling, always unsatisfactory, often attended with Difficulties in the procuring them, and Fatigue in the very Enjoyment, and too often followed by Regret and Self condemnation. What they call a Life of Pleasure among the Great, must be a very laborious Life : They spend the greatest Part of the Night in Balls and Assem blies, and fling away the greatest Part of their Days in Sleep. Their Life is too much opposed to Nature, to be capa ble of Happiness : 'Tis all a Hurry of Visits, twenty or thirty perhaps in a Day, to Persons of whom there are not above two or three that they have any real Friend ship or Esteem for (supposing them to be capable of ei

the

The Complete LETTER-WRITER. 63

ther); a perpetual feeking after what they call Diverfions; and Infipidity, and Want of Tafte, when they are
engaged in them, and a certain Languifhing and Reftleffnefs when they are without them. This is not living, but a conftant Endeavour to cheat themfelves out
of the little Time they have to live; for they generally
inherit a bad Conftitution, make it worfe by their abfurd
Way of Life, and deliver a ftill weaker and weaker
Thread down to their Children. I don't know any one
Thing more ridiculous, than the feeing their wrinkled
fallow Faces all fet off with Diamonds. Poor miftaken
Gentlewomen! they fhould endeavour to avoid People's
Eyes as much as poffible, and not to attract them; for
they are really a quite deplorable Sight, and their very
Faces are a ftanding Leffon againft the ftrange Lives
they lead.

People in a lower Life, 'tis true, do not act fo ridiculoufly as thofe in a higher, but even among them too
there's vaft Difference between the People that live well,
and the People that live ill: The former are more healthy, in better Spirits, fitter for Bufinefs, and more attentive to it; the latter are more negligent, more uneafy, more contemptible, and more difeafed.

In Truth, either in high or low Life, Virtue is
only another Name for Happinefs, and Debauchery is
the High-Road to Mifery; and this, to me, appears
juft as true and evident, as that Moderation is always
good for us, and Excefs always hurtful.

But is it not a charming Thing to have Youth and
Beauty,—to be follow'd and admir'd,—to have Prefents
offer'd from all Sides to one,—to be invited to all Diverfions, and to be diftinguifhed by the Men from all the
reft of the Company?——Yes, my dear Child. All
this would be charming, if we had nothing to do but to
dance, and receive Prefents, and if this Diftinction of
you was to laft always: But the Mifchief of it is, that
thefe Things cannot be enjoyed without encreafing your
Vanity every Time you enjoy them, and fwelling up a
Paffion in you, that muft foon be baulked and difappointed. How long is this Beauty to laft? There are
but few Faces that can keep it to the other Side of five
and twenty; and how would you bear it, after having

G 2   been

64   The Complete LETTER-WRITE

been ufed to be thus diftinguifhed and admired
Time, to fink out of the Notice of People, at
neglected, and perhaps affronted, by the very
who ufed to pay the greateft Adoration to you.

Do you remember the Gentleman that was
laft Autumn, and his prefenting you with the
Flower one Day, on his coming out of the Ga
don't know whether you underftood him or no
could read it in his Looks, that he meant it for
to you. 'Tis true, the Flower was quite a pre
but though you put it in Water, you know
and grew difagreeable in four or five Days; an
not been cropped, but fuffered to grow on in t
den, it would have done the fame in nine or ten
a Year is to a Beauty, what a Day was to that
and who would value themfelves much on the
fion of a Thing, which they are fure to lofe in
a Time.

Nine or ten Years is, what one may call the
Term of Life for Beauty in a young Woman :
Accidents, or Mifbehaviour, it may die long b
Time. The greater Part of what People call
in your Face, for Inftance, is owing to that Ai
nocence and Modefty, that is in it; if once you
fuffer yourfelf to be ruined by any bafe Man,
would foon vanifh, and Affurances and Ugliner
come in the Room of it.

And if other bad Confequences fhould fol
other bad ones there are, of more Sorts than t
would lofe your Bloom too, and then all's go
keep your Reputation, as you have hitherto kept
that will be a Beauty which fhall laft to the End
Days; for it will be only the more confirmed an
tened by Time : That will fecure your Efteem
all the prefent Form of your Face is vanifhed aw
will be always mellowing into greater and
Charms. Thefe my Sentiments you'll take as
fing, and remember they come from the Hart o
der and affectionate Mother.

The Complète LETTER-WRITER.   65·

LETTER XVI.

A Son's Letter at School to his Father.

Honoured Sir,

I AM greatly obliged to you for all your Favours; all I have to hope is, that the Progrefs I make in my Learning will be no difagreeable Return for the fame. Gratitude, Duty, and a View of future Advantages, all contribute to make me thoroughly fenfible how much I ought to labour for my own Improvement and your Satisfaction, and to fhew myfelf, upon all Occafions,

Your moft obedient, and ever dutiful Son,
ROBERT MOLESWORTH.

LETTER XVII.

A Letter of Excufe to a Father or Mother.

Honoured Sir, or Madam,

I AM informed, and it gives me great Concern, that you have heard an ill Report of me, which, I fuppofe, was raifed by fome of my School-Fellows; who either envy my Efteem, or by aggravating my Faults, would endeavour to leffen their own; though, I muft own, I have been a little too remifs in my School-Bufinefs, and am now fenfible I have loft in fome Meafure my Time and Credit thereby; but by my future Diligence, I hope to recover both, and to convince you that I pay a ftrict Regard to all your Commands, which I am bound to, as well in Gratitude as Duty; and hope I fhall ever have Leave, and with great Truth, to fubfcribe myfelf,

Your moft dutiful Son,
PHILIP COLLINS.

LETTER XVIII..

To Mr. ———.

Tunbridge.

I Think I promifed you a Letter from this Place; yet I have nothing more material to write than that I got fafe hither. To any other Man I fhould make

G 3   an

66 The Complete LETTER-WRITER.

an Apology for troubling you with an Information fo
trivial; but among true Friends there is nothing indifferent, and what would feem of no Confequence to
others, has, in Intercourfes of this Nature, its Weight
and Value. A Byftander, unacquainted with Play,
may fancy, perhaps, that the Counters are of no more
worth than they appear; but thofe who are engaged in
the Game, know they are to be confidered at a higher Rate. You fee I draw my Allufions from the Scene
before me: A Propriety which the Critics, I think,
upon fome Occafions recommend. I have often wondered what odd Whim could firft induce the healthy to
follow the fick into Places of this Sort, and lay the
Scene of their Diverfions amidft the moft wretched
Part of our Species: One fhould imagine an Hofpital
the laft Spot in the World to which thofe in Purfuit of
Pleafure would think of reforting. However, fo it is;
and by this Means the Company here, furnifh out a
Tragi-Comedy of the moft fingular Kind. While
fome are literally dying, others are expiring in Meta-
phor; and in one Scene you are prefented with the
real, and in another with the fantaftical Pains of Mankind. An ignorant Spectator might be apt to fufpect
that each Party was endeavouring to qualify itfelf for
acting in the oppofite Character; for the Infirm cannot labour more earneftly to recover the Strength they
have loft, than the Robuft to deftroy that which they
poffefs. Thus the Difeafed pafs not more anxious
Nights in their Beds, than the Healthy at the Hazard-
Tables; and I frequently fee a Game at Quadrille occafion as fevere Difquietudes as a Fit of the Gout. As
for myfelf, I perform a Sort of middle Part in this
motly Drama, and am fometimes difpofed to join with
the Invalids in envying the Healthy; and fometimes
have Spirits enough to mix with the Gay in pitying the
Splenetic.

The Truth is, I have found fome Benefit by the Waters; but I fhall not be fo fanguine as to pronounce
with Certainty of their Effects, till I fee how they enable me to pafs thro' the approaching Winter. That
Seafon, you know, is the Time of Trial with me; and
if I get over the next with more Eafe than the laft, I
fhall

shall think myself obliged to celebrate the Nymph of these Springs in grateful Sonnets.

But let Time and Seasons operate as they may, there is one Part of me, over which they will have no Power; and in all the Changes of this uncertain Constitution, my Heart will ever continue fixed and firmly yours.

I am, &c.

LETTER XIX.

From a young Apprentice to his Father to let him know how he likes his Place, and goes on.

Honoured Sir,

I Know it will be a great Satisfaction to you, and my dear Mother, to hear that I go on very happy in my Business; and my Master seeing my Diligence, puts me forward, and encourages me in such a Manner, that I have great Delight in it; and hope I shall answer in Time your good Wishes and Expectations, and the Indulgence which you have always shewn me. There is such good Order in the Family, as well on my Mistress's Part as my Master's, that every Servant, as well as I, knows his Duty, and does it with Pleasure. So much Evenness, Sedateness, and Regularity, is observed in all they injoin or expect, that it is impossible but it should be so. My Master is an honest, worthy Man; every Body speaks well of him. My Mistress is a chearful sweet-tempered Woman, and rather heals Breaches than widens them. And the Children, after such Examples, behave to us all like one's own Brothers and Sisters. Who can but love such a Family? I wish, when it shall please God to put me in such a Station, that I may carry myself just as my Master does; and if I should ever marry, have just such a Wife as my Mistress: And then, by God's Blessing, I shall be as happy as they are, and as you, Sir, and my dear Mother, have always been. If any Thing can make me happier than I am, or continue to me my present Felicity, it will be the Continuance of your's, and my good Mother's Prayers, for, honoured Sir,

Your ever dutiful Son.

L E T-

68   The Complete LETTER-WRITER.

LETTER XX.

From a Daughter to her Mother, by Way of Excuse for having neglected to write to her.

Honoured Madam,

THO' the agreeable News of your Health and Welfare, which was brought me laſt Night by the Hands of my Uncle's Man Robin, gives me an inexpreſſible Pleaſure; yet I am very much concerned that my too long Silence ſhould have given you ſo much Uneaſineſs as I underſtand it has. I can aſſure you, Madam, that my Neglect in that Particular was no Ways owing to any Want of filial Duty or Reſpect, but to a Hurry of Buſineſs, (if I may be allowed to call it ſo) occaſioned by the Honour of a Viſit from my Lady Betty Brilliant, and her pretty Niece, Miſs Charlotte, who are exceeding good Company, and whom our Family are proud of entertaining in the moſt elegant Manner. I am not inſenſible, however, that neither this Plea, nor any real Buſineſs, of what Importance ſoever, can juſtly acquit me for not writing oftener to a Parent ſo tender and indulgent as yourſelf: But as the Caſe now ſtands, I know no other Way of making Attonement, than by a ſincere Promiſe of a more ſtrict Obſervance of my Duty for the future. If therefore, Madam, you will favour me ſo far as to forgive this firſt Tranſgreſſion of the Kind, you may depend on my Word, it ſhall never be repeated by, . Honoured Madam,

Your dutiful Daughter.

LETTER XXI.

From Robin Redbreaſt *in the Garden, to Maſter* BILLY CARELESS *Abroad at School.*

Dear Maſter Billy,

AS I was looking into your Pappa's Library Window, laſt Wedneſday, I ſaw a letter lie open, ſign'd *William Careleſs*, which led my Curioſity to read it; but was ſorry to find there was not that Duty and Reſpect in it, which every good Boy ſhould ſhew to his Pappa; and this I was the more ſurpriſed at, when I found 'twas to aſk a Favour of him. Give me Leave, there-

The Complete LETTER-WRITER.   69

therefore, dear *Billy*, to acquaint you, that no one should ever write to his Pappa, or Mamma, without beginning his Letter with *Honoured Sir*, or *Honoured Madam*, and at the same Time, not forget to observe, thro' his whole Epistle, the most perfect Obedience, in a very obliging, respectful Manner. By these Means, you may not only increase your Pappa's Affection, but obtain almost any Thing from him, that you can reasonably ask, provided it be proper, and in his Power to grant; what can any good Boy desire more? But here you must permit me, dear *Billy*, to whistle an unpleasing but very useful Song in your Ear; which is, "That " you will never get so much as an Answer to any Let- "-ter that is not also wrote *handsome*, *fair*, and *large*; " which, as I know you are very capable of, am sur- " prised you will ever neglect it." And this you may depend on, for I know your Pappa extremely well, having frequently set for Hours at his Study Window, hearing him deliver his Sentiments to your Sisters, and advising them, in the most good-natured affectionate Manner, always to behave obedient to their Parents, and pretty and agreeable to every Body else, as well Abroad as at Home; and I must say it, his Advice and Commands, together with your Mamma's Care and Instruction, have had so charming an Effect, that they are beloved and admired where-ever they go; and at Home every Servant is extremely fond of them, and always ready to oblige and please them in every Thing, which I see daily, when I hop down into the Court to breakfast on the Crumbs from the Kitchen. How easy then it is for you, my dear *Billy*, who are so much older and wiser than your Sisters, to behave and write in the most dutiful and engaging Manner. And further let me advise you, never to lose Sight of the Love and Esteem of your Mamma, to whom you are all particularly obliged, for her constant Care to supply your continual Wants, which your Pappa, you are sensible, has not Leisure even to think of; besides, her good Sense and amiable Conduct, have so gained the Ascendant of your Pappa, that he does nothing relating to any of you without her Consent and Approbation; so that in gaining her Esteem, you are almost certain of his: But this
you

you are very fenfible of already, and I only juft chirp it in your Ear, to remind you of good Conduct, as well as filial Duty.

But the Morning draws on, and my Fellow Song-fters are Abroad to whiftle in the Day; fo I muft take my Leave on the Wing, and for the prefent bid you farewell; but beg I may never have Occafion again to write to you an unpleafing Letter of Rebuke; and that you will always remember, however diftant you are, or however fecret you may think yourfelf from your Friends and Relations, you will never be able to conceal your Faults; for fome of our prying tattling Tribe, will be continually carrying them Home, to be whift-led in a melancholy Strain, in the Ears of your Pappa, much to your Shame and Difcredit as well as his Diflike, and my great Concern, who am, deareft *Billy*, your ever watchful and moft affectionate Friend,

ROBIN REDBREAST.

From my Hole in the Wall,
Sun-rifing, the 1ft of June, 1767.

P. S However neglectful you may be of your Duty, I know you have too much good Senfe, as well as Good-nature, to take any Thing amifs that I have faid in this Letter, which is wrote with the Freedom and Concern of a Friend, and to which I was prompted both by Love and Gratitude, in Return for the Plenty of Crumbs I have received at your Hands, and the kind Protection you have always fhewn me, both in the Court and in the Garden, from fome of your idle Companions, who, with Sticks and Stones, have often, in your Abfence, aimed at my Life.

ROBIN REDBREAST.

LETTER XXII.

From one Sifter to another.

Dear Sifter,

EVER fince you went to London, your favourite Acquaintance Mrs. Friendly, and myfelf, have thought our Rural Amufements dull and infipid, not-withftanding we have the Players in Town, and an Af-fembly once a Week. At your Departure, if you re-member,

The Complete LETTER-WRITER.   71

member, you paffed your Word to return in a Month's Time, but inftead of that, it is now almoft a Quarter of a Year. How can you ferve us fo? In fhort, if you keep us in Sufpence much longer, we are determined to follow you, and find you out, let the Expence and Length of the Journey be what it will. We live in Hopes, however, that upon the Receipt of this Notice, you'll return without any farther Delay, and prevent our taking fuch an unmerciful Jaunt. Your Compliance with this our joint Requeft, will highly oblige, not only your moft fincere and affectionate Friends, but

Your ever loving Sifter.

L E T T E R XXIII.

In Anfwer to the foregoing.

Dear Sifter,

I Received your Summons, and can affure Mrs. Friendly, as well as yourfelf, that my long Stay in Town, notwithftanding all the good Company I have met with, and all the Diverfions with which I have been indulged, has been quite contrary to my Inclinations; and nothing but my Lady Townly's abfolute Commands not to leave her, fhould have prevented my Return to you within the Time propofed. You are fenfible I have infinite Obligations to her, and it would be Ingratitude to the laft Degree not to comply with her Injuctions. In order, however, to make you both ample Amends for that Uneafinefs which my long Abfence has given you, I fhall ufe my utmoft Endeavour to prevail with her Ladyfhip to join with me in a Vifit to you both in the Spring, and to ftay with you for a Month at leaft, if not longer. I would advife you therefore to fave an unneceffary Expence, as well as Fatigue, and reft contented where you are, till you fee,

Your ever loving,
And affectionate Sifter.

L. E T-

72　　The Complete LETTER-WRITER.

LETTER XXIV.

From Lady Goodford to her Daughter, a Girl of fourteen Years old, then under the Care of her Grandmother in the Country.

My dear Child,

THOUGH I know you want no Precepts under my Mother's Care to inſtruct you in all moral and religious Duties, yet there are ſome Things ſhe may poſſibly forget to remind you of, which are highly neceſſary for the forming your Mind, ſo as to make that Figure in the World, I could wiſh you to do:————— I am certain you will be kept up to your Muſic, Singing, and Dancing, by the beſt Maſters the Country affords; and need not doubt, but you will very often be told, that good Houſewifry is a moſt commendable Quality.————I would have you, indeed, neglect none of theſe Branches of Education; but, my Dear, I ſhould be grieved to hear you were ſo much attached to them, as not to be able to devote two Hours, at leaſt, every Day to Reading————My Father left a Collection of very excellent Books in all Languages behind him, which are yet in Being, and as you are tolerably well acquainted with the French and Italian, would have you not be altogether a Stranger to their Authors. Poetry, if it be good, (as in that Library you will find none that is not ſo) very much elevates the Ideas, and harmonizes the Soul; and well wrote Novels are an Amuſement, in which ſometimes you may indulge yourſelf: But Hiſtory is what I would chiefly recommend;————without ſome Knowledge of this, you will be accounted at beſt but an agreeable Trifler;————I would have you gay, lively, and entertaining; but then I would have you able to improve, as well as to divert the Company you may happen to fall into.

But, my dear Child, I muſt warn you to beware with what Diſpoſition you ſit down to read Books of this Nature; for if you ſlightly ſkim them over, and merely to gratify your Curioſity with the amazing Events delivered in them, the Reſearch will afford you little Advantage.————You muſt, therefore, conſider what you read;————mark well the Chain of Accidents which

bring

The Complete LETTER-WRITER. 73.

bring on any great Cataſtrophe; and this will ſhew you that nothing happens by Chance, but all is entirely governed by the Directions of an over-ruling Power:——In. diſtinguiſhing the true Cauſes of the Riſe and Fall of Empires, and thoſe ſtrange Revolutions that have happened in moſt Kingdoms of the World, you will admire Divine Juſtice, and be far from accuſing Providence of Partiality, when you find, as frequently you will, the good dethroned, all Rights both human and Divine ſacrilegiouſly trampled upon, a mock Authority eſtabliſhed in the Place of a real one, and lawleſs Uſurpation proſper; becauſe at the ſame Time, you will ſee that this does not happen till a People grown bold in Iniquity, and ripe for Deſtruction, have drawn down upon themſelves the ſevereſt Vengeance of offended Heaven, which is Tyranny and Oppreſſion; and though innocent Individuals may ſuffer in the general Calamity, yet it is for the Good of the Whole, in order to bring them to a juſt Senſe of their Tranſgreſſions, and turn them from their evil Ways?——This the Hiſtorical Part of the Bible makes manifeſt in numberleſs Inſtances; and this, the Calamities which at different Times have befallen every Kingdom and Commonwealth, evidently confirm.

I am the more particular in giving you theſe Cautions, becauſe, without obſerving them, you may be liable to imbibe Prejudices which will pervert your Judgment, and render you guilty of Injuſtice, without knowing you are ſo. As you regard therefore my Commands, which will always be for your Improvement and Emolument, never be remiſs in this Point.

Next to Hiſtory, I ſhould be glad to ſee you have ſome Smattering in Natural Philoſophy: For which Purpoſe let me recommend to your Peruſal a Work intitled, *Spectacle de là Nature*; or *Nature delineated, from the French of Abbe Le Pluche*; being very entertaining Philoſophical Converſations, wherein the wonderful Works of Providence, in the animal, vegetable, and mineral Creation are laid open, in four Pocket Volumes; in which are interſperſed, a great Variety of uſeful and explanatory Cuts.——Believe me, Child, the wide Creation preſents nothing that affords not infinite

H   Matter

74 · The Complete LETTER-WRITER.

Matter for a delightful Speculation; and the more you examine the Works of Nature, the more you will learn to love and adore the great God of Nature, the Fountain of all Pleasure.

I expect your next will be filled with no Enquiries on new Fashions, nor any Directions to your Millener; nor shall I be better satisfied with an Account of your having begun, or finished, such or such a Piece of fine Work :——This may inform you that it is other Kinds of Learning I would have you versed in,——I flatter myself with seeing my Commands obeyed, and that no Part of what I have said will be lost upon you, which a little more Time and Knowledge of the World will shew you the Value of, and prove to you more than any Indulgence I could treat you with, how very much I am   Your affectionate Mother, .   SOPHRONIA,

---

LETTER XXV.

To a young Lady, cautioning her against keeping Company
with a Gentleman of a bad Caracter.

Dear Niece,

THE sincere Love and Affection which I now have for your Indulgent Father, and ever had for your virtuous Mother, not long since deceased, together with the tender Regard I have for your future Happiness and Welfare, have prevailed on me to inform you, rather by Letter than by Word of Mouth, that the Town rings of your unguarded Conduct, and the too great Freedoms that you take with Mr. Freelove. You have been seen with him (if Fame lies not) in the Side-Boxes at both Theatres; in St. James's Park on Sunday Night, and afterwards at a certain Tavern, not a Mile from thence, which is a House (as I have been credibly informed) of no good Repute. You have both, moreover, been seen at Ranelagh Assembly, Vauxhall Gardens, and what is still more flagrant, at Cuper's Fire-Works. Don't imagine, Niece, that I am in the least prejudiced, or speak out of any private Pique; but let me tell you, your Familiarity with him gives me no small Concern, as his Character is none of the best, and as he has acted in the most ungenerous Manner by two or three very virtuous young Ladies of my Acquaintance, who entertained

tained too favourable an Opinion of his Honour. 'Tis possible, as you have no great Expectancies from your Relations, and he has an Income, as 'tis reported, of 200l. a Year left him by his Uncle, that you may be tempted to imagine his Address an Offer to your Advantage: 'Tis much to be questioned, however, whether his Intentions are sincere; for notwithstanding all the fair Promises he may possibly make you, I have heard it whispered, that he is privately engag'd to a rich, old doting Lady not far from Hackney. Besides, admitting it to be true, that he is really entitled to the Annuity above-mentioned; yet 'tis too well known, that he's deep in Debt; that he lives beyond his Income, and has very little, if any, Regard for his Reputation. In short, not to mince the Matter, he's a perfect Libertine, and is ever boasting of Favours from our weak Sex, whose Fondness and Frailty are the constant Topics of his Raillery and Ridicule.

All Things therefore duly considered, let me prevail on you, dear Niece, to avoid his Company as you would a mad Man; for notwithstanding I still think you strictly virtuous, yet your good Name may be irreparably lost by such open Acts of Imprudence. As I have no other Motive, but an unaffected Zeal for your Interest and Welfare, I flatter myself you'll put a favourable Construction on the Liberty here taken by

Your sincere Friend, and affectionate Aunt.

LETTER XXVI.

Letter of Thanks, &c.

SIR,

I Received the Favour of yours, with a very kind Present; and know not indeed, at this Time, any other Way to shew my Gratitude, than by my hearty Thanks for the same. Every Thing you do carries a Charm with it, your Manner of doing it is as agreeable as the Thing done. In short, Sir, my Heart is full, and would overflow with Gratitude, did I not stop, and subscribe myself,

Your most obliged, and

Obedient humble Servant,

JOHN WADMAN.

LETTER XXVII.

From an Apprentice to his Friends,

Honoured Father and Mother,

BY thefe I let you know, that by your good Care and Conduct I am well fettled, and pleafed with my Station, and think it my Duty to return you my hearty Thanks, and grateful Acknowledgment of your Love and tender Care of me: I will endeavour to go through my Bufinefs chearfully: And having begun well, I hope I fhall perfevere to do fo to the End, that I may be a Comfort to you hereafter, and in fome Meafure make a Return for your Love and Kindnefs to me, who am,

Your moft dutiful and obedient Son and Servant,
CHARLES SEDGLEY.

LETTER XXVIII.

From an elder Brother to a younger.

Dear Brother,

AS you are now gone from Home, and are arrived at Years of fome Difcretion, I thought it not amifs to put you in mind, that your childifh Affairs ought now to be entirely laid afide, and inftead of them more ferious Thoughts, and Things of more Confequence, fhould take Place; whereby we may add to the Reputation of our Family, and gain to ourfelves the good Efteem of being virtuous and diligent in Life, which is of great Value, and ought to be ftudied beyond any trifling Amufements whatfoever, for 'twill be an Ornament in Youth, and a Comfort in old Age.

You have too much Good Nature to be offended at my Advice, efpecially when I affure you, that I as fincerely wifh your Happinefs and Advancement in Life as I do my own. We are all, thank God, very well, and defire to be remembered to you: Pray write as often as Opportunity and Leifure will permit; and be affured a Letter from you will always give great Pleafure to all your Friends here, but to none more than

Your moft affectionate Brother
And fincere humble Servant,
EDWARD STANLEY.

LET-

LETTER XXIX.

A Letter from a Nephew to an Uncle, who wrote to him a Letter of Rebuke.

Honoured Sir,

I Received your kind Advice, and by the Contents of your Letter perceive I have been represented to you as one of immoral Principles. I dare not write you any Excuse for the Follies and Frailties of Youth, because in some Measure, I own I have been guilty of them, but not to that Degree which you have had them represented; howevever your Rebuke is not unseasonable, and it shall have the desired Effect, as well to frustrate the Designs of my Enemies, (who aim to prejudice you against me) as to please you, and obey all your Commands and Advice; which I now sincerely thank you for giving me, and promise, for the future, I will make it my Study to reform, and regain, by adhering strictly to your Instructions, the good Opinion you was once so kind to entertain of me. I beg my Duty to my Aunt, and am,

Your most obliged and ever dutiful Nephew,
HENRY MONTAGU.

LETTER XXX.

Letter from a Niece to her Aunt.

Madam,

THE Trouble I have already given you, really concerns me when I think of it, and yet I can't help intruding again upon your Goodness, for Necessity, that Mother of Invention, forces us to act contrary to our Inclinations; therefore, pray, dear Madam, excuse me if I once more intreat your Assistance in this Affair, in any Manner that you shall think proper; and I hope at least one Time in my Life, to be able to convince you that I have a thorough Sense of the many Obligations your Goodness has conferred upon

Your most dutiful and truly obliged Niece,
And very humble Servant,
JANE PEMBERTON.

H 3   LET.

LETTER XXXI.

Letter from a Youth at School to his Parents.

Honoured Father and Mother,

YOUR kind Letter of the 24th Inft. I received in due Time, and foon after the Things you therein mentioned, by the Carrier, for which I return you my fincere Thanks. They came very opportunely for my Occafions. I hope foon to improve myfelf at School, though I own it feems a little hard and irkfome to me as yet; but my Mafter gives me great Encouragement, and affures me I fhall foon get the better of the little Difficulties that almoft every Boy meets with at firft, and then it will be a perfect Pleafure inftead of a Tafk, and altogether as pleafant and eafy as it is now difagreeable and hard.

My humble Duty to yourfelves; and I beg the Favour of you to give my kind Love to my Brothers and Sifters, and remember me to all Friends and Acquaintance; and you'll oblige

Your ever dutiful and obedient Son,
CHARLES GOODENOUGH.

LETTER XXXII.

Letter from an Apprentice in Town, to his Friends in the Country.

Honoured Father and Mother,

THE Bearer, Henry Jones, came to fee me laft Night, and told me he fhould fet out for Home the next Morning. I was not willing to let flip the Opportunity of fending you a Letter by him, to let you know that I am very well, and like both my Mafter and Miftrefs, and by what I can fee of it, the Bufinefs extremely well, and do intend (pleafe God) to ufe my utmoft Endeavours to make myfelf Mafter of every Thing that belongs to it, in which I fhall have treble Satisfaction; firft, in pleafing my Mafter, fecondly in pleafing my Friends, and thirdly in benefiting myfelf. I have but little Leifure, nor do I want a great deal; but will take every Opportunity to let you know how I go on, and that I am, with great Gratitude,

Your ever dutiful and moft obedient Son, T. R.

L E T-

LETTER XXXIII.

From an elder Brother in the Country to his younger Brother put Apprentice in London.

Dear Brother,

I AM very glad to hear you are pleased with the new Situation into which the Care of your Friends has put you; but I would have you pleased not with the Novelty of it, but with the real Advantage. It is natural for you to be glad that you are under less Restraint than you were, for a Master neither has Occasion nor Inclination to watch a Youth, so much as his Parents: But if you are not careful, this, although it now gives you a childish Satisfaction, may, in the End, betray you into Mischief; nay, to your Ruin. Though your Father is not in Sight, dear Brother, act always as if you were in his Presence; and be assured, that what would not offend him, will never displease any Body.

You have more Sense, I have often told you so, than most Persons at your Time. Now is the Opportunity to make a good Use of it; and take this for certain, every right Step you enter upon now, will be a Comfort to you for your Life. I would have your Reason as well as your Fancy pleased with your new Situation, and then you will act as becomes you. Consider, Brother, that the State of Life that charms you so at this Time, will bring you to Independence and Affluence; that you will, by behaving as you ought now, become Master of a House and Family, and have every Thing about you at your own Command, and have Apprentices as well as Servants to wait upon you. The Master, with whom you are placed, was some Years ago in your Situation; and what should hinder you from being hereafter in his? All that is required, is Patience and Industry; and these, Brother, are very cheap Articles, with which to purchase so comfortable a Condition.

Your Master, I am told, had nothing to begin the World withal: In that he was worse than you; for if you behave well, there are those who will set you up in a handsome Manner. So you have sufficient Inducements to be good, and a Reward always follows it. Brother, farewell! Obey your Master, and be civil to all

80　　The Complete LETTER-WRITER.

all Persons; keep out of Company, for Boys have no Occasion for it, and most that you will meet with, is very bad. Be careful and honest, and God will bless you. If ever you commit a Fault confess it at once; for the Lie in denying it is worse than the Thing itself. Go to Church constantly; and write to us often. I think I need not say more to so good a Lad as you, to induce you to continue so.

I am your affectionate Brother.

LETTER XXXIV.

A Letter of Excuse for Silence, and Assurance 'twas not out of Disrespect.

THERE are Times, Madam, in which it is failing in Care, not to write to one's Friends; there are others in which it is Prudence. Methinks it better becomes an unhappy Man to be silent than to speak; for he tires if he speaks of his Misery, or he is ridiculous if he attempts to be diverting. I have not done myself the Honour of writing to you since my Departure, to avoid one or other of these Inconveniencies. I have too much Respect for you, Madam, to importune you with my Griefs; and I am not Fool enough to have a Mind to laugh. I know very well that there may be a Mean between these two Extremes; but, after all, the Correspondence of the unhappy are seldom pleasing to those who are in Prosperity. And yet, Madam, there are Duties with which one ought not to dispense; and it is to acquit myself of them, that I now assure you that no one can be with more Esteem and Respect than I am, Your faithful and affectionate Servant,

I. B.

LETTER XXXV.

A Letter from a Servant in London, to his Master in the Country.

SIR,

AS I find you are detained longer in the Country than you expected, I thought it my Duty to acquaint you that we are all well at Home; and to assure you

The Complete LETTER-WRITER.   81

you that your Bufinefs fhall be carried on with the fame
Care and Fidelity as if you were perfonally prefent.
We all wifh for your Return as foon as your Affairs
will permit; and it is with Pleafure that I take this Op-
portunity of fubfcribing myfelf,   Sir,
Your moft obedient, and faithful Servant,
SAM. TRUSTY.

LETTER XXXVI.

From a Father to his Son, juft beginning the World.

Dear Billy,

AS you are now beginning Life, as it were, and
will probably have confiderable Dealings in your
Bufinefs, the frequent Occafions you will have for Advice from others, will make you defirous of fingling out
among your moft intimate Acquaintance one or two,
whom you would view in the Light of Friends.

In the Choice of thefe, your utmoft Care and Caution will be neceffary; for by a Miftake here, you can
fcarcely conceive the fatal Effects you may hereafter experience. Wherefore it will be proper for you to make
a Judgment of thofe who are fit to be your Advifers by
the Conduct they have obferved in their *own Affairs*, and
the *Reputation* they bear in the World. For he who
has by his own Indifcretions undone himfelf, is much
fitter to be fet up as a Landmark for a prudent Mariner
to fhun his Courfes, than an Example to follow.

Old Age is generally flow and heavy, Youth head-
ftrong and precipitate; but there are old Men who are
full of Vivacity, and young Men replete with Difcretion; which makes me rather point out the Conduct
than the Age of the Perfons with whom you fhould chufe
to affociate; though, after all, it is a never-failing good
Sign to me of Prudence and Virtue in a young Man,
when his Seniors chufe his Company, and he delights
in theirs.

Let your Endeavours therefore be, at all Adventures,
to confort yourfelf with Men of Sobriety, good Senfe,
and Virtue; for the Proverb is an unerring one, that
fays, *A Man is known by the Company he keeps.* If fuch
Men you can fingle out, while you improve by their
Converfation,

82   The Complete LETTER-WRITER.

Converſation, you will benefit by their Advice; and be
ſure remember one Thing, that tho' you muſt be frank
and unreſerved in delivering your Sentiments, when
Occaſions offer, yet that you be much readier to hear
than ſpeak; for to this Purpoſe it has been ſignificantly
obſerved, that Nature has given a Man two Ears, and
but one Tongue. Lay in therefore by Obſervation, and
a modeſt Silence, ſuch a Store of Ideas, that you may,
at their Time of Life, make no worſe Figure than they
do; and endeavour to benefit yourſelf rather by other
People's Ills than your own. How muſt thoſe young
Men expoſe themſelves to the Contempt and Ridicule
of their Seniors, who, having ſeen little or nothing of
the World, are continually ſhutting out by open
Mouths and cloſed Ears, all Poſſibility of Inſtruction,
and making vain the principal End of Converſation,
which is Improvement! A ſilent young Man makes
generally a wiſe old one, and never fails of being reſpected by the beſt and moſt prudent Men. When
therefore you come among Strangers, hear every one
ſpeak before you deliver your own Sentiments; by this
Means you will judge of the Merit and Capacities of
your Company, and avoid expoſing yourſelf, as I have
known many do, by ſhooting out haſty and inconſide-
rate Bolts, which they would have been glad to recall;
when perhaps a ſilent Genius in Company has burſt out
upon them with ſuch Obſervations as have ſtruck Con-
ſciouſneſs and Shame into the forward Speaker, if he
has not been quite inſenſible of inward Reproach.

I have thrown together, as they occurred, a few
Thoughts, which may ſuffice for the preſent, to ſhew
my Care and Concern for your Welfare. I hope you
will conſtantly, from Time to Time, communicate to
me whatever you may think worthy of my Notice, or
in which my Advice may be of Uſe to you; for I have
no Pleaſure in this Life equal to that which the Happineſs of my Children gives me. And of this you may
be aſſured; for I am, and ever muſt be,

                              Your affectionate Father.

                                        L E T-

The Complete LETTER-WRITER. 8₃

LETTER XXXVII.

To an intimate Acquaintance to borrow Money.

PRAY favour me, Charles, with twenty Guineas, by the Bearer, who is my Servaut. I have immediate Occasion; but will repay it again whenever you please to make a Demand. This Letter will answer all the Purposes of a Note: From your obliged humble Servant, RICHARD ROLT.

LETTER XXXVIII.

To an Acquaintance to borrow a Sum of Money for a little Time.

Dear Sir,

IF it be quite convenient and agreeable to you, I'll beg the Favour of you to lend me fifty Pounds for the Space of three Months precisely: Any Security that you shall require, and I can give, you may freely ask. A less Time would not suit me; a longer, you may depend on it, I shall not desire. Your Answer will oblige, Sir, your very humble Servant,

JOHN ROBINSON.

LETTER XXXIX.

An Answer to the foregoing.

Dear Sir,

ANY Thing in my Power is always very much at your Service; the Sum you mention I have now by me, and can very conveniently spare it for the Time you fix, and you are most heartily welcome to it: Any Hour that you shall appoint To-morrow I'll be ready; and am, with the greatest Sincerity,

Your affectionate Friend and humble Servant,

CHARLES NUGENT.

LET-

LETTER XL.

Miſs J——, in Anſwer to Mrs. ——, making an Apo-
logy for not anſwering her Letter ſooner.

Madam,

'TIS paying you but an ill Compliment, to let one of the moſt entertaining Letters I've met with for ſome Years, remain ſo long unacknowledged. But when I inform you I've had a Houſe full of Strangers almoſt ever ſince, who have taken up all my Time, I'm ſure you'll excuſe, if not pity me. "Who ſteals "my Purſe, ſteals Traſh; 'twas mine, 'tis his, and "has been Slave to Thouſands: But he who filches "from me my precious Moments, robs me of that "which not enriches him, but makes me poor in "deed." 'Tis owing to this Want, I ſhould not ſay Loſs, of Time, (for the Hours have not paſs'd by unimproved or unentertaining) that I have not been able to tell you ſooner, how much I envy that Leiſure and Retirement, of which you make ſuch admirable Uſe. There 'tis the Mind unbends and enlarges itſelf; drops off the Forms and Incumbrances of this World, (which, like Garments trail'd about for State, as ſome Author has it, only hinder our Motion) and ſeizes and enjoys the Liberty it was born to. O when ſhall I ſee my little Farm! That calm Receſs, low in the Vale of Obſcurity, my Imagination ſo often paints to me! You know I am always in Raptures about the Country; but your Deſcription of Richmond is enough to intoxicate the ſoundeſt Head.

Adieu! I am interrupted, and in Haſte, ſo obliged to conclude,

Your's, &c.

LETTER XLI.

Miſs J—— to Miſs Lovelace, on the preſent Letter-Writers,
and her Opinion of a well wrote Letter.

WANT of Time, is, I think, the general Complaint of all Letter-Writers; and Yours in Haſte, concludes Wit, Buſineſs, every Thing. For my own Part my whole Life is little more than a perpe

tual

The Complete LETTER-WRITER. 85

tual Hurry, of doing nothing; and, I think, I never
had more Bufinefs of that Sort upon my Hands than
now. But as I can generally find Time to do any
Thing I've a Mind to do, fo can always contrive to be
at Leifure to pay my Refpects to Mifs L.

But the moft univerfal Complaint among Scribblers
of my Rank, is, Want of Senfe. Thefe generally begin with an Apology for their long Silence, and end
with that moving Petition, Excufe this Nonfenfe. This
is modeft, indeed; but though I'm exceffive good-natur'd, I'm refolved for the future not to pardon it entirely in any one but myfelf.

I have often thought there never was a Letter wrote
well, but what was wrote eafily; and, if I had not
fome private Reafons for being of a contrary Opinion
at this Time, fhould conclude this to be a Mafter-
Piece of the Kind, both in Eafinefs of Thought and
Facility of Expreffion. And in this Eafinefs of Writing (which Mr. Wycherly fays, is eafily wrote) methinks I excel even Mr. Pope himfelf; who is often
too elaborate and ornamental, even in fome of his beft
Letters; though it muft be confeffed he out-does me in
fome few Trifles of another Sort, fuch as Spirit, Tafte,
and Senfe. But let me tell Mr. Pope, that Letters, like
Beauties, may be over-dreft. There is a becoming Negligence in both; and if Mr. Pope could only contrive
to write without a Genius, I don't know any one fo
likely to hit off my Manner as himfelf. But he infifts
upon it, that a Genius is as neceffary towards Writing,
as Straw towards making Bricks; whereas, 'tis notorious that the Ifraelites made Bricks without that Material
as well as with.

The Conclufion of the whole Matter is this, I never
had more Inclination to write to you, and never fewer
Materials at Hand to write with: Therefore have fled
for Refuge to my old Companion, Dullnefs, who is e-
ver at Hand to affift me; and have made Ufe of all
thofe genuine Expreffions of herfelf, which are included under the Notion of Want of Time, Want of Spirit, and, in fhort, Want of every Thing, but the moft
unfeigned Regard for that Lady, whofe moft devoted

I remain, &c.

I   LET-

LETTER XLII.

To Miss L. in Answer to her Description of Windsor.

YOUR Account of the Shades of Windsor, and your Invitation to them, is equally pleasing and poetical. The first puts me in mind of the Elysian Groves, where the great Souls of Antiquity repose themselves on Beds of Flowers to the Sound of immortal Lyres; and there perhaps the Ghosts of departed Kings and Queens are still regaling themselves with soft Music, and gliding about their antient Mansions in Fresco; and the latter, of some gentle Spirit, the departed Genius of some Maid of Honour, (rather too plump for a Ghost) who beckens me into them. I'm impatient till I land in those calm Retreats, that Asylum from court'sying and Compliment, which I despair'd of arriving at in this sublunary State; where, if one can but get into the Groupe, all Distinction ceases; where, you say, I may do any Thing I have a Mind to do, without Impeachment of my Breeding; and where, disengaged from all the Forms and Incumbrances of this nether World, I'm like to be in perfect good Humour with myself, which, in most other Places, would be reckoned excessively rude.

Little did I expect to meet with you so near the Seat of polite Education, much less in King's Palaces, and among their honourable Women.————Tuesday then, I set out for the glorious Land, and the Genius that presides over it, if nothing very amazing intervenes. Many are my Thanks for your Offer of a Servant to meet me; but as I choose to give you as little Trouble as possible, shall take an Equipage along with me, to kill the Dragons and Monsters in Maidenhead Thicket. These Difficulties being overcome, shall lay my Spoils at your Feet, as Lady of the enchanted Castle, and ever after remain, Your peaceful Servant, &c.

LET-

The Complete LETTER-WRITER.   87

LETTER XLIII.

Miss J. to Miss L. from an Inn on the Road, giving an Account of her Journey.

ALAS! the Tranfition!———From Yefterday, Henrietta-Street, Mrs. L. and Mrs. ———, to a nafty Inn, the officious Mrs. Mary, damp Sheets, and perhaps the Itch before Morning. Yet fay not I want Refolution; never Virtue had more. Sick to Death from the Moment you left me, Head-Ach beyond Defcription, five Men and two Women to compliment my Way through in the Afternoon; yet boldly ruſh'd through them all, and took my Place in the Stage-Coach myfelf. After all, loft five Shillings Earneft by a Blunder, went in a wrong Coach at laft, and fuch a Morning!———But then I had a worfhipful Society! All filent and fick as myfelf; for which I thanked my Stars: For if they had fpoke, I had been murdered. Mrs. ———had almoft talked me into Non-exiftence Yefterday Morning; and I had been totally annihilated, if you had not come in and reftored me to my Identity. Pray tell her this in Revenge for my Head-Ach.

All our Friends that we took up in the Morning, we dropt gradually one by one, as we do when we fet out upon the Journey of Life; and now I've only a young Student of Oxford to finifh the Evening of my Day with; and prepare for the grand Events of To-morrow. I've juft been eating a boiled Chicken with him, and talking about Homer and Madam Roland; and am now retiring with Mrs. Mary to my Bed-Chamber, whom I fhall difmifs with her Warming-Pan in a Moment. If you do not permit me to pour out the prefent Set of Ideas upon all this Paper, I'm inconfolable; for I've no Book, and was too abfent till now to think I fhould want one.———How fudden, and how capricious are the Tranfitions of this mortal Stage! Pleafure and Pain are parted but by a fingle Moment. Windfor, Fern-Hill, Brook-ftreet, and your grey Gown, are no more; nor with Mr. Locke's Affociations, can I affociate a fingle Idea of the paft with the prefent. Even Lady ——— is defunct. And yet fhe might——But fhe is no more; Et de Mortuis nil nifi bonum.

88 The Complete LETTER-WRITER.

While Virtue fhines, or finks beneath ———

———— —— ———

—— —— —— ——

This Effort of Poetry, and that Scrap of Latin, which I don't underftand, has fo exhaufted all my Forces, that I find myfelf gradually finking into the Arms of Sleep, and muft now refign to the gentle Power of Dreams.

Farewell——and when, like me, opprefi with Care,
You to your own Aquinum fhall repair,
To tafie a Mouthful of fweet Country Air;
Be mindful of your Friend, and fend me Word
What Joys your Fountains, and cool Streams afford:
Then to affift your Rhapfodies I'll come,
And add new Spirit, when we fpeak of Rome.

JUVENAL.

LETTER XLIV.

To Mifs L. on the Exprefiions and Compliments commonly made Ufe of in Letters.

THE Money and Books came found as a Roach. *Safe* is fo common an Exprefiion, that I'm tired of telling People for ever, Things came *fafe*. We Geniufes are forced to vary our Exprefiions, and invent new Terms, as well to fhew our furprifing Compafs of Thought as our great Command of Language. This fometimes appears ftiff and affected to the Common Clafs of Readers, or Hearers, who are apt to be out of their Element, upon hearing any new or unufual Sounds; but our nicer Ears cannot always bear the fame Cadences. There's fomething peculiar in the Make and Structure of the auditory Nerve that requires Diverfification and Variety, as well as fome Skill in the Anatomy of Language, to make an Imprefiion on it, without wounding it. 'Tis for this Reafon, when I afk a Favour (a Thing I feldom chufe to do) I always felect the moft delicate Phrafes I'm Miftrefs of; but in Regard to Forms, which moft People are fick of, and yet furfeit their Friends with, thefe I vary according as

my

my own Humour or Inclination preponderates. Of Confequence, when I come towards the End, or Peroration of a Letter, I fometimes communicate my Compliments——fometimes defire they may be made known ——or where there's a large Family, and of Confequence a Number of Civilities to be paid, the laconic Stile of——my Deferences as ufual, has fometimes fucceeded beyond my Expectation. I'm fick of faying for ever, I beg my Compliments to fuch a one.——But as I propofe foon to give your Ladyfhip a particular Differtation upon Stile, and as I've many Flowers of Rhetoric yet inexhaufted, I fhall wind up the Words abovementioned into the Form of a Letter, and communicate all the Things I have to fay in the Poftfcript.

LETTER XLV.

From Mifs Jones to Lady ———.

THE firft Letter from an abfent Friend is furely the moft agreeable Thing to mufe over in Nature. Yours from Hatfield revived in me thofe pleafing Remembrances which not only enliven but expand the Heart; that very Heart, which, but the Moment before, felt itfelf mightily fhrunk and contracted at the Thoughts of your Departure. Lady H. Beauclerk partook of the Pleafure: The Moment fhe faw your Hand, fhe cried Half!———and read it moft complacently over my Shoulder.

'Tis to no Purpofe to tell you how much you are miffed by every Body that ftayed in Town; how often I caft my Eyes up at your Dreffing-Room Windows, or how many People I've run over in contemplating your Dining-Room Shutters. All I have to beg of you is, to write to me very often, to be mindful of your Health, and to order John, when I go to Town again, to tie up that Knocker. I could tell you many Stories of the fenfible Things; but of all the infenfible ones upon this Occafion, your Lamp provoked me the moft. To fee that Creature, when I've gone by in the Evening, burn fo prettily, and with fo much Alacrity, has put me out of all Patience. To what Purpofe fhould he light us into your Houfe

I 3

now? Or who'd be obliged to him for his paultry Rays?————I took a contemplative Turn or two in your Dreſſing-Room once or twice; but 'twas ſo like walking over your Grave, that I could not bear to ſtay. ————Lady H. departed two Days after you; and, in ſhort, I lived to ſee almoſt every Body I loved go before me. So laſt Saturday I made my own Exit, with equal Decency and Dignity; that is, with a thorough Reſignation of the World I left, and an earneſt Deſire after that I am now enjoying with Lady Bowyer and Miſs Peggy Stonehouſe, I ſhall begin verging towards my laſt Home, after having juſt touched upon the Confines of Lady H. B.'s World, there to ſubſide and be at Peace, where I ſhall have nothing farther to hope for, but to meet with a Letter from you.

I have implor'd St. Swithin in your Behalf; but he either not hears me, or, to pay you a greater Compliment, weeps plentifully for your Abſence. I fear you've had a terrible Journey; for ſcarce a Day has paſſed that he has not ſhed many Tears.

LETTER XLVI.

From a Tradeſman to a Correſpondent, requeſting the Payment of a Sum of Money.

SIR,

A Very unexpected Demand that has been made on me for Money, which I was in Hopes of keeping longer in my Trade, obliges me to apply for your Aſſiſtance of the Balance of the Account between us, or as much of it as you can ſpare. When I have an Opportunity to inform you of the Nature of this Demand, and the Neceſſity of my diſcharging it, you will readily excuſe the Freedom I now take with you; and as 'tis an Affair of ſuch Conſequence to my Family, I know the Friendſhip you bear me will induce you to ſerve me effectually.

I am, Sir, your moſt obedient Servant,

ROBERT JONES.

LET-

The Complete LETTER-WRITER.   9¹
LETTER XLVII.
The Answer.

SIR,

IT gives me singular Satisfaction, that I have it in my Power to answer your Demand, and am able to serve a Man I so much Esteem. The Balance of the Account is two hundred Pounds, for Half of which I have procured a Bank Note, and for Security divided it, and sent one Half by the Carrier, as you desired, and have here enclosed the other. I wish you may surmount this and every other Difficulty that lies in the Road to Happiness, and am,   Sir,   Yours sincerely,
       RICHARD TOMPKINS.

LETTER XLVIII.

To a Lady, inviting her into the Country for the Summer.

My dear Harriot,

I Don't know whether I flatter myself with an Opinion of your speaking to me the other Day with an uncommon Air of Friendship, or whether I am so happy to hold that Place, of which I should be so ambitious, in your Esteem. I thought you spoke with Concern at our parting for the Summer, on our Family's retiring into the Country. For Heaven's Sake, my Dear, what can you do all the dull Season in London?——— Vauxhall is not for more than twice; and I think Ranelagh one would not see above Half a Dozen Times in the Year. What is it then you find to entertain you in an empty Town for four or five Months together. I would fain persuade you not to be in Love with so disagreeable a Place, and I have an Interest in it; for I am a Petitioner to you to stay this Summer with us, at least I beg you will try. We go, my Dear, on Monday: Will you go with us? For there is a Place in the Coach; or will you come when we are settled? I am greatly of Opinion that it will please you. I am sure I need not tell you we shall do all we can to render it agreeable, or that you will make us very happy in complying with the Invitation.

             You

92   The Complete LETTER-WRITER.

You have not feen our Houfe; but it is a very pleafant one. There are fine Profpects from the Park, and a River runs through the Garden; nor are we quite out of the Way of Entertainment. You know there is a great deal of Company about the Place; and we have an Affembly within a Mile of us. What fhall I fay elfe to tempt you to come? Why I will tell you, that you will make us all the happieft People in the World; and that when you are tired you fhall not be teazed to ftay. Dear Harriet, think of it; you will confer an Obligation on her, who is, with the trueft Refpect,

Your affectionate Friend.

LETTER XLIX.

From a young Perfon in Trade to a Wholefale Dealer, who had fuddently made a Demand on him.

S I R,

YOUR Demand coming very unexpectedly, I muft confefs I am not prepared to anfwer it. I know the ftated Credit in this Article ufed to be only four Months; but as it has been a Cuftom to allow a moderate Time beyond this, and as this is only the Day of the old Time, I had not yet prepared myfelf. Sir, I beg you will not fuppofe it is any Deficiency more than for the prefent, that occafions my defiring a little Time of you; and I fhall not afk any more than is ufual among the Trade. If you will be pleafed to let your Servant call for one Half of the Sum this Day three Weeks; and the Remainder a Fortnight afterwards, it fhall be ready. However, in the mean Time, I beg of you not to let any Word flip of this, becaufe a very little Thing hurts a young Beginner. Sir, you may take my Word with the greateft Safety, that I will pay you as I have mentioned; and if you have any particular Caufe for infifting on it fooner, be pleafed to let me know that I muft pay it, and I will endeavour to borrow the Money; for if I want Credit with you, I cannot fuppofe that I have loft it with all the World, not knowing what it is that can have given you thefe diftruftful Thoughts concerning;

Your Humble Servant.

L E T.

LETTER L.

The Wholesale Dealer's Answer.

SIR,

I AM very forry to prefs you, but if I had not Reafon I fhould not have called upon you. It is not
out of any Difrefpect to you that I have made the Demand, but we have fo many Loffes that it is fit we
fhould take Care. However, there is fo much feeming
Franknefs and Sincerity in your Letter, that I fhall defire Leave firft to afk you whether you have any Dealing with an Ufurer in Bread-Street, and, if you pleafe,
what is his Name? Until you have given me the Satisfaction on this Head, I fhall not any farther urge the
Demand I have made upon you; but as this may be
done at once, I defire your Anfwer by the Bearer, whom
you well know; for he was, as he informs me, very
lately your Servant.

I affure you, Sir, it is in Confideration of the great
Opinion I have of your Honour, that I refer the Demand I have made to this Queftion; for it is not cuftomary, and is fuppofed not to be fair or prudent, to mention our Reafons on thefe Occafions. If this is cleared
up to me, Sir, as I wifh, but I fear it cannot be, I fhall
make no Scruple of the Time you mentioned. I beg
your Anfwer without Delay, and am fincerely,

Your Friend and Well-wifher.

LETTER LI.

*From a young Perfon juft out of his Apprenticefhip, to a Relati-
on, requefting him to lend him a Sum of Money.*

SIR,

I Can remember nothing but Kindnefs from you to our
unhappy Family ever fince my Infancy; and I flatter myfelf that I have not been guilty of any Thing
that ought to exclude me in particular from your Favour, provided you retain the fame kind Thoughts towards me. I may be miftaken in what I imagine farther, but I have always thought you had no fmall Hand
in putting me out; for I think my Father could not
have commanded fuch a Sum of Money, without the

Affiftance

94　　The Complete LETTER-WRITER.

Affiftance of fome generous Friend, and I can think of none but you. If this be the Cafe, Sir, I may be the more afhamed to write to you upon the prefent Occafion, fince it is Ingratitude to make one Benefit the Caufe of afking others : But I will venture to fay in my own Favour, that I think my Behaviour in the Time I have been with my Mafter, will not make againft me in the Application. If I afk what to you fhould feem improper, all that I farther requeft is to be pardoned.

Sir, I have at prefent before me the Profpect of being a Journeyman of a fmall Salary, and juft getting Bread, and that of being a Mafter in one of the moft advantageous Trades that can be thought of : And this is the Time of fixing myfelf in one Situation or the other. I am fenfible, Sir, you will fee the Defign of this Letter, becaufe the becoming a Mafter cannot be done without Money, and I have no where to apply for fuch an Affiftance but to your Favour : A moderate Sum, Sir, will anfwer the Purpofe ; and I think I am fo well acquainted with the Trade, as to be able foon to repay it ; at leaft, I am fure I can take Care that the Value of it fhall be always kept in Stock, fo that there can be no Rifk to lofe any Part of it. I have made the Computation, and with 200l. carefully laid out, I can make all the Shew that is neceffary, and have all Conveniencies about me. If you will be fo generous, Sir, to complete the Goodnefs you have already begun, by lending me this Sum, there is nothing fhall tempt me to endanger your lofing any Part of it ; nor fhall any Thing ever make me forget the Obligation.

　　　　　　　　I am, Sir, your moft obliged, and
　　　　　　　moft obedient humble Servant,　I. B.

　　　　　　　　　　　　　　　　　　　　　　　The

The COMPLETE

LETTER-WRITER.

PART II.

LETTERS of Courtſhip and Marriage.

LETTER I.

From a young Perſon in Buſineſs to a Gentleman, deſiring Leave to wait on his Daughter.

SIR,

I HOPE the Juſtneſs of my Intentions will excuſe the Freedom of this Letter, whereby I am to acquaint you of the Affection and Eſteem I have for your Daughter. I would not, Sir, offer, at any indirect Addreſs, that ſhould have the leaſt Appearance of Inconſiſtency with her Duty to you, and my honourable Views to her; chooſing, by your Influence, if I may approve myſelf to you worthy of that Honour, to commend myſelf to her Approbation. You are not inſenſible, Sir, by the Credit I have hitherto preſerved in the World, of my Ability, by God's Bleſſing, to make her happy; and this the rather emboldens me to requeſt the Favour of an Evening's Converſation with you, at your firſt Convenience, when I will more fully explain myſelf, as I earneſtly hope, to your Satisfaction, and take my Encouragement, or Diſcouragement, from your own Mouth. I am, Sir, in the mean Time, with great Reſpect,

Your moſt obedient humble Servant.

LET-

96　　The Complete LETTER-WRITER,
LETTER II.

From a young Lady to her Father, acquainting him with a Proposal of Marriage made to her.

Honoured Sir,

AS young Mr. Lovewell, whose Father, I am sensible, is one of your intimate Acquaintance, has, during your Absence in the Country, made an open Declaration of his Passion for me, and prest me closely to comply with his Overtures of Marriage, I thought it my Duty to decline all Offers of that Nature, however advantageous they might seem to be, till I had your Thoughts on so important an Affair; and I am absolutely determined either to discourage his Addresses, or keep him at least in Suspence, till your Return, as I shall be directed by your superior Judgment. I beg Leave, however, with due Submission, to acquaint you of the Idea I have entertained of him, and hope I am not too blind, or partial in his Favour. He seems to me to be perfectly honourable in his Intentions, and to be no Ways inferior to any Gentleman of my Acquaintance hitherto, in Regard to good Sense or good Manners. —— I frankly own, Sir, I could admit of his Addresses with Pleasure, were they attended with your Consent and Approbation: Be assured, however, that I am not so far engaged, as to act with Precipitation, or comply with any Offers inconsistent with that filial Duty, which, in Gratitude to your paternal Indulgence, I shall ever owe you. Your speedy Instruction therefore in so momentous an Article, will prove the greatest Satisfaction imaginable to,

Honoured Sir, your most dutiful Daughter.

LETTER III.

From a Daughter to her Mother upon the same Occasion.

Honoured Madam,

SOON after I left you and my Friends in the Country, I happily engaged with one Mrs. Prudence, a Governess of a noted young Ladies Boarding-School at the Court End of the Town, to act as her Assistant. She has treated me, ever since I have been with her, with

The Complete LETTER-WRITER.   97

with the utmoft Good-Nature and Condefcenfion, and has all along endeavoured to make my Service more eafy and advantageous to me than I could reafonably expect. On the other Hand, as a grateful Acknowledgment of her Favours, I have made her Intereft my whole Study and Delight. My courteous Deportment towards the young Ladies, and my conftant Care to oblige my Governefs, have not only gained me the Love and Efteem of the whole Houfe, but young Mr. Byron, the Dancing-Mafter who attends our School weekly, has caft a favourable Eye upon me fome Time, and has lately made me fuch Overtures of Marriage, as are, in my own Opinion, worthy of my Attention. However, notwithftanding he is a great Favourite of Mrs. Prudence, a Man of unblemifhed Character, and very extenfive Bufinefs, I thought it would be an Act of the higheft Ingratitude, to fo indulgent a Parent as you have been to me, to conceal from you an Affair wherein my future Happinefs or Mifery, muft fo greatly depend. As to his Perfon, Age, and Temper, I muft own, Madam, with a Blufh, that they are all perfectly agreeable; and I fhould think myfelf very happy, fhould you countenance his Addreffes. I flatter myfelf however, that I have fo much Command of my own Paffions, as in Duty to be directed in fo momentous an Affair by your fuperior Judgment. Your fpeedy Anfwer therefore will be looked upon as an additional Act of Indulgence fhewn to,   Your moft dutiful Daughter.

LETTER IV.

The Mother's Anfwer to the foregoing.

Dear Daughter,

I Received yours in regard to the Overtures of Marriage made you by Mr. Byron, and as that is a very weighty Affair, I fhall return to London as foon as poffible, in order to make all due Enquiries And in Cafe I find no juft Grounds for Exceptions to the Man, I have none to his Occupation; fince 'tis fuitable enough to that State of Life for which you feem to have a peculiar Tafte. However, tho' I fhould rejoice to fee you fettled to your Satisfaction and Advantage, and

K   tho'

tho' you feem to entertain a very favourable Opinion of
his Honour, and Abilities to maintain you in a very
decent Manner; yet I would have you weigh well the
momentous Matter in Debate: Don't be too hafty, my
Dear; confider, all is not Gold that glitters: Men are
too often falfe and perfidious; promife fair, and yet, at
the fame Time, aim at nothing more than the Gratifi-
cation of their unruly Defires. I don't fay that Mr.
Byron has any fuch difhonourable Intentions, and I
hope he has not, for which Reafon I would only have
you act with Difcretion and Referve; give him neither
too great Hopes of Succefs, nor an abfolute Denial to
put him in Defpair. All that you have to fay till you
fee me is this, that you have no Averfion to his Perfon;
but that you are determined to be wholly directed by
your Mother in an Affair of fo ferious a Concern. This
will naturally induce him to make his Application to me
on my firft Arrival; and you may depend upon it, no
Care fhall be wanting on my Side to promote your future Happinefs and Advantage.   I am,
Dear Daughter, your truly affectionate Mother.

LETTER V.

*A young Lady's Anfwer to a Gentleman's Letter, who pro-
feffes an Averfion to the tedious Forms of Courtfhip.*

SIR,

I AM no more fond of the fafhionable Modes of
Courtfhip than yourfelf. Plain Dealing I own is
beft; but methinks common Decency fhould always be
preferved.

There is fomething fo peculiar and whimfical in your
Manner of Expreffion, that I am abfolutely at a Lofs to
determine whether you are really ferious, or only write
for your own Amufement. When you explain yourfelf
in more intelligible Terms, I fhall be better able to
form a Judgment of your Paffion, and more capable of
returning you a proper Anfwer. What Influence your
future Addreffes may have over me I cannot fay; but to
be free with you, your firft Attempt has made no Impreffion on the the Heart of,   MIRA.

LET-

The Complete LETTER-WRITER. 99

LETTER VI.

The Lady's Reply to another Letter from the same Gentle-
man, wherein he more explicitly avows his Passion.

S I R,

SINCE neither of us, I perceive, is over-fond of
squandering our Time away in idle, unmeaning
Compliments, I think proper to inform you, in direct
Terms, that the Disposal of my Person is not altogether
in my own Power; and that notwithstanding my Father and Mother are both deceased, yet I transact no
single Affair of any Moment, without consulting Sir
Orlando Wiseman, of Lincoln's Inn, who is my Counsel upon all Occasions, and is a Gentleman, as I conceive, of the strictest Honour and Honesty, and one on
whose Judgment I can safely rely. I'll be so fair and
just to you, as freely to acknowledge, that I have no
Objection to your Person: If therefore you think proper to wait on him with your Proposals, and I find that
he approves them, I shall act without any mental Reser-
vation, and be very apt to encourage a Passion, that I
imagine to be both honourable and sincere.

I am, Sir, your humble Servant.

LETTER VII.

From an Aunt to her Nephew, who had complained of ill
Success in his Addresses.

Dear Nephew,

I Received your doleful Ditty, in regard to your ill
Success in your late Love Adventure with Miss
Snow. No Marble Monument was ever half so cold,
or Vestal Virgin half so coy! She turns a deaf Ear, it
seems, to your most ardent Vows! And what of all
that? By your own Account it appears, she has given
you no flat Denial; neither has she peremptorily forbid
your Visits. Really, Nephew, I thought a young Gentleman of your good Sense and Penetration, should be
better vers'd in the Arts of Love, than to be cast down
all at once, and quit the Field upon the first Re-
pulse. You should consider, that she's not only a Beau-

K 2.   ty,

ty, but a very accomplished Lady. You muſt ſurely be
very vain to imagine, that one of her Education, good
Senſe, and real Merit, ſhould fall an eaſy Victim into
your Arms. Her Affections muſt be gradually engaged; ſhe looks upon Matrimony as a very ſerious Affair, and will never give Way, I am fully perſuaded, to
the Violence of an-ill grounded Paſſion. For Shame,
Nephew, ſhake off that unbecoming Baſhfulneſs, and
ſhew yourſelf a Man. Lovers, like Soldiers, ſhould
endure Fatigues. Be adviſed: Renew the Attack with
double Vigour: for ſhe's a Lady worth your Conqueſt.
The Revolution of a Day (as the ingenious Mr. Rowe
has it) may bring ſuch Turns as Heaven itſelf could
ſcarce have promiſed. Chear up, dear Nephew, under
that Thought. When I hear from you again, a few
Weeks hence, I am not without Hopes, if you will follow my Advice, of your carrying the Siege, and making her comply with your own Terms of Accommodation. In the mean Time, depend upon it, no Stone
ſhall be left unturned on my Part, that may any Ways
contribute towards your good Succeſs, as I cannot, without Injuſtice to the Lady, but approve your Choice.

I am, your affectionate Aunt.

LETTER VIII.

*From a Daughter to a Father, wherein ſhe dutifully expoſ-
tulates againſt a Match he had propoſed to her, with a
Gentleman much older than herſelf.*

Honoured Sir,

THO' your Injunctions ſhould prove diametrically
oppoſite to my own ſecret Inclinations, yet I am
not inſenſible, that the Duty which I owe you binds me
to comply with them. Beſides, I ſhould be very ungrateful, ſhould I preſume, in any Point whatever, con-
ſidering your numberleſs Acts of parental Indulgencies
towards me, to conteſt your Will and Pleaſure. Tho'
the Conſequences thereof ſhould prove never ſo fatal, I
am determined to be all Obedience, in Caſe what I have
to offer in my own Defence ſhould have no Influence
over you, or be thought an inſufficient Plea for my A-
verſion to a Match, which, unhappily for me, you ſeem,

to

The Complete LETTER-WRITER.   101

to approve of. 'Tis very poffible, Sir, the Gentleman you recommend to my Choice, may be poffeffed of all, that Subftance, and all thofe good Qualities, that bias you fo ftrongly in his Favour; but be not angry, dear Sir, when I remind you, that there is a vaft Difproportion in our Years. A Lady, of more Experience, and of a more advanced Age, would, in my humble Opinion, be a much fitter Help-Mate for him. To be ingenuous, (permit me, good Sir, to fpeak the Sentiments of my Heart without Referve for once) a Man, almoft in his grand Climacterick, can never be an agreeable Companion for me; nor can the natural Gaiety of my Temper, which has hitherto been indulged by yourfelf in every innocent Amufement, be over-agreeable to him. Tho' his Fondnefs at firft may connive at the little Freedoms I fhall be apt to take; yet as foon as the Edge of his Appetite fhall be abated, he'll grow jealous, and for ever torment me without a Caufe. I fhall be debarr'd of every Diverfion fuitable to my Years, tho' never fo harmlefs and inoffenfive; permitted to fee no Company; hurried down perhaps to fome melancholy rural Recefs; and there, like my Lady Grace in the Play, fit penfive and alone, under a green Tree. Your long experienced Goodnefs, and that tender Regard, which you have always expreffed for my Eafe and Satisfaction, encourage me thus freely to expoftulate with you on an Affair of fo great Importance. If, however, after all, you fhall judge the Inequality of our Age an infufficient Plea in my Favour, and that Want of Affection for a Hufband is but a Trifle, where there is a large Fortune and a Coach and Six to throw into the Scale; if, in fhort, you fhall lay your peremptory Commands upon me to refign up all my real Happinefs and Peace of Mind for the Vanity of living in Pomp and Grandeur, I am ready to fubmit to your fuperior Judgment. Give me Leave, however, to obferve, that 'tis impoffible for me ever to love the Man into whofe Arms I am to be thrown, and that my Compliance with fo detefted a Propofition, is nothing more than the Refult of the moft inviolable Duty to a Father, who never made the leaft Attempt before to thwart the Inclinations of,

His ever obedient Daughter.

K 3.   L. E. T.

102·   The Complete LETTER-WRITER.

LETTER IX.

From a young Lady to a Gentleman that courted her, whom she could not like, but was forced by her Parents to receive his Visits, and think of none else for her Husband.

SIR,

IT is a very ill Return which I make to the Respect you have for me, when I acknowledge to you, that tho' the Day of our Marriage is appointed, I am incapable of loving you. You may have observed, in the long Conversation we have had at those Times that we were left together, that some Secret hung upon my Mind I was constrained to an ambiguous Behaviour, and durst not reveal myself further, because my Mother, from a Closet near the Place where we sat, could both hear and see our Conversation. I have strict Commands from both my Parents to receive you, and am undone for ever, except you will be so kind and generous as to refuse me. Consider, Sir, the Misery of bestowing yourself upon one who can have no Prospect of Happiness but from your Death. This is a Confession made perhaps with an offensive Sincerity; but that Conduct is much to be preferred to a secret Dislike, which could not but pall all the Sweets of Life, by imposing on you a Companion that doats and languishes for another. I will not go so far as to say my Passion for the Gentleman, whose Wife I am by Promise, would lead me to any Thing criminal against your Honour. I know it is dreadful enough to a Man of your Sense to expect nothing but forced Civilities in Return for your tender Endearments, and cold Esteem for undeserved Love. If you will on this Occasion let Reason take Place of Passion, I doubt not but Fate has in Store for you some worthier Object of your Affection, in Recompence for your Goodness to the only Woman that could be insensible of your Merit.   I am,

Sir, your most humble Servant,   M. H.

LET-

LETTER X.

From a young Lady to a Gentleman who courts her, and whom
she suspects of Infidelity.

SIR,

THE Freedom and Sincerity with which I have at
all Times laid open my Heart to you, ought to
have some Weight in my Claim to a Return of the
same Confidence; but I have Reason to fear that the
best of Men do not always act as they ought. I write to
you what it would be impossible to speak; but, before
I see you, I desire you will either explain your Conduct
last Night, or confess that you have used me not as I
have deserved of you.

It is in vain to deny that you took Pains to recommend yourself to Miss Peacock; your Earnestness of
Discourse shewed me that you were no Stranger to
her. I desire to know, Sir, what Sort of Acquaintance you can wish to have with another Person of Character, after making me believe that you wished to be
married to me. I write very plainly to you, because
I expect a plain Answer. I am not apt to be suspicious,
but this was too particular, and I must be either blind
or indifferent to overlook it. Sir, I am neither; though
perhaps it would be better for me if I were one or the o-
ther.   I am, yours, &c.

LETTER XI.

From a Gentleman engaged to a Lady, who had been seen talk-
ing to another, in Answer to the foregoing.

My dearest Jenny,

WHAT can have put it into your Thoughts to be
suspicious of me, whose Heart and Soul you know
are truly yours, and whose whole Thoughts and Wishes
are but on you? Sweet Quarreller, you know this: What
Afternoon have I spent from you? Or who did you ever
see me speak to without Distaste, when it prevented my
talking with you?

You know how often you have cautioned me not to
speak to you before your Uncle; and you know he was
there. But you do well to abuse me for being too obedient

dient to your Commands; for, I promife you, you fhall never get any other Caufe. I thought it moft prudent to be feen talking with another, when it was my Bufi-nefs not fo much as to look at you. Mifs Peacock is a very old Acquaintance: She knows my perfect Devotion to you, and fhe very well knew all that Civility and Earneftnefs of Difcourfe about nothing, was pretended. I write to you before I come, becaufe you commanded me; but I will make you afk my Pardon in a few Minutes for robbing me of thofe few, which might have been paffed with you, and which it has taken to write this Letter. My fweeteft Quarreller, I am coming to you. After this never doubt but that I am,

Yours moft truly.

LETTER XII.

From a Gentleman to a Lady, whom he accufes of Incon-
ftancy.

Madam,

YOU muft not be furprifed at a Letter in the Place of a Vifit, from one who cannot but have Reafon to believe it may eafily be as welcome as his Company.

You fhould not fuppofe, if Lovers have loft their Sight, that their Senfes are all banifhed: And if I re-fufe to believe my Eyes, when they fhew me your In-conftancy, you muft not wonder that I cannot ftop my Ears againft the Accounts of it. Pray let us underftand one another properly; for I am afraid we are deceiving ourfelves all this while: Am I a Perfon whom you ei-teem, whofe Fortune you do not defpife, and whofe Pre-tenfions you encourage; or am I a troublefome Cox-comb, who fancies myfelf particularly received by a Wo-man who only laughs at me? If I am the latter, you treat me as I deferve; and I ought to join with you in faying I deferve it: But if it be otherwife, and you receive me, as I think you do, as a Perfon you intend to marry, for it is beft to be plain on thefe Occafions, for Heaven's Sake, what is the Meaning of that uni-verfal Coquetry in public, where every Fool flatters you, and you are pleafed with the meaneft of them? And what can be the Meaning that I am told, you laft

Night

The Complete LETTER-WRITER.   105

Night in particular was an Hour with Mr. Marlow, and are so wherever you meet him if I am not in Company? Both of us, Madam, you cannot think of; and I should be sorry to imagine, that when I had given you my Heart so entirely, I shared yours with any Body.

I have said a great deal too much to you, and yet I am tempted to say more; but I shall be silent. I beg you will answer this, and I think I have a Right to expect that you do it generously and fairly. Do not mistake what is the Effect of the Distraction of my Heart, for Want of Respect to you. While I write this, I doat upon you, but I cannot bear to be deceived where all my Happiness is centered.

Your most unhappy.

LETTER XIII.

From a Lady to her Lover, who suspected her of receiving the Addresses of another. In Answer to the above.

SIR,

IF I did not make all the Allowances you desire in the End of your Letter, I should not answer you at all. But although I am really unhappy to find you are so, and the more to find myself to be the Occasion, I can hardly impute the Unkindness and Incivility of your Letter to the single Cause you would have me. However, as I would not be suspected of any Thing that should justify such Treatment from you, I think it necessary to inform you, that what you have heard has no more Foundation than what you have seen: However, I wonder that other Eyes should not be as easily alarmed as yours; for instead of being blind, believe me, Sir, you see more than there is. Perhaps, however, their Sight may be as much sharpened by unprovoked Malice, as yours by undeserved Suspicion,

Whatever may be the End of this Dispute, for I do not think so lightly of Lovers Quarrels as many do, I think proper to inform you, that I never have thought favourably of any one but yourself; and I shall add, that if the Fault of your Temper, which I once little suspected, should make me fear you too much to marry,

you

you will not see me in that State with any other; nor courted by any Man in the World.

I did not know that the Gaiety of my Temper gave you Uneasiness; and you ought to have told me of it with less Severity. If I am particular in it, I am afraid it is a Fault in my natural Disposition ; but I would have taken some Pains to get the better of that, if I had known it was disagreeable to you. I ought to resent this Treatment more than I do, but do not insult my Weaknefs on that Head ; for a Fault of that Kind would want the Excuse this has for my Pardon, and might not be so easily overlooked, though I should wish to do it. I should say, I will not see you To-Day, but you have an Advocate that pleads for you much better than you do for yourself. I desire you will first look carefully over this Letter, for my whole Heart is in it, and then come or not, as you please.   Yours, &c.

L E T T E R XIV.

From a young Tradesman to a Lady he had seen in Public.

Madam,

PERHAPS you will not be surprised to receive a Letter from a Person who is unknown to you, when you reflect how likely so charming a Face may be to create Impertinence; and I persuade myself that when you remember where you sat last Night at the Play-House, you will not need to be told this comes from the Person who was just before you.

In the first Place, Madam, I ask Pardon for the Liberty I then took of looking at you, and for the greater Liberty I now take in writing to you: But after this, I beg Leave to say that my Thoughts are honourable, and to inform you who I am : I shall not pretend to be any better. I keep a Shop, Madam, in Henrietta-Street, and tho' but two Years in Trade, I have tolerable Custom. I do not doubt but it will increase, and I shall be able to do something for a Family. If your Inclinations are not engaged, I should be very proud of the Honour of waiting on you; and in the mean Time if you please to desire any Friend to ask

my

The Complete LETTER-WRITER.   107

my Character in the Neighbourhood, I believe it will not prejudice you against,

Madam, Your moft humble Servant.

LETTER XV.

From a Relation of the Lady, in Anſwer to the above.

SIR,

THERE has come into my Hands a Letter which you wrote to Miſs Maria Stebbing; ſhe is a Relation of mine, and is a very good Girl; and I dare ſay you will not think the worſe of her in conſulting her Friends in ſuch an Affair as that you wrote about: Beſides, a Woman could not well anſwer ſuch a Letter herſelf, unleſs it was with a full Refuſal, and that ſhe would have been wrong to have done until ſhe knew ſomething of the Perſon that wrote it, as wrong as to have encouraged him.

You ſeem very ſincere and open in your Deſigns; and as you gave Permiſſion to enquire about you among your Neighbours, I being her neareſt Friend, did that for her. I have heard a very good Account of you; and from all that I ſee, you may be very ſuitable for one another. She has ſome Fortune, and I ſhall tell you farther, that ſhe took Notice of you at the Play, and does not ſeem perfectly averſe to ſeeing you in the Preſence of

Your humble Servant,   A. H.

LETTER XVI.

From a Lover who had Cauſe of Diſpleaſure, and determines never to ſee the Lady again.

Madam,

THERE was a Time when if any one ſhould have told me that I ſhould ever have written to you ſuch a Letter as I am now writing, I would as ſoon have believed that the Earth would have burſt aſunder, or that I ſhould ſee Stars falling to the Ground, or Trees and Mountains riſing to the Heavens. But there is nothing too ſtrange to happen: One Thing would have appeared yet more impoſſible than my writing it, which

is

is, that you fhould have given me the Caufe to have written it, and yet that has happened.

The Purpofe of this is to tell you, Madam, that I fhall
never wait on you again. You will truly know what
I make myfelf fuffer when I impofe this Command upon my own Heart; but I would not tell you of it, if it
were not too much determined for me to have a Poffibility
of changing my Refolution.

It gives me fome Pleafure, that you will feel no Uneafinefs for this, though I fhould alfo have been very
averfe fome Time ago even to have imagined that; but
you know where to employ that Attention, of which I
am not worthy the whole, and with a Part I fhall not
be contented. I was a Witnefs, Madam, Yefterday to
your Behaviour to Mr. Henly. I had often been told of
this, but I have refufed to liften to it. I fuppofed your
Heart no more capable of Deceit than my own: But I
cannot difbelieve what I have been told on fuch Authority, when my own Eyes confirm it. Madam, I take my
Leave of you, and beg you will forget there ever was fuch
a Man as

Your humble Servant,　S R.

LETTER XVII.

*From a young Lady to her Father, acquainting him with the
Addreffes of a young Tradefman.*

Honoured Sir,

I Think it my Duty to acquaint you, that a Gentleman of this Town, by Name Wills, and Bufinefs
a Linen-Draper, has made Overtures to my Coufin
Harcourt, in the Way of Courtfhip to me. My Coufin
has brought him once or twice into my Company,
which he could not well decline doing, becaufe he has
Dealings with him, and has a high Opinion of him and
his Circumftances. He has been fet up three Years, has
very good Bufinefs, and lives in Credit and Fafhion. He
is about twenty-feven Years old, a likely Man enough, feems not to want Senfe or Manners, and is
come of a good Family. He has broke his Mind to me,
and boafts how well he can maintain me: Though I affure you, Sir, I have given him no Encouragement;

but

but told him that I had no Thoughts of changing my
Condition yet a while; and ſhould never think of it but
in Obedience to my Parents; therefore deſired him to
talk no more on that Subject to me. Yet he reſolves to
perſevere, and pretends extraordinary Affection and Eſteem. I would not, Sir, by any Means omit to acquaint
you with with the Beginning of an Affair which it would be
Want of Duty in me to conceal from you, and ſhew a
Guilt and Diſobedience unworthy of the kind Indulgence
and Affection you have always ſhewn to, Sir,

Your moſt dutiful Daughter.

My humble Duty to my honoured Mother; Love to
my Brother and Siſter; and Reſpects to all Friends.
Couſin Harcourt, and his Wife and Siſter, deſire
their kind Reſpects. I cannot write enough of their
Civility to me.

LETTER XVIII.

*Her Father's Anſwer, on a Suppoſition that he does not approve
of the young Man's Addreſſes.*

Dear Polly,

I HAVE received your Letter, dated the 4th Inſt.
wherein you acquaint me of the Propoſals made to
you, thro' your Couſin Harcourt's Recommendation, by
one Mr. Wills. I hope, as you aſſure me, that you
have given no Encouragement to him; for I by no
Means approve of him for your Huſband. I have en-
quired of one of his Townſmen, who knows him and
his Circumſtances very well, and I am neither pleaſed
with them, nor with his Character; and wonder my
Couſin would ſo inconſiderately recommend him to you.
Indeed I doubt not of Mr. Harcourt's good Intentions;
but I inſiſt upon it, that you think nothing of the Matter,
if you would oblige

Your indulgent Father.

Your Mother gives her Bleſſing to you, and joins
with me in the above Advice. Your Brother and Siſter, and all Friends, ſend their Love and Reſpects
to you.

L

LET-

110 . The Complete LETTER-WRITER.

LETTER XIX.

The Father's Answer, on a Suppofition that he does approve of the young Man's Addreffes.

My dear Daughter,

IN Anfwer to yours of the 4th Inftant, relating to the Addreffes of Mr. Wills, I would have you neither wholly encourage nor difcourage his Suit; for if, on Enquiry into his Character and Circumftances, I fhall find that they are anfwerable to your Coufin's good Opinion of them, and his own Affurances, I know not but his Suit may be worthy of Attention. But, my Dear, confider that Men are deceitful, and always put the beft Side outwards; and it may poffibly, on the ftrict Enquiry, which the Nature and Importance of the Cafe demands, come out far otherwife than it at prefent appears. Let me advife you therefore, to act in this Matter with great Prudence, and that you make not yourfelf too cheap; for Men are apt to flight what is too eafily obtained. Your Coufin will give him Hope enough, while you don't abfolutely deny him: And in the mean Time, he may be told, that you are not at your own Difpofal, but entirely refolved to abide by my Determination and Direction, in an Affair of this great Importance; and this will put him upon applying to me, who, you need not doubt, will in this Cafe, as in all others, ftudy your Good, as becomes

Your indulgent Father.

Your Mother gives her Bleffing to you, and joins with me in the above Advice. Your Brother and Sifter, and all Friends, fend their Love and Refpects to you.

LETTER XX.

A modeft Lover defiring an Aunt's Favour to him for her Niece.

Good Madam,

I Have feveral Times, when I have been happy in the Company of your good Niece, thought to have fpoken my Mind, and to declare to her the true Value and Affection I have for her: But juft as I have been about

The Complete LETTER-WERITR.   111

bout to fpeak, my Fears have vanquifhed my Hopes, and I have been obliged to fufpend my Defign. I have thrown out feveral Hints, that I thought would have led the Way to a fuller difclofing of the Secret that is too big for my Breaft; and yet, when I am near her, it is too important for Utterance. Will you be fo good, Madam, to break the Way for me, if I am not wholly difapproved of by you, and prepare her dear Mind for a Declaration that I muft make, and yet know not how to begin. —— My Fortune and Expectations make me hope that I may not on thofe Accounts be deemed unworthy: And could I, by Half a Line from your Hand, hope that there is no other Bar, I fhould be enabled to build on fo defirable a Foundation, and to let your Niece know how much my Happinefs depends upon her Favour. Excufe, good Madam, I befeech you, this Trouble, and this prefumptuous Requeft, from

Your obliged humble Servant,

LETTER XXI.

The Aunt's Anfwer, fuppofing the Gentleman deferves Encouragement.

S I R,

I Cannot fay I have any Diflike, as to my own Part, to your Propofal, or your Manner of making it, whatever my Niece may have; becaufe Diffidence, is generally the Companion of Merit, and a Token of Refpect. She is a Perfon of Prudence, and all her Friends are fo thoroughly convinced of it, that her Choice will have the Weight it deferves with us all: So I cannot fay, what will be the Event of your Declaration to her: Yet fo far as I may take upon myfelf to do, I will not deny your Requeft; but on her Return To-morrow will break the Ice, as you defire, not doubting your Honour, and the Sincerity of your Profeffions; and I fhall tell her moreover what I think of the Advances you make. I believe fhe has had the Prudence to keep her Heart entirely difengaged, becaufe fhe would otherwife have told me; and is not fo mean-fpirited, as to be able to return Tyranny and Infult for true Value, when fhe is, properly convinced of it. Whoever has the Happinefs

L 2   (permit

(permit me, tho' her Relation, to call it ſo) to meet with her Favour, will find this her Character; and that it is not owing to the fond Partiality of, Sir,

Your Friend and Servant.

LETTER XXII.

From a reſpectful Lover to his Miſtreſs.

Dear Madam,

I Have long ſtruggled with the moſt honourable and reſpectful Paſſion that ever filled the Heart of Man; have often tried to reveal it perſonally, as often in is Way; but never till now could prevail upon my ars and Doubts. I can no longer ſtruggle with a cret that has given me ſo much Torture to keep, and t hitherto more when I have endeavoured to reveal it. I never entertain the Hope to ſee you without Rapture; but when I have that Pleaſure, inſtead of being animated, as I ought, I am utterly confounded. What can this be owing to, but a Diffidence in myſelf, and an exalted Opinion of your Worthineſs? And is not this a ſtrong Token of ardent Love? Yet if it be, how various is the tormenting Paſſion in its Operations? Since ſome it inſpires with Courage, while others it deprives of all neceſſary Confidence. I can only aſſure you, Madam, that the Heart of Man never conceived a ſtronger or ſincerer Paſſion than mine for you. If my Reverence for you is my Crime, I am ſure it has been my ſufficient Puniſhment. I need not to ſay my Deſigns and Motives are honourable: Who dare approach ſo much virtuous Excellence, with a Suppoſition, that ſuch an Aſſurance is neceſſary? What my Fortune is, is well known, and I am ready to ſtand the Teſt of the ſtricteſt Enquiry. Condeſcend, Madam, to embolden my reſpectful Paſſion by one favourable Line, that if what I here profeſs, and hope further to have an Opportunity to aſſure you of, be found to be unqueſtionably true, then, I hope, my humble Addreſs will not quite be unacceptable to you; and thus you will for ever oblige, r Madam,

Your affectionate Admirer, and devoted Servant.

LET·

The Complete LETTER-WRITER. 113
LETTER XXIII.
The Answer.

SIR,

IF Modesty be the greatest Glory in our Sex, surely it cannot be blameworthy in yours. For my own Part, I must think it the most amiable Quality either Man or Woman can possess. Nor can there be, in my Opinion, a true Respect where there is not a Diffidence of one's own Merit, and an high Opinion of the Person's we esteem.

To say more on this Occasion, would little become me: To say less, would look as if I knew not how to pay that Regard to modest Merit, which modest Merit only deserves.

You, Sir, best know your own Heart; and if you are sincere and generous, will receive, as you ought, this Frankness from, Sir,

Your humble Servant.

LETTER XXIV.

A Gentleman to a Lady, professing an Aversion to the tedious Formality in Courtship.

Dear Madam,

I Remember that one of the Antients in describing a Youth in Love, says, he has neither Wisdom enough to speak, nor to hold his Tongue. If this be a just Description, the Sincerity of my Passion will admit of no Dispute: And whenever in your Company I behave like a Fool, forget not that you are answerable for my Folly. Having made bold to declare thus much, I must presume to say, that a favourable Reception of this, will, I am certain, make me more worthy of your Notice; but your Disdain would be what I believe myself incapable ever to surmount. To try by idle Fallacies and airy Compliments, to prevail on your Judgment, is a Folly for any Man to attempt who knows you. No, Madam, your good Sense and Endowments have raised you far above the Necessity of practising the mean Artifices which prevail upon the less deserving of your Sex: You are not to be so lightly deceived; and if you were

L 3

give

give me Leave to fay, I fhould not think you deferving of the Trouble that would attend fuch an Attempt.

This, I muft own, is no fafhionable Letter from one who, I am fure, loves up to the greateft Hero of Romance: But as I would hope, that the Happinefs I fue for fhould be lafting, it is certainly moft eligible to take no Step to procure it but what will bear Reflection; for I fhould be happy to fee you mine, even when we have both out lived the Tafte of every Thing that has not Virtue and Reafon to fupport it. I am, Madam, notwithftanding this unpolifhed Addrefs,

Your moft refpectful Admirer,

And obedient humble Servant.

L E T T E R XXV.

The Lady's Anfwer, encouraging a farther Declaration.

S I R,

I AM very little in Love with the fafhionable Methods of Courtfhip: Sincerity with me is preferable to Compliments; yet I fee no Reafon why common Decency fhould be difcarded. There is fomething fo odd in your Stile, that when I know whether you are in Jeft or Earneft, I fhall be lefs at a Lofs to anfwer you. Mean Time, as there is abundant Room for rifing, rather than finking, in your Complaifance, you may poffibly have chofen wifely to begin firft at the lower End. If this be the Cafe, I know not what your fucceeding Addreffes may produce: But I tell you fairly, that your prefent make no great Impreffion, yet perhaps as much as you intend, on,

Your humble Servant.

L E T T E R XXVI.

The Gentleman's Reply, more openly declaring his Paffion.

Dear Madam,

N O W I have the Hope of being not more defpifed for my acknowledged Affection, I declare to you with all the Sincerity of a Man of Honour, that I have long had a moft fincere Paffion for you; but I have feen

Gentlemen

The Complete LETTER-WRITER. 115

Gentlemen led fuch Dances, when they have given up
their Affections to the lovely Tyrants of their Hearts,
and could not help themfelves, that I had no Courage
to begin an Addrefs in the ufual Forms, even to you, of
whofe good Senfe and Generofity I neverthelefs had a
good Opinion. You have favoured me with a few
Lines, which I moft kindly thank you for. And I do,
affure you, Madam, if you will be pleafed to encourage
my honourable Suit, you fhall have fo juft an Account
of my Circumftances and Pretenfions, as I hope will
intitle me to your Favour in the honourable Light in
which I profefs myfelf, dear Madam,

Your moft obliged and faithful Admirer.

Be fo good as to favour me with one Line more to encourage my perfonal Attendance, if not difagreeable.

LETTER XXVII.

The Lady's Anfwer to his Reply, putting the Matter on a.
fudden Iffue.

SIR,

AS we are both fo well inclined to avoid unneceffary
Trouble, as well as unneceffary Compliments, I
think proper to acquaint you that Mr. Dunford, of
Winchefter, has the Management of all my Affairs;
and is a Man of fuch Probity and Honour, that I do nothing in any Matters of Confequence without him. I
have no Diflike to your Perfon; and if you approve of
what Mr. Dunford can acquaint you with in Relation
to me, and I approve of his Report in your Favour, I
fhall be far from fhewing any Gentleman that I have either an infolent or a fordid Spirit, efpecially to fuch as
do me the Honour of their good Opinion.

Andover.   I am, Sir,

Your humble Servant.

LET-

116   The Complete LETTER-WRITER.

LETTER XXVIII.

A facetious young Lady to her Aunt, ridiculing her serious Lover.

Dear Aunt,

I AM much obliged to you for the Kindnefs you intended me, in recommending Mr. Richards to me for a Hufband : But I muft be fo free to tell you, he is a Man no Ways fuited to my Inclination. I defpife, 'tis true, the idle Rants of Romance; but I am inclinable to think there may be an Extreme on the other Side of the Queftion.

The firft Time the honeft Man came to fee me, in the Way you was pleafed to put into his Head, was one Sunday after Sermon Time. He began with telling me, what I found at my Finger Ends, that it was very cold; and politely blowed upon his. I immediately perceived that his Paffion for me could not keep him warm ; and in Complaifance to your Recommendation, conducted him to the Fire-Side. After he had pretty well rubbed Heat into his Hands, he ftood up with his Back to the Fire, and, with his Hands behind him, held up his Coat that he might be warm all over; and looking about him, afked, with the Tranquility of a Man a Twelvemonth married, and juft come off a Journey, how all Friends did in the Country? I faid, I hoped very well; but would be glad to warm my Fingers. Cry Mercy, Madam! ——And then he fhuffled a little further from the Fire; and after two or three Hems, and a long Paufe———

I have heard, fays he, a moft excellent Sermon juft now: Dr. Thomas is a fine Man truly: Did you ever hear him, Madam? No, Sir, I generally go to my own Parifh-Church. That's right, Madam, to be fure: What was your Subject To-day? The Pharifee and the Publican, Sir. A very good one truly: Dr. Thomas would have made fine Work upon that Subject. His Text To-day was Evil Communications corrupt good Manners. A good Subject, Sir, I doubt not but the Doctor made a fine Difcourfe upon it. O, ay, Madam, he can't make a bad one upon any Subject.

I rung

The Complete LETTER-WRITER.   117

I rung for the Tea-Kettle, for, thought I, we shall have all the Heads of the Sermon immediately.

At Tea he gave me an Account of all the religious Societies, unasked; and how many Boys they had put out 'Prentices, and Girls they had taught to knit, and sing Psalms. To all which I gave a Nod of Approbation, and was just able to say, (for I began to be most horribly in the Vapours) it was a very excellent Charity. O, ay, Madam, said he again, (for that's his Word I find) a very excellent one truly; it is snatching so many Brands out of the Fire. You are a Contributor, Sir, I doubt not. O, ay, Madam, to be sure, every good Man would contribute to such a worthy Charity, to be sure. No Doubt, Sir, a Blessing attends upon all who promote so worthy a Design. O, ay, Madam, no Doubt, as you say: I am sure I have found it; blessed be God! And then he twang'd his Nose, and lifted up his Eyes, as if in an Ejaculation.

O, my good Aunt, what a Man is here for a Husband! At last came the happy Moment of his taking Leave; for I would not ask him to stay Supper: And, moreover, he talked of going to a Lecture at St. Helens. And then (tho' I had an Opportunity of saying little more than Yes, and No, all the Time; for he took the Vapours he had put me into, for Devotion, or Gravity; at least, I believe so) he pressed my Hand, looked frightfully kind, and gave me to understand, as a Mark of his Favour, that if, upon further Conversation, and Enquiry into my Character, he should happen to like me as well as he did from my Behaviour and Person, why, truly, I need not fear in Time, being blessed with him for my Husband!

This, my good Aunt, may be a mighty safe Way of travelling towards the Land of Matrimony, as far as I know, but I cannot help wishing for a little more Entertainment on our Journey. I am willing to believe Mr. Richards an honest Man; but am, at the same Time, afraid his religious Turn of Temper, however in itself commendable, would better suit with a Woman who centers all Desert in a solemn Appearance, than with, dear Aunt,

Your greatly obliged Kinswoman.

L E T-

LETTER XXIX.

Her Aunt's Anfwer, rebuking her Indicrous Turn of Mind.

Coufin Jenny,

I AM forry you think Mr. Richards fo unfuitable a Lover. He is a ferious, fober, good Man: And furely when Serioufnefs and Sobriety make a neceffary Part of the Duty of a good Hufband, a good Father, and a good Mafter of a Family, thofe Characters fhould not be the Subject of Ridicule, in Perfons of our Sex efpecially, who would reap the Advantages from them. But he talks of the Weather when he firft fees you, it feems; and would you have had him directly fall upon the Subject of Love the Moment he beheld you?

He vifited you juft after the Sermon on a Sunday; and was it fo unfuitable for him to let you fee, that the Duty of the Day had made proper Impreffions upon him?

His Turn for promoting the religious Societies, which you fpeak fo flightly of, deferves more Regard from every good Perfon; for that fame Turn is a Kind of Security to a Woman, that he who had a benevolent and religious Heart, could not make a bad Man, or a bad Hufband. To put out poor Boys to 'Prentice, to teach Girls to fing Pfalms, would be with very few a Subject for Ridicule; for he that was fo willing to provide for the Children of others, would take ftill greater Care of his own.

He gave you to underftand, that if he liked your Character on Enquiry, as well as your Perfon and Behaviour, he fhould think himfelf very happy in fuch a Wife; for that, I dare fay, was more like his Language, than what you put in his Mouth: And, let me [t]ell you, it would have been a much ftranger Speech, had [fo] cautious and ferious a Man faid, without a thorough [kn]owledge of your Character, that at the firft Sight he [wa]s over Head and Ears in Love with you.

I think, allowing for the ridiculous Turn your airy Wit gives to this firft Vifit, that, by your own Account, he acted like a prudent, ferious and worthy Man, as he is, and like one who thought flafhy Compliments beneath him in fo ferious an Affair as this.

I think, Coufin Jenny, this is not only a mighty fafe Way, as you call it, of travelling towards the Land

The Complete LETTER-WRITER. 119

of Matrimony, but to the Land of Happiness, with Respect as well to the next World as this. And it is to be hoped, that the better Entertainment you so much wish for on your Journey, may not lead you too much out of your Way, and divert your Mind from the principal View which you ought to have at your Journey's End.

In short, I should rather have wished that you could bring your Mind nearer to his Standard, than that he should bring down his to your Level. And you'd have found more Satisfaction in it than you imagine, could you have brought yourself to a little more of that solemn Appearance, which you treat so lightly, and which, I think, in him is much more than meer Appearance.

Upon the Whole, Cousin Jenny, I am sorry, that a Woman of Virtue and Morals, as you are, should treat so ludicrously, a serious and pious Frame of Mind, in an Age wherein good Examples are so rare, and so much wanted; tho', at the same Time, I am far from offering to prescribe to you in so arduous an Affair as a Husband; and wish you and Mr. Richards, too, since you are so differently disposed, matched more suitable to each other's Mind than you are likely to be together: For I am

Your truly affectionate Aunt.

LETTER XXX.

A Sailor to his Sweetheart.

My dear Peggy,

IF you think of me half so often as I do of you, it will be every Hour; for you are never out of my Thoughts; and when I am asleep, I constantly dream of my dear Peggy. I wear my Half-Bit of Gold always at my Heart, tied to a blue Ribbon round my Neck; for True-Blue, my dearest Love, is a Colour of Colours to me. Where, my dearest do you put yours? I hope you are careful of it: For it would be a bad Omen to lose it.

I hope you hold in the same Mind still, my dearest Dear: For God will never bless you if you break the

Vows

Vows you have made to me. As to your ever faithful William, I would fooner have my Heart torn from my Breaft, than it fhould harbour a Wifh for any other Woman befides my Peggy. O, my deareft Love! you are the Joy of my Life! my Thoughts are all of you; you are with me in all I do; and my Hopes and my Wifhes are only to be yours. God fend it may be fo!

Our Captain talks of failing foon for England; and then, and then, my deareft Peggy!—O how I rejoice, how my Heart beats with Delight that makes me I cannot tell how, when I think of arriving in England, and joining Hands with my Peggy, as we have our Hearts before, I hope! I am fure I fpeak for one.

John Arthur, in the good Ship Elizabeth, Captain Winterton, which is returning to England, as I hope we fhall foon, promifes to deliver this into your own dear Hand; and he will bring you too, fix Bottles of Citron Water, as a Token of my Love It is fit for the fineft Lady's Tafte, it is fo good; and is, what they fay, Ladies drink, when they can get it.

John fays he will have one fweet Kifs of my deareft Peggy, for his Care and Pains. So let him, my beft Love; for I am not of a jealous Temper. I have a better Opinion of my Deareft, than fo. But oh! that I was in his Place!—One Kifs fhould not ferve my Turn, tho' I hope it may his——Yet if he takes two, I'll forgive him, one for me and one for himfelf. For I love John dearly; and fo you may well think Well, what fhall I fay more?— or rather what fhall I fay next? For I have an hundred Things crowding in upon me, when I write to my Deareft; and alas, one has fo few Opportunities but yet I muft leave off; for I have written to the Bottom of my Paper. Love then to all Friends, and Duty to both our Mothers, conclude me,

Your faithful lover till Death.

LETTER XXXI.

Her Anfwer.

Dear William,

FOR fo I may call you now we are fure; and fo my Mother fays; this is to let you know that nothing
fhall

The Complete LETTER-WRITER.   121

shall prevail upon me to alter my Promife made to you when we parted: With heavy Hearts enough, that's true: And yet I had a little Inkling given me, that Mr. Alford's Son, the Carpenter, would be glad to make Love to me: But do you think I would fuffer it? No, indeed! For I doubt not your Loyalty to me; and do you think I will not be as loyal to you?—To be fure I will. Thefe Sailors run fuch fad Chances, faid one, that you and I both know. They may return and they may not. Well, I will truft in God for that, who has returned fafe to his Friends, their dear Billy fo many a Time, and often. They will have a Miftrefs in every Land they come to, faid they. All are not fuch naughty Men, faid I; and I'll truft Billy Oliver all the World over. For why cannot Men be as faithful as Women, tro'? And for me, I am fure no Love fhall ever touch my Heart but yours.

God fend us a happy Meeting! Let who will fpeak againft Sailors, they are the Glory and the Safeguard of the Land. And what would become of Old England long ago but for them? I am fure the lazy, good-for-nothing Land-lubbers would never have protected us from our cruel Foes. So Sailors are, and ever fhall be, efteemed by me; and of all Sailors, my dear Billy Oliver, Believe this Truth from

Your faithful, &c.

P. S. I had this Letter writ in Readinefs to fend you as I had Opportunity. And the Captain's Lady undertakes to fend it with hers. That's very kind and condefcending: Is it not?

LETTER XXXII.

Mifs Molly Smith to her Coufin, giving her an Account of a very remarkable Inftance of Envy, in one of her Acquaintance who lived in the City of York.

Dear Coufin,

I Promifed, you know, to write to you, when I had any Thing to tell you: And as I think the following Story very extraordinary, I was willing to keep my Word.

122 The Complete LETTER-WRITER.

Some Time ago there came to settle in this City, a Lady whose Name is Dison: We all visited her: But she had so deep a Melancholy, arising, as it appeared, from a settled State of ill Health, that nothing we could do, could afford her the least Relief, or make her chearful. In this Condition she languished among us five Years, still continuing to grow worse and worse.

We all grieved at her Fate. Her Flesh was withered away; her Appetite decayed by Degrees, till all Food became nauseous to her Sight; her Strength failed her; her Feet could not support her tottering Body, lean and worn away as it was; and we hourly expected her Death. When at last, she one Day called her most intimate Friends to her Bedside, and as well as she could, spoke to the following Purpose: " I know you " all pity me: But, alas! I am not so much the Ob- " ject of your Pity, as your Contempt; for all my Mi- " sery is of my own seeking, and owing to the Wick- " edness of my own Mind. I had two Sisters, with " whom I was bred up; and I have all my Life-Time " been unhappy, for no other Cause but for their Suc- " cess in the World. When we were young, I could " neither eat nor sleep in Peace, when they had either " Praise or Pleasure. When we grew up to be Wo- " men, they were both soon married much to their " Advantage and Satisfaction. This galled me to the " Heart, and though I had several good Offers, yet " as I did not think them in all Respects equal to my Sis- " ters, I would not accept them; and yet was inwardly " vexed to refuse them, for fear I should get no better. " I generally deliberated so long that I lost my Lovers, " and then pined for that Loss. I never wanted for " any Thing; and was in a Situation in which I might " have been happy, if I pleased. My Sisters loved me " very well; for I concealed, as much as possible, from " them, my odious Envy; and yet never did any poor " Wretch lead so miserable a Life as I have done; " for every Blessing they enjoyed was a Dagger to my " Heart. 'Tis this Envy that has caused all my ill " Health, has preyed upon my very Vitals, and will now " bring me to my Grave."

In

The Complete LETTER-WRITER.   123

In a few Days after this Confession she died; and her Words and Death made such a strong Impression on my Mind, that I could not help sending you this Relation; and begging you, my dear Sukey, to remember how careful we ought to be to curb in our Minds, the very first Rising of a Passion so detestable, and so fatal, as this proved to poor Mrs. Dison. I know I have no particular Reason for giving you this Caution; for I never saw any Thing in you, but what deserved the Love and Esteem of,

Your ever most affectionate Cousin,
M. SMITH.

LETTER XXXIII.

The following Letter is from an unknown Lady, to a young Gentleman, on whom she had unfortunately fixed her Affections; but as she never had it in her Power to make any proper Impressions on him, or a better Opportunity of having her Inclinations signified to him, she wrote as follows:

SIR,

I RELY on your Goodness to redress and conceal the Misfortunes I now labour under; but oh! with what Words shall I declare a Passion which I blush to own? It is now a Year and a Half since I first saw, and (must I say) loved you, and so long I have strove to forget you; but frequent Sight of what I could not but admire, have made my Endeavours prove vain. I dare not subscribe to this Letter, lest it should fall into Hands that may possibly expose it; but if you, Sir, have any Curiosity or Desire to know who I am, I shall be in the Park To-morrow, exactly at two o'Clock. I cannot but be under Apprehensions, lest you should come more out of Curiosity than Compassion; but, however, that you may have some Notion of me, if you do come, I will give you a short Description of my Person, which is tall and slender, my Eyes and Hair dark; perhaps you will think me vain, when I tell you that my Person altogether is, what the flattering World calls handsome; and as to my Fortune, I believe you will have no Reason to find Fault with it. I doubt you will think such a Declaration as this, from a Woman, ridiculous;

M 2

but

but, you will confider, 'tis Cuftom, not Nature, that makes it fo. My Hand trembles fo, while I Write, that I believe you can hardly read it.

LETTER XXXIV.

The Gentleman did not give himfelf the Trouble to meet the Lady, but took great Pains to expofe and ridicule her Letter, though reproved for it by his Acquaintance; which coming to the Lady's Knowledge, fhe fent him the following,

SIR,

YOU will the more eafily pardon this fecond Trouble from a flighted Correfpondent, when I affure you it fhall be the laft

A Paffion like mine, violent enough to break through cuftomary Decorums, cannot be fuppofed to grow calm at once; but I hope I fhall undergo no feverer Trials, or Cenfures, than what I have done by taking this Opportunity of difcharging the Remains of a Tendernefs, which I have fo unfortunately and imprudently indulged. I would not complain of your Unkindnefs and Want of Generofity in expofing my Letter, becaufe the Man that is fo unworthy of a Woman's Love, is too inconfiderable for her Refentment; but I can't forbear afking you, what could induce you to publifh my Letter, and fo cruelly to fport with the Mifery of a Perfon whom you know nothing worfe of, than that fhe had entertained too good, too fond an Opinion of you?

For your own Sake, I am loth to fpeak it, but fuch Conduct cannot be accounted for, but from Cruelty of Mind, a Vanity of Temper, and an incurable Defect of Underftanding; but whatfoever be the Reafon, amidft all my Difappointments, I cannnot but think myfelf happy in not fubfcribing my Name, for you might perhaps have thought my Name a fine Trophy to grace your. Triumph after the Conqueft; and how great my Confufion muft have been, to be expofed to the Scorn, or at leaft to the Pity of the World, I may guefs from the Mortifications I now feel from feeing my Declarations and Profeffions returned without Succefs, and

in

in being convinced by the rafh Experience I have made, that my Affections have been placed without Difcretion. How ungenerous your Behaviour has been, I had rather you were told by the Gentlemen, (who I hear univerfally condemn it) than force myfelf to fay any Thing fevere; but although their kind Senfe of the Affair muft yield me fome Satisfaction under my prefent Uneafinefs; yet it furnifhes me with a frefh Evidence of my own Weaknefs, in lavifhing my Efteem upon the Perfon that leaft deferved it.

I hope the Event will give me Reafon not only to forgive, but to thank you for this ill Ufage. That pretty Face, which I have fo often viewed with a miftaken Admiration, I believe I fhall be able to look on with an abfolute Indifference; and Time, I am fenfible, will abundantly convince me, that your Features are all the poor Amends which Nature hath made you for your Want of Underftanding, and teach me to confider them only as a decent Cover for the Emptinefs and Deformity within. To cut off all Hopes of your difcovering who I am, if you do not yet know, I have taken Care to convey this by a different Hand from the former Letter, for which I am obliged to a Friend, on whofe Goodnefs and Fidelity I can fafely rely. And it is my laft Requeft, that you would make this Letter as public as you have done the former: If you don't, there are other Copies ready to be difperfed; for though I utterly defpair of ever fhewing it to yourfelf, yet I am very fure of making it plain to every one elfe, that you are a Coxcomb. Adieu.

LETTER XXXV.

Lydia *to* Harriot, *a Lady newly married.*

My dear Harriot,

IF thou art fhe, but oh, how fallen, how changed, what an Apoftate! How loft to all that's gay and agreeable! To be married, I find is to be buried alive; I can't conceive it more difmal to be fhut up in a Vault to converfe with the Shades of my Anceftors, than to be carried down to an old Manor-Houfe in the Country, and confined to the Converfation of a fober Hufband

and

and an aukward Chambermaid. For Variety, I suppose, you may entertain yourself with Madam in the Grogram Gown, the Spouse of your Parish Vicar, who has by this Time, I am sure, well furnished you with Receipts for making Salves and Possets, distilling cordial Waters, making Syrups, and applying Poultices.

Blest Solitude! I wish thee Joy, my Dear, of thy loved Retirement, which indeed, you would persuade me is very agreeable, and different enough from what I have here described: But, Child, I am afraid thy Brains are a little disordered with Romances and Novels. After six Months Marriage to hear thee talk of Love, and paint the Country Scenes so softly, is a little extravagant; one would think you lived the Lives of the Sylvan Deities, or roved among the Walks of Paradise, like the first happy Pair. But prithee leave these Whimsies and come to Town, in order to live and talk like other Mortals. However, as I am extremely interested in your Reputation, I would willingly give you a little good Advice at your first Appearance under the Character of a married Woman: 'Tis a little insolent in me, perhaps, to advise a Matron; but I am so afraid you'll make so silly a Figure as a fond Wife, that I cannot help warning you not to appear in any public Place with your Husband, and never to saunter about St. James's Park together. If you presume to enter the Ring at Hyde Park together, you are ruined for ever; nor must you take the least Notice of one another at the Play-house or Opera, unless you would be laughed at as a very loving Couple, most happily paired in the Yoke of Wedlock. I would recommend the Example of an Acquaintance of ours to your Imitation; she is the most negligent and fashionable Wife in the World; she is hardly ever seen in the same Place with her Husband, and if they happen to meet, you would think them perfect Strangers. She never was heard to name him in his Absence, and takes Care he shall not be the Subject of any Discourse that she has a Share in. I hope you'll propose this Lady as a Pattern, though I am very much afraid you'll be so silly to think Porcia, Sabine, &c. Roman Wives, much brighter Examples. I wish it may never come into your Head to imitate those

antiquated

The Complete LETTER-WRITER.   127

antiquated Creatures fo far, as to come into public in the Habit, as well as Air, of a Roman Matron. You make already the Entertainment at Mrs. Modifh's Tea-Table; fhe fays, fhe always thought you a difcreet Perfon, and qualified to manage a Family with admirable Prudence She dies to fee what demure and ferious Airs Wedlock has given to you; but fhe fays fhe fhall never forgive your Choice₁ of fo gallant a Man as Bellmour, to transform him to a mere fober Hufband; 'twas unpardonable: You fee, my Dear, we all envy your Happinefs, and no Perfon more than

Your humble Servant,

L Y D I A.

LETTER XXXVI.

Harriot's *Anfwer to the above.*

BE not in Pain, good Madam, for my Appearance in Town; I fhall frequent no public Places, or make any Vifits where the Character of a modeft Wife is ridiculous. As for your wild Raillery on Matrimony, 'tis all Hypocrify; you and all the handfome young Women of your Acquaintance, fhew themfelves to no other Purpofe, than to gain a Conqueft over fome Men of Worth, in order to beftow your Charms and Fortune on him. There's no Indecency in the Confeffion, the Defign is modeft and honourable, and all your Affectation can't difguife it.

I am married, and have no other Concern but to pleafe the Man I love; he's the End of every Care I have; if I drefs, 'tis for him; if I read a Poem or a Play, 'tis to qualify myfelf for a Converfation agreeable to his Tafte: He's almoft the End of my Devotion; Half my Prayers are for his Happinefs——I love to talk of him, and never hear him named, but with Pleafure and Emotion. I am your Friend, and wifh your Happinefs; but am forry to fee by the Air of your Letter, that there are a Set of Women who are got into the Common-place Raillery of every Thing that is fober, decent, and proper. Matrimony and the Clergy, are the Topics of People of little Wit and no Underftanding. I own to you, I have learned of the Vicar's Wife

all

128 The Complete LETTER-WRITER.

all you tax me with: She is a discreet, ingenious, pleasant, pious Woman; I wish she had the handling of you and Mrs. Modish; you would find, if you were too free with her, she would make you blush as much as if you had never been fine Ladies. The Vicar, Madam, is so kind as to visit my Husband, and his agreeable Conversation has brought him to enjoy many sober happy Hours when even I am shut out, and my dear Husband is entertained only with his own Thoughts. These Things, dear Madam, will be lasting Satisfactions, when the fine Ladies and the Coxcombs, by whom they form themselves, are irreparably ridiculous, ridiculous. even in old Age.

I am, Madam,
Your most humble Servant,
H A R R I O T.

L E T T E R XXXVII.

The following pretty entertaining Letter was written by our Poet Waller, *to the Lady* Sidney, *on the Marriage of her Sister.*

To my Lady Lucy Sidney, *upon the Marriage of my Lady* Dorothy *to my Lord* Spencer.

Madam,

IN the common Joy at Penshurst * I know none to whom Complaints may come less unseasonable than to your Ladyship; the Loss of a Bedfellow being almost equal to that of a Mistress; and therefore you ought, at least, to pardon if you consent not to the Imprecations of the deserted; which just Heaven no Doubt will hear!

May my Lady Dorothy, (if we may yet call her so) suffer as much, and have the like Passion for this young Lord, whom she has preferred to the rest of Mankind, as others have had for her: And may this Love, before the Year goes about make her taste of the first Curse imposed on Woman-kind, the Pains of becoming a.

They were married, as we are informed, at Penshurst, July 11, 1739.

Mother

The Complete LETTER-WRITER. 129

Mother! May her Firſt-born be none of her own Sex!
Nor ſo like her, but that he may reſemble her Lord as
much as herſelf?

May ſhe that always affected Silence and Retirednefs,
have the Houſe filled with the Noiſe and Number of
her Children; and hereafter of her Grand-Children!
And then may ſhe arrive at that great Curſe ſo much
declined by fair Ladies,——Old Age! May ſhe live to
be very old, and yet ſeem young; be told ſo by her
Glaſs, and have no Aches to inform her of the Truth!
And when ſhe ſhall appear to be mortal, may her Lord
not mourn for her, but go Hand in Hand with her to
that Place, where we are told, there is neither marrying nor giving in Marriage; that being there di-
vorced, we may have all an equal Intereſt in her again!
My Revenge being immortal, I wiſh all this may alſo be-
fall their Poſterity to the World's End and afterwards!

To you, Madam, I wiſh all good Things; and that
this Loſs may in good Time be happily ſupplied with
a more conſtant Bedfellow of the other Sex.

Madam, I humbly kiſs your Hand, and beg Pardon
for this Trouble, from your Ladyſhip's moſt humble
EDMUND WALLER.

LETTER XXXVIII.

The Wit and Spirit which gave Lady Mary Wortley
Montague, *during her Life, ſuch Rank in the polite
World, was in no Inſtance more happily diſplayed than in
the following Letter. We think the polite Reader will be
of Opinion with us, that there is no Letter in the Collection lately publiſhed, and ſuppoſed to have been wrote by
the ſame Lady, where the Life and Spirit of the Writer is
to be more admired, or the Sentiments more approved.*

A Letter from Lady Wortley Montague, *againſt a Maxim
of Monſ.* Rochefaucault's, " *That Marriages are con-
" venient, but never delightful."*

IT appears very bold in me to attempt to deſtroy a
Maxim eſtabiſhed by ſo celebrated a Genius as
Monſ. de Rochefaucault, and implicitly received by a
Nation which calls itſelf the only perfectly polite in the
World.

World, and which has, for fo long a Time, given Laws
of Gallantry to all Europe.

But, full of the Ardour which the Truth infpires, I
dare to advance the contrary, and to affert, boldly, that
it is Marriage-Love only which can be delightful to a
good Mind,

We cannot tafte the Sweets of perfect Love but in
a well-fuited Marriage. Nothing fo much diftinguifhes
a little Mind as to ftop at Words. What fignifies that
Cuftom (for which we fee very good Reafons) of making the Name of Hufband and Wife ridiculous? A Hufband fignifies, in the general Interpretation, a jealous
Mortal, a quarrelfome Tyrant, or a good Sort of Fool,
on whom me may impofe any Thing; a Wife is a Do-
meftic Dæmon, given to this poor Man to deceive and
torment him. The Conduct of the Generality of People fufficiently juftifies thefe two Characters. But I
fay, again, What fignify Words: A well-regulated
Marriage is not like thofe of Ambition and Intereft: It
is two Lovers who live together. Let a Prieft pronounce
certain Words, let an Attorney fign certain Papers; I
look upon thefe Preparations as a Lover does on a Lad-
der of Cords, that he fixes to the Window of his Miftrefs.

I know there are fome People of falfe Delicacy, who
maintain that the Pleafures of Love are only due to
Difficulties and Dangers. They fay, very wittily, the
Rofe would not be the Rofe without Thorns, and a
Thoufand other Trifles of that Nature, which make fo
little Impreffion on my Mind, that I am perfuaded, was
I a Lover, the Fear of hurting her I loved would make
me unhappy, if the Poffeffion was accompanied with
Dangers to her. The Life of married Lovers is very
different, they pafs it in a Chain of mutual Obligations
and Marks of Benevolence, and have the Pleafure of
forming the entire Happinefs of the Object beloved; in
which Point I place perfect Enjoyment.

The moft trifling Cares of Œconomy become noble and delicate, when they are heightened by Sentiments of Tendernefs. To furnifh a Room is no longer furnifhing a Room, it is ornamenting the Place
where I expect my Lover; to order a Supper is not
simply

The Complete LETTER·WRITER. 131

simply giving Orders to a Cook, it is amusing myself in regaling him I love. These necessary Occupations, regarded in this Light by a Lover, are Pleasures infinitely more sensible and lively than Cards and public Places, which make the Happiness of the Multitude incapable of true Pleasure. —A Passion happy and contented, softens every Movement of the Soul, and gilds each Object that we look on.

To a happy Lover (I mean one married to his Mistress) if he has any Employment, the Fatigues of the Camp, the Embarrassments of a Court, every Thing becomes agreeable when he can say to himself, It is to serve her I love. If Fortune is favourable, (for that does not depend on Merit) and gives Success to his Undertaking, all the Advantages he receives are Offerings due to her Charms, and he finds, in the Success of his Ambition, Pleasure much more lively and worthy a noble Mind, than that of raising his Fortune, or of being applauded by the Public. He enjoys his Glory, his Rank, his Riches, but as they regard her he loves; and it is her Lover she hears praised when he gains the Approbation of the Parliament, the Praises of the Army, or the Favour of his Prince. In Misfortune, it is his Consolation to retire to a Person who feels his Sorrow, and to say to himself in her Arms, " My Happiness does not depend on the Caprice of " Fortune; here is my assured Asylum against all " Grief; your Esteem makes me insensible to the " Injustice of a Court, or the Ingratitude of a Master. I feel a Sort of Pleasure in the Loss of my " Estate, as that Misfortune gives me new Proofs of " your Virtue and Tenderness. How little desirable " is Grandeur to Persons already happy ? We have " no Need of Flatterers or Equipage; I reign in your " Heart, and I possess in your Person all the Delights " of Nature." In short, there is no Situation of which the Melancholy may not be softened by the Company of the Person we love. Even an Illness is not without its Pleasures, when we are attended by one we love. I should never have done, was I to give you a Detail of all the Charms of an Union in which we find, at once, all that flatters the Senses in the most delicate

and

and moft extended Pleafure; but I cannot conclude without mentioning the Satisfaction of feeing each Day increafe the amiable Pledges of our tender Friendfhip, and the Occupations of improving them according to their different Sexes. We abandon ourfelves to the tender Inftinct of Nature refined by Love. We admire in the Daughter the Beauty of the Mother, and refpect in the Son the Appearances of Underftanding and natural Probity which we efteem in the Father. It is a Pleafure of (which God himfelf according to Mofes) was fenfible, when feeing what he had done, he found it good.

A propos of Mofes, the firft Plan of Happinefs infinitely furpaffed all others, and I cannot form to myfelf an Idea of Paradife more delightful than that State in which our firft Parents were placed: That did not laft, becaufe they did not know the World; (which is the true Reafon that there are fo few Love-Matches happy.) Eve may be confidered as a foolifh Child, and Adam a Man very little enlightened. When People of that Sort meet, they may, perhaps, be amorous at firft, but that cannot laft. They form to themfelves, in the Violence of their Paffions, Ideas above Nature; a Man thinks his Miftrefs an Angel, becaufe fhe is handfome; a Woman is enchanted with the Merit of her Lover, becaufe he adores her. The firft Change of her Complexion takes from him his Adoration, and the Hufband ceafing to adore her, becomes hateful to her, who had no other Foundation for her Love; by Degrees they are difgufted with one another, and, after the Example of our firft Parents, they throw on each other the Crime of their mutual Weaknefs; afterwards Coldnefs and Contempt follow a great Pace, and they believe they muft hate each other becaufe they are married; their fmalleft Faults are magnified in each others Sight, and they are blinded to their mutual Perfections. A Commerce eftablifhed upon Paffion can have no other Attendants. A Man when he marries his Miftrefs, ought to forget that fhe then appears adorable to him; to confider that fhe is but a fimple Mortal, fubject to Difeafes, Caprice, and Ill-Humour. He muft prepare his Conftancy to fup-

port

port the Loſs of her Beauty, and collect a Fund of
Complacency, which is neceſſary for the continual
Converſation of the Perſon who is moſt agreeable, and
the leaſt unequal. The Woman, on her Side, muſt
not expect a Continuance of Flatteries and Obedience. She muſt diſpoſe herſelf to obey agreeably, a Sci-
ence very difficult, and conſequently, of great Merit to a Man capable of feeling. She muſt ſtrive to
heighten the Charms of a Miſtreſs by the good Senſe and
Solidity of a Friend. When two Perſons, prepoſſeſſed
with Sentiments ſo reaſonable, are united by eternal Ties,
all Nature ſmiles upon them, and the common Objects
become charming.

I eſteem much the Morals of the Turks, an ignorant People, but very polite, in my Opinion. A Gallant convicted of having debauched a married Woman,
is looked upon by them with the ſame Horror as an
abandoned Woman by us; he is ſure never to make
his Fortune; and every one would be aſhamed to give
a conſiderable Employment to a Man ſuſpected of
being guilty of ſo enormous a Crime.——What would
they ſay in that moral Nation, were they to ſee one
of our Anti-Knight-Errants who are always in Purſuit
of Adventures to put innocent young Women in Diſtreſs, and to ruin the Honour of Women of Faſhion;
who regard Beauty, Youth, Rank, and Virtue, but as
ſo many Spurs to incite their Deſire to ruin, and who
place all their Glory in appearing artful Seducers, forgetting that, with all their Care, they can never attain
but to the ſecond Rank, the Devils having been long
ſince in Poſſeſſion of the firſt!

I own, that our barbarous Manners are ſo well calculated for the Eſtabliſhment of Vice and Miſery,
(which are inſeparable from them) that they muſt have
Hearts and Heads infinitely above the common, to enjoy the Felicity of a Marriage ſuch as I have deſcribed.
Nature is ſo weak, and ſo given to change, that it is
difficult to ſupport the beſt-founded Conſtancy, amidſt
thoſe many Diſſipations that our ridiculous Cuſtoms
have rendered inevitable. A Huſband, who loves his
Wife, is in Pain to ſee her take the Liberties which
Faſhion allows; it appears hard to refuſe them to her

N   ar

and he finds himſelf obliged to conform himſelf to the polite Manners of Europe; to ſee, every Day, her Hands a Prey to every one who will take them; to hear her diſplay, to the whole World, the Charms of her Wit; to ſhew her Neck in full Day; to dreſs for Balls and Shows, to attract Admirers, and to liſten to the idle Flattery of a Thouſand Fops. Can any Man ſupport his Eſteem for a Creature ſo public, or, at leaſt, does ſhe not loſe much of her Merit.

To return to the Oriental Maxims, where the moſt beautiful Women content themſelves with limiting the Power of their Charms to him who has a Right to enjoy them; they have too much Honour to wiſh to make other Men miſerable, and are too ſincere not to own they think themſelves capable of exciting Paſſion.

I remember a Converſation I had with a Lady of great Quality at Conſtantinople, the moſt amiable Woman I ever knew in my Life, and for whom I had afterwards the moſt tender Friendſhip, ſhe owned ingenuouſly to me, that ſhe was content with her Huſband. What Libertines you Chriſtian Women are! (ſhe ſaid;) it is permitted for you to receive Viſits from as many Men as you pleaſe; and your Laws permit you, without Limitation, the Uſe of Wine. I aſſured her ſhe was very much mis-informed, that it was true we received Viſits, but thoſe Viſits were full of Form and Reſpect, and that it was a Crime to hear a Man talk of Love, or for us to love any other than our Huſbands. Your Huſbands are very good (ſaid ſhe, laughing) to content themſelves with ſo limited a Fidelity. Your Eyes, your Hands, your Converſation, are for the Public, and what do you pretend to reſerve for them? Pardon me, my beautiful Sultana, (added ſhe, embracing me) I have all poſſible Inclination to believe what you ſay, but you would impoſe upon me Impoſſibilities. I know the amorous Complexion of you Infidels, I ſee you are aſhamed of them, and I will never mention them to you more.

I found ſo much good Senſe and Truth in all ſhe ſaid, that I could ſcarcely contradict her; and I owned at firſt, that ſhe had Reaſons to prefer the Morals of
                                                              the

The Complete LETTER-WRITER. 135

the Muſſulmen to our ridiculous Cuſtoms, which are
ſurpriſingly oppoſite to the ſevere Maxims of Chriſti-
anity. And notwithſtanding our fooliſh Manners, I am
of Opinion, that a Woman, determined to find her Happineſs in the Love of her Huſband, muſt give up the
extravagant Deſire of being admired by the Public; and
that a Huſband who loves his Wife, muſt deprive himſelf of the Reputation of being a Gallant at Court. You
ſee that I ſuppoſe two Perſons very extraordinary; it is
not, then, very ſurpriſing ſuch a Union ſhould be rare in
a Country, where it is neceſſary, in order to be happy, to
deſpiſe the eſtabliſhed Maxims.

I am, &c.

The

The COMPLETE

LETTER-WRITER.

PART III.

Familiar Letters of Advice and Inſtruction, &c. in many Concerns of Life.

LETTER I.

A Letter from Judge Hale, *Lord Chief Juſtice of England, to his Children ; on the ſerious Obſervance of the Lord's Day, (commonly called Sunday) when he was on a Journey, which well deſerves our Attention.*

I AM now come well to ——, from whence I intend to write ſomething to you on the Obſervance of the Lord's Day ; and this I do for theſe Reaſons ; 1ſt, Becauſe it has pleaſed God to caſt my Lot ſo, that I am to reſt at this Place on that Day, and the Conſideration therefore of that Duty is proper for me and you, viz. The Work fit for that Day. 2dly, Becauſe I have by long and ſound Experience found, that the due Obſervance of that Day, and the Duties of it, have been of ſingular Comfort and Advantage to me ; and I doubt not but it will prove ſo to you. God Almighty is the Lord of our Time and lends it us ; and it is but juſt we ſhould conſecrate this Part of that Time to him ; for I have found by a ſtrict and diligent Obſervation that a due Obſervance of the Duty of this Day, has ever had joined to it a Bleſſing on the reſt of my Time ; and the Week that hath been ſo begun has been bleſſed and proſperous to me.

On.

On the other Side, when I have been negligent of the
Duty of this Day, the reft of the Week has been unfuccefsful and unhappy to my own fecular Employment;
fo that I could eafily make an Eftimate of my Suc-
ceffes the Week following, by the Manner of my paffing this Day; and this I do not write lightly or inconfiderately, but upon a long and found Obfervation
and Experience.

LETTER II.

*The Earl of Stafford to his Son, juft before his Lordfhip's
Execution.*

My deareft Will,

THESE are the laft Lines that you are to receive
from a Father that tenderly loves you. I wifh
there was a greater Leifure to impart my Mind unto
you; but our merciful God will fupply all Things by
his Grace, and will guide and protect you in all your
Ways; to whofe infinite Goodnefs I bequeath you;
and therefore be not difcouraged, but ferve him, and
truft in him, and he will preferve and profper you in
all Things. Be fure you give all Refpects to my
Wife, that hath ever had a great Love unto you, and
therefore will it be well becoming you. Never be wanting in your Love and Care to your Sifters, but let
them ever be moft dear unto you: For this will give
others Caufe to efteem and refpect you for it, and is a
Duty that you owe them in the Memory of your
excellent Mother and myfelf: Therefore your Care
and Affection to them muft be the very fame that you
are to have of yourfelf; and the like Regard muft you
have to your youngeft Sifter; for indeed you owe it
her alfo, both for her Father's and Mother's Sake. Sweet
Will, be careful to take the Advice of thofe Friends,
who are, by me, defired to advife you for your Education. Serve God diligently Morning and Evening,
and recommend yourfelf unto him, and have him before your Eyes in all your Ways. With Patience hear
the Inftructions of thofe Friends I leave with you,
and diligently follow their Counfel. For, till you
come by Time to have Experience in the World, it

N 3   will

will be far more fafe to truft to their Judgment than
your own. Lofe not the Time of your Youth, but
gather thofe Seeds of Virtue and Knowledge which
may be of Ufe to yourfelf, and Comfort to your Friends
for the reft of your Life. And that this may be the
better effected, attend thereto with Patience, and be
fure to correct and reftrain yourfelf from Anger. Suffer not Sorrow to caft you down, but with Chearfulnefs and good Courage go on the Race you have to
run in all Sobriety and Truth. Be fure with an hal-
lowed Care to have Refpect to all the Commandments
of God, and give not yourfelf to neglect them in the
leaft Thing, left, by Degrees, you come to forget
them in the greateft; for the Heart of Man is deceitful
above all Things. And in all your Duties and Devotions towards God, rather perform them joyfully
than penfively; for God loves a chearful Giver. For
your Religion, let it be directed according to that which
fhall be taught by thofe who are in God's Church,
the proper Teachers thereof, rather than that you
either fancy one to yourfelf, or be led by Men that
are fingular in their own Opinion, and delight to go in
Ways of their own finding out: For you will certainly
find Sobernefs and Truth in the one, and much Unftea-
dinefs and Vanity in the other. The King, I truft,
will deal gracioufly with you; reftore you thofe Honours, and that Fortune, which a diftempered Time
hath deprived you of, together with the Life of your
Father; which I rather advife might be by a new Gift
and Creation from himfelf, than by any other Means,
to the End you may pay the Thanks to him, without
having Obligations to any other. Be fure to avoid, as
much as you can, to enquire after thofe that have been
fharp in their Judgments towards me, and I charge you
never to fuffer Thought of Revenge to enter into your
Heart; but be careful to be informed who were my
Friends in this Profecution, and to them apply yourfelf
to make them your Friends alfo; and on fuch you may
rely, and beftow much of your Converfation amongft
them. And God Almighty of his infinite Goodnefs,
blefs you and your Childrens Children; and his fame
Goodnefs blefs your Sifters in like Manner; perfect you

in

The Complete LETTER-WERITR.   139

in every good Work, and give you right Underftanding in all Things. *Amen.*

Your moft loving Father,
T. WENTWORTH.

LETTER III.

From a Gentleman at Lifbon, *immediately after the Earth-quake, to his Son in* London.

My dear Son,

ERE you receive this from your unhappy Father, you will have heard of the Deftruction of this Place, and of the calamitous Situation of its few remaining miferable Inhabitants. God, in his infinite Mercy, protect us! All that you have heard will fall fhort of what I have feen; for no Words have Energy fufficient to convey an Idea of a Scene fo amazingly dreadful.—Your poor Mother is no more! afk me not for your Sifters! and as for myfelf, I am a Vagabond, and condemned to feek my Bread from thofe who can ill afford to feed me. But *the Lord gave, and the Lord hath taken away*—I am fatisfied.—All may be for the beft, and our Friends are, I doubt not, removed to a more permanent City, whofe Foundations are not to be fhaken, and where Sorrow is no more. Let us, my dear Child, prepare to follow them; and that we may do fo, let us live here that we may fear no Diffo-lution, nor dread what may happen hereafter. Let us always be prepared for the worft, and not depend on a Death-bed Repentance; for you fee we have not a Moment that we can call our own. St. AUSTIN fays, *We read of one Man who was faved at the laft Hour, that none may defpair, and of but one, that none may prefume.* How unfafe, how foolifh, therefore, it is, to put off that until To-morrow which is fo effentially neceffary to be done To-day? To-morrow may never come!—Oh think of that! you may be fnatched away in an Inftant, as Thoufands here have been, for there is no withftanding the Arms of the Almighty: No! the Attempt would be vain, would be prefumptuous, would be impious, and you will find, my dear Son, (I hope not too late) that the only Security, aginft Accidents.

cidents of this Sort, is the leading a religious and good Life.

I am,

Your truly affectionate Father.

LETTER IV.

To Amelia, *with a Gold Thimble.*

Sept. 28, 1764.

CAN you believe me, my little Friend, when I say that the Present I now make you may be of more Service to you in the Course of your Life than the Ring of Gyges, and that I deserve your Thanks as much as if I had given you the Cap of Fortunatus. Perhaps you may have heard only of the latter, I will explain to you the Virtues of the Ring: This, my little Fair, would render you invisible whenever you chose to be so; you might then range through the Apartments of your Play-fellows unseen, play Ten Thousand little Tricks which at present it is not in your Power to do; but indeed the greatest Advantages of the Ring are reserved for another Age, when you may be present with your Lover, and discover the true Sentiments of his Heart, perplex your Rival, hide her Brussels and her Jewels the Night before a Ball, and torment her with all the Arts of ingenious Mischief. These are Advantages which at present, perhaps, may not tempt you; the Cap, as I can easily imagine, to be rather the Object of your Wishes; but tell me, you say, how this Thimble can be of such infinite Service.

At your Age, my little Friend, Employment is of the utmost Use; to be busy, if it be not learning to be virtuous, will at least protect you from the contrary Impressions: Whilst your Imagination is employed how best to shade a Rose, or your Fancy determines the Colours of the various Parts of your Work, Vanity will scarce have Time to whisper in your Ear, that you have more Beauty than another, or inspire you with too early a Love of Gaiety and Pleasure.

When you have lived to that Age in which your Reason shall be ripened, you will, perhaps, perceive that those little Follies which your Sex are guilty of,

proceed

The Complete LETTER-WRITER.   14ĭ

proceed from a Fault in their Education, and that Idle-
nefs is the Parent of Vice. Thus then, in the early
Years of Life, whilft you place the Thimble on your
Finger, you are guarding your Bofom againft the Ap-
proach of Foibles which might banifh thofe from your
Society, who were attracted by the Charms of your
Perfon.

Another of its Virtues, which, in all Probability,
you can never want to experience, is, that if properly applied, it contains a Charm againft the Calamities of Poverty. I have known many a Female, who,
by its Affiftance has fupported herfelf with Decency, and
felt the Pleafure of living without depending on the Bene-
ficence of others.

A few Years hence, when the Youth whom your Eyes
have wounded, fhall beg your Acceptance of fome Trifle
in the warmeft Terms imaginable, he will intreat you
to preferve it; but I, on the contrary, fhall defire you to
be frequent in the Ufe of this, and to wear it out for my
Sake.   I am, &c.

LETTER V.
On the Viciffitudes of human Life.

REMEMBER, my Son, that human Life is the
Journey of a Day. We rife in the Morning of
Youth, full of Vigour, and full of Expectation; we
fet forward with Spirit and Hope, with Gaiety and with
Diligence, and travel on a while, in the ftraight Road
of Piety, towards the Manfions of Reft. In a fhort
Time we remit our Fervour, and endeavour to find fome
Mitigation of our Duty, and fome more eafy Means
of obtaining the fame End. We then relax our Vigour, and refolve no longer to be terrified with Crimes
at a Diftance, but rely upon our own Conftancy, and
venture to approach what we refolve never to touch.
We thus enter the Bowers of Eafe, and repofe in the
Shades of Security. Here the Heart foftens, and Vigilance fubfides; we are then willing to enquire, whether another Advance cannot be made, and whether we
may not, at leaft, turn our Eyes upon the Gardens of
Pleafure. We approach them with Scruple and Hefi-
tation; we enter them, but enter timorous and trem-
bling.

bling, and always hope to pass through them without
losing the Road of Virtue, which we, for a while, keep
in our Sight, and to which we propose to return. But
Temptation succeeds Temptation, and one Compliance prepares us for another; we, in Time, lose the
Happiness of Innocence, and solace our Disquiet with
sensual Gratifications. By Degrees we let fall the Remembrance of our original Intention, and quit the only
adequate Object of rational Desire. We entangle ourselves in Business, immerge ourselves in Luxury, and
rove through the Labyrinths of Inconstancy, till the
Darkness of old Age begins to invade us, and Disease
and Anxiety obstruct our Way. We then look back
upon our Lives with Horror, with Sorrow, with Repentance; and wish, but too often vainly wish, that
we had not forsaken the Ways of Virtue. Happy are
they, my Son, who learn not to despair, but shall remember, that though the Day is past, and their Strength
is wasted, there yet remains one Effort to be made;
that Reformation is never hopeless, nor sincere Endeavours ever unassisted; that the Wanderer may at
Length return after all his Errors; and that he, who
implores Strength and Courage from above, shall find
Danger and Difficulty give Way before him.

LETTER VI.

From a Father *to his* Son, *on his Admission into the University.*

My dear Son,

YOU are now going into the wide World. Every
Step you take is attended with Danger, and requires Caution. My Eye is upon you no longer, and
the Vigilance of Governors, and the Care of Tutors,
cannot follow you every where. Few will have Concern or Affection enough to advise you faithfully.
Your Conduct must be a good deal regulated by your
own Reflections. The only secure Paths are those of
Religion and Virtue, in which it will not be difficult
for you to walk, if you live agreeably to that Simplicity
of Life, which the Rules of Academical Societies prescribe. Mix not Intemperance with your growing
Years,

The Complete LETTER-WRITER.   143

Years, nor treasure up Infirmities against an Age the fittest for Employment. You have received Health from your Parents, and you owe it to your Children. Be careful in the Choice of your Company, pay Civility to all; have Friendship with few; not too quickly with any: An idle Companion will corrupt and disgrace you while you associate with him, and asperse and expose you when you shall shake him off. In this, be advised by those whom I trust to, to do all good Offices for you. Whenever you find yourself with Persons of superior Age, or Quality, or Station, or Endowments, pay a Deference to them; so much is due to their Experience and Character. Modesty is the most amiable Virtue, especially in a young Man who professes himself a Learner. Possibly, in a large Society, you may meet with some bold young Men, who will think to arrogate to themselves a Value amongst their ill-bred Companions, by daring to say and do abusive Things to their Governors: But do not you imitate such Examples: For Prudence is not Magnanimity. A brave Mind is seen in persevering through the Difficulties of a virtuous Course; in the Conquest of irregular Appetites and Passions, and in scorning to do any Thing that is mean or base. Have nothing to do with Politics, which, when you shall have studied all your Life, you will not have found out what will hereafter be the Humours or Resentments, or private Interests or public Views of Men in Power: A Study, which, as it is generally directed, rather leads from Virtue, is foreign to your present Purpose, and in which, if you could really have any Skill, at your Age it would seem to be affected. Take the proper Advantages of living in a Society. Observe the different Tempers and Dispositions of Men; shun their Vices, imitate their Virtues, make Use of their Learning, and let the many Eyes that are upon you, the Consciousness of your Duty, and the Indignation to be insignificant, raise an Emulation in you to excell in some Kind of Art or Knowledge, that may hereafter be useful to the Public. From the Moment of your Entrance take Care of your Reputation. Let not one Exercise go out of your Hands that hath not employed your utmost Diligence.

Not-

144 The Complete LETTER-WRITER.

Notwithstanding the Affection I have for you, I shall
not be able to do you the Service I desire, unless you
assist me with your Character. And, in all doubtful
Cases, let not your Father, who loves you best, and
your Governors, who are well able to direct you, be the
only Friends that you will not consult.

I am, &c.

LETTER VII.

To Demetrius, *with a Present of Fruit, on early rising.*

June 28, 1766.

YOU would have received a much larger Quantity
of Fruit, but to say the Truth, my Band of Mu-
sicians have made bold with more of it this Summer
than usual; however, when I consider that 'tis the
only Wages I pay them, I am no otherwise displeased
with it, than as it prevents me from obliging my Friends
in Town as I could wish.

My Lucinda, you know, is extremely fond of Birds,
and she says it would be cruel to deprive them of their
Liberty, when we can be entertained with their Songs
without it; to encourage then their Residence amongst
us, they are not denied a great Share of the Productions
of my Garden.

We were this Morning at Six o'Clock in our Garden,
an Hour which you are totally unacquainted with, and
which, notwithstanding, affords the noblest Scene which
a human Creature can be present at.

The Sun, my Demetrius, was just risen above the
Horison, and all the Eastern Sky was tinged with Blushes,
the Zephyrs, as they passed, were fraught with Fragrance from the opening Flowers, and the feathered Song-
sters were waked to their respective Parts, in their Morning Hymn to the Author of Nature.

Whilst my Lucinda and I were walking, like a fond
old-fashioned Couple, Arm in Arm, I could not but
recollect that Part of the Paradise lost, where Milton
has described our first Parents as rising to their Labours,
and addressing their grateful Orisons to the bounteous Father of every Blessing.

These

The Complete LETTER-WRITER.   145

There is indeed something which at this Time inspires us with Gratitude to our Maker, and produces Sentiments in almost every Bosom, like those which are given to Adam.

Thefe are thy glorious Works, Parent of Good,
Almighty, thine this univerfal Frame,
Thus wondrous fair; thyfelf how wondrous then!
Unfpeakable, who firft above thefe Heavens
To us invifible or dimly feen,
In thefe thy loweft Works, yet thefe declare
Thy Goodnefs beyond Thought, and Pow'r divine.

There is likewife fomething which muft create a grateful Senfe of our Obligation to Heaven, when we wake again to Life, with the Bleffing of Health, and recollect that many have paffed the Night in all the Anguifh of Pain and Difeafe. As for myfelf, I fhould retire to Sleep with no little Anxiety, if I were not affured that we are protected in thofe Hours by our Maker, when we are not confcious of our own Exiftence. There cannot furely be a more comfortable Reflection than being convinced that a Power who commands and directs all Nature is our Guard, without whofe Knowledge no Action is committed, nor even the moft fecret Thought can arife.

With this Confidence of Security the good Man commits himfelf to the Arms of Sleep, where all befides muft fear it, and feels Serenity where every other Breaft muft be difcompofed.

The unufual Serenity of the Morning, which infpired every Warbler with Chearfulnefs, detained us in the Garden, till our little Boy came running to inform us that the Breakfaft waited.

' Is it not extremely abfurd, faid Lucinda, as we
' returned, for Mankind to complain of the fhort Du-
' ration of their Lives, when they even refufe to live
' a Number of Hours which Providence has beftowed
' on them. How many can we recollect amongft our
' Acquaintance, who have been loft to every Joy this
' Morning has afforded us, and who may, notwith-
' ftanding, before Night affert, that the Age which
' Men in general attain to, ferves only to conduct
' them to a fuperficial Knowledge of the Sciences, or,

O   ' that

' that old Age approaches almoſt as ſoon as we begin
' to live.'

Such indeed is frequently the Language of human
Creatures, who loſe the moſt valuable Parts of every
Day. Such too have I heard from your Mouth, but then
indeed you riſe——by Eleven.

Lucinda and myſelf, who are great Advocates for
early Hours, want much to try whether we cannot
reform you, as we have already done Leontes; and
ſhould therefore rejoice to ſee you amongſt us; there
is then ſome Probability of your ſeeing the Sun riſe,
which I ſincerely believe you have not done for many
Years, and which is one of the moſt pleaſing Scenes upon
the Theatre of Nature.   I am, &c.

LETTER VIII.

To Lucinda, *on the Happineſs of a domeſtic Matrimonial
Life.*

July 5, 1766.

AFTER ſo many Years which we have paſſed, my
Lucinda, almoſt without Separation, one would
naturally imagine that the few Days Abſence I have
known ſhould not be diſpleaſing, and yet believe me,
I am already tired of the Town, and am preparing to
leave it with the utmoſt Expedition to return to domeſtic
Joys.

When I reflect on my Diſpoſition, I am greatly thankful to Providence that the ſame Diſlike for public Pleaſures has always prevailed in Lucinda as myſelf, and
that we have been actuated by the ſame Inclinations
during the Tenor of our Lives.

Though I own myſelf in general but little fond of
the Town, yet I never fail of ſeeing Objects in it which
remind me of my own Felicity, and increaſe the Love
I bear you. Alas! my Dear, the faſhionable Tenor of
matrimonial Lives is ſo little ſuited to my Turn of
Mind, that I muſt have been wretched with what is
now called a very good Wife. I could by no Means
have endured to ſee the Heart of the Woman I loved,
entirely devoted to Pleaſure, nor have even been content to ſhare it with the King of Trumps.

The Complete LETTER-WRITER. 147

It is however, happy for Mankind, that the same Delicacy does not univerfally prevail, as there are now many Couples who are thought to be happy, becaufe the Wife has never tranfgreffed the Bounds of Virtue, nor the Hufband treated her with Language which he would be afhamed to ufe to a Stranger Their Amufements are diftinct from each other, they know nothing of that heart-felt Joy which arifes from being with thofe they love, fecluded from every Eye, and breathing the Sweets of the balmy Evening. Their only Care is refining thofe Pleafures which Repetition has rendered dull, and inventing new Arts to pafs the tedious Day, which, notwithftanding their Endeavours, affords fome Hours in which that moft impertinent of all Companions, called *Self*, never fails of Intrufion.

There are many Women in the World, I believe, to whom I might have made a good Hufband; but I do not recollect any one but my Lucinda who could have made me a happy one. How greatly then am I indebted to thy amiable Difpofition and Virtues, fince Indifference and Content are to be incompatible in the Marriage State. To Heaven, likewife my fincereft Thanks are due, for preferving its beft and moft valuable Gift to blefs my Life. For as Milton elegantly expreffes it,

With thee converfing I forget all Time;
All Seafons and their Change, all pleafe alike
Sweet as the Breath of Morn, her Rifing fwee,
With Charm of earlieft Birds; pleafant the Sun,
When firft on this delightful Land he fpreads
His orient Beams, on Herb, Tree, Fruit and Flower,
Glift'ring with Dew; fragrant the fertile Earth
After foft Show'rs; and fweet the coming on
Of grateful Evening mild; then filent Night,
With this her folemn Bird, and this fair Moon,
And thefe the Gems of Heaven, her ftarry Train:
But neither Breath of Morn, when fhe afcends
With Charm of earlieft Birds; nor rifing Sun
On this delightful Land; nor Herb, Fruit, Flower,
Glift'ring with Dew; nor Fragrance after Showers;
Nor grateful Evening mild; nor filent Night,

With this her folemn Bird, nor Walk by Moon,
Or glittering Starlight without thee is fweet.

Having once begun thofe beautiful Lines of my Lu-cinda's favourite Poet, I found it impoffible to break off fooner; nay, I was pleafed to be able to exprefs fo ele-gantly the Language of my Heart.

Aranthes, who is juft come in, and has looked over my Shoulder, upon feeing fo much Poetry, cried out, very fine, truly, I fhall take the firft Opportunity to inform Lucinda of this, I affure you. If you have any Thing, I replied, to acquaint Lucinda with, you may make Ufe of me, for I am now writing to her. How's this, fays Aranthes, what larding your Letters with Poetry after more than twenty Years Marriage? I concluded you were addreffing fome other Fair One, and endeavouring to foften her inexorable Heart by the Mufe's Affiftance. But come with me to Lady ——'s Not a Word, however, of Lucinda all Night; to be feen with fuch an old-fafhioned Creature as you, would fpoil my Reputation entirely, if your Character fhould once be known.

You know, Aranthes, my Lucinda extremely well, and will perceive by this that he is ftill the fame Man as ever. He defires me to apologize for his taking me from you, as he calls it, and at the fame Time to fend you his Compliments. My Bleffing to the Chil-dren, whom I fhall make happy by fome little Prefents at my Return; to thee, my Love, I fhall bring a Heart more truly thine than ever, more intimately acquainted with thy Virtues, and more perfectly convinced of its own Felicity. Believe me, &c.

LETTER IX.

To Cleanthes, *on Friendfhip, Age, and Death.*

Nov. 15, 1765.

IT is no fmall Alleviation of that Anxiety which the Lofs of a Friend produces, to reflect that the fame Virtues which procured him our Efteem, will likewife entitle him to eternal Happinefs. This Con-folation I received upon clofing the Eyes of Ariftus, the

The Complete LETTER-WRITER. 149

the laſt and moſt melancholy Office which Friendſhip can perform.

At Length, my Cleanthes, that Friendſhip which we once divided is now confined to ourſelves. We have ſeen thoſe who advanced with us along the Vale of Life, ſink into the Grave, and have lived to be the only Links of the Chain of Friendſhip which we helped to conſtitute at our Entrance on the World. We have together, in the Hours of Youth, looked back and deſpiſed the Toys of Infancy, in our Manhood we have ſmiled at the Pleaſures of our Youth, and are now come to that Age in which we look back on all alike, and conſider every Proſpect that terminates on this Side the Grave as beneath our Notice or Regard.

At this Seaſon of Life, one of the moſt conſiderable Pleaſures which remains to human Nature, is the Recollection of the Moments which are paſt. Now, whilſt I write, my Cleanthes, I recall with Satisfaction the Time in which we were induced, by a Parity of Sentiments, to form the ſocial Connexion, and the ſteady Union in which we have paſſed from that Hour to the preſent. The Time approaches which muſt put a Period to our Friendſhip, none hope that Providence will extend their Lives to an unuſual Length but thoſe who fear to die; as for ourſelves, we have reached that Age which few are born to attain, and which, in the Language of an admired Writer, requires a great deal of Providence to produce. I flatter myſelf that our Days have been ſo ſpent that we have no Reaſon to tremble at the Thought of our laſt, nor embitter the remaining Part of our Life with Apprehenſion for the inevitable Hour to come.

We have lent the Tear of Pity to Diſtreſs, and alleviated the Misfortunes of our Fellow Creatures, we have neither indulged our Paſſions, nor neglected the Praiſe we owe the Author of our Mercies. Why, therefore, ſhould we tremble? We leave a World whoſe Pleaſures we are no longer capable of poſſeſſing, we have paſſed through its Enjoyments, and have found them vain, we leave it for the happineſt of States: And yet the tender Tie of Parents holds us; we muſt leave thoſe whom Nature obliges us to love: Yet let us remem-

member

member that we leave them to the Care of a divine Providence, and be thankful that we were not called whilft their
Minds were yet unformed, or we had conducted them from
the Budding to the Bloom of Reafon.

If at any Time a Kind of Wifh arifes which would defer the Hour that Heaven has allotted for my laft, 'tis
when I am furrounded by my Family, and obferve the
Looks of Tendernefs which they gratefully beftow on me;
yet fometimes their being prefent has the oppofite Effect,
and I am apprehenfive left the Moment fhould not arrive
till I mourn the Lofs of a Child.

I know not that any Thing would give more confiderable Amufement than our reviewing together our
paft Lives, and recollecting the Dangers we have paft
from the Storms of our Paffions, when now Time has
lulled them to Reft. It would not be unentertaining,
I imagine, to collect the various Opinions and Ideas
we have had of the fame Object, and mark the Progrefs of the human Mind through the different Stages of
Life. Cleanthes, therefore, who enjoys the Blefling
of Health in a more eminent Degree than his Friend,
will haften to fee and give him the greateft Satisfaction he
can poffibly know.

I write this from the Grotto which Lucinda's Fancy
decorated, and where we have paffed fo many happy
Hours. Providence has taken Care to wean us from
the Love of Life by Degrees. Scarce have we reached
the ripened Age of Manhood before we have more
Friends in the Grave than furviving, and from that
Moment, which is almoft the firft of ferious Reflection, we begin to perceive the Vanity of human
Happinefs. It was the Will of Heaven that I fhould
mourn the Lofs of my Lucinda, and feel the Pang of
Separation, yet not till we had grown old in Love,
and fweetened the greateft Part of our Lives with con-
nubial Happinefs Since the Retrofpect Part of our
Lives prefents us with nothing which fhould terrify our
Imagination, let us pafs the remaining Days which Heaven fhall allot us in calm Serenity, and in Refignation to
the divine Will.

Whenever

The Complete LETTER-WRITER. 151

Whenever the deftined Hour fhall come, my Cle-anthes, may we fink contented from the World, and in the perfect Affurance of eternal Happinefs.

I am, &c.

LETTER X.
A Letter from Bifhop Atterbury *to his Son* Obadiah, at Chriftchurch *College, in* Oxford.

[*Containing fome ufeful Hints in regard to writing Letters.*]

Dear Obby,

I Thank you for your Letter, becaufe there are manifeft Signs in it of your endeavouring to excel yourfelf, and of Confequence to pleafe me. You have fucceeded in both Refpects, and will always fucceed, if you think it worth your while to confider what you write, and to whom, and let nothing, tho' of a trifling Nature, pafs through your Pen negligently; get but the Way of writing correctly and juftly, Time and Ufe will teach you to write readily afterwards; not but that too much Care may give a Stiffnefs to your Stile, which ought in all Letters, by all Means, to be avoided. The Turn of them fhould be always natural and eafy, for they are an Image of private and familiar Converfation. I mention this with Refpect to the four or five firft Lines of yours, which have an Air of Poetry, and do therefore naturally refolve themfelves into Blank Verfes. I fend you your Letter again, that yourfelf may now make the fame Obfervation. But you took the Hint of that Thought from a Poem, and it is no Wonder, therefore, that you heightened the Phrafe a little when you were expreffing it. The reft is as it fhould be; and particularly there is an Air of Duty and Sincerity, which, if it comes from your Heart, is the moft acceptable Prefent you can make me. With thefe good Qualities an incorrect Letter would pleafe me, and without them the fineft Thoughts and Language will make no lafting Impreffion on me. The great Being fays, you know——*My Son give me thy Heart,* implying, that without it all other Gifts fignify nothing. Let me conjure you, therefore, never to fay any Thing, either in a Letter, or common Converfation, that you do not think; but always to

let

let your Mind and your Words go together on the moſt trivial Occaſions. Shelter not the leaſt Degree of Inſincerity under the Notion of a Compliment, which, as far as it deſerves to be practiſed by a Man of Probity, is only the moſt civil and obliging Way of ſaying what you really mean; and whoever employs it otherwiſe, throws away Truth for Breeding: I need not tell you how little his Character gets by ſuch an Exchange.

I ſay not this as if I ſuſpected that in any Part of your Letter you intended to write what was proper, without any Regard to what was true; for I am reſolved to believe that you were in Earneſt from the Beginning to the End of it, as much as I am, when I tell you that I am,

Your loving Father, &c.

LETTER XI.

From a young Lady in one of the Canary Iſlands, *to her Siſter in* England, *whom ſhe had never ſeen; containing a preſſing Invitation to her to come over, and deſcribing the Beauties of the Place, in order to prevail on her.*

MUST we for ever, my dear Siſter, converſe only at this unhappy Diſtance?———Are we born of the ſame Parents, to be eternal Aliens to each other——— I have been told Wonders of your Wit, Ingenuity, and Good-Nature———Muſt Strangers, or at leaſt very diſtant Kindred, reap all the Benefit of theſe amiable Qualities, while thoſe who are neareſt, and ought, methinks, to be deareſt, mourn the Want of it.———They ſay there is a ſecret Sympathy between Perſons of the ſame Blood, and I am ſure I feel it; how is it then with you?———Have you never any of thoſe Earnings, thoſe Longings, to ſee the Daughter of your Father and your Mother, which ſo powerfully agitate me in my daily Muſings and my nightly Dreams?——If not Affection, Pity ſhould make you wiſh to be with a Siſter, who ſtands ſo much in Need of your Aſſiſtance. You know, my Father's great Affairs ſuffer him ſeldom to be with his Family;———Death has deprived me of my Mother, and Devotion of her Siſter; but ſhe forſakes me only to

join

The Complete LETTER-WRITER. 153

join herself to her Creator; you have no such Plea:
And as you are six Years older than myself, and of a
much superior Understanding, it is a Kind of Duty in
you to be with me, to correct the Errors of my un-
experienced Youth, and form my Mind by the Model
of your own.———Believe me, I would be most obedient
to your Instructions, and love the Precepts for the
Teacher's Sake.———What can with-hold you from
coming to a Place where your Presence is so ardently
desired?———What can you find so pleasing to you in
a Kingdom rent with internal Divisions?———Where
Father against Son, and Brother against Brother, maintain unnatural Contest!———A Kingdom, where Pride,
Injustice, Luxury, and Profaneness, are almost universal, and Religion become a Reproach to the Profession!———A Kingdom, sinking by swift Degrees into
Misery and Contempt, yet infatuated so far as to doat
on the Cause of their Undoing.——— At least this is
the Account we have of it.———Can this be agreeable to
a Person of your nice and distinguishing Taste!——— O,
my dearest Sister! listen to the Dictates of Reason, of
Duty, and of Nature, all join to call you from that
worse than *Egypt* into the Land of *Canaan*———Here
Peace and Innocence go Hand in Hand, and all the
Graces, all the Pleasures, wait upon their Steps———No
foreign Wars, no home-bred Jars, no Envy, no Dis-
trust, disturb the soft Serenity of these blissful Seats,
but all is Harmony and Love.———Eternal Zephyrs watch
our Morning Wakings, bringing ten thousand Odours
on their Wings, and tempt us to the Groves from
whence they spring———In Troops we wander through
the *Jessamine* Lanes, or sit in *Orange Bowers*, where
Fruits, ripe and in Blossom, charm our Smell and
Taste———Sometimes on Mules we take short Journies
to *Teneriffe*, and on the Foot of that stupendous
Mount, recline on Banks of Roses umbrella'd over with
spreading Myrtles:———Then change the Scene, and view
the spacious Vineyards, where huge Alcoves of clustering Grapes hang pendant over our Heads.———Sometimes we roam through a long Gallery of stately Pines,
whose loaded Boughs present us every Kind of Fruit
in one.———But there is no describing Half the vari-

154　　The Complete LETTER-WRITER.

Sweets which Nature, with a lavish Hand, pours on
these Isles, which justly have the Name of *Fortunate!*
nor (I flatter myself) will there be any Need of farther
Arguments, to bring you to us; —my Father has just
now informed me, that Captain *** carries his positive
Orders for your coming, and I may now rest in an
assured Hope of enjoying the Happiness I so long, and
so earnestly have wished; yet I am craving still more—I
would fain, methinks, imagine, if I could, that with
your Obedience to our Father, some little Share of
Love for me was mingled, and that you will embark with
the more Readiness, by the Thoughts that you will embrace one who has so tender an Affection for you, and
thinks it the greatest Blessing to subscribe herself,

My dear Sister,
Your most affectionate and most obedient Servant,
M A R I A B O Y L E.

LETTER XI.

From *** to Cleora, *on the Pleasures of Retirement.*

Madam,

IT is certainly better for yourfelf, and more for the Security of Mankind, that you fhould live in fome rural Abode, than appear in the World; fuch Perfons as you, are fatal to the public Tranquility, and do Mifchief without ever defigning it: But I muft own, when Belles and Beaux retire to Country Shades for the Sake of Heavenly Contemplation, the World will be well reformed. A Hermit's Life might be tolerable while the ferious Hours are divided between Hyde-Park and the Opera; but a more diftant Retreat, in the full Pride of your Charms and Youth, would be very extraordinary. To be convinced by fo early Experience, that Mankind are amufed only with Dreams and fantaftic Appearances, muft proceed from a fuperior Degree of Virtue and good Senfe. After a Thoufand Convictions of the Vanity of other Purfuits, how few know the Emphafis of thefe few Lines:

> *Sweet Solitude! when Life's gay Hours are paft,*
> *Howe'er we range, in thee we fix at laft:*

Tofs'd

The Complete LETTER-WRITER. 185

Tofs'd thro' tempeſtuous Seas, (the Voyage now o'er)
Pale we look back, and blefs the friendly Shore.
Our own ſtriĉt Judges, our paſt Life we ſcan,
And aſk if Virtue has enlarged the Span:
If bright the Proſpeĉt we the Grave defy,
Truſt future Ages and contented die. TICKEL.

Nothing, perhaps, is more terrible to the Imagination than an abſolute Solitude ; yet I muſt own ſuch
a Retreat as diſengages the Mind from thoſe Intereſts
and Paſſions which Mankind generally purſue, appears
to me the moſt certain Way to Happineſs ; quietly to
withdraw from the Crowd, and leave the Gay and Ambitious to divide the Honours and Pleaſures of the World,
without being a Rival or Competitor in any of theſe
Advantages, muſt leave a Perſon in perfeĉt and un-
envied Repoſe.

Without any Apology, I am going to talk to myſelf;
and what follows, may be properly called a Digreſſion.

Let me loſe the Remembrance of this buſy World,
and hear no more of its diſtraĉting Tumults! Ye vain
Grandeurs of the Earth! ye periſhing Riches and fan-
taſtic Pleaſures! what are your proudeſt Boaſts? Can
you yield undecaying Delights, Joys becoming the Dignity of Reaſon, and the Capacities of an immortal
Mind? Aſk the happy Spirits above, at what Price
they value their Enjoyments; aſk them, if the whole
Creation ſhould purchaſe one Moment's Interval of
their Bliſs? No:——One Beam of celeſtial Light ob-
ſcures, and caſts a Reproach on all the Beauty this
World can boaſt.

This is talking in Buſkins, you will think; and,
indeed, I may reſign Crowns and Scepters, and give
up the Grandeurs of the World, with as much ima-
ginary Triumph, as a Hero might fight Battles, and conquer Armies, in a Dream.

In the Height of this romantic Inſult, I am,
Madam,
Your moſt obliged humble Servant.

R 3 LET-

186　　The Complete LETTER-WRITER.

LETTER XII.

In the Stile of a Lady, by Mr. Pope.

PRAY what is your Opinion of Fate? for I muft confefs, I am one of thofe that believe in Fate and Predeftination——No, I can't go fo far as that; but, I own, I am of Opinion one's Stars may incline, tho' not compel one; and that is a Sort of Freewill; for we may be able to refift Inclination, but not Compulfion.

Don't you think they have got into the moft prepofteıous Fafhion this Winter that ever was, of flouncing the Petticoat fo very deep, that it looks like an entire Coat of Luteftring?

It is a little cool indeed for this Time of the Year, but then, my Dear, you'll allow it has an extream clean pretty Look.

Ay, fo has my Muflin Apron; but I would not chufe to make it a Winter's Suit of Cloaths.

Well, now I'll fwear Child, you have put me in Mind of a very pretty Drefs; let me die if I don't think a Muflin Flouuce made very full, would give one a very agreeable Flirtation Air.

Well, I fwear it would be charming! and I fhould like it of all Things———Do you think there are any fuch Things as Spirits?

Do you believe there is any fuch Place as the Elyfian Fields! O Gad, that would be charming! I wifh I were to go to the Elyfian Fields when I die, and then I fhould not care if I were to leave the World Tomorrow: But is one to meet there with what one has lov'd moft in this World?

Now you muft tell me this pofitively. To be fure you can, or what do I correfpond with you for, if you won't tell me all; you know I abominate Referve.

LETTER XIII.

To Mrs. Rowe, *on the Vanity of all fublunary Enjoyments.*

PEOPLE feem at prefent more bufily employed in preparing for the King's Birth-Day, than for their own laft; and appear to be in greater Anxiety for a Seat in the Dancing-Room, than for a Seat in Paradife.

I

British and American Letter Manuals, Volume 3

I was laſt Night with———; a Barge of Muſick followed us; but in the Midſt of this Gaiety your Letter
was not the only Thing that put me in Mind of Mor-
tality: I had ſuch a violent Pain in my Head, that neither the Wit of the Company, the Softneſs of the Muſic, nor the Beauty of the Evening could give me any
ſincere Delight.———If Pleaſure be the Lot of Man, it
muſt be in ſomething beyond the Grave; for on this
Side, conſtant Experience tells us, all is Vanity.

But this Confeſſion has hardly any Influence on human Conduct; for People in a high Rank muſt often
act againſt their Reaſon, to avoid being thought un-
faſhionable; and for Fear of being thought mad by the
modiſh World, moſt act in a Manner which they are
ſenſible is being truly ſo, to be in Vogue with their polite
Cotemporaries.

I cannot forbear thinking with myſelf, that if a Being, endued with Reaſon and a Capacity of judging,
(an Inhabitant of another Planet, and an utter Stranger
to our Nature) could take a View of our Actions, he
would be at a Loſs what to imagine we were; and had he
no Informer, but was to judge by our Conduct, he would
certainly either imagine that we were a Species who
were inſured always to live in the World we now inha-
bit; or elſe, that after enjoying ourſelves here as long
as we could, we were to be inſenſible for ever, without
the leaſt Expectation of a future Judgment, Puniſhment,
or Reward.

You would hardly make an Apology for deſiring me to
write to you, if you knew how much Pleaſure the Injunction gives to

Yours unalterably, CLEORA.

LETTER XIV.

From Mr. Locke directed thus:
For Anthony Collins, *Eſq; to be delivered to him after my*
Deceaſe.

Dear Sir,

BY my Will you will ſee that I had ſome Kindneſs
for ***. And I know no better Way to take care
of him than to put him and what I deſigned for him,
into

188   The Complete LETTER-WRITER.

into your Hands and Management: The Knowledge I have of your Virtue of all Kinds, fecures the Truft which, by your Permiffion, I have placed in you; and the peculiar Efteem and Love I have obferved in the young Man for you, will difpofe him to be ruled and influenced by you; fo that of that I need fay nothing. But there is one Thing, which it is neceffary for me to recommend to your efpecial Care and Memory ***.

May you live long and happy, in the Enjoyment of Health, Freedom, Content, and all thofe Bleffings, which Providence has beftowed on you, and your Virtue intitles you to. I know you loved me living; and will preferve my Memory, now I am dead. All the Ufe to be made of it is, that this Life is a Scene of Vanity, that foon paffes away; and affords no folid Satisfaction, but in the Confcioufnefs of doing well, and in the Hopes of another Life. This is what I can fay upon Experience, and what you will find to be true, when you come to make up the Account: Adieu: I leave my beft Wifhes with you.

JOHN LOCKE.

LETTER XV.

Earl of Rochefter *to the Honourable* Henry Saville.

Harry,

YOU cannot fhake off the Statefman entirely; for, I perceive you have no Opinion of a Letter, that is not almoft a Gazette: Now to me, who thinks the World as giddy as myfelf, I care not which Way it runs, and am fond of no News, but the Profperity of my Friends, and the Continuance of their Kindnefs to me, which is the only Error I wifh to continue in them: For my own Part, I am not at all ftung with my Lord M———'s mean Ambition, but I afpire to my Lord L———'s generous Philofophy: They who would be great in our little Government, feem as ridiculous to me as School-Boys, who with much Endeavour, and fome Danger, climb a Crab-Tree, and venture their Necks for Fruit, which folid Pigs would difdain, if they were not ftarving. Thefe Reflections, how idle

foever

foever they feem to the bufy, if taken into Confideration, would fave you many a weary Step in the Day,
and help G----y to many a Hour's Sleep, which he
wants in the Night: But G----y would be rich;
and, by my Troth, there is fome Senfe in that: Pray remember me to him, and tell him, I wifh him many
Millions, that his Soul may find Reft. You write me
Word, that I'm out of Favour with a certain Poet,
whom I have ever admired, for the Difproportion of
him and his Attributes. He is a Rarity which I cannot
but be fond of, as one would be of a Hog that could
fiddle, or a finging Owl. If he falls upon me at the
Blunt, which is his very good Weapon in Wit, I will
forgive him if you pleafe, and leave the Repartee to
Black Will, with a Cudgel. And now, my dear Harry, if it may agree with your Affairs to fhew yourfelf
in the Country this Summer, contrive fuch a Crew together as may not be afhamed of paffing by Woodftock,
and if you can debauch Alderman G----y, we will
make a Shift to delight his Gravity. I am forry for the
declining D----fs, and would have you be generous
to her at this Time: For that is true Pride, and I delight
in it.

ROCHESTER.

LETTER XVI.

Earl of Rochefter *to the Honourable* Henry Saville.

Dear Saville,

THIS Day I received the unhappy News of my
own Death and Burial. But, hearing what Heirs
and Succeffors were decreed in my Place, and chiefly in
my Lodgings, it was no fmall Joy to me that thofe Ti-
dings proved untrue. My Paffion for living is fo increafed, that I omit no Care of myfelf, which, before, I never thought Life worth the Trouble of taking. The
King, who knows me to be an ill-natured Man, will not
think it an eafy Matter for me to die, now I live chiefly
out of Spite. Dear Mr. Saville, afford me fome News
from your Land of the Living. And tho' I have little
Curiofity to hear who's well, yet I would be glad my

few

few Friends were fo, of whom you are no more the
leaft than the leaneft. I have better Compliments for
you, but that may not look fo fincere as I would have
you believe I am, when I profefs myfelf

Your faithful affectionate humble Servant,
ROCHESTER.

LETTER XVII.

To CLEORA.

August 11, 1756.

THO' it is but a few Hours fince I parted from my
Cleora, yet I have already, you fee, taken up
my Pen to write to you: You muft not expect, however, in this, or in any of my future Letters, that I fay
fine Things to you, fince I only intend to tell you true
ones. My Heart is too full to be regular, and too fincere to be ceremonious. I have changed the Manner,
not the Stile, of my former Converfation: And I write
to you, as I ufed to talk to you, without Form or Art.
Tell me then, with the fame undiffembled Sincerity,
what Effect this Abfence has upon your ufual Chearfulnefs? As I will honeftly confefs, on my own Part,
that I am too interefted to wifh a Circumftance, fo little
confiftent with my Repofe, fhould be altogether re-
concileable to yours. I have attempted, however, to
purfue your Advice, and divert myfelf by the Subject
you recommend to my Thoughts: But it is impoffible,
I perceive, to turn off the Mind at once from an Object
which it has long dwelt upon with Pleafure. My Heart,
like a poor Bird which is hunted from her Neft, is ftill returning to the Place of its Affections, and, after fome
vain Efforts to fly off, fettles again where all its Cares
and all its Tendernefs are centered.   Adieu.

LET-

British and American Letter Manuals, Volume 3

The Complete LETTER·WRITER. 191

LETTER XVIII.

To Colonel R****s, *in* Spain.

From his Lady in England.

BEFORE this can reach the beft of Hufbands, and the fondeft Lover, thofe tender Names will be of no more Concern to me; the Indifpofition in which you, (to obey the Dictates of your Honour and Duty,) left me, has increafed upon me; and I am acquainted, by my Phyficians, I cannot live a Week longer. At this Time my Spirits fail me, and it is the ardent Love I have for you that carries me beyond my Strength, and enables me to tell you the moft painful Thing in the Profpect of Death is that I muft part with you; but let it be a Comfort to you I have no Guilt hangs upon me, no unrepented Folly that retards me; but I pafs away my laft Hours in Reflection upon the Happinefs we have lived in together, and in Sorrow that it is fo foon to have an End. This is a Frailty which, I hope, is fo far from being criminal, that methinks there is a Kind of Piety in being fo unwilling to be feparated from a State which is the Inftitution of Heaven, and in which we have lived according to its Laws. As we know no more of the next Life, but that it will be an happy one to the Good, and miferable to the Wicked, why may we not pleafe ourfelves, at leaft, to alleviate the Difficulty of refigning this Being, in imagining that we fhall have a Senfe of what paffes below, and may poffibly be employed in guiding the Steps of thofe with whom we walked with Innocence when mortal? Why may not I hope to go on in my ufual Work, and though unknown to you, be affiftant in all the Conflicts of your Mind: Give me Leave to fay to you, O beft of Men! that I cannot figure to myfelf a greater Happinefs than in fuch an Employment; to be prefent at all the Adventures to which human Life is expofed; to adminifter Slumber to the Eye-lids in the Agonies of a Fever; to cover thy beloved Face in the Day of Battle; to go with thee a Guardian Angel, incapable of Wound or Pain, where I have longed to attend thee, when a weak, a fearful Woman. Thefe, my Dear, are the Thoughts with which

192   The Complete LETTER-WRITER.

which I warm my poor languid Heart; but indeed I
am not capable, under my prefent Weaknefs, of bearing the ftrong Agonies of Mind I fall into, when I form
to my myfelf the Grief you muft be in, upon your firft hearing of my Departure. I will not dwell upon this, becaufe your kind and generous Heart will be but the more
afflicted, the more the Perfon for whom you lament
offers you Confolation. My laft Breath will, if I am myfelf, expire in a Prayer for you. I fhall never fee your
Face again. Farewell for ever.

MANUALS PUBLISHED IN GLASGOW, NEW YORK AND NEW HAVEN

H. W. Dilworth, *The Complete Letter Writer; or Young Secretary's Instructor. Containing a Great Variety of Letters on Friendship, Marriage, Duty, Amusement, Love, Bussiness [sic], &c. To Which Are Prefixed Plain Instructions for Writing Letters on All Occasions* (Glasgow: Peter Tait, 1783), pp. 3–96. British Library, shelfmark 10921. a.30.

H. W. Dilworth, *The Complete Letter Writer, or Young Secretary's Instructor. Containing a Great Variety of Letters on Friendship, Marriage, Duty, Amusement, Love, Business, &c. To Which Are Prefixed Plain Instructions for Writing Letters on All Occasions* (New York: Benjamin Gomez, 1793), title page, pp. 101–20. British Library, shelfmark 10921.a.8.

This manual began life in London as *The Familiar Letter-Writer or Young Secretary's Instructor* (1758), but fell stillborn from the press, and was printed only once. Peter Tait's Scottish abridgement, given below (pp. 177–272), relaunched it in 1783, after which its history became entirely provincial, with several editions of the manual appearing under its new Scottish title both in Glasgow and in New York during the 1790s. There was also a late New Haven edition of 1809. The New York editions all worked from Tait's abridgement, reprinting this more or less as they found it but adding some supplementary letters at the end. The second extract below consists of the letters Benjamin Gomez added to Tait's Dilworth in his New York edition of 1793.

Like *The Complete Letter-Writer; or Polite English Secretary*, this manual culled letters from Richardson and Hallifax. American printers seeking to supplement Tait's abridgement generally took their letters from these sources too, or from the rival *Complete Letter or Polite English Secretary* and Hill's *Young Secretary's Guide* (see Volume 2). Consequently there are letters common to the various collections. But due to culling and sequencing, the two *Complete Letter-Writers* are also very different in focus and target audience.

The Glasgow Dilworth is far more focused on the world of work than *The Complete Letter Writer; or Polite English Secretary*. Compiled after the American War of Independence when Glasgow was suffering acutely from loss of the American trade, Tait's abridgement of Dilworth addressed issues of debt and failure. Geared primarily to the struggling urban trading and commercial classes, it described better business practices aimed at avoiding bankruptcy, and provided a series of model letters which dealt with bankruptcy by having creditors come together to keep debtors out of prison, and enable them to repay their debts over time. Many of these letters were later culled by other American manuals, such as the one at the end of this volume. Inasmuch as it was also addressed to mechanics and artisans, Tait's version of Dilworth focused on issues of education and upward social mobility.

New York editions generally added models of the kind of letters Tait's abridgement had excised: courtship letters for young ladies, letters between siblings, some letters of ceremony (such as thanking friends for kindnesses or congratulating friends on their success) and letters of commerce for thriving businesses. However, they often omitted all outwork, including Dilworth's brief directions about letter writing.

THE COMPLETE

LETTER WRITER;

OR,

YOUNG SECRETARY'S INSTRUCTOR.

CONTAINING

A great Variety of LETTERS

ON

FRIENDSHIP,	MARRIAGE,
DUTY,	AMUSEMENT,
LOVE,	BUSSINESS, &c.

To which are prefixed,

PLAIN INSTRUCTIONS for WRITING LETTERS on all occasions.

By H. W. DILWORTH, M. A.

GLASGOW:

PRINTED BY PETER TAIT, BOOKSELLER.

M.DCC.LXXXIII.

{ 3 }

INTRODUCTION.

THERE is nothing more commendable, and at the same time more useful in life, than to be able to write letters on all occasions with elegance and propriety. When you write to a friend, your letter should be a picture of your heart, the style loose and irregular; the thoughts themselves should appear naked, and not dressed in the borrowed robes of rhetoric; for a friend will be more pleased with that part of a letter which flows from the heart, than that which is the product of the mind. I would not be understood to mean, that the passions themselves may not be dress'd in wit, provided it sits easy and natural, and seems rather expressive of the thoughts, than placed there for any beauty of its own.

When you write merely out of compliment, it is done more to please your correspondent than yourself; and therefore you should endeavour to hit his taste: but at the same time never forget to make choice of that subject, if possible, you are the greatest master of. When the subject is determined, you must be careful to fix your eyes on the brightest part of it, that when you have taken all the pains in your power to adorn it, you may have the satisfaction to see it appear pleasing and graceful.

In writing to a stranger, the first thing necessary to be observed, is your correspondent's station in life, and the ceremonies proper to be observed, that every thing may be conducted accordingly. But be his condition what it will, you should be very careful to let an air of good breeding and humanity appear in every expression, which will give a pleasing beauty to the whole.

When you write letters on the common concerns of life, elegance is not required; ease and perspicuity are the only beauties you should study. Write freely, but not hastily; let your words drop from your pen,

A 2

4 INTRODUCTION.

as they would from your tongue when speaking deliberately on a subject of which you are master, and to a person with whom you are intimate.

But be sure to think closely on the subject of your letter before you sit down to write. This is a caution which may perhaps appear unnecessary; but I will venture to say, that hundreds appear ridiculous on paper thro' hurry and want of thought, for one that is really so for want of understanding.

Before you begin any sentence, ponder the whole in your mind, and make use of the first words that offer themselves to express the meaning; for they are the most natural; and will, in general, best answer your purpose. Forced expressions will spoil the easy flow of your diction, and render the whole stiff and awkward. But above all things learn to write correct, and never fail to give your letter a careful perusal before you send it. Nor never be ashamed to amend anything you find amiss, even when you have not time to transcribe your letter; for a blot in the writing is by no means so bad as a blunder in the sense.

With regard to letters of business, they should be plain, concise, and to the purpose; but at the same time full and sufficient to express your meaning; for it is a most ridiculous piece of vanity to write in so concise a manner as to render your letter doubtful, and perhaps unintelligible. In short, your language, in all letters of business, should be so natural, that the thoughts may seem to have been conceived in the very words they are expressed in, and your sentiments to have sprung up naturally like the lillies of the field, whose natural beauty exceeds all the dress of human art.

(5)

THE COMPLETE
LETTER WRITER;

O' R;

YOUNG SECRETARY'S INSTRUCTOR.

LETTER I.

A Son's Letter at School to his Father.

Honoured Sir;

I AM greatly obliged to you for all your favours;
all I have to hope is, that the progress I make in
my learning will be no disagreeable return for the
same. Gratitude, duty, and a view of future advantages, all conspire to make me thoroughly sensible
how much I ought to labour for my own improvement and your satisfaction, and to shew myself upon
all occasions,

Your most obedient,
and ever dutiful Son,
ROBERT REID.

LETTER II.

A Letter of excuse to Father or Mother.

Honoured Sir,

I AM informed, and it gives me great concern, that
you have heard an ill report of me, which I suppose was rais'd by some of my school-fellows, who either envy my happiness, or by aggravating my faults,
would be thought to seem less criminal themselves;

A 3

6 THE COMPLETE

though I muſt own I have been a little too remiſs in my ſchool buſineſs, and am now ſenſible I have loſt, in ſome meaſure, my time and credit thereby; but by my future diligence, I hope ſoon to recover both; and to convince you that I pay a ſtrict regard to all your commands, which I am bound to as well in gratitude as duty, and hope I ſhall ever have leave, with great truth, to ſubſcribe myſelf,

Your moſt dutiful Son,
WILLIAM COLLINS.

LETTER III.

A Young Gentleman's Letter abroad, to his Father in England.

Honoured Sir;

THIS is the ſixth letter I have ſent you by divers ſhips, ſince Michaelmas laſt; which I hope, all came ſafe to hand. I have nothing new or particular to communicate, only beg you will conceive ſo favourable an opinion of me, as to believe I proſecute my ſtudies with the utmoſt application, well knowing that will prove the beſt recommendation to your favour at preſent, and moſt real ſervice to myſelf in time to come. All our friends here preſent their beſt reſpects to you; and that you may continue in health and happineſs, is the conſtant prayer of,

Sir,
Your moſt dutiful Son,
HENRY JONES.

LETTER IV.

From a Young Apprentice to his Father, to let him know how he likes his place, and goes on.

Honoured Sir,

I KNOW it will be a great ſatisfaction to you and my dear mother, to hear that I go on very happily in my buſineſs; and my maſter ſeeing my diligence, puts me forward, and encourages me in ſuch a man-

LETTER WRITER.   7

ner, that I have great delight in it, and hope I shall answer in time your good wishes and expectations, and the indulgence which you have always shewn me. There is such good order in the family, as well on my mistress's part as my master's, that every servant, as well as I, knows his duty, and does it with pleasure. So much evenness, sedateness, and regularity is observed in all they enjoin or expect, that it is impossible but it should be so. My master is an honest worthy man; every body speaks well of him. My mistress is a cheerful sweet temper'd woman, and rather heals breaches than widens them: and the children, after such examples, behave to us all like one's own brothers and sisters. Who can but love such a family? I wish, when it shall please God to put me in such a station, that I may carry myself just as my master does; and if I should ever marry, have just such a wife as my mistress: and then, by God's blessing, I shall be as happy as they are; and as you, Sir, and my dear mother have always been. If any thing can make me happier than I am, or continue to me my present felicity, it will be continuance of yours and my good mother's prayers for, honoured Sir and Madam,

Your very dutiful Son,

LETTER V.

Letter from a Youth at School to his Parents.

Honoured Father and Mother,

YOUR kind letter of the 24th instant I received in due time, and soon after the things you therein mentioned by the carrier, for which I return you my sincere thanks. They came very opportunely for my occasions. I hope soon to improve myself at school, though I own it seems a little hard and irksome to me as yet; but my master gives me great encouragement, and assures me I shall soon get the better of the little difficulties that almost every boy meets with at first, and then it will be a perfect plea-

8 THE COMPLETE

fure inftead of a tafk, and altogether as pleafant and eafy as it is now irkfome and hard

My humble duty to yourfelves: and I beg the favour of you to give my kind love to my brothers and fillers, and remember me to all friends and acquaintances, which is at prefent all from

Your ever dutiful and obedient Son,
CHARLES GOODENOUGH.

LETTER VI.

Letter from an Apprentice in Town to his Friends in the Country.

Honoured Father and Mother,

THE bearer, Harry Jones, came to fee me laft night, and told me he fhould fet out for home the next morning. I was not willing to let flip the opportunity of fending you a letter by him, to let you know that I am very well, and like both my mafter and miftrefs, and, by what I can fee of it, the bufinefs extremely well, and do intend (pleafe God) to ufe my utmoft endeavours to make myfelf mafter, of every thing that belongs to it, in which I fhall have treble fatisfaction; firft, in pleafing my mafter; fecondly, in pleafing my friends, and thirdly, in benefiting myfelf. I have but little leifure, nor do I want a great deal, but will take every opportunity to let you know how I go on, and that I am, with great gratitude,

Your ever dutiful and moft obedient Son,
T. R.

LETTER VII.

To a Mother, to thank her for her Care and Tendernefs.

Honoured Madam,

I Have written twice to my brother, and not doubting but that he would inform you of my being well, I have taken the liberty to omit writing

LETTER WRITER.   9

to you. I beg you will be pleaſed to hear the reaſons that weighed with me againſt a very earneſt inclination, that whether you tell I was right or nor,
you may acquit me of the charge of diſobedience, or
want of reſpect as well as gratitude.

The pain with which I ſaw you part from me on
the road, has made an impreſſion on my heart, which
time will never wear out ; and I hope as it will always keep in my remembrance your tenderneſs as well
as care for me, the beſide the natural right all your
commands have to obedience from me, I ſhall, on a-
nother principle, avoid every thing that is wrong,
leſt it ſh uld give you diſquiet.

I ſhould be unnatural and unpardonable not to
have the moſt ſincere regard for the peace of your
mind, and for its compoſure: God prevent that I
ſhould do any thing that might affect the firſt, and I
ſhall hope my true concern will guard me againſt the
latter: indeed, madam the care of this prevented
my writing; I feared that a letter from me, be the
contents ever ſo indifferent, might, recal my remembrance too fully before you, and that the ſame pain
might attend it; as did your parting with me. This
was the only reaſon of my not writing to you before;
and in the moſt ſincere truth, I have done violence to
myſelf in omitting that teſtimony of my duty and reſpect.

As to occaſions of writing, I have yet none, more
than to tell you that I do not forget to whom I owe
my attention ; and to ſay how great an happineſs it
will be to me to receive your farther thoughts as to
things that are about me. I have yet entered into
no acquaintance with them, being determined, ſo far
as my youth and ſcanty judgment may allow of it, to
conſider them before I mix myſelf among them: for
this purpoſe I have hitherto kept within the houſe,
where partly from the converſation of my relations,
and partly from that of other perſons of their acquaintance who viſit them, and ſome of whom are
perſons of very reſpectable talents, I ſettle in myſelf
ſome character of the ſeveral perſons I am likely to-

10 THE COMPLETE

meet with and of the occurrences which may fall in my way :. but of all this, having not yet eſtabliſhed within myſelf any firm opinion, I ſhall take the freedom to write to yon.

The greateſt ſubjects of my conſideration, madam, are the inſtructions and the cautions you gave me; theſe will never be out of my remembrance; and although perhaps the tenderneſs of the parent, or the fears of the mother may have repreſented ſome of theſe in ſtronger lights then they are ordinarily ſeen, yet when I compare them with the obſevations I have yet had opportunities of making, I find them all moſt perfectly juſt, and all very neceſſary.

No perſou I am ſure ever had the happineſs of a more affectionate mother; and I am fully perſwaded, that the great experience you have had of the world, will render you, more then moſt people, able to judge of the courſe of things; I think it a great happineſs that ſo excellent an adviſer is ſo much concerned in my welfare ; and I do promiſe you madam, in the moſt ſincere manner, that I will always prefer to all other conſiderations in the world; the admonitions which you ſhall be pleaſed to give me. I ſhall alſo look upon myſelf as accountable for the laſt articles of my conduct to vou, as well as to God and my own heart ; and it will ſcarce be a greater obligation upon me to do in every thing as I ought, that the eye of that all ſeeing Judge is upon me, than that any wrong ſtep in my behaviour will, beſides throwing myſelf into difficultiis, make you unhappy.

You cannot know, madam, how much and how gratefully I think of your care in placing me where I now am ; where, under the eye of a good and prudent perſon, I have an opportunity to conſider of my future conduct, and to ſee things before I am placed among them, and to conſider this great world before I may be ſaid to make a part of it. I ſee it as a terrible as well as a profitable ſcene of action : I have already ſet down many things which I ſhall avoid like death and which I ſhall elſe perhaps have fallen into heedleſsly : I hope my experience will

LETTER WRITER.   11

shew me many more. Indeed, on the little that I see at present, I cannot wonder that of the youths who at my unthinking and rash time of life, are let loose into the danger, and never consider it till they are in the midst of it, if they ever consider it at all, the greater part are ruined. I hope I shall profit even by their misfortunes; but whatsoever advantages I have over the rest of the young men I meet withal, I shall always remember, with a due gratitude, that I owe them to you.

I pray daily that you may continue in all respects happy. You'll let my brother know, madam, that I shall endeavour to think of all things as he would have me; he has taught me to write long letters; but if be not tedious to you, I cannot think the time it has taken me could be more worthily employed; nor can I count that a trouble which besides that it is a duty and a satisfaction to myself, will give you pleasure.

I am honoured Madam,
with all Duty and Affection,
Your obedient Son.

LETTER VIII.

From a Mother to her Son, in answer to the former.

Dear Child,

I Have this moment read your letter, and I am set down to write to you. Where corresponding is trouble, people may defer it to the latest hour; but why should I deny myself a moment the pleasure of conversing with you? My dear, continue in the thought you have at present, and you will add all that can be now thrown into the portion of my happiness. I interrupt myself by casting my eye over and over your letter, and the fulness of my heart prevents my informing you of its sensations. If you should see more blots than this which is just now made in my writing, do not wonder, or be uneasy. I will not dissemble to you that they are made by tears; but, dearest son, these are tears that flow from transport, which has no other expression. Sure no mother was ever happier in her children. Your brother is esteemed, nay, he is almost adored by every body: your sister is settled to an advantage that was beyond my utmost expectations, and yet she is so good a woman, that her husband thinks himself under everlasting obligations. You, my dear Jack, was my only care; and I had more fear for you than all; as the youngest, that is child, as the latest remembrance of your honoured father, you had a larger share of my tenderness than either, and you was destined to a scene of the greatest danger. Heaven alone can tell what have been my anxieties and fears about you, and how continual my prayers for your security They are all granted; and instead of being, as I feared you would, an occasion of continual alarm to me, you are adding more than any of them to my contentment. I know your good heart, and I can see what a joy it is to you to perceive you make me happy: in such a mind as your's, there can be wanting no other motive to be good beside the excellence of virtue, but I am sure if this were not sufficient, that the very thought that your mother's peace depended upon your conduct, would keep you in the way of goodness.

My dear child, regard your brother; no person is so able to advise you, and he loves you with more than the common affection of the relation; he admires your good sense, and he esteems your principles. Dear son, think what an honour to have the esteem of so excellent a man; think what a happiness it is to have so fine a character at so tender a age as your's; and as you shew me how much my satisfaction is an object of your concern, remember what a transport it must be to me to hear of you so favourably.

I shall not repeat to you, my dear, the cautions which I gave you, for I see you will not need to be put again in remembrance; only reverence truth, be acquainted with no one till you know that he deserves it, and avoid bad women.

LETTER WRITER.   13

If I can give you fatisfaction, and I am fure it will do fo, to hear that every thought of your heart has my perfect approbation, you hear it truly; but altho' there is not any the leaft part of your conduct that does not give me pleafure, there is, although you will be furprized to hear it, fomething in your brother's with refpect to you, that gives him pain. He told me of your afking his advice upon an inconfiderable fubject, and his giving it to you rather honeftly than elegantly. Dear child, take care of your heart, and you may be lefs uneafy about your expreffion; let your thoughts be good, and never be uneafy about the words you put them in. The books recommend-ed to you may be good for nothing, but you have no occafion for any; nor is it a pin matter in the affairs of life, whether you put every word where it fhould be. But this is all a trifle, nor fhall I pretend to en-ter into the matter; if it be worth any confideration, he is the beft judge, fo pray mind him; but what I fpeak of is the manner in which he fays he wrote of your coufin.

My dear, always refpect your elders, and do not let any little fchool boy's leffon put you above them in your own opinion, becaufe they have forgotten it; nor becaufe your coufin is a plain man, do you fup-pofe he is lefs capable to advife you. He is a perfon of undoubted probity and uprightnefs of heart, and that is worth all the Greek and Latin of Weftminfter and Eton: he has made his way to a plentiful for-tune, and he has the refpect and efteem of all that he ever was concerned with. Would you wifh for a bet-ter character or better fortune? God fend you may conduct yourfelf through the world juft as he has done: I that would weary heaven with prayers for you, wifh you nothing better: I do not pretend to fay your brother is wrong in his judgement about this matter, for I do not underftand the nature of it, all that I know is, you will never write a letter that will pleafe me more than this you have fent already: and I think had I been in his place I would not have

B

14   THE COMPLETE

put any thing into your mind upon an occasion of such little confequence, that fhould have abated your regard for a perfon whofe advice will be of fervice to you. But I know you will not do fo. Preferve, I defire you, that refpect for him which his years, and his integrity, and his fuccefs in the world require: and whatfoever you may think about this trifle, do not let it leffen your efteem for one whom your mother recommends to you.

My dear, I have faid the more upon this fubject, becaufe it feems the only one on which you are in danger to err; and I have thought it the more necef- fary to fay fo, becaufe the regard I defired you to pay to your brother, might have rendered it a kind of duty to go into this error, I have fpoke to him a- bout it, and he defires me to fay that he is perfectly of my opinion.

Farewel, my deareft boy; you have a very eafy tafk before you; feeing you are already fo good, that you need only go on in the fame path, to make all that love you happy.

          I am,

              Your affectionate mother.

LETTER IX.

From Mafter Billy, relating the particulars of a fignal Efcape.

I Should not now have written this letter; and per- haps fhould never have given you the uneafinefs of knowing the danger I have been in, if my mafter had not been hafty in fending you a piece of news, which I am fure has greatly afflicted you, and which muft render every thing I can write agreeable, fince you will be glad to find that I can write at all. This being the King's birth day, we had a holiday; and I took a walk with feveral of my companions in the meadow, attended by the ufher. We there found fe- veral workmen repairing an old wooden bridge acrofs

the river, who foon left their work, and went home
to dinner, only firft throwing fome loofe boards over
a large hole they were preparing to mend.   Some of
my companions croffed over into the other field, and
I was following them, when one of thofe boards on
which I ftepp'd, tilting up, I fell into the middle of
the river, and was immediately driven away by the
fwiftnefs of the current.   They all ran to the water
fide, calling out for help, and ftriving to give me affiftance, but in vain, and at laft gave me up for loft,
and were returning flowly home, when they faw honeft Robin, whom in his neceffity I had, by your affiftance, relieved with a few fhillings.   They mentioned my name, pointing to the river, again burft
into tears, and begged him to help me.   He flew to
my relief; and ftripping off his coat, leaped from the
top of the bank, and foon brought me fenfelefs on
fhore; then taking me in his arms, ran with me to a
public houfe, and begged the people to put me into
a warm bed.   As no body expected I fhould ever recover, fome of the fcholars went to inform my mafter of what had happened; and the ufher returning
with the fame news, and the poft being ready to fet
out, he too haftily fent you the melancholy account.
All thefe particulars I was informed of afterwards.

The firft perfon I faw when I opened my eyes, was
the honeft man who had faved my life, and who imagining that he had felt fome motion about my heart,
was rubbing me all over with brandy and warm
cloths, and at the fame time was lamenting as if I
had been his own child.   I found myfelf very fick,
but having emptied my ftomach grew much better,
and was thinking of getting up, when I faw my fhirt
very bloody; but my furprife was foon removed by
the people's telling me that a furgeon had attended
to bleed me; but as he could only get a few drops,
every body apprehended I was dead, they neglected
to bind up my arm.   However, this was now done,
and through the goodnefs of God I was foon pretty
well, and found no other diforder but a little faint-

B 2

ness. I was then advised to drink a glass of hot wine, which I readily complied with, and at the same time ordered some for my deliverer, and soon after fell a-sleep for about an hour, when I waked not only much refreshed, but in a manner quite well.

Dear Sir, dear Madam, dear Sister, forgive the uneasiness I have occasioned. My heart is filled with gratitude to God for prolonging my life, and I have no other concern but what you feel for me. I was but just awake, when my master and the usher, with some of the scholars, having heard of my recovery, came into the room and embraced me; but having told me what they had written to you, I insisted on getting up immediately, and contradicting the letter, which I have done with as much dispatch as I was able; and finding that the post had not been gone three-hours, I got the landlord to send a man and horse, who, if he cannot overtake the post, is to deliver the letter to you. The man is already mounted, and I have only time to assure you that I am quite well, and ever will be,

Dear Papa and Mamma, most dutifully yours.

L E T T E R   X.

The Answer.

My dear Child,

WE all rejoice, and bless God for your recovery. You see, my dear, how precarious life is, and how suddenly we may be snatched into that world where our everlasting fate will be finally determined. Seriously reflect on this important truth; let it put a check upon the follies of youth, and lead you to think on the necessity and advantages of a religious and virtuous life, which will be able to support you under every difficulty here, and render death itself, however sudden, the entrance into never fading felicity. I hope you will make this use of your recovery; for this your gratitude to the Almighty requires

LETTER WRITER.   17

from you. God, like a tender parent only defires your happinefs; and all the return you can make to him is to live fo as to be happy for ever.

We are all greatly pleafed with the gratitude of the honeft man, who has been the inftrument of your prefervation. You fee that kind and generous actions are frequently rewarded even in this life: and that none are fo mean as not to be worth making our friends. The loweft human being is your fellow crea‧ ture, and may equal, and perhaps exceed us in virtue. I have fent the good man a prefent of five guineas, and would have you tell him, that when his bufinefs leads him to town, I fhall be glad to fee and thank him.

Your eagernefs to change our grief into joy, by fending a man and horfe with your letter, was at once a convincing proof of your confidence in our love, and the generous fenfibility of your heart; and my dear, we all thank you for the kind concern you have fhewn for our grief, and the method which your good fenfe has prompted you to put a ftop to it. I will not fay how much I was affected at opening Mr. Thompfon's letter. Your mother and fifter were prefent, and feeing me lay it down to wipe my eyes, eagerly caft a look upon it, and immediately burft into tears, and the moft affecting lamentations. Alas! I was but little able to comfort them! we were all in deep diftrefs: but, juft as I was ftruggling with my forrow, in order to perfuade your poor mother to be more compofed, the man arrived with your letter, which he refufed to deliver to any body but me: I therefore ordered him to be called in, and received it from him at the parlour door, when over-hearing your mother's fighs, and your fifter's more audible complaints, he cried, as I put the letter carelefsly in my pocket, Sir, that letter brings good news. I then defired him to ftay and refrefh himfelf in the kitchen, faw with joy the fuperfcription written with your own hand, and turned to dry up their tears by reading to them the contents, which, like precious balm, rems-

B 3

d the agony of our minds, and filled us with extasy.

My dear son, God bless and preserve your precious life, and may you long live a comfort to us all, is the constant prayer of

Your affectionate Father.

LETTER XI.

From Master Billy Lewis to his Father in Reply.

Dear and ever honoured Sir,

I Can find no words to express the sense I have of your's, my mamma's, and my sister's goodness. I read your kind letter with many tears, and could not help being much, very much concerned for the grief I have occasioned I do not know how to make you sensible of the duty and gratitude that fills my heart; but what is wanting in words, the actions of my whole life shall better explain. I will therefore leave them to speak for me. The man, my deliverer, was surprised at your generosity, when I gave him the money, and told me that he was never worth so much money at any one time in his life. He sends you a thousand thanks; and on my telling him that you would be glad to see him when he came to town, he offered to walk thither on purpose; but I told him I was sure you did not expect him to neglect his business. The honest man has just brought his wife and children, all dressed in new clothes, that are coarse, plain and neat, to thank me, and desire me to return their thanks to you.

I am, dear Sir, with the tenderest brotherly affection for my Sister,

Your and my Mamma's ever dutiful Son.

P. S. I have sent my sister a specimen of my drawing I am also much pleased with the study of geography, and no diversion gives me half the pleasure I find in examining and comparing the situation

LETTER WRITER.   19

of places on my mafter's terreftrial globe, and in re-
folving the problems he has taught me.

LETTER XII.

From a Daughter to her Father, wherein fhe dutifully expoftulates againft a Match he had propofed to
her, with a Gentleman much older than herfelf.

Honoured Sir,

THO' your injunctions fhould prove diametrically
oppofite to my own fecret inclinations, yet I
am not infenfible that the duty which I owe you binds
me to comply with them. Befides I fhould be very
ungrateful, fhould I prefume, in any point whatever,
confidering your numberlefs acts of parental indulgence towards me, to conteft your will and pleafure.
Though the confequence, therefore, fhould prove
never fo fatal, I am determined to be all obedience,
in cafe what I have to offer in my own defence fhould
have no influence over you, or be thought, an infufficient plea for my averfion to a match, which, unhappily for me, you feem to approve of. 'Tis very
poffible, Sir, the gentleman you recommend to my
choice may be poffeffed of all that fubftance, and all
thofe good qualities, that bias you fo ftrongly in his
favour; but be not angry, dear Sir, when I remind
you, that there is a vaft difproportion in our years.
A lady of more experience, and of more advanc'd age,
fhould, in my humble opinion, be a much fitter help
mate for him. To be ingenious, (permit me, good
Sir, to fpeak the fentiments of my heart without referve for once) a man almoft in his grand climacterick, can never be an agreeable companion for me;
nor can the natural gaiety of my temper, which has
hitherto been indulged by yourfelf in every innocent
amufement, be ever agreeable to him. Though his
fondnefs at firft may connive at the little freedoms I
fhall be apt to take; yet, as foon as the edge of his
appetite fhall be abated, he'll grow jealous, and for

ever torment me without a caufe. I fhall be debar-
red of every fituation fuitable to my years, tho' never
fo harmlefs and innoffenfive; permitted to fee no
company; hurried down, perhaps, to fome melancholy rural recefs; and there, like my lady Grace in
the play, fit penfive, and alone, under a green tree.
Your long experienced goodnefs, and that tender regard which you have always exprefs'd for my eafe
and fatisfaction, encourage me thus freely to expoftulate with you on an affair of fo great importance.
If, however, after all you fhall judge the inequality
of our age any plea in my favour, and that want of
affection for a hufband is but a trifle, where there is a
large fortune and a coach and fix to throw into the
fcale; if, in fhort, you fhall lay your peremptory
commands upon me to refign all my real happ'nefs
and peace of mind, for the vanity of living in pomp
and grandeur, I am ready to fubmit to your fuperior
judgement. Give me leave, however, to obferve,
that 'tis impoffible for me ever to love the man into
whofe arms I am to be thrown; and that my compliance with fo detefted a propofition, is nothing more
than the refult of the moft inviolable duty to a father,
who never made the leaft attempt before to thwart the
inclination of

His ever obedient Daughter.

LETTER XIII.

To a Young Lady, cautioning her against keeping
Company with a Gentleman of a bad Character.

Dear Niece,

THE fincere love and affection which I now have
for your indulgent father, and ever had for
your virtuous mother, not long fince deceafed, together with the tender regard I have for your future
happinefs and welfare, have prevailed on me to inform you, rather by letter than by word of mouth,
that the town rings of your unguarded conduct, and

LETTER WRITER.   21

the too great freedom that you take with Mr. Trippet. You have been seen with him (if fame lies not) in the side boxes of both theatres, at the blue-coat hospital on a Sunday night, and afterwards at a certain tavern, not à mile from thence, which is a house (as I have been credibly informed) of no good repute. You have both, moreover, been seen at Ranelagh assembly, Vauxhall gardens; and what is still more flagrant, at Cuper's fire works, Don't imagine, niece, that I am in the least prejudiced, or speak out of any private pique; but let me tell you, your familiarity with him gives me no small concern, as his character is none of the best, and as he has acted in the most ungenerous manner to two or three very virtuous young ladies of my acquaintance, who entertain'd a too favourable opinion of his honour. 'Tis possible, as you have no great expectation from your relations, and he has an annuity, as 'tis reported, of 200 l. a year left him by his uncle, that you may be tempted to imagine his addresses an offer to your advantage. 'Tis much to be questioned, however, whether his intentions are sincere; for, notwithstanding all the fair promises he may possibly make you, I have heard it whispered that he's privately engaged to a rich, old doating lady, not far from Hackney. Besides, admiting it to be true, that he is really entitled to the annuity above mention'd, yet 'tis too well known that he is deep in debt; that he lives beyond his income, and has very little, if any, regard for his reputation. In short, not to mince the matter, he's a perfect libertine, and is ever boasting of favours from our weak sex, whose fondness and frailty are the constant topics of his raillery and ridicule.

All things therefore duely consider'd, let me prevail on you, dear niece, to avoid his company as you would avoid a mad man; for, notwithstanding I still think you strictly virtuous, yet your good name may be irreparably lost by such acts of imprudence. As I have no other motive but an unaffected zeal for your interest and welfare, I flatter myself you'll

22   T H E   C O M P L E T E

put a favourable construction on the liberty here taken, by

Your sincere Friend,
and affectionate Aunt.

L E T T E R   XIV.

From an elder Brother in the Country, to his younger Brother put Apprentice in London.

Dear Brother,

I Am very glad to hear you are pleased with the new situation into which the care of your friends has put you; but I would have you pleased not with the novelty of it, but with the real advantage. It is natural for you to be glad that you are under less re-straint than you were; for a master neither has occasi-on nor inclination to watch over a youth so much as his parents: But if you are not careful, this altho' it now gives you a childish satisfaction, may, in the end, betray you into mischief; nay, to your ruin. Tho' your father is not in sight, dear brother, act always as if you were in his presence; and be assured, that what would not offend him, will never displease any body.

You have more sense, I have often told you so, than most persons at your time. Now is the oppor-tunity of making a good use of it: and take this for certain, every right step you enter upon now will be a comfort to you for life. I would have your reason as well as your fancy, pleased with your new situa-tion, and then you will act as becomes you. Consi-der, brother, that the state of life that charms you so at this time will bring you to independence and af-fluence, and that you will, by behaving as you ought now, be at one time master of a house and family; have every thing about you at your command, and have apprentices as well as servants to wait upon you. The master with whom you are now placed was some years ago in your situation; and what would hinder you from being in his? All that is required, is patience and industry; and these, brother, are a very cheap price at which to purchase so comfortable a condition.

Your master, I am told, had nothing to begin the world withal: in that he was worse than you; for, if you behave well, there are those who will set you up in a handsome manner: So you have a sufficient inducement to be good, and a reward always follows it. Brother, farewel. Obey your master, and be civil to all persons; keep out of company, for boys have no occasion for it, and most that you will meet with is very bad. Be careful and honest, and God will bless you. If ever you commit a fault, confess it at once; for the lie in denying it is worse than the thing itself. Go to church constantly; and write to us often. I think I need not say more to so good a lad as you, to induce you to continue so.

I am your affectionate Brother.

LETTER XV.

Advice from a Father to a young Beginner, what Company to chuse, and how to behave in it.

Dear Robin,

AS you are now entering into the world, and will probably have considerable dealings in your business, the frequent occasion you will have for advice from others, will make you desirous of singling out, among your most intimate acquaintance, one or two, whom you would view in the light of friends.

In the choice of these, your utmost care and caution will be necessary; for, by a mistake here, you can scarcely conceive the fatal effects you may hereafter experience. Wherefore it will be proper for you to make a judgement of those who are fit to be your advisers, by the conduct they have observed in their own affairs, and the reputation they bear in the world. For he who has by his own indiscretions undone himself, is much fitter to be set up as a land mark for a prudent mariner to fhun his courfes, than an example to follow.

Old age is generally flow and heavy, youth head-ftrong and precipitate; but there are old men who are full of vivacity, and young men replete with dif-cretion; which makes me rather point out the con-duct than the age of the perfons with whom you fhould chufe to affociate; though, after all, it is a never failing good fign to me of prudence and virtue in a young man, when his feniors chufe his company, and he delights in theirs.

Let your endeavours therefore be, at all adven-tures, to confort yourfelf with men of fobriety, good fenfe, and virtue; for the proverb is an unerring one that fays, A man is known by the company he keeps. If fuch men you can fingle out, while you improve by their converfation, you will benefit by their ad-vice: And be fure remember one thing, that though you muft be frank and unreferved in delivering your fentiments, when occafions offer; yet that you be much readier to hear than to fpeak; for to this pur-pofe it has been fignificantly obferved, that nature has given a man two ears, and but one tongue. Lay in therefore, by obfervation and modeft filence, fuch a ftore of ideas, that you may, at their time of life, make no worfe figure than they do; and endeavour to benefit yourfelf rather by other people's ills than your own. How muft thofe young men expofe them-felves to the contempt and ridicule of their feniors, who, having feen little or nothing of the world, are continually fhutting out, by open mouths and clofed ears, all poffibility of inftruction, and making vain the principal end of converfation, which is improvement? A filent young man makes generally a wife old one, and never fails of being refpected by the beft and moft prudent men, when, therefore, you come among ftrangers, hear every one fpeak before you deliver your own fentiments; by this means you will judge of the merit and capacities of your company, and a-void expofing yourfelf as I have known many do, by fhooting out hafty and inconfiderable bolts, which

LETTER WRITER.   25

they would have been glad to recal; when, perhaps, a silent genius in company has burst out upon them with such observations, as have struck consciousness and shame into the forward speaker, if he has not been quite sensible of inward reproach.

I have thrown together, as they occurred, a few thoughts which may suffice for the present, to shew my care and concern for your welfare. I hope you will constantly, from time to time, communicate to me whatever you shall think worthy of my notice, or in which my advice may be of use to you: for I have no pleasure in this life equal to that which the happiness of my children gives me. And of this you may be assured; for I am and ever must be,

Your affectionate Father.

LETTER XVI.

To a Friend, on Occasion of his not answering his Letters.

Dear Sir,

IT is long since I had the favour of a line from you that I am under great apprehensions in relation to your health and welfare. I beg you Sir, to renew to me the pleasure you used to give me in your correspondence, for I have written three letters to you before this; to which I have had no answer, and am not conscious of having any way disobliged you. If I have, I will most willingly ask your pardon; for no body can be more than I am,

Your affectionate and faithful
Friend and Servant.

LETTER XVII.

In Answer to the preceeding

Dear Sir,

YOU have not, cannot disoblige me; but I have greatly disobliged myself, in my own faulty re-

C

26   T H E   C O M P L E T E :

miffnefs : I cannot account for it as I ought. To fay
I had bufinefs one time, company another, was diftant from home a third, will be put poor excufes,
for not anfwering one of your kind letters in four long
months.   I therefore ingenioufly take fhame to myfelf, and promife future amendment and that nothing
fhall ever, while I am able to hold a pen, make me
guilty of the like neglect to a friend I love, Forgive
me then, my good, my kind, my generous friend;—
and believe me ever,

> Your highly obliged humble Servant.

L E T T E R XVIII.

*From a Father to a Son, on his Negligence in his
Affairs.*

Dear Jemmy,

YOU cannot imagine what a concern your careleffnefs and indifferent management of your affairs give me. Remiffnefs is inexcufable in all men,
in none fo much as in a man of bufinefs, the foul of
which is induftry, diligence, and punctuality.

Let me beg of you to fhake off the idle habits you
have contracted : quit unprofitable company, and un-
feafonable recreation, and apply to your compting
houfe with diligence. It may not yet be too late to
retrieve your affairs. Infpect therefore your gains,
and caft up what proportion they bear to your expences ; and then fee which of the latter you can, and
which you cannot contract. Confider, that when once
a man fuffers himfelf to go backward in the world,
it muft be an uncommon fpirit of induftry that retrieves him, and puts him forward again.

Reflect, I befeech you, before it be too late, upon
the inconveniences which an impoverifh'd trader is
put to, for the remainder of his life, which too many
happen to be the prime part of it ; the indignities he
is likely to fuffer from thofe whofe money he has
unthinkingly fquandered ; the contempt he will meet

LETTER WRITER. 27

with from all, not excepting the idle companions of his folly; the injustice he does his family, in depriving his children, not only of the power of raising themselves, but of living tolerably; and how on the contrary, from being born to creditable expectation he sinks them into the lowest class of mankind, and exposes them to the most dangerous temptations.——— What has not such a father to answer for! and all this for the sake of indulging himself in an idle, a careless, a thoughtless habit, that cannot afford the least satisfaction beyond the present hour, if in that; and which must be attended with deep remorse, when he comes to reflect. Think seriously of these things, and in time, resolve on such a course as may bring credit to yourself, justice to all you deal with, peace and pleasure to your mind, comfort to your family; and which will give, at the same time, the highest satisfaction to

> Your careful and loving Father.

LETTER XIX.

From a Young Gentleman at the University, to a Family Acquaintance, to borrow Money.

SIR,

THE death of my father soon after his putting me to this place of education, and many other accidents in which my own conduct has had no concern, have involved me in difficulties, which threaten altogether to impede my progress in my studies, and prevent the means which I hoped were in my power to get my bread; for through the utter want of friends, under which I labour, I cannot expect preferment. But with this, Sir, I should be satisfied. The reason of my writing to you upon the melancholy occasion is, Sir, what I have already mentioned, is my entire want of friends. I know you are so distant a relation, that I can have no right to expect any

C 2

THE COMPLETE

28

favour from you upon that account; but I have heard my father often mention your name, and always with the greatest respect. Sir, if you entertain the same remembrance of him that he always did for you; and if your fortune is so plentiful as I am told, perhaps you will not only pardon the present application, as strange as it may seem from one you never saw, but may comply with my request of supplying me with fourteen pounds seven shillings, which will answer all my present demands, and, perhaps before new difficulties fall upon me, I may find some friend to relieve me farther. I only request of you, Sir, if you decline this, not to be offended at the presumption of the application; because I would avoid nothing so carefully, as offending those whom my father valued. I am,

With the greatest respect,

S I R,

Your most obedient humble servant.

L E T T E R XX.

From a substantial Tradesman to a very distant Relation asking Money. In Answer to the former.

Dear Cousin,

IF you knew what was the nature of that friendship with which your father honoured me, your letter would have been written in a style of less humility: or if I had known he had a son unprovided for the occasion of such a letter would have been prevented.

Sir, whatsoever be the case of my present circumstances, I owe it all to your father, and God forbid I should not return it to you. Your father, Sir, advanced the money with which I was put out; and when I was out of my time, the same friend lent me the sum with which I set up, and assisted me afterwards in all my difficulties; it is true, I repaid him the money, but the obligation can never be re-paid.

LETTER WRITER. 29

I have ordered twenty pounds to be paid to the
ftage coachman, who will take charge of it, and
bring it to you ; and I pray you to let me know the
nature of your affairs at college, for my low education has given me no knowledge of this, and whatever is neceffary, you fhall moft willingly receive from
me. Look no farther, Sir, for a friend, for you
fhall want no other. When it is your time of coming
away for your holidays, let my houfe be your home?
and, dear young man, if you can condefcend to humble yourfelf fo far, be for the future my fon. A
wife reftriction from your father prevented my marrying when I was very young ; fince that time my
mind has been taken up with bufinefs; and at the
years I am now, I am fure I never fhall. He little
fuppofed, that in preventing my marrying foolifhly,
he was providing a father for a deftitute fon of his
own ; but heaven orders all things right. Pray write
to me again immediately.

I am,

Your faithful Friend.

LETTER XXI.

From a Town Tenant to his Landlord, excufing
Delay of Payment.

Honoured Sir,

I Am under a great concern that I cannot at prefent anfwer your juft expectation. I have fuftained fuch heavy loffes, and met with fo many
difappointments of late, that I muft intrude another
quarter upon your goodnefs. Then, whatever fhifts
I am put to, you fhall hear to more fatisfaction than
at prefent, from,

SIR,

Your moft humble Servant.

C 3

30   THE COMPLETE

LETTER XXII.

From a Country Tenant to the same purpose.

Honoured Sir,

THE season has been so bad, and I have had such unhappy accidents to encounter with in a sick family, loss of cattle, &c. that I am obliged to trespass upon your patience a month or two longer. The wheat harvest, I hope, will furnish me with the means to answer your just expectations, which will be a great contentment to,

Your honest Tenant,
and humble Servant.

LETTER XXIII.

The Landlord's Answer.

Mr. Williams,

I Have your's: I hope you will be as good as your word, at the expiration of the time you have mentioned. I am unwilling to distress any honest man; and I hope that I will not meet with the worse usage for my forbearance; for lenity abused, even in generous tempers, provoke returns, that some people would call severe; but should not be deemed such, if just.

I am, Your's, &c.

LETTER XXIV.

A young Woman in town to her Sister in the country, recounting her narrow escape from a snare laid for her on her arrival, by a wicked Procuress.

Dear Sister,

WE have often by our good mother, been warned against the dangers that would probably

LETTER WRITER. 31

attend us on coming to London? though I must own her admonitions had not always the weight I am now convinced they deserved.

I have had a deliverance from such a snare, as I never could have believed would have been laid for a person free from all thought of ill, or been so near succeeding upon one so strongly on her guard, as I imagined myself. And thus, my dear sister, the matter happened.

Returning, on Tuesday, from seeing my cousin Atkins, in Cheapside, I was overtaken by an elderly gentlewoman, of a sober and creditable appearance, who walked by my side some little time before she spoke to me; and then guessing, by my asking the name of the street, that I was a stranger to the town, she very courteously began a discourse with me: and, after some other talk, and questions about my country, and the like, desired to know, if I did not come to town with a design of going into some genteel place? I told her, if I could meet with a place to my mind, to wait upon a single lady, I should be very willing to embrace it. She said, I looked like a creditable, sober, and modest body; and, at that very time, she knew one of the best gentlewomen that ever lived, who was in great want of a maid to attend upon her own person; and that if she liked me, and I her, it would be a lucky incident for us both.

I expressed myself so thankfully, and she was so very much in my interest, as to intreat me to go instantly to the lady, lest she should be provided, and acquaint her I was recommended by Mrs. Jones; not doubting, as she said, but on inquiry, my character would answer my appearance.

As that, you know, was partly my view in coming to town. I thought this a happy incident, and determined not to lose the opportunity; and so, according to the direction she gave me, I went to enquire for Mrs. C————, in J————'s Court, Fleet Street. The neighbourhood looked genteel, and I soon found the house. I asked for Mrs. C————: she came to me dreffed in a fplendid manner; I told her what I came about; fhe immediately defired me to walk into the parlour, which was elegantly furnifhed; and after afking me feveral queftions, with my anfwer to which fhe feemed very well pleafed, a fervant foon brought in a bowl of very warm liquor, which fhe called negus, confifting of wine, water, orange, &c. which fhe faid was for a friend or two fhe expected prefently; but as I was warm with walking, fhe would have me drink fome of it, telling me it was a pleafant innocent liquor, and fhe always ufed her waiting maids as fhe did herfelf: I thought this very kind and condefcending, and being warm and thirfty, and fhe encouraging me, I took a pretty free draught of it, and thought it very pleafant, as it really was. She made me fit down by her, faying, pride was not her talent, and that fhe fhould always indulge me in the like manner, if I behaved well, when fhe had not company; and then flightly afked what I could do, and the wages I required. With my anfwers fhe feemed well fatisfied, and granted the wages I afked, without any offer of abatement.

And then I rofe up, in order to take my leave, telling her I would, any day fhe pleafed of the enfuing week, bring my clothes and wait upon her.

She faid, that her own maid being gone away, fhe was in the utmoft want of another, and would take it kindly, if I would ftay with her till next day, becaufe fhe was to have fome ladies to pafs the evening with her. I faid this would be pretty inconvenient to me; but, as fhe was fo fituated, I would oblige her, after I had been with my aunt, and acquainted her with it. To this fhe replied, that there was no manner of occafion for that, becaufe fhe could fend the cook for what I wanted, who could at the fame time, tell my aunt how matters ftood.

I thought this looked a little odd; but fhe did it with fo much civility, and feemed fo pleafed with her new maid, that I fcarcely knew how to withftand her: but the apprehenfion I had of my aunt's anger, for

LETTER WRITER.   33.

not afking her advice, in what so nearly concerned me, made me infift upon going tho' I could perceive difpleafure in her countenance when fhe faw me refolved.

She then plied me very clofe with the liquor, which fhe again faid was innocent and weak; but I believe it was far otherwife; for my head began to turn round, and my ftomach felt a little difordered. I entreated the favour of her to permit me to go, on a firm promife of returning immediately; but then my miftrefs began to raife her voice a little, affuring me, I fhould on no account whatever ftir out of her houfe. She left the room in a fort of pet; but faid fhe would fend the cook to take my directions to my aunt; and I heard her take the key out of the outward door.

This alarmed me very much; and in the inftant of my furprize, a young gentlewoman entered the parlour, dreffed in white fattin, and every way genteel: fhe fat down in a chair next me, looked earneftly at me a while, and feemed going to fpeak feveral times, but did not. At length fhe rofe from her chair, bolted the parlour door; and, breaking into a flood of tears, expreffed herfelf as follows:

" Dear young woman, I cannot tell you the pain I feel on your account: and from an inclination to ferve you, I run a hazard of involving myfelf in greater mifery than I have yet experienced, if that can be. But my heart is yet too honeft to draw others, as I am defired to do, into a fnare which I have fallen into myfelf. You are now in as notorious a brothel as any in London; and if you efcape not in a few hours, you are inevitably undone. I was once as innocent as you feem to be. No apprehenfion you can be under for your virtue, but I feel as much; my reputation was as unfpotted, and my heart as unverfed in ill, when I firft entered thefe guilty doors, whither I was fent on an errand, much like what I underftand has brought you hither, I was by force detained the whole night as you are defigned to be: was robbed of my virtue; and knowing I should hardly be forgiven by my friends for staying out without their knowledge, and in the morning being at a lofs, all in confufion as I was, what to do, before I could refolve on any thing, I was obliged to repeat my guilt, and hardly time afforded me to reflect upon its fatal confequences. My liberty I intreated to no purpofe, and my grief ferved for the cruel fport of all around me: In fhort, I have been fo long confined, that I am afhamed to appear among my friends and acquaintance. In this dreadful fituation, I have been perplexed with the hateful importunities of different men every day; and though I long refifted to my utmoft, yet downright force never failed to overcome. Thus in a fhameful round of guilt and horror, have I lingered out ten months; fubject to more miferies than tongue can exprefs. The fame fad lot is intended you, nor will it be eafy to fhun it: however, as I cannot well be more miferable than I am, I will affift you what I can; and not as the wretched procurefs hopes, contribute to make you as unhappy as myfelf.

You may guefs at the terror that feized my heart, on this fad ftory, and my own danger. I trembled in every joint, nor was I able to fpeak for fome time; at laft, in the beft manner I could, I thanked my unhappy new friend, and begged fhe would kindly give me the affiftance fhe offered; which fhe did; for the firft gentleman that came to the door, fhe ftepped up herfelf for the key to let him in, which the wretched procurefs gave her; and I took that opportunity, as fhe directed, to run out of the houfe, and that in fo much hurry and confufion, as to leave my hood, fan, and gloves behind me.

I told my aunt every circumftance of my danger and efcape, and received a fevere reprimand for my following fo inconfiderately, in fo wicked a town as this, the direction of an entire ftranger.

I am fure, fifter, you rejoice with me for my deliverance; and this accident may ferve to teach us to

LETTER · WRITER.   35

be upon our guard for the future, as well against the
viler part of our own sex, as that of the other.

   I am,
    Dear Polly,
     Your truely affectionate Sister.

N. B   This shocking story is taken from the
mouth of the young woman herself, who so narrow-
ly escaped the snare of the vile procurefs, and is fact
in every circumstance.

LETTER XXV.

From a Maid-Servant in Town; acquainting her Father and Mother in the Country with a proposal of
Marriage, and asking their Consents.

Honoured Father and Mother,

I Think it my duty to acquaint you that I am addressed to for change of condition by one Mr.
John Brittle, who is a glazier, and lives in the
neighbourhood by us.   He is a young man of a fober character, and has been set up about two years;
has good bufinefs for his time, and is well beloved,
and spoken well of by every one.   My friends here
think well of it, particularly my master and mistrefs;
and he says, he doubts not, by God's blefling on his
industry, to maintain a family very prettily: and I
have fairly told him how little he has to expect with
me.   But I would not conclude on any thing, however, till I had acquainted you with his propofals,
and asked your bleffings and confents; for I am, and
ever will be,

   Your dutiful Daughter,
    ANNE LOVEGLASS.

96   T H E   C O M P L E T E

L E T T E R   XXVI.

From the Parents in Anſwer to the preceeding.

Dear Nanny,

WE have received your dutiful letter. We can
  only pray to God to bleſs and direct you in all
your engagements.   Our diſtance from you muſt
make us leave every thing to your own diſcretion;
as you are ſo well ſatisfied in Mr. Brittle's character,
as well as all your friends, and your maſter and miſtreſs, we give our bleſſings and conſents with all our
hearts: We are only ſorry we can do no more for
you; But let us know when it is done, and we will do
ſome little matter, as far as we are able, towards
houſe keeping. Our reſpects to Mr. Brittle. Every
body joins with us in our wiſhes for your happineſs;
and God bleſs you, is all that can be ſaid by,
          Your truely loving Father and Mother.

L E T T E R   XXVII.

From the ſame, acquainting her Parents with her
Marriage.

Honoured Father and Mother,

I Write to acquaint you, that laſt Thurſday I was
  married to Mr. Brittle, and am to go home to
him in a fortnight. My maſter and miſtreſs have
been very kind, and have made me a preſent towards
houſe keeping of three guineas. I had ſaved twenty
pounds in ſervice, and that is all. I told him the naked truth of every thing; and indeed, did not intend
to marry ſo ſoon; but when I had your letter, and
ſhewed it to him, he would not let me reſt till it was

LETTER WRITER. 37

done. Pray do'nt ſtraiten yourſelves out of love to me. He joins with me in ſaying ſo, and bids me preſent his duty to you, and tell you, that he fears not to maintain me very well, I have no reaſon to doubt of being very happy. And your prayers for a bleſſing on both our induſtry, will, I hope be a means to make us more ſo. We are, and ever ſhall be, with reſpect to all friends.

Your moſt dutiful Son and Daughter.

LETTER XXVIII.

From a Country Chapman beginning Trade, to a City Dealer, offering his Correſpondence.

S I R,

THE time of my apprenticeſhip with Mr. Walker of this town being expired, I am juſt going to begin for myſelf in Preſton, having taken a ſhop there for that purpoſe. And as I know the ſatisfaction you always gave to my maſter in your dealings, I make an offer to you of my correſpondence, in expectation that you will uſe me as well as you have done him, in whatever I may write to you for. And this I rather expect, as you cannot diſoblige Mr. Walker by it, becauſe of the diſtance I ſhall be from him; and I ſhall endeavour to give you equal content with regard to my payments, &c. Your ſpeedy anſwer, whether or no you are diſpoſed to accept of my offer, will oblige   Your humble ſervant.

LETTER XXIX.

In anſwer to the foregoing.

S I R,

I Have received your's of October 20; and very chearfully accept the favour you offer me. I will

D

take care to serve you in the best manner I am able, and on the same footing with Mr. Walker, not doubting you will make as punctual returns as he does; which intitles him to a more favourable usage than could otherwise be afforded. I wish you such cess with all my heart, and am,

Your obliged Servant.

LETTER XXX.

A pressing and angry Letter from a City Dealer, to his Correspondent in the Country.

Mr. Thomson,

I Am sorry your ill usage constrains me to write to you in the most pressing manner. Can you think it is possible to carry on business after the manner you act by me? You know what promises you have made me, and how, from time to time, you have broken them; and can I depend upon any new ones you make? if you use others as you have done me, how can you think of carrying on business? if you do not, what must I think of a man, who deals worse with me than he does with any body else? if you think you may trespass more upon me, than you can on others, that is a very bad compliment to my prudence, or your own gratitude; for surely good usage should be entitled to good usage. I know how to allow for disappointments as well as any man; but can a man be disappointed for ever? trade is so dependent a thing, you know, that it cannot be carried on without mutual punctuality. Does not the merchant expect it from me, for these very goods I send you? And can I make a return to him, without receiving it from you? what end can it answer to give you two years credit, and then be at an uncertainty for goods, which I sell at a small profit, and

LETTER WRITER.   59

have not six months credit for myself? indeed, Sir, this will never do. I must be more punctually used by you, or else must deal as little punctually with others; and what then must be the consequence? In short, Sir, I expect a handsome payment by the next return, and security for the remainder; and shall be very loth to take any harsh methods to procure this justice to myself, my family, and my own creditors. For I am, if it be not your own fault,

Your faithful Friend and Servant.

LETTER XXXI.

In answer to the preceeding.

SIR,

I Must acknowledge I have not used you well, and can give no better answer to your just expostulations, then to send you the inclosed draught for fifty pounds, which you will be pleased to carry to my credit; and to assure you of more punctual treatment for the future. Your letter is no bad lesson to me; I have conned it often, and hope I shall improve by it. I am ready to give you my bond for the remainder, which I will keep paying every month something till all is discharged; and what I write to you for in the interim, shall be paid for on receipt of the goods. This, I hope Sir, will satisfy you for the present. If I could do better, I would; but shall be straitened to do this: but, I think in return for your patience, I cannot do less, to convince you that I am now at last in earnest. I beg you will continue to me the same good usage and service I have met with from you hitherto; and that you will believe me to be unfeignedly, Your obliged humble servant.

D 2

LETTER XXXII.

From an Insolvent Debtor, to desire the Acceptance of a Composition.

SIR,

IT is with the greatest concern I now inform you, that some losses I have lately suffered render it impossible for me to carry on business any longer. I am sorry, Sir, that your debt is so large, and the composition I am able to make so small; for I am able to pay but five shillings in the pound. I have, however, the comfort of being conscious that my intentions were always honest, and that it would have given the highest pleasure to me fully to have discharged every debt I have contracted. If, upon the inspection of my books, you will accept of such a dividend as I am able to make, my other creditors, I have reason to hope will fol'ow your example. They are to have a meeting next Tuesday at the Feathers in our town, and a favourable line from you, who are my principal creditor, will have much weight with them, and lay me under the greatest obligation; and I shall think myself bound in honour and conscience, if ever providence should place me in a prosperous situation, to make good what you and my other creditors will lose by accepting the composition.

I am SIR,

Your most unhappy, and most humble servant.

LETTER XXXIII.

The Answer.

SIR,

I Am really concerned for your unhappy situation, and readily consent to accept of the composition ton mention. I have appointed Mr. Lawson, a very honest attorney of your town, to act for me in your affairs, and have wrote to him accordingly. I always thought you a very honest man, and have defired him to exert himfelf in your behalf with your other creditors, in order to bring them to amicable terms. He is alfo to examine your books, and to make fuch enquiries as he fhall judge necessary; and if every thing turns out as I wish, I shall readily give you fresh credit. I heartily wish you better days; and am

Your real friend,

William Lewis.

LETTER XXXIV.

From a Gentleman in London, to his Friend in the Country, on the New Year.

Dear Sir,

IT is now the feafon to wish you a good end of one year, and a happy beginning of another; but both thefe you know how to make yourfelf, by only continuing fuch a life as you have been long accustomed to lead. As for good works they are things I dare not name, either to thofe that do them, or to thofe that do them not; the first are too modest, and the latter too felfish, to bear the mention of what are become either too old-fashion'd or too private, to constitute any part of the vanity of reputation of the prefent age. However, it were to be wished people would now and then look upon good works as they do upon old wardrobes, merely in cafe any of them should by chance come into fashion again; as antient fardingales revive in modern hoop'd petticoats, which may be properly compared to charities, as they cover a multitude of fins.

D 5

They tell me that at Coleshill certain antiquated charities and obsolete devotions are yet subsisting; that a thing called Christian Chearfulness (not incomparible with christmas pies and plum broth) whereof frequent is the mention in old sermons and almanacks, is really kept alive and in practice: that feeding the hungry, and giving alms to the poor, do yet make a good part of house keeping, in a latitude not more remote from London than fourscore miles: and lastly, the prayers and roast beef actually made some people as happy as a whore and a bottle. But here in town, I assure you, men, women and children have done with these things. Charity not only begins but ends at home. Instead of the four cardinal virtues, now reign four courtly ones: we have cunning for prudence, rapine for justice, time serving for fortitude, and luxury for temperance. Whatever you may fancy, where you live in a state of ignorance, and see nothing but quiet religion, and good humour, the case is just as I tell you where people understand the world, and know how to live with credit and glory.

I wish that heaven would open the eyes of men, and make them sensible which of these is right; whether, upon a one conviction, we are to quit faction, and gaming, and high feeding, and all manner of luxury, and take to your country way; or you to leave prayers and alms giving, and reading and excercise, and come into our measures. I wish (I say) that this matter were as clear to all men, as it is to

Your affectionate, &c.

LETTER XXXV.

From a young Tradesman to a Lady he had seen in Public.

Madam,

PErhaps you will not be surprised to receive a letter from a person who is unknown to you, when you reflect how likely so charming a face may be to create impertinence; and I persuade myself that when you remember where you sat last night at the play house, you would not need to be told this comes from the person who was just before you.

In the first place, madam, I ask pardon for the liberty I then took of looking at you, and for the greater liberty I now take in writing this letter: But after this I beg leave to tell you that my thoughts are honourable, and to inform you who I am: I shall not pretend to be any better. I keep a shop, madam, in Henrietta Street, and though but two years in trade, I have tolerable custom: I do not doubt but it will increase, and I shall be able to do something for a family. If your inclinations are not engaged, I should be very proud of the honour of waiting on you, and in the mean time, if you please to desire any friend to ask my character in the neighbourhood, I believe it will not prejudice you against

Madam, your most humble Servant,

LETTER XXXVI.

From a Relation of the Lady, in answer to the last.

SIR,

THere has come into my hands a letter which you wrote to Miss Maria Stebbing: she is a relation of mine, and is a very good girl; and I dare say you will not think the worse of her for consulting her friends in such an affair as that you wrote about. Besides, a woman could not well answer such a letter herself, unless it was with a full refusal, and that she would have been wrong to have done until she knew something of the person that wrote it; as wrong as to have encouraged him.

44   THE COMPLETE

You seem very sincere and open in your designs; and as you gave permission to enquire about you among your neighbours, I being her nearest friend did that for her. I have heard a very good account of you; and from all that I see, you may be very suitable for one another. She has some fortune; and I shall tell you further, that she took notice of you at the play, and does not seem at all disinclined to think favourably of you.

I am with respect,

Sir,

Your friend and Servant.

LETTER XXXVII.

An offer of Assistance to a Friend, who had received great Losses by a Person's Failure.

Dear Sir,

I am exceedingly concerned at the great loss you have lately sustained by the failure of Mr Potts. I hope you behave under it like the man of prudence you have always shewn yourself, and as one who knows how liable all men are to misfortunes. As I am really desirous of giving you consolation, I chearfully offer my service to answer any present demand, and you are at liberty to draw upon me to the amount of 200 l. which you may have the use of for a twelvemonth or more, if your affairs require it. In accepting of which you will give great pleasure to

Your Sincere Friend.

LETTER XXXVIII.

The Friend's Answer, on accepting the generous offer.

My dear Friend,

I Am at a loss to find words to express the grateful sense I have of this instance of true generous friend-

LETTER WRITER.   45

ship, My lofs indeed is heavy ; but I find that fo kind a friend is capable of making it light.   I thankfully accept of a part of your generous offer, and am ready to give my bond for 100 l. payable in a year. This fum is all I fhall have occafion for; and if I did not know I could then return it, I would not accept of your favour.   I am dear Sir,

Your moft faithful
and obliged humble Servant.

LETTER XXXIX.

The fame Offer being alfo made to another Friend, who had no Occafion for the Money, he returned the following anfwer.

Dear Sir,

I Return you a thoufand thanks for your generous offer.   I have indeed been much affected at the unexpected failure of a man, whom I thought in very happy circumftances ; but at prefent have no occafion for your friendly affiftance. If I fhould, I know no one in the world to whom I fhould fooner choofe to be obliged, I am, Sir, with warmeft gratitude,

Your moft obliged,
and moft humble Servant.

LETTER XL.

From a young Woman juft gone to Service, to her Mother at home.

Dear Mother,

TIS a fortnight this very day that I have been at Mr. Johnfon's; and, I thank God, I begin

46   T H E C O M P L E T E

to find myself a little easier than I have been: but indeed, I have suffered a great deal, since I parted from you and all the rest of my friends. At our first coming hither, I thought every thing look'd so strange about me; and when John got upon his horse, and rode out of the yard, methought every thing look'd stranger and stranger; so I got up to the window, and looked after him, 'till he turned into the London road, (for you know we live a quarter of a mile on the farther side of it) and then I sat down and cried; and that always gives me some relief. Many a time have I cried since; but I do my best to dry up my tears, and to appear as chearful as I can.

Dear mother, I return you a thousand thanks for all the kind advice you were so good as to give me at parting, and I think it over often and often; but yet, methinks, it would be better if I had it in writing; that would be what I should value above all things. But I am afraid to ask for what would give you so much trouble. So with my duty to you and my father, and kind love to all friends, I remain ever,

Your most dutiful Daughter.

L E T T E R XLI.

Her Mother's Answer.

My dear Child,

I Am very sorry that you have suffered so much since we parted: but 'tis always so at first; and will wear away in time. I have had my share too, but I bear it now pretty well; and hope you will endeavour to follow my example in this as you used to say you loved to do in every thing. You must consider, that we should never have parted with you had it not been for your good. If you conti-

true virtuous and obliging; all the family will love
and esteem you. You will get new friends there and
I think I can assure you, that you will lose no love
here; for we all talk of you every evening; and e-
very body speaks of you as fondly, or rather more
fondly than ever they did. In the mean time keep
yourself employed as much as you can; which is the
best way of wearing off any concern. Do all the bu-
finess of your place; and be always ready to assist your
fellow servants where you can in their business. This
will both fill up your time, and help to endear you to
them; and then you will soon have as many friends
about you there, as you used to have here. I don't
caution you against speaking ill of any body living,
for I know you never used to do it: but if you hear
a bad story of any body, try to soften it all you can;
and never tell it again, but rather let it slip out of
your mind as soon as possible. I am in great hopes,
that all the family are kind to you already, from the
good character I have heard of them; but I should
be glad to see it confirmed by your next; and the
more particular you are in it the better. If you have
any time to spare from your business, I hope you will
give a good share of it to your devotions: that's an
exercise which gives comfort and spirits without tiring one. My prayers you have daily; I might have
said hourly: and there is nothing that I pray for with
more earnestness, than that my dearest child may do
well. You did not mention any thing about your
health in your last: but I had the pleasure of hearing
you are well, by Mr Yates, a young man, who said
he called upon you in his way from London, and
that you looked as fresh as a rose, and as bonny as a
black bird—You know James's way of talking—However. I was glad to hear you was well; and desire you
would not forget to mention your health yourself in
your letter. Your father desires his blessing, and your
brothers their kind love to you: heaven bless you,

my dear child, and continue you to be a comfort to us all, and more particularly to

Your affectionate Mother.

LETTER XLII.

Upon the Death of a near Friend, from a Relation.

Dear Madam,

THough I am sensible that to a real grief nothing can be so impertinent as the ceremony of condolence, yet I think from relations and friends so strictly united as we have been, something may be allowed, because a great deal is required of them. When I judge by myself, I consider with what distaste and aversion I should look upon the ceremony of grief from those who neither knew the deceased enough for me to be concerned about it; yet when I consider how true a satisfaction any notice from you would be in that melancholy situation; nay, when I recollect (for it assuredly would be so)that this would be one of the greatest comforts of which I was capable, I cannot deny myself the mournful indulgence of writing to you.

I am not about to blame that sorrow which shuts you from the day-light, and from the company even of your nearest friends; the cause is worthy of it; and you owe no less to his memory, who would have paid no less to yours. Do to his remembrance this justice; but remember when you have paid the tribute, that something is also due to yourself; or could you suppose that you might neglect that, to your children.

You have no right to impair your own health; and in a constitution so tender as yours, 'tis easily done; nor had you, could you answer it to those who want

LETTER WRITER.   49

a guide and guardian, and who can have none fo interefted in their good, or fo able to promote it as you,
if you negle&t any care of yourfelf.

I know to reafon with you would be to engage with
an antagonift too powerful for me on any occafion;
but I alfo know, that when I prefs this on you as a
duty, and affured!y I have a right fo to do, you will
be convinced, and yield to the fuperiority of the caufe.
Dear coufin, we are all interefted in this, and therefore you muft give me leave to prefs the confideration upon you.   Difcharge your duty to the dead, but
remember, you owe it alfo to the living; and that thefe
little ones have a claim to your care of your own
health.   I fhall fay no more: perhaps, lefs would
have become me better; but you will excufe a fault,
if it be one, which has fo honeft a motive.   Give me
leave to affure you, that none is more folicitous of your
welfare than,   Dear Madam,
          Your moft obedient and humble Servant.

LETTER XLIII.

To a Friend gone for the Summer into the Country.

Dear Sir,

YOU left me your commands, when you took your
     leave of us, to write to you once in a fortnight,
and give you the news of the town; but you that
make the news are gone; and what is there worth
your attention among the inconfiderable people thet
remain here? Shall I write you word the king is gone
to Kenfington: you know he refolved it before you
went; or that the duke is at Windfor; you are as well
acquainted with that as I am. Shall I defcribe to you
the new equipage of the princefs of Wales; the news-
papers have done it already: or if I were inclined to

E

THE COMPLETE

give you the fcandal of the people that are left in this
defolate place, the pamphleteers have fpread that alfo.
The French parliament had bribed Madam de Pompadour on their fide; but the king difcovered the con-
fpiracy, and he forbade the one his fight, and turned
the other out of doors. The clergy were a match for
the lay antagonift in this occafion. If only a miftrefs
was to affect the matter, the holy panders did not
fcruple to do the office : and his moft Chriftian Ma-
jefty is at this moment probably; for it is morning
though I am writing to you, at reft in the arms of
the daughter of an Irifh fhoemaker. O ill ftarr'd Fan-
ny, that did not ftay for fuch an incident; but fhe
was never in favour with the churchmen.

Mr Sullen is more than ever out of humour with
his wife; but he cannot be more eager to get rid of
her, than her lover is to get her. The lady will not
be long without a protector. It is expected that it will
come to this; but when, no mortal can tell. She is
agreeable, though fhe is a baggage; and the hufband
is in the condition of Prior's thief, who often took
leave, but was loth to depart.

I do not know that there is any thing elfe here to
tell you of. As to your friends, you have moft of
them with you, and the reft are not here. What remains in Grofvenor-Sreet are well; but had better
be well in any other part of the earth. I am apt to
believe that we are as much in love with green trees,
as you are tired of them. With all your boaft of
eafe, and folitude, and retirement, and contemplation, I fancy you would be very glad to change the
fcene for buftle and bufinefs, if they were any people
to make it. But you feem all of you to have betray-
ed yourfelves, and one another; to have got away
from town in purfuit of what you do not find in the
country, now you are no more together in it. Dear
Sir, I have written, as you will perceive, rather becaufe it was proper I fhould write, than that I had

LETTER WRITER.   51

any thing to fay.   But there is a merit in obedience ;
and when it is your commands, there will always be
a pleafure alfo in it, to   Your moft obedient and
                              moft humble Servant.

LETTER XLIV.

From a Friend in the Country, to an Acquaintance
in Town, in Anfwer.

My dear Sir,

I Do not know that when I engaged you to write to
me twice a month, I promifed to anfwer you as
often : at leaft I imagine none nearer you expected to
have any thing to hear, nor I to have any thing to
write from the country, more than we are all well and
at your fervice, and we thank you, and pray tell us the
news.   But I find the turns of bufinefs have changed
hands; and this is the place of buftle, while you are
quiet.

The contefts between the French king and his parliament, are nothing to thofe of our mayor and his
court of aldermen.   The reprefentative of the town
intereft has been taking the neceffary and ufual methods to prepare for the enfuing election; but whether the aldermen have had their minds poifoned by
fome bad reports, or whether they have, in their own
hands, reafons as weighty as Mr Mayor's.   I cannot
tell ; they are determined to oppofe the re-election of
this worthy gentleman.   They fay they do not know
who will offer in this place; but this I am afraid is
apocryphal.

The game affociation have alfo created as much
confufion as the election ; and they are in this particular circumftance united with it.   The reprefenta-

E 2

tive has been one of the ftar and garter club; and he has, I think, forfeited his feat at Weftminfter, to preferve the hares and patridges about his feat in the country. Whether he will, think himfelf a gainer by this exchange, his banner will, I fuppofe, inform us.

You will fay peace and quietnefs are not what we retire to in the country; but to people ufed to contefts between parties and their heads, between power and power, and in which the fate of kingdoms are involved, this buftle about it is amufing. My dear Sir, farewel. Continue to write to me as I requefted you; for when you have leaft to fay, you ftill have fomething.

Yours moft truly.

LETTER XLV.

The Daughter to her Mother.

Dear Mother,

THough we begin to have fuch cold weather, I am got up into my chamber to write to you. God be thanked I am grown quite eafy, which is owing to my following your good advice, and the kindnefs that is already fhewn me in the family. Betty and I are bed fellows: and fhe, and Robin, and Thomas, are all fo kind to me, that I can fcarce fay which is the kindeft. My mafter is fixty years of age next April; but by his look you would not think him fifty. He has always an eafy, fmiling look; and is very good to all his fervants. When he has happened to pafs by me, as I have been dufting out the chambers, or in the paffage, he generally fays fomething to encourage me; and that makes one's work go on the more pleafantly. My miftrefs is thin as my mafter is plump; not much fhort of him in age; and more apt to be a little peevifh. Indeed that may

eafy be ; for I have never yet heard my mafter fay a
fingle word to any of us, but what was kind and encouraging. My mafter they fay is vaftly rich ; for
he is a prudent man, and laid up a great deal of money while he was in bufinefs, with which he purchafed this eftate here, and another in Suffex, fome time
before he left off: and they have, I find, a very good
houfe in London, though I don't at all defire to go
there.   As to my fellow fervants, 'tis thought Betty
(who is very good natured, and as merry as the day
is long) is to be married to the jovial landlord over
the way; and, to fay the truth, I am apt to believe
that they are actually promifed to one another.   Our
coachman, Thomas, feems to be a truly good worthy man ; you may fee by his eyes, that it does his
heart good whenever he can do a kind thing for any
of the neighbours.   He was born in the parifh, and
his father has a good farm of his own in it, and rents
another.   Robin the footman is good-natur'd too ; he
is always merry, and loves to laugh as much as he
loves to eat ; and I am fure he has a good ftomach.
But I need not talk of that, for now mine is come a-
gain, I eat almoft as hearty as he does.   With fuch
fellow fervants, and fuch a mafter, I think it will be
my own fault, if I am not eafy.   Well in health I
am, and begin to be pretty well in fpirits, only my
heart will heave a little ftill every time I look towards
the road that goes to your houfe.   Heaven blefs you
all there ! and make me a deferving daughter of fo
good a mother.   M.   C.

LETTER XLVI.

The Mother's Anfwer, and Advice.

Dear Child,

" THE next piece of advice that I give you's to
" think often how much a life of virtue is to

" be perferred to a life of pleafure; and how much " better, and more lafting, a good name is than beauty." If we called things by their right name, there is nothing that deferves the name of pleafure fo truly as virtue, but one mult talk as people are ufed to talk; and I think, by a life of pleafure, they generally mean a life of gaiety. Now our gaieties, God knows, are at beft very trifling: always unfatisfactory; often attended with difficulties in the procuring them, and fatigue in their very enjoyment; and too often followed by regret and felf condemnation. What they call a life of pleafure, among the great, muft be a very laborious life: they fpend the greateft part of their nights in balls and affemblies; and fling away the greateft part of their days in fleep. Their life is too much oppofed to nature, to be capable of happinefs; 'tis all a hurry of vifits, twenty or thirty perhaps in a day, to perfons for whom there are not above two or three that they have any real friendfhip or efteem (fuppofing them to be capable of either;) a perpetual feeking after what they call diverfions; and infipidity: and want of tafte, when they are engaged in them, and a certain languifhing and reftleffnefs when they are without them. This is not living; but a conftant endeavour to cheat themfelves out of the little time they have to live; for they generally inherit a bad conftitution, make it worfe by their abfurd way of life, and deliver a ftill weaker and weaker thread down to their children. I don't know any one thing more ridiculous than the feeing their wrinkled fallow faces all fet out with diamonds. Poor miftaken gentlewomen; they fhould endeavour to avoid peoples eyes as much as poffible, and not to attract them; for they are really a quite deplorable fight; and their very faces are a ftanding leffon againft the ftrange lives that they lead.

People in lower life, 'tis true, do not act fo ridiculoufly as thofe in higher: but even among them too

LETTER WRITER. 55

there's a vast difference between the people that live well, and the people that live ill; the former are more healthy, in better spirits, fitter for business, and more attentive to it; the latter are more negligent, more uneasy, more contemptible, and more diseased.

In truth, either in high or low life, virtue is only another name for happiness, and debauchery is the high road to misery; and this, to me appears just as true and evident, as that moderation is always good for us, and excesses always hurtful.

But is it not a charming thing to have youth and beauty, to be followed and admired? to have presents offered from all sides to one? to be invited to all diversions, and to be distinguished by the men from all the rest of the company? Yes, my dear child, all this would be charming, if we had nothing to do but to dance, and receive presents, as if this distinction of you was to last always. But the mischief of it is, that these things cannot be enjoyed without increasing your vanity every time you enjoy them, and swelling up a passion in you, that must soon be baulked and disappointed. How long is this beauty to last? there are but few fair faces that can keep it to the other side of five and twenty: and how would you bear it, after having been used to be thus distinguished and admired for some time, to sink out of the notice of people, and be neglected, and perhaps affronted by the very persons who used to pay the greatest adoration to you?

Do you remember the gentleman that was with us last autumn, and his presenting you with that pretty flower one day, on his coming out of the garden? I don't know whether you understood him or not; but I could read it in his looks, that he meant it for a lesson to you. 'Tis true, the flower was quite a pretty one; but though you put it in water, you know it faded, and grew disagreeable in four or five days; and had it not been cropp'd, but suffered to grow on in

the garden, it would have done the fame in nine or
ten.   Now a year is to a beauty, what a day was to
the flower : and who would value themfelves much on
the poffeffion of a thing, which they are fure to lofe
in fo fhort a time ?

Nine or ten years is what one may call the natural
term of life for beauty in a young woman : but by
accident, or mifbehaviour, it may die long before its
time.   The greater part of what people call beauty
in your face, for inftance, is owing to that air of innocence and modefty that is in it: if once you fhould
fuffer yourfelf to be ruined by any bafe man, all that
would foon vanifh, and affurance and uglinefs would
come in the room of it.

And if other confequences fhould follow, (for o-
ther bad ones there are, of more forts than one) you
would lofe your bloom too, and then all is gone. But
keep your reputation, as you have hitherto kept it :
and that will be a beauty which will laft to the end
of your days; for it will be the more confirmed and
brightened by time.   That will fecure you efteem,
when all the prefent form of your face is vanifhed a-
way; and will be always mellowing in greater and
greater charms.   Thefe my fentiments you'll take as
bleffings, and remember they come from the heart of
a tender and affectionate mother.

E. T.

LETTER XLVII.

**From an Apprentice who married without the Confent
of his Relations, to his Uncle.**

Honoured Uncle,

YOUR great kindnefs and affection, which I have
fo often experienced, by the favour of which I
have hardly been fuffered to feel the lofs of my father
and mother, emboldens me to write to you upon an

occafion which gives me the greateft trouble of mind, and which I have too long kept fecret ; in that, adding to the fault I at firft committed.

Sir, not to prefume to keep you in fufpence, I moft humbly confefs to you that I am married. The perfon I have chofen is not of family, nor poffeffed of any fortune ; wherefore I have hitherto kept it a fecret, fearing your difpleafure, but at prefent I cannot retain it fo any longer ; and altho your difpleafure, which I greatly fear, may make me repent of what I have done, I have no other caufe to be forry.

Sir, it is now more than a year that I have been married, in which time having had fufficient opportunities of feeing the conduct and temper of my wife, and that fomething under difficult and not agreeable circumftances, I have reafon to fay that fhe is one of the beft and worthieft women I ever knew. I wifh, Sir, I may find it as eafy to reconcile you to this match, as I find it to make myfelf content with the advantages of a fortune, which I might have obtained with another, and twice with fuch a one would propably have fpent.

The occafion, Sir, of my writing to you at this time, is the fame which rendered it neceffary for me to confefs my marriage to you, which otherwife I fhould have feared to do ; and this, Sir, I hope you will confider favourably. This allowance you are pleafed to make me for my pocket, together with the induftry of my wife, has very well fupported us hitherto ; for loving only her company, I have no other expence but the care of her. But Sir, fhe is now near her lying in, and the neceffary charge of fuch a time is more than I have had opportunities to provide.

I am not ignorant, fir, that too many having thofe opportunities to do ill, perhaps unperceived, that I have, would have kept this fecret ftill at the expence of their honefty; but there is no hazard I fhall not run perferably to this; not even the incurring your difpleafure, which fhould, it happen, would break my heart, I have prefumed, Sir, to trouble you with a long letter, and I am afraid the leaft agreeable to you in its contents of any that I have written. You will fee, Sir, that although there is fcarce any thing I would not do rather than venture to difpleafe you; yet I have run that hazard perferably to the being dif. honeft. To reconcile you to my marriage there is only one way, which is, that you will be pleafed to fee my wife; but, as fhe is not in a condition to travel at this time, I prefume to beg of you fome little affiftance towards the expence which is coming upon me.

Sir, I dread your anfwer, and yet, I muft wifh for it immediately; I muft humbly requeft of you not to exprefs your difpleafure at a thing which, although it were wrong, is now paft, and cannot be recovered, and which I am to bear. I dare not trefpafs further upon your patience but beg leave to fubfcribe my. felf, Honoured Sir,

Your moft dutiful Nephew,

LETTER XLVIII.

From an Uncle to his Nephew, who had married imprudently.

Nephew,

I Have read your letter with the greateft concern; it is a grief to me not lefs than it would have been to your father, were he living, that you have done the only act of difobedience that cannot be forgiven. I fhall not refufe you the triffle you afk of me, becaufe I pity the perfon you have married, although I cannot think you deferve that confideration. You will receive by the coach a parcel, in which are fifteen

LETTER WRITER.   59

guineas. I have paid the coachman for taking charge of it; fo fee that you find it there: and God blefs you,

I would not write cruelly to you, for I am inclined to love you tenderly; but at the fame time cannot help telling you, that you muft expect nothing more from me: nor muft you flatter ycurfelf that a reconciliation can ever be brought about. Here was a match provided for you, and when you fhould have been of a proper age, you would have heard of it. This would have made us all happy: but if I could get thofe who had intended you fo favourably to overlook the difappointment,—and forgive the infult, for they ftill confider it as no other, yet it would be impoffible to receive into our families and acquaintance a mean perfon, for fo your filence on that head, befide what you have conffeffed, declare your wife to be; and it is therefore impoffible you can be received upon the footing that you have been among them.

You fee that I am not influenced by any ftart of paffion or refentment in what I write to you. This is the natural light in which the thing muft be feen; an indifcretion. I wifhed and expected to have feen you, a credit to your friends by your induftry and fuccefs, although in a fphere below theirs; and to have met you every where well received by them: but it is impoffible. For my own part, I am, as you very well know, under no obligations to provide for you; but your good behaviour, and my own good opinion of you, prevailed with me to do fo much as has been done. You are now very nearly out of your apprenticefhip, and, as a journeyman, will be in a fituation to earn as much as I have been ufed to allow you; therefore that charge upon me is no longer neceffary, nor muft you expect it. I hoped to have feen you in a better ftation; but this is what you have chofen for yourfelf, and I am afraid is what you are moft fit for.

60   T H E   C O M P L E T E

I wifh you not to write to me after this, for I have
given you my thoughts at large in this letter ; and,
as they are not the effects of paffion, they will not
be altered by any thing you can add to what you
have already faid, I am truely concerned for you,
and am,

Your's, &c.

L E T T E R   XLIX.

From a Friend who had undertaken to adjuft a Difference, on the part of the Aggreffor.

S I R,

THERE may require many apologies from an
entire ftranger, who prefumes to write to you
on a fubject, in which, although it is of fome confequence to you, he has no immediate concern : but if
I had not heard greatly of your candour, I fhould
not have written at all, and as that has been the occafion of my adventuring to do it, the lefs an excufe
feems neceffary.

Not to detain you with ceremony, Mr. Nichols,
for whom I have a particular friendfhip, and who was
once honoured with your efteem, has been fpeaking
in fuch a manner, of fome unpleafing things which
have lately paffed between you, that, I am fure, if
you heard him, you would have forgotten every
thing in which he may have been to blame.

I have always found, that animofities between
thofe who have been friends, are carried on with the
greateft violence : nor is this a wonder, fince we naturally regard an offence lefs in profpect to itfelf,
than to the relation in which the perfon ftood with
us, who was guilty of it.   I believe, if you pleafe to
recollect without paffion, (for though all cannot do

LETTER WRITER.   61

this under provocations, yet I have been very imperfectly informed concerning you, if you have not that command of yourself) if you will reflect coolly, I believe you will find, that where resentments, on ever so just occasions, have been carried to the greatest lengths, the consequences have been such as neither of the persons would have wished, when out of the influence of passion; and I cannot doubt, but you will rather do yourself justice by receiving an honourable submission, than pursue a resentment, even upon a justifiable foundation, to the last extremity.

You will pardon me, Sir, that my good will to the person who has given you offence has carried me thus far: he is sensible that he was to blame, and he is willing to acknowledge it. It was my opinion, that a third person could better speak on such an occasion than himself: and he has joined with me in it. Though I have not the honour to be known to you, I flatter myself my name is. If you will permit me to wait on you on this occasion, I shall be happy to be the instrument of honourable satisfaction; and (for I cannot doubt but that will be the consequence) of a perfect reconciliation between two persons, who, notwithstanding this unlucky misunderstanding, I do believe to be the most worthy in the world of each other's friendship.

I am with the greatest respect,

Sir,

Your very humble Servant.

LETTER L.

Upon receiving the Offer of a Submission, in consequence of an Offence; in Answer.

Sir,

MR. Nichols could take no step in this matter so agreeable to me as the applying to you; since

F

62 THE COMPLETE

whatfoever is agreed by your advice, cannot but be to both our honours. I am also happy; that the effect of so disagreeable an incident is, that I shall have the honour to see a person to whom I have always thought it a misfortune that I was not perfonally known.

It gives me great pleafure that this matter will be accommodated with a man with whom I have had fo long a friendfhip, and for whom I entertain fo true an efteem; nor fhall I think him lefs the man of honour for confeffing a miftake, than if he had, knowing ti to be wrong, defended it with obftinacy. I impatiently expect the honour of your vifit.

And am, with the greateft refpect,
Sir,
Your obedient Servant,

LETTER LI.

To a Friend, whofe Indifcretion had engaged him in a difpute likely to end in Law.

Dear Charles,

I Take the liberty of writing to you, though I know before hand my letter muft be difagreeable; but it is to ferve, and not humour you in a thing where you are wrong. You know I was prefent when there happened to pafs fome words between you and Mr Nicholas, and I hear fince that he is confulting an attorney, to know if what you faid was not actionable. You never have been in law, elfe you would be in more care than you feem about it. Take it for granted, trying a caufe is like ending our a difpute; which ever gets the better, both are heartily beaten.

As to the words you faid, they certainly reflected upon his character, and therefore you may depend upon it he will have his remedy. I grant you it was

LETTER WRITER. 63

all true that you spoke; but that is the reason why he feels so much. People are always nicest about their characters who have no characters at all: and one thing I must tell you, what very likely you do not know already, which is, that a thing is not less scandal in law because it is true.

I say all this to you first, dear Charles, that you may take my advice about your conduct. I would have you make it up by any means in the world, before it goes farther. Ask his pardon at the club where you spoke it, own you was in liquor, or you should not have said it, and if this will not do; offer him ten pounds to drop it, for he is a dirty fellow, and will take it. It is more, perhaps, than he would get by a verdict, but then it would cost you an hundred.

I know, dear Charles, you are of a passionate temper, and you will not be ready to give up a point, especially when you are in the right; but it is better to do that, than be plagued with a law suit that will take up all your time, and cost you heaven knows what into the bargain. Do be advised, and get the better of yourself, though you are in the right; for it is much better to do so, than to be ruined by one's obstinacy. I beg you will do as I desire you, for your family's sake: for if you once get into the lawyers hands, you know not what will be the end of it.

I am, Dear Charles,
Your Friend and Servant,

LETTER LII.

From a Person engaged in a Dispute with a bad Man, to a Friend whom he desires to interfere.

My dear Friend,

I Received your letter, and am convinced you are in the right. It is the most unfortunate thing in the

F 2

64　THE COMPLETE

world to have to do with bad people in any respect,
and nothing is worse than to quarrel with them. I am
sure all I said was true, and I can bring proof of it:
but notwithstanding that, I am sensible of the prudence of your advice, and am resolved to follow it. I
am willing to do any thing that is necessary to make
up the matter; and will give more money than you
mention, if that be necessary; but I do not know how
to speak to the fellow myself. As you have been so
kind in your advice, I beg you will talk to him. Whatever you settle with him I will agree to; and shall always remember how much I am obliged to your
friendship, 　I am,

Dear Sir,

Your most humble Servant.

LETTER LIII.

*From a Son to a Father, asking his Advice about of-
fering himself a Candidate for a Place in the Gift
of a Number.*

Honoured Sir,

MY neighbour, Mr Wilkins, is dead since I wrote
to you last, and as he was in possession of a post
under the governors of the London hospital, and
many of the most considerable live in this ward, I have
been advised by my friends to offer myself as a candidate to succeed him. I have reason to think I am
respected in the place; and I am sure I have some
friends that will assist me: but I am quite unexpe-
rienced in the thing, and know not how to go about
it. I would not attempt any thing that should make
my name public in this manner without your approbation; and for that reason, as well as my inexperience in such matters, I make it the first thing to write

you word of it. I beg, Sir, you will first tell me
whether you approve of my attempting it; and then,
if you do so, that you will give me your advice in what
manner I am to do it; but in this I beg you would
not lose any time; because if any application be made,
it must be immediately, as others will be ready to
make it; and often a first request carries it, though
made by a stranger. I beg you will be pleased to answer me this morning.

I am,

honoured Sir,

Your obedient Son.

LETTER LIV.

From a Father to a Son, asking his Advice about
putting up for a Place. In answer to the former.

Dear Son,

I Think you cannot do better than to follow the
advice of your friends on this occasion. I heartily
recommend it to you to put up, and will take all the
pains possible among my friends to speak to those they
know. It is always right to try, where it is no difcredit to lose; and as to the making your name public, it is nothing but advantage. You did not intend
to practise your business in private, and the more
people know of you, the better; besides, it is some
credit to stand for a thing which it is so much credit
to obtain. Use your own and your friends interest
thoroughly, and beg of them all to be in earnest in
their recommendation. Consider, if you do not succeed in this, still it is being made known to many families, and that in the most favourable manner; and
they may employ you afterwards.

E 3

66 **THE COMPLETE**

My dear Harry, you will find every thing of this kind depends upon the general good behaviour of the perfon; therefore I should recommend it to all young people to try often for fuch employments. You do not need any cautions or guards upon your conduct, but they will do you no harm. I do not fuppofe you will fucceed, for few, I believe, ever have on the firft attempt; but you will make yourfelf an intereft: you are young enough to fee more vacancies: and if you preferve that intereft you fet out with, the advantage of fo many votes at the next, is always a recommendation to thofe that have ftood before.

You now fee my thoughts fully upon this matter, and you will find that I fhall give you more than my advice; for I will do every thing that is poffible to ferve you. You muft be induftrious in your application; for this rule, my dear fon, that in all things to be obtained from a number of votes, the moft buftling man generally carries it, whether he be the moft deferving or not. God fend you fuccefs!

I am,

Your affectionate Father.

LETTER LV.

From a Father to his Son in Trade, at the Time of an approaching Election.

Dear James;

YOU have hitherto fhewn every mark of prudence that your friends could expect of you in the management of bufinefs, and in your behaviour. You may be fure it is a pleafure to me to fee this, and that I have no fatisfaction like the hearing others fpeak of it. An affable behaviour, James, I always told you, was more than every thing in the conduct

LETTER WRITER.   67

of life; and you have found that it is truth; There is a way of refusing what is required of you, that yet will not give the person who is refused opportunity to be angry; and you have found the way to this among other articles of prudence; for tho' I know you have been led by prudence to deny credit to some that asked you, which is certainly the most difficult thing in the world, yet I hear every one speak kindly of you.

I give you no more commendation than I find you have deserved in the particular; but I must give you advice in a thing that you have not yet experienced; there will be request made to you now, which will be the most difficult of all others to be denied; and yet, if it be possible, you must refuse them. You have occasion for all the caution that can be given you with respect of these, for they will be pressed upon you with the greatest warmth; and to a young person, as you are, will seem to be the most friendly in the world, and you will expect the greatest consequences from them; but you will find none, at least no good ones.

The election of a member of parliament is coming off at your own; and it is the request of your vote about which I am giving you this caution. It will be asked by both candidates, and they will get their friends to ask it of you also; but, if it be possible, James, you should give it to neither. There are places where the whole town is divided into parties, as violent and outrageous as if they were enemies at war; but this is not quite the case with yours; and therefore I think you may with conduct keep yourself from making enemies, but it will require all your prudence to do this. In many places hatreds of the most implacable kinds arise from this source; and the feuds of one election do not subside till another; but, it is not quite so with you: You are too young to have experience of this, and therefore I advise you fo fully upon it.

The gentlemen who are candidates are strangers to you, therefore you may eafily refufe them both. If you tell them, that it is not for want of refpect, but that you wifh to make yourfelf no enemies, and affure them that you fhall not vote on the other fide; you will decline the requeft as civilly as it is made to you, and they will perhaps neither of them take offence If you are preffed by your cuftomers of confequence to vote on either fide, according to the intereft, the more ftrong the folicitation is, the more prudent it is to decline: becaufe in proportion to that, you are fure to difoblidge the party againft whom you gave it In this cafe, I would have you wait upon the principal cuftomers of each party, and tell them how much you are afked alfo by the other. Reprefent to them that your fingle vote can be of no confequence either way, and how fearful you are of giving offence where you are fo much obligated, You have fo good a way of making an excufe, that I hope you will prevail; I am fure any man who has candour will approve of your conduct: and it is happy for you, as I faid before, that yours is not one of the moft violent towns on this fubject. If all this fail, and you find you muft give a vote on one fide, for fear of difobliging both; it is better to lofe half your cuftomers than lofe them all; fo do it. In this cafe, mind not the promifes on either fide; but you will know what are the principles of each of the candidates; and I charge you give your vote according to your confcience.

You will have great promifes from both but you are not to mind either. No good ever came of elections; at leaft, it is very little good that ever came of them, and that to the worft people in the world: and I am fure you never will get it in the manner they have done. You will lofe by voting; you muft chufe the leaft of the two evils. To declare yourfelf on one

LETTER WRITER.   69

fide, is always to difoblige: and then you lofe them all. I have given you my thoughts at large upon it; and as this is what experience has fhewn me. I hope you will regard it. Conduct yourfelf with prudence in this, elfe all you have done already is nothing.

I am,

Dear James,

Your affectionate Father.

LETTER LVI.

To a Widow Lady in London, to diffuade her from a Marriage.

Dear Coufin,

I WAS accidentally in company the other day, where you was mentioned with great refpect; but it was faid that you were about to marry again. I may be impertinent in what I have to fay on this fubject, becaufe the obfervations may come too late: yet I think that can hardly be the cafe, becaufe this is the firft time I have heard of your defigning it, and then but cafually. I know how ready the world is to interpret the flighteft acquaintance into courtfhips; and I think, had his been any more, I fhould have heard of it earlier, and with more certainty; nay, I will not believe but you would have written to me of it yourfelf.

As I will perfuade myfelf from thefe reafons, that you have not gone fo far in this matter, if you have made any ftep in it, as to have made it too late to go back, I fhall with all that freedom which our acquaintance and affinity fupport me in ufing, give you my reafons why I think you do wrong. You are very happy at prefent, and thofe who do not know when they are well commonly change for the worfe.

It is a maxim among gamesters, that nobody ought to play but those who have nothing to lose; and I it ought to hold as good with those who marry after they are thirty. When there is a bloom of youth upon the face, a man must be tempted to do a great many things to purchase it; but when that is gone, I shall be always afraid that the desire of winning the bet might go further than the love of play. If that is the matter, wretched is she who is caught; for the winner will be as ready in this case, as the loser in the other, to break the tables.

But to talk in plain words, and argue the matter like people of this world, I should imagine that any woman who had been married a dozen of years, let it have been ever so happily, would have seen enough of the condition not to be in humour to enter upon it again when the best season is over. I talk very freely to you, cousin, but I love you, and you know it; you will therefore excuse me; nay, I believe you will thank me. I advise you against marriage, but I do not know who you are going to marry. There is one test of affections and there is but one; and if your lover's affairs will bear that, why I shall give up half my objections. The man who has nothing may deceive you when he says he loves you, whether you have nothing or have a fortune; for in the one case he may just like you enough for a month's living together, and, as it is all one to him where he lives, he may resolve upon bidding good bye to you afterwards; in the other, he may very reasonably be in love with your fortune, and may think no incumbrance of your person too much for the advantage. But if the lover have a fortune more than equal to your own, take it for granted he is in earnest, and give yourself no trouble but about his constancy. It would not be worth while to marry a man you was sure liked you to day, but who it was fifty to one, might change his mind to morrow: and as to him, whom it was

LETTER WRITER.   71

impossible to know, whether he liked you or no, you, who will be too wise to fall into absolute green sickness love, would be distracted to venture upon it.

Which of these, or whether either of these descriptions belongs to your present admirer, I am entirely ignorant   You see I am a great enemy to your marrying at all; but I have told you there is a sort of a man that I think you may venture upon; she will have good luck, however, that finds him.

It would be easy to be grave upon this subject; but dear cousin, it is not easy to be grave without being dull; and I have not a mind you should throw away my letter without reading it. You have a great many years probably to come, and you have a right to be happy in them. You have the means in your own hands, and in the name of wisdom keep them there. You have relations who will want your money, when you can make no more use of it; and should you rob them of it in favour of a stranger? besides, I have that true affection for you, that I should be unhappy to see you in difficulties; and why should you wish to make a man miserable, because he deserves better at your hands?

Consider all these things, for you have gratitude and generosity; and consider yourself, for you have prudence? you may be happy in yourself, and a blessing to others these forty years; or you may be miserable, and a burthen to your relations; this is the chance, and, I protest, I believe the choice is now before you. Dear cousin, farewell; I only repeat to you, consider.   Yours most affectionately,

LETTER LVII.

From a Lady to a stranger, enquiring the Character of an upper Maid Servant.

Madam,

I Think myself unhappy that I have not the pleasure of being known to you, as I have a request to

72   THE COMPLETE

make; on your complying with which I place a great
dependance. The occasion of this letter is nothing
more than the comon form of enquiring the character of a fervant; and I am very fenfible that in the
general way this fignifies little; for whatever was the
fault the perfon committed, fhe begs pardon when
fhe goes away, and her lady promifes her a character
upon a belief that fhe will mend.

But, Madam, I beg leave to mention to you, that
I am too fenfible how much injury may be done by
the tatling of one of thofe creatures, much more by
her wickednefs, if fhe is bad enough to take bribes
from defigning perfons. Madam, I have a daughter
grown up to a woman's eftate, who is as dear to me
as a child can be to a parent; I have ommitted no
care in her education; and I think fhe wants no kind
of goodnefs. I fhall be very unhappy to fee fuch a
character facrificed to the malice of a fervant; or the
child (for fhe has fome fortune) attempted by needy
perfons. becaufe they can command enough to engage
fuch a perfon in their fervice.

I beg pardon for troubling you with fo long a letter on fuch an occafion: but I intreat the favour of
you to inform me whether the perfon whom you difcharged a fortnight fince, Sufannah Clark by name,
is fit for me.

I have the honour to be,
with the greateft refpect,
Your moft obedient Servant.

LETTER LVIII.

From a Lady, giving the Character of an upper Maid-
Servant. In anfwer to the forgoing.

Madam,

AFTER the letter you have written to me, I
fhould be unpardonable to fay any thing to you

LETTER WRITER. 73

but the moſt perfect truth. I know it is a cuſtom with ladies to be too favourable to diſcharged ſervants, but it is a bad one. I would not be too kind to them on this occaſion, in any caſe; but at preſent I ſhall think it a duty to ſpeak without the leaſt reſerve.

The ſervant who has offered herſelf to you, madam, has left my place about ſix weeks ago; the occaſion of her being diſcharged, was ſome expreſſions that I thought did not carry a proper reſpect; but they were ſpoken to me, and not behind my back. I will do her the juſtice alſo to acknowledge, that perhaps ſhe might have ſome provocation. However, if I had been ſenſible I was in fault myſelf, I would not have kept the ſervant afterwards. As to the circumſtances you mention, I have no cauſe to ſuſpect them; I believe her to be very diſcreet and honeſt. How far what I have mentioned may plead againſt her, I cannot ſay; you are the judge of it; but I think as it is all that can be objected to a perſon, otherwiſe very deſireable, and is all I have to charge her with, who have had opportunities of ſeeing whatever faults ſhe has, I ſhould not as the world of ſervants goes, expect a better,

I am,

Madam,

Your very humble Servant,

LETTER LIX.

To a Stranger, aſking the Character of a Servant.

Sir,

A Perſon, whoſe name is James Wilkins, has applied to me, on hearing there was a vacancy in my family to ſerve as footman. His greateſt recommendation is, that he lived a conſiderable time with you, and behaved himſelf well in your ſervice; if this

G

be true, it is indeed fufficient; but this, as well as his occafion of leaving you, (which he fays, was to fee his friends) is fo common an account for people to give of themfelves, that I place no value upon it, till I am favoured with a confirmation of it by you.

I know it is too common in gentlemen of humane difpofitions, to promife a better character to fervants than they have deferved, upon their promife of amending the fault, they had been guilty of; but I am afraid this is oftener kept on the firft part, than on the latter. Sir, I have troubled you thus far only to acquaint you that mine is a family, into which it would be particularly improper to take a bad man: and having faid fo much, I fhall perfectly depend upon what you are pleafed to tell me in refpect of him.

I am, Sir,

your obedient,

and very humble Servant.

LETTER LX.

The Anfwer: containing the Character of a Servant.

I Am very fenfible of the propriety of all you fay in refpect to the abufe in characters given with fervants. If there were not the particular occafion which you intimate in this cafe, I fhould ftill, after fuch a letter as you have written to me, be careful to fay no more or lefs of the man than he deferves; fince I think that candour from one gentleman to another, is more neceffary than partiality to fervants.

The perfon you mention lived in my family about ten months; a time perhaps, not fo long as he is willing to have it thought; and the occafion of my difcharging him was fome difagreements with the other fervants: this Sir, is the truth of it. As the excufes he has made to you are very common. I think if I were in your place, I should not construe them particularly to his advantage. The time that he was with me is sufficient to judge, in some degree, of a person in his station: and from that I think very well of him, I should not have parted with him on my own account; nor do I know who was to blame in the dispute which occasioned my discharging him; only as the other servants have lived with me, I was less inclined to part with them. This, Sr, is exactly the truth, as to his behaviour, while with me, and as to his leaving me. I believe he will make you a very good servant, and am,

Sir,
Your very obedient humble Servant.

L E T T E R LXI.

From a Person in Trade to his late Master, on Account of a bad Debt.

Honoured Sir,

THERE is but one thing in the management of my business, in which I find myself now at a loss for your instructions; but there is no one to whom I can so properly apply for advice. The only part of your conduct, of which you left me uninformed, was that with respect to the getting in your bills; and this I am sensible the secrecy that is due to those who are indebted is a sufficient reason never to divulge. I beg you, however, now, Sir, to instruct me in my own affairs, although I had no right to enquire into yours. I am in great uneasiness about a debt that is due to me, and I will relate the circumstances. The person I have trusted so deeply is a physician; he seems to be considerably in business, and is very much respected by every body: but I have heard some whispers that he has answered some demands

G 2

but very indifferently. A part of my debt is money lent out pocket. This I can leſs afford to loſe than the money due in trade ; and the time of paymentis elapſed a conſiderable time ago. I have aſked him more than once, and he has put me off for a ceitain time, and when that time is expired, I am not at all nearer than I was. I muſt confeſs that it would be a very difficult thing for me to ſpare the money, and I beg you'll tell me what ſtep I ſhould take. I am preſſ-ed by one or two who know the matter to arreſt him ; but I have no mind to do ſuch a thing.

    I beg you to tell what is the beſt courſe I can take. I hope you will not, Sir take amiſs this application, for I believe there is no perſon who wiſhes me better than you do. I return my humble thanks for your many favours, and am,

Sir,

Your moſt obedient,
and humble Servant,

LETTER LXII.

The Anſwer,

Dear William,.

THERE is one very good rule I ſhall give you, about what you aſk, and that is, to take care never to make bad debts. I aſſure you, this has been the great ſecret of my conduct, and I owe what ſuc-ceſs I have had in the world more in this than any thing elſe whatever. Nobody in trade ever refuſed ſo many cuſtomers as I have done ; but, William, one bad debt runs away with the profit of many good ones : for this reaſon I have leſs experience than you think in theſe matters, but I ſhall give you my advice as well as I can.

    I am not of opinion you ſhould arreſt the gentle-

LETTER WRITER.   97

man by any means. It is a very good method where people have money and will not pay; but there are two reasons against it in such a case as you speak of: it is cruel, and it answers no purpose. Instead of getting the money now, it will prevent his ever being able to pay you at all? for a man that has nothing but his business, will never make much of that in the rules of a prison. Never lend money to your customers for the future: for it is a common maxim, and it is true, that those who borrow money seldom pay it.

I would have you depend in this matter upon frequent asking for your money; and tell the gentleman that you are distressed in your own circumstances. I have known some people, who, when they were uneasy about a large debt, have insisted upon the debtor's finding some persons to be security that he should pay them; this is getting bail without going to law; but I believe it is very seldom that they are able to obtain this. A man would sooner bid them do their worst, and give in bail to an action, because he can then pretend some dispute about the demand, and it is an excuse for asking, and the law will give him as much time as the creditor is generally inclined to allow: for if you arrest the gentleman to morrow, you will not be able to recover your money this twelvemonth: nay, most likely you would never get it at all; for the laws allows all that delay; and then the debtor, if he cannot pay, is only to live in St George's Fields, or the Borough a place that thousands of people chuse.

Take care, William, how you have any dealings, for the future, with people that are at all dubious: if you get them into your books, never let them get far; and, whatever you do, never lend money to those who are in your debt already. These are the best rules I can give for your future conduct: as for the present it is my opinion, the best way is to dun

G 3

78 THE COMPLETE

continually. Plead the neceffity of your own affairs ; and take any thing, if it be ever fo little at a time : he will find that he is obliged to you not to diftrefs him farther : and as you never defign to do it, never threaten; this is the greateft of all folly in a creditor ; if he defigns to proceed to law, he never fhould tell the perfon of it before hand, for it is bidding him keep out of the way; and if he does not intend to do it, it is only making him hate him as well as fear him, and never anfwers any purpofe. By civil behaviour and conftant application, you will get in your money by degrees, as faft as he can pay it, and, in the mean while, you will have him for a cuftomer with ready money.

I have wrote you a long letter; but, as you afked my advice, I was willing to give you my reafons for it ; befides, I think you have a right to know every thing that I do, relating to trade ; and if you had not, I have a refpect for you that would make me comply with any fuch requeft; or readily do any thing to ferve you.

> I am,
>> Your faithful Friend.

LETTER LXIII.

A Letter of Advice to a Perfon in Trade, from the Mafter to whom he ferved his Apprenticefhip.

Dear William,

YOU will forgive me that I addrefs you by a name which calls up my remembrance of your good qualities, though Mr Aylworth might feem a title of more refpect; I mean this as a name of friendfhip : befides, I defign to advife you, and therefore may be fuppofed ftill to keep up fomething of the mafter.

LETTER WRITER.   79

I meet with you upon change every day, and you seem th. busiest man at the place; I know your affairs cannot be so very numerous there; nor indeed are they who have the most numerous those whom one sees in the greatest bustle in transacting them. I am afraid you confuse yourself in all this bustle; and fearing that I have in this article omitted to give you the due instructions while you was with me, I hold it an act of duty as well as friendship to do it now. I believe you have seldom seen me perplexed and hurried by my business, and yet nobody knows better than you how considerable a share I have had of it; and you know also that I have gone thro' it well. The method I used was always to set down in the morning what was to be done in the day, and the order in which it was to be done; and he that does this will always be doing only one thing at a time, and he will know what to do next.

I will set it right before you in a very plain instance; suppose you were making interest for a place, and were to wait upon a great number of persons in different parts of the town; you would take a list of their names, and run from one to another at random; and when you had seen one, the time it would take to go to the next would be lost in settling which you should next go to   Now, if another man of more years and experience was to set about the same thing, he would spend the first morning in taking a new list of them in their divisions, according as they ly, so as to go readily from one to another. Your hurrying temper would think this time lost; but though you get twenty before him the first day, he would have gone thro' the whole before you had done half; it is just so in business. If you only remember, in a general manner, confused which to set about next, and leave half of them undone; but if you bestow one quarter of an hour thus in the morning you will never be hurried in the rest of the day. You well know three things that contain all the secrets of business; first, what you have to do that day; and how much of it you can do that day; and thirdly what time to set about each part of it.

I am under some concern to see you pushing every body about the change, and all in heat and hurry the whole time; when you see Mr Gordon, who has a hundred times your business, walking about as leisurely as if he was in his compting house, and yet doing it all; while your's is left undone, though there is so little for it.

I hope you will take this friendly, as it was meant, and as you used to observe me when it was a duty, that you will now do it by choice.

I am,
Your sincere friend.

LETTER LXIV.

From a Person in Trade to his late Master, thanking him for friendly Advice. In Answer to the former.

Sir,

I Should be wanting in civility, as well as gratitude if I did not take the first opportunity of returning you my thanks for your kind advice. Sir, I look upon it as the greatest obligation, and shall obey it strictly. I have been used to hear persons say, that when the doctor knows his disease, he is half way towards the cure of it; and this, I assure you, is fairly the case between you and me. I am sensible that what you say is exactly the case with me, and I shall begin to morrow to pursue the course which you prescribe for the cure.

I do not wonder you have taken notice of my hur-

ry upon the change; I have been many times afhamed
of it, but I never knew to what it was owing till you
told me.   I fhall fhew my gratitude in the beft manner by avoiding it for the future, and I am with the
greateft fincerity.

Sir,

Your moft obliged Servant.

LETTER LXV.

To a Perfon who had done a bad Thing by an unex-
perienced Servant.

Mr James,

I Have a great deal of good will for you, and that is
the occafion of my writting this letter. You know
I faw you win the money of lady Philip's fervant;
and I have feen the young man, fince, and can tell you,
you muft take care of yourfelf, for I fear what is doing. The man does not fufpect any harm of you, but
there are thofe that will.   He told me all the matter,
and I would advife you, for your own fake, to give
him the money again, if you expect to ftay in your
place, or get a character.

The money that he paid you, he told you was his
lady's; and that's the truth.   He is afraid to be called
to an account, and has wrote to his father to come
and fpeak to his lady about it. You may be fure this
will come to your mafter's ears, and if he does not
turn you away, it is well if you are not taken up for
winning the money in an unlawful manner.   As I
hear the ftory, it is altogether againft you.   I have
nothing to do in it, only as I wifh you well, I tell you
what you ought to do.

Your humble Servant.

THE COMPLETE

LETTER LXVI.

From a Perfon who had done a bad thing, fenfible of it, and defirous to make amends. In confequence of the former.

Mr William,

I AM very fenfible now how bad a thing I did in infifting upon your paying me the money which belonged to your lady, when I won fo much of you at cards. If you will come to our houfe, I am defirous to make it up with you, and will give you any fatisfaction you pleafe to require. As to the money you won of me, I let you get it on purpofe to make you play more; and all that I have won of you, I won fairly: but, however, as you cannot play the game at all, it was not an even match, and I fhall willingly return it.

Whereas, I hear you have fent for your father out of the country, to come up and fpeak to your miftrefs about it; I defire you will not let him fay any thing concerning it; as I fhall make you fatisfaction, your lady will not know any thing that has happened, and it would only hurt my character to have it talked of. I am fure it will make your father eafy to fee all is well on your fide, and I dare fay it will be example enough to you as it is; and as for my part, I fhall never do fo foolifh a thing again. So all things being made up, I defire of you as the greateft favour, that nothing may be faid about it, and am

Your humble Servant,

LETTER LXVI.

From a refpectful Lover to his Miftrefs.

Dear Madam,

I Have long ftruggled with the moft honourable and refpectful paffion that ever filled the heart of man;

LETTER WRITER. 83

I have often try'd to reveal it perfonally; as often in this way: but never till now could prevail upon my fears and doubts. But I can no longer ftruggle with a fecret that has given me fo much torture to keep, and yet hitherto more, when I have endeavoured to reveal it. I never entertain the hope to fee you, without rapture; but when I have that pleafure, inftead of being animated as I ought, I am utterly confounded. What can this be owing to, but a diffidence in myfelf, and an exalted opinion of your worthinefs, and is not this one ftrong token of ardent love? yet if it be, how various is the tormenting paffion in its operations? fince fome it infpires with courage, whilft others it deprives of all necefary confidence. I can only affure you, Madam, that the heart of man never conceived a ftronger or fincerer paffion than mine for you. If my reverence for you is my crime, I am fure it has been my fufficient punifhment. I need not fay my defigns and motives are honourable: who dare approach fo much virtue and excellence, with a fuppofition that fuch an affurance is necefary? what my fortune is, is well known; and I am ready to ftand the teft of the ftricteft enquiry. Condefcend, Madam, to embolden my refpectful paffion, by one favourable line; that if what I here profefs, and hope further to have an opportunity to affure you of, be found to be unqueftionable truth, then my humble adrefs will not quite be unacceptable to you; and thus you will for ever oblidge, Dear Madam,

Your affectionate admirer,
and devoted Servant.

LETTER LXVII.

The Anfwer.

Sir,

IF modefty be the greateft glory of our fex furely it cannot be blame worthy in yours. For my own

part, I muſt think it the moſt amiable quality either
man or woman can poſſeſs. Nor can there be, in my
opinion, a true reſpect where there is not a diffidence
of one's merit, and an high opinion of the perſons we
eſteem.

To ſay more, on this occaſion, would little become
me; to ſay leſs, would look as if I knew not how to
pay that regard to modeſt merit, which modeſt merit
only deſerves.

You, Sir, beſt know your own heart; and if you
are ſincere and generous, will receive as you ought
this frankneſs from

Your humble Servant.

LETTER LXIX.

A Gentleman to a Lady, profeſſing an Averſion to
the tedious Formality in Courtſhip:

Dear Madam,

I Remember that one of the antients, in deſcribing
a youth in love, ſays, he has neither wiſdom e-
nough to ſpeak nor hold his tongue. If this be a juſt
deſcription, the ſincerity of my paſſion will admit of
no diſpute; and whenever, in your company, I behave like a fool, forget not that you are anſwerable
for my incapacity. Having made bold to declare thus
much, I muſt preſume to ſay, that the favourable reception of this, will, I am certain make me more worthy of your notice: but your diſdain would be what
I believe myſelf incapable ever to ſurmount. To try
by idle falacies, and airy compliments, to prevail on
your judgment, is a folly for any man to attempt
who knows you. No Madam, your good ſenſe and
endowments have raiſed you far above the neceſſity of
practiſing the mean artifices which prevail upon the

L E T T E R   W R I T E R.   85

lefs deferving of your fex: you are not to be fo lightly deceived; and if you were, give me leave to fay,
I fhould not think you deferving of the trouble that
would attend fuch an attempt.

This, I muft own, is no fafhionable letter from one
who, I am fure, loves up to the greateft heroe of romance: but as I would hope that the happinefs I fue
for fhould be lafting, it is certainly moft eligible to
take no ftep to procure it but what will bear reflection; for I fhould be happy to fee you mine, when we
have both outlived the tafte for every thing that has
not virtue and reafon to fupport it. I am, madam,
nothwithftanding this unpolifhed addrefs,

Your moft refpectful admirer,
and obedient humble Servant.

L E T T E R   LXX.

The Lady's Anfwer, encouraging a further Declaration.

Sir,

I Am very little in love with the fafhionable methods
of courtfhip: fincerity with me is preferable to
compliments; yet I fee no reafon why common decency fhould be difcarded. There is fomething fo
odd in your ftile, that when I know whether you are
in jeft or earneft, I fhall be lefs at a lofs to anfwer you.
Mean time, as there is abundant room for rifing, rather than finking, in your compliance, you may poffibly have chofen wifely to begin firft at the loweft
end. If this be the cafe, I know not what your fucceeding addreffes may produce: but I tell you fairly,
that your prefent make no great impreffion, yet perhaps as much as you intended, on

Your humble Servant.

H

86 # THE COMPLETE

LETTER LXXI.

The Gentleman's Reply, more openly declaring his Paſſion.

Dearest Madam,

NOW I have the hope of being not more deſpiſed for my acknowledged affection. I declare to you, with all the ſincerity of a man of honour, that I have long had a moſt ſincere paſſion for you; but I have ſeen gentlemen led ſuch dances when they have given up their affections to the lovely tyrants of their hearts, and could not help themſelves, that I had no courage to begin an addreſs in the uſual forms, even to you, of whoſe good ſenſe and generoſity I had nevertheleſs a great opinion. You have favoured me with a few lines, which I moſt humbly thank you for. And I do aſſure you, madam, if you will be pleaſ'd to encourage my humble ſuit, you ſhall have ſo juſt an account of my circumſtances and pretenſions, as I hope will entitle me to your favour in the honourarable light in which I profeſs myſelf, dear madam,

Your moſt obliged
and faithful Admirer

P. S. Be ſo good as to favour me with one line more to encourage my perſonal attendance, if not diſagreeable.

LETTER LXXII.

The Lady's Anſwer to his Reply, putting the matter on a ſudden Iſſue.

Sir,

AS we are both ſo well inclined to avoid unneceſſary trouble, as well as unneceſſary compli-

LETTER WRITER. 87

ments, I think proper to acquaint you, that Mr Richardson of Winchester, has the management of all my affairs; and is a man of such probity and honour, that I do nothing in any matters without him. I have no dislike to your person; and if you approve of what Mr Richardson can acquaint you with, in relation to me, and I approve of his report in your favour, I shall be far from shewing any gentleman, that I have either an insolent or a sordid spirit, especially to such as do me the honour of their good opinion.

I am, Sir,

Your humble Servant.

LETTER LXXIII.

A facetious young Lady to her Aunt, ridiculing her serious Lover.

Dear Aunt,

I Am much obliged to you for the kindness you intended me; in recommending Mr Slyboots to me for a husband: but I must be so free as to tell you, he is a man no way suited to my inclination. I despise, 'tis true, the idle rants of romance; but am inclinable to think there may be an extreme on the other side of the question.

The first time the honest man came to see me in the way you were pleased to put into his head, was one Sunday after sermon-time. He began telling me, what I found at my finger ends, that it was very cold; and politely blow'd upon his. I immediately perceived, that his passion for me could not keep him warm; and in compliance to your recommendation, conducted him to the fire side. After he had pretty well rubbed heat into his hands, he stood up with his

H 2

back to the fire, and, with his hands behind him, held
up his coat, that he might be warm all over; and looking about him, afked, with the tranquility of a man
a twelve-month married, and juft come off a journey,
how all friends did in the country? I faid, I hoped
very well; but would be glad to warm my fingers.
Cry mercy madam?—And then he fhuffled a little
farther from the fire; and after two or three hems,
and a long paufe.——

I have heard, faid he, a moft excellent fermon juft
now; Dr Thomas is a fine mad truly; did you ever
hear him, madam? No fir, I generally go to my own
parifh church. That's right, madam, to be fure:
what was your fubject to day? The pharifee and publican Sir. A very good one truly: Dr Thomas would
have made fine work upon that fubject His text to
day was evil communications corrupt good manners.
A good fubject, Sir; I doubt not the good Doctor
made a fine difcourfe upon it. O, aye, madan, he
cant make a bad one upon any fubject. I rung for the
tea-kettle; for thought I, we fhall have all the heads
of the fermon immediately.

At tea he gave me an account of all the religious
focieties, unafked: and how many boys they had put
out 'prentices, and girls they had taught to knit and
fing pfalms. To all which I gave a nod of approbation, and was juft able to fay (for I began to be
horribly in vapours) it was a very excellent charity.
O, aye, madam, faid he again (for that's his word I
find) a very excellent one truly; it is fnatching fo
many brands out of the fire. You are a contributor
Sir, I doubt not. O, aye, madam, to be fure. No
doubt, Sir, a bleffing attends upon all who promote
fo worthy a defign. O, aye, Madam, no doubt, as
you fay: I am fure I found it: bleffed be God! and
then he twang'd his nofe, and lifted up his eyes, as
if in an ejaculation.

O my good aunt, what a man is here for an huf-

LETTER WRITER.   89

band! At laſt came the happy moment of his taking
eave; for I would not aſk him to ſtay ſupper; and
moreover he talked of going to a lecture at St He-
len's. And then (though I had an opportunity of
ſaying little more than yes, and no, all the time; for
he took the vapours he had put me into, for devotion
or gravity, (at leaſt, I believe ſo) he preſs'd my hand,
look'd frightfully kind, and gave me to underſtand
as a mark of his favour, that if, upon further converſation, and enquiry into my character, he ſhould
happen to like me as well as he did from my behaviour and perſon; why, truly, I need not fear in time
being bleſſed with him for my huſband!

This, my good aunt, may be a mighty ſafe way of
travelling towards the land of matrimony, as far as
I know; but I cannot help wiſhing for a little more
entertainment on our journey. I am willing to believe Mr Slyboots an honeſt man, but am, at the
ſame time, afraid this religious turn of temper, however in itſelf commendable, would better ſuit with a
woman who centers all deſert in a ſolemn appearance,
than with, dear Aunt,

Your greatly obliged Kinſwoman.

LETTER LXXIV.

Her Aunt's Anſwer, rebuking her ludicrous turn of
Mind.

Couſin Jenny,

I Am ſorry you think Mr Slyboots ſo unſuitable a
lover. He is a ſerious, ſober good man: And
ſurely when ſeriouſneſs and ſobriety make a neceſſary
part of the duty of a good huſband, a good father,
and a good maſter of a family; thoſe characters ſhould

H 3

THE COMPLETE

not be the subjects of ridicule, in persons of our sex especially; who would reap the greatest adventage from them. But he talks of the weather when he first sees you, it seems: and would you have him directly fall upon the subject of love the moment he beheld you?

He visited you just after sermon, on a Sunday: and was it so unsuitable for him to let you see, that the duty of the day had made proper impressions upon him.

His turn for promoting the religious societies, which you speak so slightly of, deserves more regard from every good person; for that same turn is a kind of security to a woman, that he who had a benevolent and religious heart, could not make a bad man, or a bad husband. To put out poor boys to 'prentice, to teach girls to sing psalms, would be with very few a subject for ridicule: for he that was so willing to provide for the children of others, would take still greater care of his own.

He gave you to understand, that if he liked your character on enquiry, as well as your person and behaviour, he should think himself very happy in such a wife: for I dare say this was more like his language, than what you put in his mouth: and let me tell you, it would have been a much stranger speech, had so cautious and serious a man said, without a thorough knowledge of your character, that at the first sight he was over head and ears in love with you.

I think, allowing for the ridiculous turn your airy wit gives to this first visit, that by your own account, he acted like a prudent, a serious, and worthy man, as he is, and like one that thought flashy compliments beneath him, in so serious an affair as this.

I think, cousin, Jenny, this is not only a mighty safe way, as you call it, of travelling toward the land of matrimoney, but the land of happiness, with respect as well to the next world as this. And it is to

LETTER WRITER.   91.

be hoped, that the better intertainment you fo much
wifh for on your journey, may not lead you too much
out of your way, and divert your mind from the
principal view which you ought to have to your journey's end.

In fhort, I could rather have wifhed, that you could
bring your mind nearer to this ftandard, than that he
fhould bring down his to your level. And you'd
have found more fatisfaction in it than you imagine,
could you have brought yourfelf to a little more of
that folemn appearance, which you treat fo lightful-
ly, and which, I think, in him is much more than
mere appearance.

Upon the whole, coufin Jenny, I am forry that a
woman of virtue and morals, as you are, fhould treat
fo ludicoufly a ferious and pious frame of mind, in
an age, wherein good examples are fo rare, and fo
much wanted ; though at the fame time I am far
from offering to prefcribe to you in fo ardous an affair
as a hufband ? and wifh you and Mr Slyboots too,
fince you are fo differently difpofed, matched more
fuitably to each other's mind, than you are likely to
be together: for I am

　　　　　　Your truely affectionate Aunt.

LETTER LXXV.

**To a Father, on his Neglect of his Childrens Edu-
cation.**

Dear Sir.

I Am under a concern to fee fuch a remiffnefs, as e-
very body takes notice of, in the education of your
children. They are brought up, 'tis true, to little
offices in your bufinefs, which keep them active, and
may make them in fome degree of prefent, though

poor, ufe to you: but I am forry to fay, of none to
themfelves with, regard to their future profpects,
which is what a worthy parent always has in view.

There is a proper time for every thing: and if children are not early initiated into their duty, and
and thofe parts of learning which are proper to their
particular years, they muft neceffarily be difcouraged,
and fet behind every one of their fchool fellowsthough
much younger than themfelves; and you know not,
Sir, what a laudable emulation you may by this
means deftroy, than which nothing is of greater force
to children, to induce them to attend to their books;
nor what difgrace you involve them in with refpect
to children among children, for the biggeft and eld-
eft to be fo much outdone by the leaft and youngeft.

Nor is the confequence of this defect confined to
the fchool age, as I may call it; for as they grow
up, they will be looked upon, in an equally difcou-
raging and difadvantageous light, by all who converfe with them: which muft of courfe throw them
into the company of the dregs of mankind; for how
will they be able to converfe or correfpond with thofe
whofe acquaintance it is moft worth their while to
cultivate: and indeed they will probably be fo confcious of their unfitnefs to bear a part in worthy converfation, that, to keep themfelves in countenance,
they will, of their own accord fhun the better company, and affociate with the worft: and what may
be the confequence of this, a wife man, and a good
father, would tremble to think of, especially when he
has to reflect upon himfelf as the caufe of it, let it be
what it will.

Then, Sir, it is to confidered, that without a tolerable education they can be only fit for mean and fordid employments. Hear what the wife men fay to
this very purpofe: "How can he get wifdom that
holdeth the plow, and that glorieth in the goad, that
driveth the oxen, and is occupied in their labours, and

LETTER WRITER. 93

whofe talk is of bullocks? He giveth his mind to make
urrows, and is diligent to give the kine fodder. So
every carpenter and workmafter, that laboureth night
and day—The fmith alfo fitting by the anvil, and
confidering the iron warm, the vapour of the fire waft-
eth his flefh—The noife of the hammer and anvil is
ever in his ears—So doth the potter fitting at his
work, and turning the wheel about with his feet—
He fafhioneth the clay with his arm, and boweth down
his ftrength before his feet." Thefe as be obferves,
are ufeful in their way; but their minds being wholly engroffed by their labours, "they fhall not be
fought for in public council, nor fit high in the con-
gregation --they cannot declare juftice and judgment,
and they fhall not be found where parables are fpoken." That is, they fhall be confined to the drud-
gery of their own fervile ftation, and will be entitled
neither to honour and refpect, as they might have
been, had they had an education to qualify them for
more refpectable bufineffes. And you will confider,
Sir, in clofer fight, as to us who live in the prefent
age, and in this great city, that there is hardly a creditable or profitable employment in London, where
a tolerable knowledge of accounts and penmanfhip,
in a particular, is not required. Confider alfo, what
opportunities they may lofe by this neglect of their
education, in cafe they fhould fail in the bufinefs they
are put to, of getting a comfortable and genteel fupport in fome merchants compting houfe, or in fome
one of the feveral offices about this great metropolis; as book-keepers, clerks, accomptants. &c.

And with regard more immediately to yourfelf,
how can you expect, when they know you could do
better for them, but that their behaviour to you will
be of a piece with the reft? for if they are not polifhed
by learning, but are left to a kind of inftinct rather, is
it to be expected that they fhould behave to you, and
their mother, with that fenfe of their obligations which

94   THE COMPLETE

learning inculcates? Nor, indeed, will they have those obligations to you, which other children have to their parents, who take care to give them opportunities of improvement, which are denied to yours. Consider, dear sir, what a contemptible character, even among the sordid vulgar, that of an illiterate fellow is; and what respect, on the contrary, a man of letters is treated with, by his equals, as well as inferiors. And when you lay all these plain reasons and observations together, I make no doubt but you will endeavour to retrieve lost time and be advised in this material point (which I can have no interest in) by,

Your sincere Friend and Servant.

LETTER LXXVI.

From a young Maiden, abandoned by her Lover for the sake of a greater Fortune.

Mr John,

I Must take up my pen and write, though perhaps you will only scoff at me for so doing; but when I have said what I have to say, then I shall have eased my mind, and will endeavour to forget you for ever, I have had so many cautions given me against the false hearts of men, and was so often told how they vow and forswear themselves, that I ought to have been on my guard, that's true: and indeed, so I was a great while; you know it well. But you courted me so long, vowed so earnestly, and seemed so much in love with me, that it was first pity in me, that made me listen to you; and, oh! this hasty pity, how soon did it bring—But I won't say love neither. I thought, if all the young men in the world besides proved false, yet it was impossible you should. Ah! poor silly creature that I was, to think, though every

LETTER WRITER.   95

body flattered me with being sightly enough, I could hold a heart so sordidly bent on interest, as I always saw yours to be! but that, thought I, though 'tis a meaness I don't like, yet it will be a security of his making a frugal husband in age so fruitful of spendthrifts.

But at length it has proved, that you can prefer Polly Bambridge, and leave poor me only because she has a greater portion than I have.

I say nothing against Polly. I wish her well. Indeed I do. And wish you no harm neither. But as you knew Polly before, why could you not have made to you a merit with her, without going so far with me? What needed you so often begg'd and pray'd, sigh'd and vow'd never leaving me day nor night) till you had got me foolishly to believe and pity you? And so, after your courtship was made a town talk, then you could leave me to be laughed at by every one, I slighted for you? Was this just, was this well done, think you?

Here I cannot go out of doors but I have some one or other simpering and sneering at me? and I have had two willow-garlands sent me; so I have—But what poor stuff, in some of my own sex, is this, to laugh at and deride me for your baseness? I can call my heart to witness to my virtue in thought, in word, and in deed; and must I be rediculed for a false one, who gives himself airs at my expence, and at the expence of his own truth and honour? Indeed you cannot say the least ill of me, that's my comfort. I defy the world to say any thing to blast my character; why then should I suffer, in the world's eye, for your baseness?

I seek not to move you to return the fidelity you have vowed; for by this time, mayhap, you'd be as base to Polly as you have been to me, if you did I wish her no willow garlands I'll assure you. But yet, let me desire you to speak of me with decency. This is

96 **THE COMPLETE** &c.

no more than I deferve, well you know. Don't (to brave through the perfidy you have been guilty of) mention me with fuch fleers, as, I hear, you have done to feverals; and pray call me no more of your poor dear girls!—And, I hope fhe wont take it to heart, poor thing!—with that infolence that fo little becomes you, and I have fo little deferved I thought to have appealed to confcience, on what has paffed between us when I began. I thought to have put the matter home to you! But I have run out into this length, and now don't think worth while to write much more; for what is confcience to a man who could vow as you have done, and act as you have done?

Go then, Mr John, naughty man as you are! I will try to forget you for ever. Rejoice in the fmiles of your Polly Bambridge, and glad your heart with the poffeffion of an hundred or two of pounds more than I have; and fee what you'll be the richer or happier a few years hence. I wifh no harm to you. Your confcience will be a greater trouble to you than I wifh it to be, if you are capable of reflecting. And for your fake, I will henceforth fet myfelf up to be an advifer to all my fex, never to give ear to a man, unlefs they can be fure his intereft will be a fecurity for his pretended affection to them. I am, tho' greatly injured and deceived, naughty Mr John,

Your Well-Wifher.

F I N I S.

☙

THE COMPLETE
LETTER WRITER,

OR

YOUNG SECRETARY's
INSTRUCTOR.

CONTAINING

A great Variety of LETTERS,

ON

FRIENDSHIP,	MARRIAGE,
DUTY,	AMUSEMENT,
LOVE,	BUSINESS, &c.

To which are prefixed,

Plain Inftructions for Writing LETTERS
on all Occafions.

By H. W. DILWORTH, A. M.

NEW-YORK:
Printed for BENJAMIN GOMEZ,
Bookfeller and Stationer, No. 32, Malden Lane.
1793.

LETTER-WRITER. 101

LETTER LXX.

From a Gentleman to his mistress who seeing no hopes of Success, respectfully withdraws his Suit.

Madam,

I Make no doubt but this will be the welcomest letter that you ever received from me; for it comes to assure you, that is the last trouble you will ever have from me. Nor should I have so long with held from you this satisfaction, had not the hope your brother gave me, that in time I might meet with an happier fate, made me willing to try every favor. But I see all the hopes given me by his kind consideration for me, and those that by my own presumption have made me entertain, are all in vain: and I will rid you of so troublesome an importuner, have nothing to offer now, but my ardent wishes for your happiness; and these madam, I will pursue you with to my life's latest date.

May you, whenever you shall change your condition meet with a heart as passionately, and as sincerely, devoted to you as mine! and may you be happy for many, very many years, in the man you can honor with your love! For, give me leave to say madam, that in this, my end will be in part answered, because it was most sincerely your happiness I had in view, as well as my own, when I presumptuously hoped by contributing to the one, to secure the other. I am madam, with the highest veneration,

Your most obedient humble Servant,

I 2

L E T T E R   LXXI.

From a Lady to a Gentleman, who had obtained all her Friends Consent urging him to decline his Suit to her.

Sir,

Y O U have often importuned me to return marks of that confideration for you, which you profefs for me.   As my parents, to whom I owe all duty, encourage your addrefs, I wifh I could.   I am hardly treated by them, becaufe I cannot.   What fhall I do ? Let me apply to you, Sir, for my relief, who have much good fenfe, and I hope generofity.   Yes, Sir, let me befpeak your humanity to me, and juftice to yourfelf, in this point; and that fhall be all I will afk in my favour.   I own you deferve a much better wife than I fhall ever make : but yet, as love is not in one's own power, if I have the misfortune to know I cannot love you, will not juftice to your-felf, if not pity to me, oblige you to abandon your prefent purpofe ?

. But as to myfelf, Sir, why fhould you make a poor creature unhappy in the difpleafure of all her friends at prefent, and ftill more unhappy, if, to avoid that fhe gives up her perfon, where fhe cannot beftow her heart ? If you love me, as you profefs, let me afk you, Sir, is it more for for my fake, or is it your own ?——If for mine, how can it be; when I muft be miferable, if I am forced to marry where I cannot love ?——If for your own, reflect, Sir, on the felfifhnefs of your

LETTER-WRITER.   103

love, and judge if it deserves from me the return you wish.

How sadly does this love already operate!—You love me so well, that you make me miserable in the anger of my dearest friends!—Your love has already made them think me undutiful; and instead of the fondness and endearment I used to be treated with by them, I meet with nothing but chidings, frowns, flights and displeasure.

And what has this love of yours to do for me hereafter?—Why hereafter, Sir, it will be turned into hatred, or indifference at least; for then, though I cannot give you my heart, I shall have given you a title to it, and you will have a lawful claim to its allegiance. May it not then, nay, ought it not to be treated on the foot of a rebel and expect punishment as such, instead of tenderness even were I to be treated with mercy, with goodness, with kindness by you, and could not deserve or return it, what a wretch would your love make me! how would it involve me in the crying sin of ingratitude? how would it destroy my reputation in the world's eye that the best of husbands had the worst of wives! the kindest of men, the unkindest of women.

Cease then I beseech you, this hopeless, this cruel pursuit! make some worthier person happy in your addresses, that can be happier in them by this means you will restore me (if you decline as of your own motion) to the condition you found me in, the love of my parents and the esteem of my friends. If you really love me, this will be a hard task, but it will be a most gene-

rous one—and there is some reason to expect it ;
for who that truly loves, wishes to make the object of his love miserable ? this must be, if you
persist in your addresses ; and I shall know by
your conduct, on occasion of this uncommon request, how to consider it; and in what light to
place you, either as the most generous, or the
most generous of men. Meantime I am, Sir, most
heartily, though *I* cannot be what you would
have me,

Your Well Wisher, and humble Servant.

LETTER LXXII.

*The Gentleman's Answer to the Lady's uncommon
Request.*

Dear Madam,

I Am exceedingly concerned, that I cannot be
as acceptable to you· as I have the good fortune , [undeservedly] to find myself to your honoured parents. If, Madam, I had good reason to think it was owing to your prepossession,
in some happier man's favour, I should utterly
despair of it, and should really think it would be
unjust to myself, and ungenerous to you, to continue my address. As therefore you have, by
your appeal to me, in so uncommon a way, en-
deavored to make me a party against myself, and
I have shewn so much regard to you, as to be
willing to oblige you, as far as I can, may I not
hope the favor of you to declare so generously,
whether I owe my unhappiness to such a prepos-

LETTER-WRITER.   105

feſſion, and whether your heart is given to ſome other? If this be the caſe, you ſhall find all you wiſh on my part: And I ſhall take a pride to plead againſt myſelf, let me ſuffer ever ſo much by it, to your father and mother; but if not, and you have taken any other diſguſts to my perſon or behaviour, that there may be hope my utmoſt affection and aſſiduity, are a contrary conduct, may in time, get the better of, let me implore you to permit me ſtill to continue my zealous reſpects to you; for this I will ſay, that there is not a man in the world who can addreſs you with a ſincerer and more ardent ſlame, than dear Madam, your affectionate admirer, and humble ſervant.

LETTER LXXIII:

The Lady's Reply in caſe of a Prepoſſeſſion.

Sir,

I Thank you for your kind aſſurance, that you will befriend me in the manner *I* wiſh; and *I* think *I* owe it to your generoſity to declare, there is a perſon in the world, that, might *I* be left to my own choice. *I* ſhould prefer to all other men. To this, Sir, it is owing that your addreſs cannot meet with the return it might otherwiſe deſerve from me. Yet are things ſo circumſtanced, that while my friends prefer you and know nothing of the other, *I* ſhould find it very difficult to obtain their conſent. But your generous diſcontinuance, without giving their true reafon for it, will lay an obligation greater than *I* can exprefs, on

Your humble Servant.

LETTER LXXIV.

The Lady's Reply in cafe of no Prepoffeffion, or that fhe choofes not to avow it.

Sir,

I AM forry to fay, that my difapprobation of your addrefs is infupportable—Yet *I* cannot but think myfelf beholden to you for the generofity of your anfwer to my earneft requeft. *I* muft beg you, Sir, to give over your application; but how can *I* fay, while *I* cannot help being of this mind, that it is, or is not owing to a prepoffeffion; when you declare, that in the one inftance (and that is very generous too) you will oblige me; but in the latter you will not? if *I* cannot return love for love, be the motive what it will, pray Sir, for your own fake as well as mine, difcontinue your addrefs —*In* cafe of prepoffeffion, you fay you can, and you will oblige me. Let my unworthinefs, Sir, have the fame effect upon you, as if that prepoffeffion were to be avowed. This will infpire me with a gratitude that will always make me

Your humble Servant.

LETTER-WRITER.   107

LETTER LXXV:

To a Lady, inviting her into the Country for the Summer.

My dear Harriot.

I Do not know whether I flatter myself with an opinion of your speaking to me the other day with an uncommon air of friendship, or whether I am so happy to hold that place, of which I should be so ambitious, in your esteem. I thought you spoke with concern at our parting for summer, on our family's retiring into the country. For heavens sake, my dear, what can you do all the dull season in London? Vauxhall is not for more than twice; and I think Ranelagh one would not see above half a dozen times in the year. What is it then you find to entertain you in an empty town for four or five months together? I would fain persuade you not to be in love with so disagreeable a place, and I have an interest in it; for I am a petitioner to you to stay the summer with us; I beg you will try. We go, my dear, on Monday. Will you go with us? for there is a place in the coach; or will you come when we are settled? I am greatly of opinion that it will please you. I am sure I need not tell you we shall do all we can to render it agreeable, or that you will make us very happy in complying with the invitation.

You have not seen our house, but is a very pleasant one. There are fine prospects from the park, and a river runs through the garden; nor are we quite out of the way of entertainment. You know there is a great deal of company about that place; and we have an affembly within a mile of us. What fhall I fay elfe to tempt you to come? why, *I* will tell you that you will make us all the happieft people in the world, and that when you are tired you fhall not be teazed to ftay. Dear Harriot, think of it; you will confer an obligation on her, who is, with the trueft refpect,

Your moft affectionate Friend.

LETTER LXXV.

To a Lady inviting her to a Party of Pleaſure.

Dear Madam,

PEOPLE are interfted who invite you to be of their parties, becaufe you are fure to make them happy. This is the reafon why you will not pethaps always comply when you are afked to be of them; but it is certainly a caufe of your being folicited oftener than any woman in the world. After you were gone yefterday, Mr. Bohun propofed an expedition to Richmond for to-morrow, and he requefted me (for he thought he had no title to fuch a liberty himfelf,) to tell you, that we all underftood you to be of the party, though you happened to be out of the way when it was propofed.

I hope you are not engaged; the weather promifes to be favorable, and your company you know how we value. *I* need not tell you that

LETTER-WRITER.   109

we shall suppose it a matter of form, if you are absent. What we shall think of it if you go with us, you will know when you remember what every body thinks, who has the pleasure of your company. I beg you will not invent an excuse, but go with us,

> I am, with the greatest sincerity.
> Dear Madam,
> Your most obedient humble Servant.

LETTER LXXVI.

To Colonel R——s, in Spain, from his Lady just before her Death.

My Dear,

BEFORE this can reach the best of husbands and the fondest lover, those tender names will be no more of concern to me. The indisposition in which you, to obey the dictates of your honor and duty, left me, has since increased upon me; and I am acquainted by my physicians I cannot live a week longer. At this time my spirits fail me; and it is the ardent love I have for you that carries me beyond my strength, and enables me to tell you the most painful thing in the prospect of death is, that I must part with you. But let it be a comfort to you, that I have no guilt hanging upon me, no unrepented folly that retards me; but I pass away my last hours in reflection upon the happiness we have lived in together, and in sorrow that it is so soon to have an end. This is a frailty which I hope is so far

K

from criminal, that methinks there is a kind of piety in being so unwilling to be separated from a state which is the institution of heaven, and in which we have lived according to its laws. As we know no more of the next life, but that it will be a happy one to the good, and miserable to the wicked, why may we not please ourselves at least to alleviate the difficulty of resigning this being, in imagining that we shall have a sense of what passes below, and may possibly be employed in guiding the steps of those with whom we walked with in innocence, when mortal? why may I not hope to go on in my usual work, and though unknown to you, be assistant in all the conflicts of your mind? Give me leave to say to you, O best of men, that I cannot figure to myself a greater happiness than such an employment! To be present at all the adventures to which human life is exposed; to administer slumber to thy eye-lids in the agonies of a fever, to cover thy beloved face in the day of battle; to go with thee a guardian angel, incapable of wound or pain, where I have longed to attend thee when a weak and fearful woman: These, my dear, are the thoughts with which I warm my poor languid heart; but indeed I am not capable, under my present weakness, of bearing the strong agonies of mind I fall into, when I form to myself the grief you will be in upon your first hearing of my departure. I will not dwell upon this, because your kind and generous heart will be but the more afflicted, the more the person for whom you lament, offers you consolation. My last breath will, if I am myself, expire in a prayer for you, I shall never see thy face again. Farewell for ever.

LETTER LXXVII.

To a young Gentleman on the Death of his Father.

Dear Sir,

I KNOW no part of my life more impertinent than the office of administring consolation : I will not enter upon it, for I cannot but applaud your grief. The virtuous principles you had for that excellent man whom you have lost, have wrought in you as they ought, to make a youth of three and twenty incapable of comfort, upon coming into the possession of a great fortune. I doubt not but you will honour his memory by a modest enjoyment of his estate; and scorn to triumph over his grave, by employing in riot, excess and debauchery, what he purchased with so much industry, prudence, and wisdom. This is the true way to shew the sense you have of your loss, and to take away the distress of others upon the occasion. You cannot recal your father by grief, but you may revive him to your friends by your conduct.

LETTER LXXVIII:

To a Country Gentleman, requesting a Balance of Accompts.

Sir,

I Find myself unavoidably obliged, by a present exigence, to desire the favor of your balancing the accompt between us. For though matters have run into some length, I would not have applied to you had I known how to answer my present occasions so well any other way. If it does not suit you, Sir, to pay the whole, I beg you will remit me as much towards it as you can, without prejudice to your own affairs, which will greatly oblige,

Sir,
Your *most humble Servant*.

LETTER LXXIX.

The Answer.

Sir,

I AM very glad it is in my power to send you immediately the enclosed draught for £.10c, on the accompt between us, and will in a few days remit the balance of your whole demand, which will be accompanied with a fresh order

I am very sincerely,
Your most humble Servant.

LETTER LXXXI.

From a Lady to her Niece, on the Subject of dress.

Dear Bibby,

I AM much of your opinion, that the make of a woman's mind, greatly contributes to the ornament of her body. Behold lady Vicars' she has the largest share of simplicity of manners,

perhaps in her whole fex. This makes every
thing look native about her; and her cloaths
are fo exactly fitted, that they appear, as it were,
part of her perfon   Every one that feeks her,
knows her to be of quality; but her diftinction
is ow'ng to her manner, and not to her habit.
Her beauty is full of attraction, but not of allurement,   There is fuch a compofure in her looks;
and propriety in his drefs, that you would think
it impoffible fhe fhould change the garb you one
day fee her in, for any thing fo becoming, till
you next day fee her in another,   There is no
myftery in this, but that however fhe is apparel-
led, fhe is herfelf the fame; for there is fo imme
diate a relation between our thoughts and geftures, that a woman muft think well to look well
this I have no doubt of your endeavoring to do,
my dear: which will give the utmoft fatisfaction
to,

Your affectionate and tender Aunt.
LETITIA.

LETTER LXXXII.

Acknowledging a Kindnefs received.

Dear Sir,

HOW can *I* without blufhes, make you fo
poor a return as thanks for the many and
weighty obl'gations you have laid upon me? Yet
fhould I be wanting in making an acknowledgment of your kindnefs, not only you, but all

K 2

mankind, might juftly tax me with ingratitude, from the imputation of which, above all other crimes I defire to be molt free. I muft entreat you therefore, to fuffer this my flender offering to approach you, and in fome meafure infinuate itfelf, into your good opinion, till fuch time as my abilities may fpeak louder, what my defires with willingnefs are framing; and fo, Sir, with all imaginable refpect, begging to be excufed for my no better performance. I muft till a more feafonable requital offers itfelf, lye under the weight of your favors, and fubfcribe myfelf,

Your moft dutiful and obliged Servant.

I. F.

L E T T E R LXXXIII.

Thanks for profered kindne's.

Sir,

LET me firft beg your pardon, before I tell you that I muft make myfelf fo unhappy, as not at prefent to ftand in need of your kindnefs, and I dare fay unfeigned profer of love and affiftance. Indeed my neceffities, not many days fince, did require it; but I fuppofe before they reached your ear, I was fupplied by another hand yet fhould not *I* pay you the fame acknowledgment for the care you exprefs of my welfare, as if *I* had really accepted the kindnefs, I might with good reafon, be termed ungrateful, and not worthy to be numbered in the lift of your real

LETTER-WRITER. 113

friends : wherefore I resolve whilst I live, not only to confess your kindness, but remain,

Yours to serve you in what I may.

J. J.

LETTER LXXXIV.

Advice to a Friend.

Sir,

UNDERSTANDING you have left the town I thought it convenient to inform you how things are carried on ; especially in relation to trade, a particular account of which *I* have enclosed in this paper. I would indeed have communicated to you, in writing, but that I found it done to my hand. Our friends are in a perfect enjoyment of health, and kindly at present (especially such as I have had lately the opportunity to converse withal) their love and kind respects to you, and your good lady. As for your affairs in London, as far as I can see, or enquire into them they go on prosperously; and for news we have none of moment : wherefore not to trouble you with a tedious epistle, I only make it my request, that a good correspondence may be maintained between us as heretofore, and that I may still be ranked in the number of your friend desiring always to be, whilst my own.

Yours, in all friendship and respect

J. M.

116 THE COMPLETE

LETTER LXXXV.

Advice to a Friend, &c.

Sir,

THE cause of my writing (though the news perhaps, may be unwelcome to your ears) is to let you know that T. B. of D. with whom I understand you had considerable dealings is dead and has left as I hear and fear, his estate and effects much incumbred and imbezelled, to the no small admiration of his neighbors who all along imagined it fared with him far otherwise; though indeed it is a common saying, "That few know what a man is worth until he dies." This though unrequired, I thought fit to advertise you of, and so leaving the further prosecution to your discretion, whom it mainly concerns, I remain,

Your Friend and Servant.
P. W.

LETTER LXXXVI.

Complaining of Injury.

Sir,

NOtwithstanding the injury you have done me against the very laws of friendship, yet you may see my good nature is such, that I cannot so slightly shake off on my part, the bonds of amity, but must with a gentle reproof, instead of complaining to others softly and in silence,

complain to yourself, that you may be the more
sensible what kindness you have abused and
slighted, nay, I will make the moderatest construction, and that what was done proceeded from
rashness, or some misunderstanding, created by
false report. However, the fault is not so great
as to make me call off a friend, whose unfeigned
acknowledgment and moderate repentance may
atone for his fault; and where the offended is
of so facile and mild a disposition the offender
surely can do no more than relent; wherefore,
Sir, in hopes you will answer u - expectation, I
close my letter, subscribing myself,

As yet your Friend,

T. C.

LETTER LXXXVII.

In Answer to the foregoing.

Sir,

YOUR mild way of proceeding, has entirely
conquered and subdued my rough nature,
so that I find myself constrained to an acknowledgment of my rashness; and therefore, with
blushes for what I have done, I have sent this letter to entreat your pardon, hoping you will sign
it when I shall wait on you (which will be shortly), personally to acknowledge my offence; and
in the mean time, I take the boldness to subscribe
myself,

Your unworthy Friend,

B. T.

118 ## THE COMPLETE

LETTER LXXXIX.

Counsel to a Friend in a doubtful Matter.

Dear Friend,

UNderstanding you had entangled yourself in a business of so much importance as ——, I thought it my duty to assist you with my advice; not that I presume my counsel can exceed what you have already had; but more out of a friendly office that you may see how ready I am always to communicate any thing to you, that may redound to your advantage. The advice I gave for the better securing of it from prying eyes upon the casual breaking of a letter, which many times falls out, I have sealed up in a paper by itself; neither would I have you altogether neglect it; for we oftentimes see where one thing has failed; another less suspected has succeeded; but, however, having done my duty in this case, I submit the rest to your more knowing and discerning judgment; taking leave only to subscribe myself,

Your faithful Friend to serve you,

J. F.

LETTER CX.

Congratulating a Person upon his Marriage.

Sir,

THE news I received of the happy change of your condition, did not a little revive me from the melancholy, that is too much accus-

tomed to opprefs my fpirits, efpecially upon the
knowledge of the happy election you have made
of one whofe difcretion, parentage, and good
education, muft be fuitable to your humour. In
which fatisfaction, as a true friend, I am not
wanting to participate in civility, being very much
pleafed, that you have now divided the power
which you had obtained over my affections, ho-
noring your fecond felf, with that equality of
refpect, that was heretofore entirely your own;
for certain it is; that your good and ill fortune
ftand with me in an equal balance, in which, as
a true friend, actually or reciprocally, I muft intereft myfelf, being perfuaded you will make no
more doubt of it, than of the paffion I have to
ferve you in the quality of,

Sir,
Yours and your Lady's
very humble Servant,

J. R.

LETTER XC.

*From one young Man to another, to requeft a
Kindnefs.*

Dear Friend,

RELYING upon the long familiarity that has
paffed between us, and your large protef-
tations of fincerity and friendfhip, urged by neceffity, and the hafte that my occafions require,
I have made bold to let you know, that I ftand
in need of ———, with which if you can poffi-

bly furniſh me, without prejudice or hindrance to your own affairs, I ſhall take it as an extraordinary kindneſs; and if it ſtand with your conveniency, pray ſend it by the bearer, or by ſome other ſpeedy hand; and in ſo doing, you will very much oblige him who is,

        Your very humble Servant,

             T. S.

L E T T E R CVI.

The Anſwer.

Dear Tom,

I WAS not a little glad, upon the peruſal of your letter, that you would be ſo kind at leaſt as to put it into my power to do you any manner of ſervice, whereby I might more immediately ſignalize ſome marks of true friendſhip; nor indeed could you have required it a more ſeaſonable time. Wherefore, not to give you any delay, I have ſent by the bearer what you demand, and ſhall always be proud to oblige you in this kind, ſo far as my abilities will extend; and ſo with my hearty good will towards you, and my good wiſhes for the proſperity of your affairs, I remain

        Your unfeigned Friend,

            A. W.

F I N I S.

David Fordyce, *The New and Complete British Letter-Writer; or Young Secretary's Instructor in Polite Modern Letter-Writing* (London: C. Cooke, [1790?]), title page, pp. 5–14, iv–v, 25–65. British Library, shelfmark 1086. b.36.(1).

David Fordyce (1711–51) was Professor of Moral Philosophy at Marischal College in Aberdeen, Scotland from 1742 until his death. He was also a well known public figure – the much respected author of *Dialogues Concerning Education* (1741 and 1747), which was a notable success on both sides of the Atlantic; and of 'Elements of Moral Philosophy' which appeared in Dodsley's *Preceptor* (1745), a school text that was widely used both in Britain and America, as well as separately. Where education, morals and conduct were concerned, Fordyce's *Complete British Letter-Writer* reproduced and popularized positions Fordyce had taken in his other more philosophical works.

Written in a perfectly limpid and perspicuous simple style, Fordyce's letter collection is also interesting for its emphasis on empire. The letters promote emigration abroad, demonstrate the wide range of benefits Scots could gain from participating commercially, professionally and administratively in the British Empire, and offer worldly and very practical conduct book advice about how to make or mend one's fortune in the imperial world. They also model the kinds of commercial letters that Scottish, American and Scottish-American merchants and factors used in the course of their transatlantic trade.

This *Complete Letter-Writer* appears to have been published posthumously, but when remains uncertain. It may well have circulated in manuscript in Scotland before being sent to a printer in London, perhaps by Fordyce's brother James Fordyce who was himself a conduct book writer, and the executor of David's literary estate. For more about this manual, see Eve Tavor Bannet, 'Empire and Occasional Conformity: David Fordyce's *Complete British Letter-Writer*', *Huntington Library Quarterly*, 66:1 and 2 (2003), pp. 55–79.

THE

NEW AND COMPLETE

Britiſh Letter-Writer;

OR,

YOUNG SECRETARY's INSTRUCTOR

IN

POLITE MODERN LETTER-WRITING.

CONTAINING NEAR FOUR HUNDRED
Original, Plain, Eaſy, Inſtructive, and Entertaining
LETTERS *on the moſt uſeful and important* SUBJECTS,

PARTICULARLY

EDUCATION,	MARRIAGE,	COMPLIMENTS,
BUSINESS,	WIT AND HUMOUR,	CONDOLANCE,
FRIENDSHIP,	INSTRUCTION,	RELIGION AND
LOVE AND COURTSHIP,	ADVICE,	MORALITY, &c.&c.

TOGETHER WITH
LETTERS to and from PARENTS, CHILDREN, BROTHERS,
SISTERS, and other RELATIONS,
As well as in every other intereſting Subject throughout Life.
The WHOLE calculated to enable the Reader to write Letters on
all Occaſions, without any further Inſtructions.

WITH
A Conciſe and Familiar ENGLISH GRAMMAR.

TO WHICH ARE ADDED,
DIRECTIONS *for addreſſing* PERSONS *of all* RANKS *either in*
WRITING OR DISCOURSE.

AND
A SET OF GENTEEL COMPLIMENTARY CARDS.

LIKEWISE
THE PETITIONER's INSTRUCTOR,
CONTAINING
The ART *of* WRITING PETITIONS *to* SUPERIORS;
Alſo USEFUL FORMS of LAW, as WILLS, BONDS, &c. &c.
And other inſtructive Articles, neceſſary to be known by all Perſons.

By DAVID FORDYCE, M. A.

LONDON:
PRINTED *for* C. COOKE, No. 17, PATER-NOSTER-ROW,
And ſold by all other Bookſellers in Great-Britain.
(PRICE TWO SHILLINGS BOUND.)

CONTENTS.

A Concise and familiar Englifh Grammar　　　15
　　Inftructions for Letter-Writing　　　　　24
　　　　LETTERS on EDUCATION, &c.
LETTER
I. From a Gentleman to the Mafter of an Academy　　25
II. The Mafter's Anfwer　　　　　　　　ibid
III. From a young Gentleman to his Father　　26
IV. From the Father to the Son　　　　　ibid
V. From a Lady to her Daughter at Boarding-fchool, reprehending her
　　for neglect of Writing　　　　　　27
VI. The young Lady's Anfwer　　　　　　ibid
VII. A Mother to her Daughter on Female Education　ibid
VIII. The Anfwer　　　　　　　　　28
IX. From a Father to his Son, cenfuring him for an undue Fondnefs
　　for one of his Children in particular　　ibid
X. From a Tradefman to his Son at School, recommending what may
　　beft qualify him for the Man of Bufinefs　29
XI. The Son's Anfwer　　　　　　　ibid
XII. From a Father to his Son, foon after his having been bound
　　Apprentice　　　　　　　　　30
XIII. The Anfwer　　　　　　　ibid
XIV. From a Guardian in the Country to a Youth apprenticed to a
　　Tradefman in London　　　　　　31
XV. The Youth's Anfwer　　　　　ibid
XVI. From an Officer to his Son on his going abroad　32
XVII. The Son's Anfwer　　　　　ibid
XVIII. From a Father to his Son, defiring him to inftil religious
　　Education in his Children　　　　ibid
XIX. From a young Gentleman at School to his Parents, as a Speci-
　　men of his Improvement in Writing　33
XX. The Father's Anfwer.　　　　ibid
XXI. From a Youth at School to his Parents, in Acknowledgement
　　of Favours received　　　　　34
XXII. From a Youth to his Father, expreffing Concern at not having
　　heard from him for fome time　　ibid
XXIII. From a Youth at an Academy to his Father, requefting Per-
　　miffion to learn fome of the Sciences　ibid
XXIV. The Father's Anfwer　　　　36
XXV. From a Youth at an Academy to his Parents, requefting their
　　Permiffion to learn to dance　　ibid
XXVI. The Anfwer from the Father　39
XXVII. From a Youth at an Academy to his Sifter　ibid
XXVIII. From a Youth at a Boarding-School to his Parents, re-
　　quefting their Prefence at a publick Examination　ibid

LETTERS *relating to Trade, Commerce, Family Occurrences, and various
　　　　other Subjects.*

XXIX. From a Father to his Son, juft fet up in Bufinefs　37
XXX. From a young Beginner to a Wholefale Dealer　38
XXXI. The Anfwer　　　　　　ibid

A 3　　　　　　　XXXII. From

6 . CONTENTS.

XXXII. From a Retail Dealer to a Wholesale one, complaining of Injuries received in Trade - ibid

XXXIII. The Answer - - ibid

XXXIV. Letter of Reproof from a Wholesale Dealer to a Shopkeeper, who had been backward in his Remittances 39

XXXV. The Answer - - ibid

XXXVI. From a Tradesman requesting a Payment 40

XXXVII. The Answer - ibid

XXXVIII. From a young Man to a distant Relation, requesting the Loan of a Sum of Money 41

XXXIX. The Answer - - ibid

XL. From a Country Tradesman to a Dealer in London, excusing Remissness in Payment - - ibid

XLI. The Answer - - 42

XLII. From a Tradesman to a Wholesale Dealer, on his demanding Cash before the usual Time for Payment - ibid

XLIII. The Answer - 43

XLIV. From an embarrassed Tradesman to one of his Creditors, requesting his Concurrence in a Letter of Licence ibid

XLV. The Answer - - ibid

XLVI. From a Tradesman to a principal Creditor, requesting his Acceptance of a Composition - 44

XLVII. The Answer - ibid

XLVIII. Offering Assistance to a Friend in Distress 45

XLIX. The Answer - - ibid

L. From a Merchant's Clerk to his Master - ibid

LI. The Answer - - 46

LII. From a Country Tradesman to a Friend, requesting him to purchase Goods for him - ibid

LIII. The Answer - ibid

LIV. To a Landlord, on delaying Payment of Rent 47

LV. The Answer - ibid

LVI. From a Country Tenant on the same Occasion ibid

LVII. A Merchant at Hamburg to another in London 48

LVIII. The Answer - - ibid

LIX. From a young Man bred to the Sea, requesting of a Relation a small Sum of Money, to enable him to proceed on a Voyage 49

LX. The Answer - - ibid

LXI. To a Friend, limiting the Re-payment of a Sum of Money to a certain time - 50

LXII. To a Friend who had promised lending Money on an Exigence - ibid

LXIII. Apology to a Person wanting to borrow Money 51

LXIV. To the same Purport - ibid

LXV. Recommending a Man Servant ibid

LXVI. Requesting the Character of a Housekeeper ibid

LXVII. The Answer - 52

LXVIII. Enquiring the Character of a Cook-Maid ibid

LXIX. The Answer - ibid

LXX. To a Friend on Breach of Promise, in the Neglect of repaying a Sum lent - ibid

LXXI. From a Merchant in London to a young Man going to the West-Indies - 53

LXXII. The

CONTENTS

7

LXXII. The young Man's Anſwer after his Arrival there — ibid

LXXIII. From a Gentleman to his Nephew, a young Man going to the Eaſt-Indies — — 54

LXXIV. The Anſwer — — 55

LXXV. From a young Man going to ſettle at Oporto to an Uncle, who had retired from Buſineſs — ibid

LXXVI. The Anſwer — — 56

LXXVII. From a Rider to his Employer in London — ibid

LXXVIII. The Anſwer — 57

LXXIX. From a Tradeſman to a Country Correſpondent — ibid

LXXX. The Anſwer — — 58

LXXXI. From a Merchant at Liſbon, to his Correſpondent in London ib.

LXXXII. The Anſwer — — 59

LXXXIII. From a Clerk at Bengal, to his Father — ibid

LXXXIV. The Anſwer — — 60

LXXXV. From a wholeſale Dealer in London, to a Correſpondent at Birmingham — — ibid

LXXXVI. The Anſwer — — 61

LXXXVII. From a young Man who had failed in Buſineſs to a Gentleman of Fortune — — ibid

LXXXVIII. The Anſwer — — ibid

LXXXIX. From a Tradeſman deſirous of retiring from Buſineſs 62

XC. The Anſwer — — ibid

XCI. To a Merchant, giving Orders for ſhipping Goods . 63

XCII. Anſwer to the foregoing, written under the Bill ibid

XCIII. From a wholeſale Dealer in London to a Country Shopkeeper, who had left him for another — ibid

XCIV. From a Shopkeeper, deſiring to be informed of the Prices of ſeveral Commodities. — 64

XCV. The Anſwer — — ibid

XCVI. With a Bill of Exchange — ibid

XCVII. The Anſwer — — ibid

LETTERS on Love, Courtſhip, Gallantry, Marriage, &c.

XCVIII. From a young Gentleman to his Father, pleading Excuſe for ſome Indiſcretions into which he had fallen through the Paſſion of Love — — 65

XCIX. Diſcloſing the Paſſion of Love to a Female in a plain conciſe Manner — — 66

C. From a reſpectable young Man to a Lady, with whom he fell in Love at a public Place — ibid

CI. From the Lady's Aunt to the above — 67

CII. To a young Lady on the Power of Love — ibid

CIII. From a Lover to a Father, diſcloſing his Paſſion for the Daughter 68

CIV. The Father's Anſwer — ibid

CV. From the Lover to the Daughter, acquainting her that he had obtained her Father's Conſent — 69

CVI. The Daughter's Anſwer — ibid

CVII. From a young Lady to a Suitor impoſed by her Father 70

CVIII. From a Father to a Daughter, reprehending her Inclination to marry at too early a Period. — ibid

CIX. From a young Lady to her Father, ſubmitting a Propoſal of Marriage to his Opinion — 71

CX. The Father's Anſwer — ibid

A 4

CXI. From

CONTENTS.

CXI. From a Lady to her Suitor, on his Falfehood   72

CXII. From a Lover to a Lady who conceived herfelf treated with Coolnefs   ibid

CXIII. From a Lover, requefting the Exertion of a Female Relative's Influence with the Lady of his Affections   73

CXIV. The Aunt's Anfwer   ibid

CXV. Advice from a Relation to a young Lady who admitted a Suitor of diffolute Character.   ibid

CXVI. From a Daughter to her Father, in Behalf of her Sifter, who had difpleafed him in Marriage   74

CXVII. From the Friend of a young Lady to a troublefome Suitor   75

CXVIII. From a young Tradefman, propofing Marriage to a Lady in the Neighbourhood   ibid

CXIX. The Anfwer   76

CXX. From a Gentleman to a young Widow   ibid

CXXI. From a young Lady to her Father on the bad Effects of Marriage between Youth and Age   77

CXXII. From a young Woman to her Parents, to obtain Confent to a Marriage   78

CXXIII. The Anfwer   ibid

CXXIV. From the Daughter to her Parents, upon the Appointment of the Wedding-Day   79

CXXV. From a young Gentleman in the Army to a Lady with whom he is enamoured   ibid

CXXVI. From a Suitor to his Mother, on being unfuccefsful in his Addreffes   80

CXXVII. The Anfwer   81

CXXVIII. To a Lady from her Lover, congratulating her on Recovery from a dangerous Indifpofition   ibid

CXXIX. To a Lady from a jealous Lover   82

CXXX. To a Lady without Fortune, from a Gentleman in affluent Circumftances   ibid

CXXXI. From a young Lady to an old Female Bufy Body   83

CXXXII. To a Lady from a Gentleman declining his Suit   ibid

CXXXIII. From a Gentleman in Chaftifement of a Coquette   84

CXXXIV. The Anfwer   ibid

CXXXV. From a Father to his Daughter, advifing her not to encourage the Addreffes of a Serjeant   85

CXXXVI. Congratulating a Lady on her Marriage   86

CXXXVII. To a Lady by Way of Confolation and Advice, on having met with a perfidious Suitor   ibid

CXXXVIII. The Anfwer   87

CXXXIX. To a Friend in Love   88

CXL. From a Friend to a Lover, affigning a Caufe why he fhould fupprefs his Paffion   89

CXLI. From a young Lady to an old Gentleman, defiring him to defift from his Addreffes   ibid

CXLII. From a Lady juft recovered from the Small-Pox to a former Lover   90

CXLIII. The Anfwer   ibid

CXLIV. From a young Woman to a Lover, who had abandoned her from interefted Views   ibid

CXLV. To a Country Lady, from her Town Lover   91

CXLVI. From

CONTENTS. 9

CXLVI. From a young Officer on board a Ship of War at Plymouth, to a Lady in London - - 92

CXLVII. The Lady's Anfwer. - 92

CXLVIII. From the Officer to the Father - ibid

CXLIX. The Father's Anfwer - 93

CL. From a Gentleman to a young Lady without Fortune, whom he had known in early Life. - - ibid

CLI. The Anfwer - - 94

CLII. From a Clergyman to a new-married Couple, on the reciprocal Duties of the conjugal State - 95

CLIII. From a Lady to her Suitor, expreffing Concern at being abfent when he firft came to vifit her - ibid

CLIV. From the fame on her going into the Country - 96

CLV. To a Lady of exquifite Beauty, on the Ufefulnefs of exterior Ornaments - ibid

CLVI. From a Lover complimenting a Lady - 97

CLVII. To a Lady on the real Evidence of Love - ibid

CLVIII. The Lady's Anfwer - ibid

CLIX. To a Lady after the Day of Marriage was fixed - 98

CLX. To a Lady on the Power of Beauty - ibid

CLXI. To a Lady from a paffionate Lover - ibid

CLXII. From a Lady reprehending her Lover for Jealoufy - 99

CLXIII. From the Mate of an Eaft-India Ship to his Sweetheart in London - ibid - 100

MISCELLANEOUS LETTERS *on various, inftructive, and important Subjects.*

CLXIV. On the Subject of Friendfhip - 101

CLXV. A Difplay of Friendfhip after Death - 102

CLXVI. The Anfwer - ibid

CLXVII. From a Father to his Son, advifing him to be cautious in contracting a Friendfhip - 103

CLXVIII. To a Friend on the Importance of Secrecy in certain particular Inftances - 104

CLXIX. To a young Man on Difobedience to Parents - ibid

CLXX. On the Permanency of fincere Friendfhip - 105

CLXXI. To a young gentleman on referved Behaviour in Company ibid

CLXXII. Communicating a particular Circumftance, as a Plea for the Requeft of a Favour - 106

CLXXIII. The Friend's Anfwer - ibid

CLXXIV. To a Friend on Remiffnefs in Correfpondence - 107

CLXXV. The Anfwer - ibid

CLXXVI. To a Friend on the Improvement of Time - 108

CLXXVII. From a Lady to another whofe Beauty had been impaired by the Ravages of the Small-Pox - ibid

CLXXVIII. To a Friend on ceremonious Vifits - 109

CLXXIX. On the Effects of a fudden Change of Fortune - ibid

CLXXX. Diffuafive from Female Indelicacy - 110

CLXXXI. On rural Life from a Lady of a volatile Turn in the Country to her Friend in Town - ibid

CLXXXII. The Anfwer - 111

CLXXXIII. To a Friend in confinement for Debt - 112

CLXXXIV. The Anfwer - ibid

A 5　　　　　CLXXXV. On

CONTETNS.

10

CLXXXV. On the Abfurdity of too great a Partiality to Relations 113

CLXXXVI. On the bad Effects of a prevailing Paffion for Mufic 114

CLXXXVII. In Praife of Benefits generoufly conferred ibid

CLXXXVIII. To a Friend on temporal Happinefs 115

CLXXXIX. To a Friend on Pride - 116

CXC. From a well-difpofed young Woman to a Lady, who had rendered her many Services - - ibid

CXCI. The Lady's Anfwer - - 117

CXCII. On the Excellence of mental Qualifications ibid

CXCIII. From a young Gentleman in London, to a Friend in the Country, on the prevailing Vices and Temptations of the Metropolis - - 118

CXCIV. The Anfwer - - ibid

CXCV. The means of obtaining ufeful Knowledge, and the Improvement to be gained by Converfation - 119

CXCVI. On the bad Effects of Prejudice - 120

CXCVII. From a Gentleman, who had lately loft his Wife, to his Friend, a reverend Divine - - 121

CXCVIII. The Anfwer - - 122

CXCIX. To a Friend on Virtue and Charity - 124

CC. From a diftreffed Widow in the Country, to her Friend a Man of Rank in London - 125

CCI. The Anfwer - - 126

CCII. Anfwer to a Letter of Compliment - ibid

CCIII. Invitation to a Party of Pleafure - ibid

CCIV. The Anfwer - 127

CCV. From a Widow in the Country to a generous Friend in London - - ibid

CCVI. The Anfwer - - 128

CCVII. On the bad Effects of a litigious Difpofition ibid

CCVIII. To a Nephew on his going to College - 129

CCIX. From a Father to his Son entering upon commercial Life, on the Choice of Friends - - 130

CCX. On the fatal Effects of drinking - ibid

CCXI. To a Relation on his Extravagance - 131

CCXII. On the fatal Confequences of youthful Follies 132

CCXIII. To a friend on the Force of Habit - 133

CCXIV. On epiftolary Correfpondence - 134

CCXV. Defcribing the Character of a Friend, &c. ibid

CCXVI. On the grand Defign of Learning in general - 135

CCXVII. On the excellent Effects of the Union of a good Head and a good Heart - 136

CCXVIII. From a Father to his Son on his bad Conduct ibid

CCXIX. From the Son to the Father - 137

CCXX. From a Gentleman to a Lady on Compliments ibid

CCXXI. From a Lady to a Gentleman of the Law, on his poetical Commendation of her Beauty - - 138

CCXXII. To a Gentleman on Pedantry ibid

CCXXIII. To a young Gentleman from his Tutor, on Affectation 139

CCXXIV. To a Son on the Death of his Father - 140

CCXXV. To a Man of Rank, in Acknowledgement of a Letter of Confolation and Condolance - ibid

CCXXVI. Acknowledging the Receipt of a Prefent ibid

CCXXVII. From

CONTENTS. 11

CCXXVII. From a Gentleman to a Person of Rank, returning Thanks for Favours - - 141

CCXXVIII. Acknowledging the Condescension of a Superior in the Acceptance of a Present - - ibid

CCXXIX. On the Folly of a magnificent Appearance in common People only - - ibid

CCXXX. On the Choice of a Mode of Life - 142

CCXXXI. To a Lady from a Gentleman, who having broken her Looking-Glass presents her with another - 143

CCXXXII. Recommending a Relation to a Man of Rank ibid

CCXXXIII. Recommending a Son to an intimate Friend . ibid

CCXXXIV. The Answer - - 144

CCXXXV. To a Gentleman entreating his Interest in his official Department - - ibid

CCXXXVI. From a Gentleman in Retirement, on Account of the ill State of his Health - ibid

CCXXXVII. Condoling a Female Friend - 145

CCXXXVIII. From a young Lady, with a Present ibid

LETTERS on the most common Occurrences of Life.

CCXXXIX. From a Youth on a Visit in the Country, to his Father in London - - 146

CCXL. From a Servant in London to his Parents ibid

CCXLI. From a young Man in Town to his Uncle in the Country, requesting a Favour - 147

CCXLII. The Answer - - ibid

CCXLIII. From a young Man who had deserted his Master's Service to his Father, requesting his Interposition to obtain his Readmission - - 148

CCXLIV. The Father's Answer - 149

CCXLV. The Father's Letter to the Master - ibid

CCXLVI. The Master's Answer - 150

CCXLVII. From a young Woman to her Aunt, requesting a Favour ibid

CCXLVIII. From an Apprentice to his Guardian, on a Matter of the most serious Concern . - ibid

CCXLIX. The Answer - - 151

CCL. From a young Woman just entered on a Service in Town to her Aunt in the Country - ibid

CCLI. The Aunt's Answer 152

CCLII. From a Son to his Father, requesting Consent to his Marriage - ibid

CCLIII. The Answer - - 153

CCLIV. From a Father to a Daughter on hasty Marriages ibid

CCLV. From a young Man at Service in Town, to his Father in the Country - - 154

CCLVI. The Answer - 155

CCLVII. From a seafaring Man to his Wife ibid

CCLVIII. Rebuking a young Man for Remissness, &c. 156

CCLIX. The Answer - ibid

CCLX. From a young Lady in the Country to a Brother in Town, reproving him for Neglect of filial Duty - 157

CCLXI. The Answer - 158

CCLXII. To a Gentleman congratulating his good Fortune ibid

    CCLXIII. From

12   C O N T E N T S.

CCLXIII. From a Gentleman to a Lady with whom he had been at
a Party the Night before   -   -   159
CCLXIV. The Anſwer   -   -   ibid
CCLXV. From a Gentleman to a Lady, with a Preſent of Tickets
for a Concert   -   ibid
CCLXVI. The Lady's Anſwer   -   160
CCLXVII. From a Gentleman in London to a Servant in the Country,
whom he is deſirous of hiring   -   ibid
CCLXVIII. The Countryman's Anſwer   -   161
CCLXIX. From a Relation of one Servant, reproving another for
leading him into a criminal Practice   -   ibid
CCLXX. From the Servant reproved in the former, to the young
Man whom he had over-reached   -   162
CCLXXI. From a female Relation to a young Lady who diſcovered a
Partiality for a Man of bad Character.   -   ibid
CCLXXII. The young Lady's Anſwer   -   163
CCLXXIII. From a Lady to a Friend on her being brought to Bed of
a Son and Heir   -   -   164
CCLXXIV. To a Gentleman on his Return from abroad   ibid
CCLXXV. To a Clergyman, on his Preferment in the Church   165
CCLXXVI. To an Officer on his Preferment in the Army   ibid
CCLXXVII. To an Officer on his Preferment in the Navy   ibid
CCLXXVIII. To a Friend on the Wiſdom of bearing what are called
the adverſe Occurrences of Life with Fortitude and Reſignation 166
CCLXXIX. To a Friend. Remarks on travelling   168
CCLXXX. To a Friend on the Tedioufnefs and Embarraſments at-
tending Law-Suits   -   -   169
CCLXXXI. To the ſame on the foregoing Subject   ibid
CCLXXXII. From a Lady to her Friend, on female Vanity   170
CCLXXXIII. To a Friend on the Folly of Peeviſhnefs   171
CCLXXXIV. On the Government of the Paſſions, particularly that of
Anger   -   -   -   ibid
CCLXXXV. On the Benefits which are ſometimes derived from alarm-
ing Strokes of Providence   -   172
CCLXXXVI. To a Friend. Deſcription of a ſingular Character 173
CCLXXXVII. To a Friend in a very perplexed State   174
CCLXXXVIII. On the Prudence of Wives conforming themſelves to
the Conditions of their Huſbands   -   175
CCLXXXIX. From a Man of Fortune, purporting laudable Reſolu-
tions reſpecting his Country Tenants   .   176
CCXC. From a Merchant to his Friend at Leghorn   ibid
CCXCI. To a Lady, congratulating her on her Marriage   177
CCXCII. To a Lady, inviting her into the Country   178
CCXCIII. The Anſwer   -   -   ibid
CCXCIV. From a young Woman, lately come to London for a Place,
to her Mother in the Country, giving an Account of her Situation 179
CCXCV. From another young Woman who had lately come to Town
for a Place, to her Mother in the Country   180
CCXCVI. From the Mother to her Daughter in Anſwer   181
CCXCVII. From a Lady on Peeviſhnefs of Temper   182
CCXCVIII. The Anſwer   -   -   183
CCXCIX. From a young Lady to a Gentleman whom her Parents had
compelled to receive as a Suitor   -   184
                                    CCC. From

C O N T E N T S. 13

CCC. From a young Lady to her Father, who had promifed her in Marriage to a Gentleman whom fhe could not love 185

CCCI. From the Wife of an Officer to her Hufband abroad, a few Days before her Death ibid

CCCII. From a Lady to her Friend on her Illnefs 186

CCCIII. From a Lady to her Niece, on the deftructive Ufe of Beauty-Wafhes, &c. - - 187

CCCIV. From the fame to the fame, with directions to make a Cofmetic, which was never known to fail - 188

CCCV. From a Lady to her Friend, acquainting her of a Sifter's Death 189

CCCVI. From the Lady to her Sifter, the Night before her Death 191

CCCVII. From a Lady to another, on Diffidence in Love 192

CCCVIII. From Mifs Courtney to Mifs Southern, humouroufly expofing the injudicious Fondnefs of Parents to Children ibid

CCCIX. Humourous Letter of Advice on Marriage 195

CCCX. To a Friend on his Recovery from Illnefs 197

CCCXI. On the fame Occafion - ibid

CCCXII. In Anfwer to the Preceding - ibid

CCCXIII. A young Woman in Town to her Sifter in the Country, recounting her narrow Efcape from a Snare laid for her on her firft Arrival, by a wicked Procurefs - 198

CCCXIV. To a Bottle Companion abroad, defcribing the State of a Club to which they belonged - 202

CCCXV. From the fame to the fame, defcribing the State of the Neighbourhood - - 203

CCCXVI. From the fame to the fame on Politics - 204

CCCXVII. An Offer of Affiftance to a Friend who had received great Loffes by a Perfon's Failure - 205

CCCXVIII. The Friend's Anfwer, accepting the kind Offer ibid

CCCXIX. Of Confolation to a Friend in Prifon for Debt 206

CCCXX. In Anfwer to the preceding - 207

CCCXXI. From a young Gentleman on a Vifit to his Uncle in the Country, defcribing the Town - ibid

CCCXXII. From the fame, defcribing various Places about London 208

CCCXXIII. From the fame, defcribing a Paffage down the River, with the Humours of Greenwich-Park at Holiday-times 210

CCCXXIV. To a Country Gentleman, defcribing a public Execution in London - - 211

CCCXXV. From a Tradefman, under Confinement at the Suit of a mercilefs Creditor - - 213

CCCXXVI. From a furly old Fellow, on a Vifit in London, to a Country Neighbour - - 214

CCCXXVII. From a Ufurer to his Son, in London 215

CCCXXVIII. A Father to a Daughter in Service, on hearing of her Mafter's attempting her Virtue - ibid

CCCXXIX. The Daughter's Anfwer - 216

CCCXXX. Humourous Letter to a Friend, advifing him to turn Quack - - ibid

CCCXXXI. From a prodigal Spendthrift, to his Comrade, on coming into Poffeffion of a capital Fortune - 217

CCCXXXII. Diffuading a Friend from going to Law ibid

COMPLIMENTARY CARDS - 220

PETITIONS

CONTENTS.

14

PETITIONS

From a Person under Sentence of Death for a Robbery or a Burglary 221

From a decayed Tradesman, to the President and Governors of Christ's
Hospital, for the Admission of a Boy on that Foundation   222

From a poor Woman, whose Husband was lately dead, soliciting for a
weekly Pension from the Parish   -   223

To the Right Honourable the First Lord Commissioner of the Treasury,
for a Tide Waiter's Place in the Custom-House   ibid

From a poor reduced Widow, to a Lady, with whom she had lived as
a Servant   -   224

To the India Company, from a young Gentleman, to be Surgeon's
Mate on Board one of their Ships   -   ibid

From an aged and decayed Tradesman, to be admitted a Pensioner in
the Charter-House   -   -   225

From a poor distressed Man, to a Gentleman in the same Neighbourhood   ibid

From a Tradesman under great Difficulties, to his principal Creditors,
for a Letter of Licence   -   -   226

From an unfortunate young Woman, to be admitted into the Magdalen ibid

From a Mechanic to the Trustees of a Charity-School, in Behalf of a
Boy   -   ,   -   227

From a Prisoner for a small Debt, to a Gentleman celebrated for his
Humanity   -   -   ibid

From a disabled Seaman to be admitted on the Chest at Chatham   228

From a disbanded old Soldier, to be admitted into Chelsea Hospital   ibid

From a poor Citizen, to be admitted into Bancraft's Alms-Houses 229

From a poor Woman, to the Churchwardens of C. for the Christmas
Bounty of Coals   -   -   ibid

From a Vintner's Widow, to be admitted into the Company's Alms-
Houses   ,   -   -   ibid

From a Sailor, late in the Merchants Service, to be admitted as a
Pensioner   -   -   230

From a poor Sailor's Sister, praying that his Daughter might be admitted into the Asylum   -   ibid

From a Person afflicted with Illness, to be admitted into an Hospital 231

From a poor labouring Man, who had been impressed for Sea Service ibid

From a poor Man, whose Goods had been seized for Rent, to a worthy
Gentleman in the same Neighbourhood   -   ibid

FORMS of LAW, &c.

A Bond   -   232
Letter of Attorney   -   233
A Letter of Attorney by a Seaman; or a Will and Power   234
A Will   -   235
An Indenture for an Apprentice   ibid
A Bill of Sale of Goods   237
A General Release   ibid
Notes of Hand   -   238
Bill of Exchange   -   ibid
Suitable Directions for addressing Persons of all Ranks, either in
Writing or Discourse   -   239

PREFACE.

AS the principal part of social and commercial correspondence is carried on by means
of letters; it is a kind of reproach to any person,
in the present improved and enlightened age, not
to have attained a proper knowledge of an art
tending so essentially to our general reputation and
emolument.

Many efforts have been made at works similar
to this we now lay before the public; but they
have not been adequate to the important object
they had in view: we do not, however, mean to
comment on their imperfections, but with great
deference offer one of our own, as an improvement upon others.

By carefully avoiding prolixity, we consequently
give a greater diversity of matter; nay, nearly
double the quantity will be found comprized in
this single volume, than almost in any other two
volumes of the same size; and as the subjects are
various, there will be found a necessary variety
in the stile, or mode of delivering the sentiments;
for as our imagination acts and conceives, so our
stile expresses and explains. In general our stile
ought to be plain, simple, easy, and unaffected.

Some persons make use of strained allusions,
redundant descriptions, high-sounding words, &c.
but use the expressions so improperly, that the
reader can either affix no meaning at all to them,
or he may affix any meaning he pleases.

A 2   Young

P R E F A C E.

Young writers too often ufe a ftile very un-connected. To fuch perfons this volume will be found infinitely ufeful, as it will teach them to make a proper choice of words, and to exprefs them with purity and perfpicuity, which are two very effential objects of a learner's attention.

A freedom and eafe, both of thought and ex-preffion, will be found in the contents of this vo-lume; in fhort, the reader will find every advan-tage he can wifh, both in point of ftile and fubject; the firft being carefully adapted to the refpective occafions on which the letters are written, and the laft as carefully appropriated to the various oc-currences of life.

To facilitate practice by the aid of theory, we prefent the reader with an ufeful and compendious Grammar of the Englifh Language; which, we think, is laying the bafis of our work judicioufly, as the rudiments of a language being once ob-tained, a fmooth and regular procefs is made to the thorough attainment of it. We have alfo given directions for addreffing perfons of all ranks, either in writing or converfation; and to render our work as complete as poffible, we have introduced forms for genteel complimentary cards, and the art of writing petitions to fu-periors; and alfo fome ufeful forms in law, as Wills, Bonds, &c. &c. neceffary to be known by all perfons.

Such is the nature of our undertaking; and we fubmit it to that public candour which is never remifs in countenancing works of real merit.

[25]

LETTERS on EDUCATION, &c.

LETTER I. — *From a Gentleman to the Master of an Academy.*

SIR,

AS I hold the education of youth to be one of the most important concerns of parents and guardians, respecting not only the welfare of individuals, but society in general, I have spared no pains in my enquiries for a person capable of the various duties incumbent on the character of a preceptor. I cannot therefore but be happy to find, from the assurance of a friend whose son has been some time under your care, that you possess the qualifications necessary for your profession, and propose shortly to add my son to the number of your scholars. To dictate to a person of ability and discretion may seem presumptuous; but candour will admit a parent to recommend such treatment as to him appears most agreeable to the genius and disposition of a child. Of these, however, you will judge from experience, and proceed accordingly. I shall only add, that being as solicitous for my son's becoming a good citizen as a good scholar, your views I hope will be equally directed to those grand objects. I am, Sir,   Your most humble servant, &c.

LETTER II. — *The Master's Answer.*

SIR,

I WAS favoured with your's, and desire to express due acknowledgement of your candour and liberality. You have concisely pointed out the two main ends of education, which you recommend as the grand objects of my professional regard. As these can only be attained by the improvement of the mind in knowledge and virtue, to which instruction conveyed with care, and precept enforced by example, are indispensably necessary, I have always endeavoured to frame my conduct upon those principles. You may rest

B   assured,

affured, that nothing fhall be wanting on my part to promote your good intentions in committing your fon to my
care and inftruction.   I am, Sir,

Your obliged and very humble fervant:

LETTER III.—*From the young Gentleman at the Academy
to his Father.*

Honoured Sir,

IN compliance with your defire, that I would let you
hear from me as foon as I was fettled in my new fituation, I take this opportunity of acquainting you, that I am
happy in a mafter and miftrefs, and indeed in my fchool-
fellows in general. We have our hours fet apart for learning and amufement, fo that I am feldom tired. Our mafter
is not very fevere in punifhing, except in bad cafes. As
your fatherly care has placed me in this fituation, it fhall
be my conftant endeavour fo to improve as to promote your
good intentions to your utmoft wifhes. Prefent my duty
to mamma, and believe me to be, Honoured Sir,

Your dutiful fon.

LETTER IV.—*From the Father to the Son.*

Dear Boy,

IT affords me great pleafure to find you are happy in
your fituation.   According to my fincere defire, that
you may become a good man as well as a good fcholar, I
hope you are frequently called upon to read fome paf-
fages of the Bible, a book I have ever enjoined you to
hold in preference, becaufe it contains truths effential to
your prefent and future welfare. You would do well alfo
to read at leifure a paper or two of the Spectators I fent
with you, in order to acquire a general knowledge of men
and things, and a purity of ftyle in fpeaking and writing.
Indeed, I know not any Englifh profe fo eafy, familiar, and
yet fo correct, as that I now recommend. Your mafter
acts perfectly agreeable to my notion of education, in
adopting punifhments to the nature of crimes.   In a
word, my advice is, that you be obedient to your mafter,
attentive to your learning, and obfervant of your duty, in
every refpect, both to God and man. I remain, with ten-
dereft regard,

Your affectionate father.

LET-

AND ENTERTAINING LETTERS.   *27*

LETTER V.—*From a Lady to her Daughter at boarding-school, reprehending her for neglect of writing.*

Dear Charlotte,

NOT hearing from you for some time, I am anxious to enquire concerning your welfare, which I believe you are perfuaded is the principal object of my concern. If fo, why are you negligent in a matter of fuch moment? Is your vacant time all taken up in attention to trifles? Cannot you fpare a leifure moment to inform me of the ftate of your health, and your advancement in learning and female accomplifhments? To promote thefe ends, I placed you under the care of a governefs, and have therefore a parental right to know how far they are anfwered.

I remain,   Your affectionate parent, &c.

LETTER VI.—*The young Lady's Anfwer.*

Dear Mamma,

NOTHING gives me fo much pain as your difpleafure. You will however permit me to intreat your pardon of my neglect, when I affure you it fhall be my conftant care in future to obey your commands in every inftance. I have enjoyed a good ftate of health ever fince I had the happinefs of feeing you laft, and though it does not become me to praife myfelf, hope you will have a pleafing account from my governefs of my improvement in the feveral branches of education. Agreeable to my duty, it fhall be my endeavour to fhew, upon every occafion, with what profound refpect I am,

Your dutiful and obedient daughter, &c.

LETTER VII.—*From a Mother to her Daughter on female education.*

Dear Caroline,

AS the education of the female part of your family comes more immediately under your care in the relationfhip of a mother, I have taken upon me to offer fome fhort hints upon that fubject, which may probably be of ufe to you in future. You may remember, that in early life care was taken to inftil into your mind notions confiftent with your rank; to train you to houfewifery, and to endow you with the principal qualifications for a good wife and a good mother. I have therefore to enjoin you, from an affectionate concern for the welfare of you and your's, to follow the fteps of a parental guide, fo far as they may

B 2   appear

28   FAMILIAR, USEFUL, INSTRUCTIVE,

appear worthy of imitation. Be not led by fashion into the paths of folly, avoid extremes, and teach your children to consider themselves as what they are, not as what they are not, nor ever can be. Be yourself an example of modesty, prudence, and industry, and then you may reasonably expect they will imitate so amiable a pattern.
I am,   Your's most affectionately.

LETTER VIII.—*The Answer*.

Dear Madam,

YOUR last favour I received as a fresh instance of your affectionate regard, shewn not only to me, but those whom by the ties of nature I am bound to hold most near and dear. From my small knowledge of the world, I can subscribe to the truth of your remarks, and intend to observe it as a lesson with respect to the education of the female part of our family in particular. Our eldest daughter is sent to a boarding-school, from whence, according to the determination of her father, and my hearty approbation, she is to be taken at the age of twelve years, in order to be instructed in those rules of domestic œconomy, which lead to the prudent management of a family. This is the plan we propose to pursue in the course of the education of our females, trusting it will effectually promote their welfare, and the comfort of those to whom they are related. I remain, with the sincerest thanks for your counsel,   Your dutiful daughter.

LETTER IX.—*From a Father advanced in years to his Son, censuring him for an undue fondness for one of his children in particular..*

Dear Son,

THOUGH I would not wish to be thought a busy meddling old fellow, the affection I bear you compels me to give you a word of advice concerning one instance of your conduct, that will, if persisted in, most probably be attended with disagreeable, if not injurious consequences. The particular I allude to is the indulgence of your elder son William, whom I find you frequently mount on a poney to accompany you, when you make occasional excursions. This practice in a tradesman is highly imprudent, though his prospect in life may be promising; because it gives a boy a turn for extravagant pleasure, and too often excites an aversion to the pursuit of learning; so that when

he

he reaches to years of maturity, he proves a blockhead, contemptible in himself, and useless to society. You will deliberate on this, and, if convinced of an error, I presume you will amend it. I remain, as ever,

Your affectionate father.

LETTER X.—*From a Tradesman to his Son at school, recommending such pursuits in learning, as may best qualify him for the man of business.*

Dear Tom,

AS you are now turned of thirteen, and must shortly fix on some commercial business to be put to in the course of another year, you will give me leave to remind you of the necessity of applying to such pursuits, as seem most probable to qualify you for the same. These, from experience, I have found to be a considerable progress in arithmetic, the writing a good hand, and being correct in spelling. You have, I must confess, made some advance in each of these pursuits; but as there is still room for amendment, as your time of continuance at school is short, and you may, by assiduous application, make greater improvement in the course of one year than you could in three years at your beginning, I recommend to you double diligence, by which you cannot fail to acquire those branches of learning, that will prove useful and ornamental in future life. I am, Your affectionate father,   THO. TRADELOVE.

LETTER XI.—*The Son's Answer.*

Honoured Sir,

YOUR kind advice demands my thanks, and every attention to it within the compass of my power. I must do my master the justice to say, he has taken much pains to forward me in the branches of learning you particularly recommend; nor has he been wanting in pointing out to me their usefulness in that station of life for which you design me. I hope you will find, from the letter you are now reading, that I write an easy, legible hand, suited to correspondence, and that my spelling is not erroneous. Of my progress in arithmetic you will form a judgment, when you see my last book of merchants accompts. However, at all events, I shall not fail to keep your advice constantly in view, because I am persuaded it is both my duty and interest to follow it. I remain, Your dutiful son,   THOMAS TRADELOVE.

30 FAMILIAR, USEFUL, INSTRUCTIVE,

LETTER XII.—*From a Father to his Son, soon after his having been bound apprentice.*

My Dear Boy,

YOU doubtless recollect the advice I gave you the latter part of the time of your being at school; indeed, from your compliance with it, I am persuaded it is impressed on your memory. Hence I am encouraged to offer a few hints to your observation, now you have entered upon a new scene of life. I put you to school to qualify you for business; I put you to business to qualify you for obtaining the means to render you happy in yourself, and respectable in society. To these great ends, the same diligence is necessary in attending to the concerns of the one as the other, without which you could not be a proficient in either, or reasonably expect they could answer my design. Consider, you have passed the state of childhood; throw aside toys, and devote your mind to the substantial pursuits of business. Be obedient to your master; attend to his advice and example; and aspire to excellence in your business; remembering, that ambition in laudable attainments is a virtue. I remain,

Your affectionate father.

LETTER XIII.—*The Answer.*

Honoured Sir,

FROM the kind concern you intimate for my success in my present state of life, I find myself bound to be attentive to your advice. I know your good nature and candid disposition will make allowance for the inexperience and flightiness of youth, and induce you to overlook some little faults which may fall to its share. I take the liberty to mention this, as I have not yet the vanity to think myself free from them; while at the same time I assure you, that in the main point of business, I shall endeavour to be as serious and as solid as those of riper years, keeping constantly in mind the counsel of so excellent a parent, and so good a master.

I am, honoured Sir,

Your dutiful and much obliged son.

LET.

AND ENTERTAINING LETTERS.   3ĩ

LETTER XIV.—*From a Guardian in the country to a Youth apprenticed to a tradesman in London.*

Dear Billy,

AS the care of a parent devolved on me at the death of your worthy father, by which you became an orphan, I trust I have hitherto performed the duties of one. You received your education under my immediate inspection, and I think in some degree it has been my happiness to promote it. You are now put to a trade in London, at a distance from me, and exposed to many temptations. I hope your morals continue good, and your principles uncorrupt; but as mankind in general are frail, and youth in particular liable to be seduced, I must caution you against an inclination to go out of your master's house at night, as it is often injurious to young people, and has in many instances been attended with fatal consequences. Shun idle company, and the society of those unthinking boys, who wish to be their own masters before they have discretion to guide their conduct, and glory in those things which are their disgrace, and ought to be their shame. Neglect not publick worship on Sundays, nor suffer reprobates to laugh you out of your duty to God and man. If you always remember that *to be good is to be happy*, and guide your actions by that unerring maxim, it will certainly lead you to present comfort and future bliss. I am,   Your's sincerely.

LETTER XV.—*The Youth's Answer.*

Dear Sir,

YOUR kind attention follows me wherever I go. I may truly say, that since the death of my worthy parents, you have been to me indeed a father, and should deem myself highly ungrateful, if I neglected your advice in any instance. The counsel given me in your last, I receive most cordially, and shall as punctually observe it. I have hitherto been very recluse, and therefore have not had the opportunity of seeing much of this great world; but as you warn me of the vices which prevail in it, I shall be very cautious how I engage in it, and for the present let the duties you recommend employ my time.

I am, dear Sir,

Your's most respectfully.

32   FAMILIAR, USEFUL, INSTRUCTIVE,

LETTER XVI.—*From an Officer to his Son at school, previous to his departure on foreign service.*

Dear Child,

I INTENDED to have called on you at school before I embarked on the expedition to which I am appointed; but find myself so straitened for time, that I must not indulge that pleasing satisfaction. The only means left is to supply my absence by my advice, which I hope will be fixed in your mind. I must, my dear Boy, enjoin you to attend to your learning, because on it depends your success in life. Now is the season for improvement; this the space for acquiring that which you can never lose, and laying up a treasure which cannot be exhausted. I have, however, made such a reserve, as will not only defray the expences attending your education and apprenticeship, but enable you to set forward in life in a respectable light. I beg you will pay a proper attention to the advice of Mr. Trusty, whom I have appointed by will my sole executor, and to whose care you are solemnly recommended, from my having a firm persuasion of his integrity. When I arrive at the place of my destination, I will write to you, and shall expect an immediate answer. Farewell, remember the advice of

An affectionate father.

LETTER XVII.—*The Son's Answer.*

Honoured Sir,

I CANNOT but be greatly affected by the information of your sudden departure; and as the present time will not admit my saying so much as I could wish, shall only observe, that, next to my obedience and duty to you, I shall pay a due regard to the precepts of Mr. Trusty. I hope to hear from you as often as possible, assuring you that it will be the greatest happiness that can be felt by,

Your most dutiful son.

LETTER XVIII.—*From a Father to his Son, desiring him to instil religious education in his children.*

Dear Son,

I THINK I may conscientiously affirm, that from the earliest period of your life to the present hour, I have entertained a most serious concern for the promotion of your temporal and eternal interests. I endeavoured to convince you of the great importance of religion, pointed out to you the excellence of the Bible, as comprising a perfect
system

fyftem of faith and morals, and recommended it to you as an infallible guide. Nor was I difappointed in my view: you foon imbibed juft notions of your duty to your Creator, and the defign of your creation; and your conduct in life has, in a great meafure, been conformable to the fame. As you are now become a father, I fincerely recommend to you, in this particular inftance, to follow my example, as the moft probable means of fecuring the permanent felicity of your immediate defcendants. Perfevere in the practice of thofe duties to your children which I taught you; leave the event to an All-wife Providence; and then, whatever it may be, you will enjoy the confolation of an approving confcience. I remain,   Your's moft affectionately.

LETTER XIX.—*From a young Gentleman at fchool to his Parents, as a fpecimen of his improvement in writing.*

Honoured Parents,

PURSUANT to the cuftom of our fchool, I prefent you with this fpecimen of my writing, in which, on comparifon with former letters, I hope you will obferve I have made fome improvement. You may reft affured that it fhall be my conftant endeavour to advance not only in this, but every other branch of education, to which you may judge it expedient for me to apply, as it is my earneft defire, upon all occafions, to teftify with what profound reverence I am,   Your moft dutiful fon.

LETTER XX.—*The Father's Anfwer.*

Dear Son,

WITH infinite fatisfaction I received the late inftance of your filial duty, which was as pleafing to your mother as myfelf. I much approve your mafter's plan for the regulation of his fchool, as it refpects ftated fpecimens of your writing, and thereby excites a laudable emulation in young minds, to excel in that ufeful and ornamental art; nor can I withhold my approbation of the very vifible improvement you have made in it. Go on to deferve, and you fhall never want my favour and encouragement, fince my grand aim is to qualify you in your earlier days for fuch purfuits in more advanced life, as may promote your own intereft, and the good of fociety in general. I remain,   Your moft affectionate father.

LETTER XXI.—*From a Youth at school to his Parents, in acknowledgment of favours received.*

Honoured Parents,

YOUR very kind letter came duly to hand, as did the neceſſaries you were pleaſed to ſend me by the ſtage-coach. For theſe and all other favours I can only ex-preſs a moſt grateful acknowledgement, and promiſe, as the beſt return I can make, to pay the ſtricteſt attention to my learning, and follow the wholeſome advice you have ſo often given me reſpecting my conduct in general. My maſter preſents his compliments, and will write to you in a few days, when I hope you will have the ſatisfaction of hearing from him the progreſs I have made in the ſeveral ſtudies to which I have applied myſelf under his care and direction. I ſubſcribe myſelf, honoured parents,

Your moſt dutiful ſon.

LETTER XXII.—*From a Youth to his Father, expreſſing concern at not having heard from him for ſome time.*

Honoured Sir,

AS a conſiderable time is elapſed ſince I had the plea-ſure of receiving your laſt kind letter, I cannot help entertaining a diſagreeable apprehenſion, that I have in-curred your diſpleaſure, though I am perſuaded it muſt have been from an involuntary cauſe. Sometimes I have imputed the omiſſion of your ſtated favours in writing to indiſpoſition, and therefore, being as anxious for the ſtate of your health as the continuance of your approbation, permit me to expreſs a moſt earneſt deſire of hearing from you, that I may diſmiſs thoſe doubts and fears which at preſent perplex and render me unhappy. I remain, ho-noured Sir,   Your ever dutiful ſon.

LETTER XXIII.—*From a Youth at an academy to his Father, requeſting permiſſion to learn ſome of the ſciences.*

Much honoured Sir,

AS I have had the pleaſure of receiving your approba-tion of ſpecimens of my attainments in the acquiſition of the ſeveral branches of Engliſh, French, writing, and accounts, I am encouraged to ſolicit the favour of your permiſſion to enter upon ſome new ſtudies. I am alſo in-duced to prefer this requeſt, from a deſire of being placed on a level with thoſe of my ſchool-fellows, who learn geo-graphy,

graphy, the ufe of the globes, and drawing : thefe branches are reprefented in the moſt approved treatifes on education, not only as ufeful and ornamental, but abfolutely neceſſary for perfons defigned to fill ſome public ſtations in life. If therefore you are pleafed to grant my requeſt, nothing ſhall be wanting on my part to render your defigns in my education as accompliſhed as poſſible, fince it will ever be my higheſt ambition to approve myfelf,

.Honoured Sir,   Your moſt dutiful fon.

LETTER XXIV.—*The Father's Anſwer.*

Dear Son,

THE purport of your laſt letter affordedme great fatis-faction. From the learning you have already obtain-ed, I am readily induced to comply with your requeſt. Prefent my compliments to your maſter, and tell him, that in the profecution of the ſtudies propofed, I ſhall rely on his known prudence for your direction. To encourage your induſtry and diligence in thofe purfuits to which you feem fo much inclined, I have remitted your maſter a note, in order to accommodate you with whatever may be deemed neceſſary for that purpofe. I am, Your moſt loving father.

LETTER XXV.—*From a Youth at an academy to his Parents; requeſting their permiſſion to learn to dance.*

Honoured Father and Mother,

FROM the care and expence with which my education has hitherto been attended, I flatter myfelf nothing will be wanting on your part to render it complete. Hence I prefume to remind you, that upon my uncle's mention-ing at table, when I was laſt at home, how proper it was for young people to acquire the ufeful and ornamental ac-compliſhments of the perfon as well as the mind, you pro-miſſed that I ſhould learn dancing, as requifite to complete the gentleman. There are very few in this academy who do not enter upon this polite art, when they have attained to the age of ten or twelve years. You will permit me therefore to requeſt the fame opportunity for improvement, efpecially when I aſſure you that to merit the continuance of your indulgence in this, as well as every other refpect, ſhall be the conſtant endeavour of, honoured parents,

Your moſt dutiful fon.

LET-

56   FAMILIAR, USEFUL, INSTRUCTIVE, &c.

LETTER XXVI.—*The Anſwer from the Father.*

Dear Son,

I RECEIVED your's, requeſting the fulfilment of my promife that you ſhould learn dancing. To convince you
therefore that I would by no means difcourage you from the
purfuit of any thing that might recommend you in future
life, you have my permiffion to enter upon it immediately.
I have only to warn you to be careful, that the purfuit of
this accomplifhment does not divert your attention from
more important objects, and fubfcribe myfelf,

Your affectionate father.

LETTER XXVII.—*From   a Youth at an academy to his
Siſter at a boarding-fchool.*

Dear Siſter,

I WAS extremely concerned to hear by the laſt letter with
which I was favoured from our honoured father, that
you have had an attack of the fever. Anxious therefore
for the ſtate of your health, I impatiently wait to know
how you are at prefent, and whether I may promife myfelf
the happinefs of feeing you at home next Whitfuntide.
Though our feparation is wifely ordered by our parents for
our benefit and advantage, occafional interviews muſt be
very pleafing to a brother and fifter, whofe affection I truſt
has and will be mutual. Entreating to hear from you
without delay, I fubfcribe myfelf   Your loving brother.

LETTER XXVIII.—*From a Youth at a boarding-fchool
to his Parents, requeſting their prefence at a publick examination, before the vacation takes place.*

Honoured Father and Mother,

A CCORDING to the ſtated rules of our fchool, Thurf-
day next is the day appointed for our public examination in the feveral branches of education upon which we have
entered. As I fhould be very happy to fee you both upon
that occafion, I have prefumed to fend you the inclofed, and
which muſt be produced in order to gain admittance. From
my foliciting the honour of your prefence, you will I apprehend be pretty confident I fhall acquit myfelf in fuch a
manner as not to put you to the bluſh, but on the contrary
brighten your profpect of my future progrefs in every valuable acquifition. I remain with profound reverence, honoured parents,   Your moſt dutiful fun.

LETTERS *relating to* Trade, Commerce, Family *Occurrences, and various other Subjects.*

LETTER XXIX.—*From a Father to his Son, just set up in business.*

Dear George,

YOU must be sensible that my concern for your welfare has attended you through your progress in life. My first care was that of your education; my next, that of your apprenticeship; and now succeeds, in course, that of your commencing business. I have discharged the duties of a parent with respect to the two former, and am anxious for doing the same with respect to the latter. To this end, upon this important occasion, I must first repeat the admonition I have so frequently given you to industry and sobriety, and urge them as the chief qualifications of the man of business, without which no views of success can be reasonably entertained. I now recommend to your consideration the choice of proper persons for your connections in social and commercial life. Be it your constant endeavour to associate with men of sobriety, good sense, and virtue, remembering that the character of a man of business in particular, is greatly benefitted or injured by the company he keeps. You will, I hope, also attend to the œconomy of your domestic affairs, and in the regulation of your family expences, nor foolishly aspire to begin life as you should end it; a vanity that has proved the ruin of thousands of young beginners. These hints I offer as proofs of my zeal for your welfare. You will, I trust, communicate to me, from time to time, every particular in which you may need my advice, resting assured that my great pleasure is the promotion of the happiness of my children. I am,

Your affectionate father.

LET-

38   FAMILIAR, USEFUL, INSTRUCTIVE,

LETTER XXX.—*From a Young Beginner in business to a Wholesale Dealer.*

SIR,   *Reading, Dec.* 5.

FROM the general character you have long maintained, and your approved integrity in all your dealings with my master, justice and prudence dictate the propriety of my application to you at my outset in life. Having fulfilled the articles of my apprenticeship, I hope to the entire satisfaction of the parties concerned, my worthy father has enabled me to begin business for myself, to which purpose I have taken a shop in this town, and now propose to you my correspondence, from the motives already assigned, not doubting but you will treat me on the same terms as you have done my master. I shall endeavour to be as punctual in my payments as possible, and have therefore only to request your pleasure by return of post, which will oblige

Your humble servant.

LETTER XXXI.—*The Answer.*

SIR,   *London, Dec.* 7.

YOUR's of the 5th instant came duly to hand; and, pursuant to request, I take the earliest opportunity of assuring you that I cordially accept of your connection in business, from the character you acquired and preserved in your apprenticeship. You may rely on just dealings from me, and, as I doubt not the sincerity of your endeavours to be as punctual in your returns, shall make a point of sending you the best articles of each assortment you may order on the most reasonable terms. With wishes for the continuance of your health, and prosperity in business, I am,

Your obliged servant.

LETTER XXXII.—*From a Retail Dealer in the country to a capital house in town, stating injuries received from the badness of their commodities.*

Gentlemen,   *Upton.*

NECESSITY, from a desire of preserving that reputation I have acquired, obliges me to inform you, that though your commodities have till now been as good in quality as could possibly be procured, yet lately they have been generally indifferent, and frequently so bad, as to subject me to loss of character as well as property. The only reparation you can make is to send me immediately the con-

tents

tents of my laſt order in prime goods, which may be admitted by my cuſtomers as ſome compenſation for former diſappointments, not to ſay injuries, as well as contribute to retrieve my charaćter, on which my ſucceſs totally depends.
Your compliance will be the only means of continuing our
correſpondence, as in caſe of neglećt I muſt have recourſe
to another quarter, being determined to vend no goods
which are any way exceptionable.   I am, Gentlemen,

     Your's, &c.   DANIEL DOWNRIGHT.
Meſſ. *Surface* and Co. *London.*

LETTER XXXIII.—*The Anſwer.*

SIR,

WE are very ſorry that the neglećt or miſtake of ſervants has given you juſt cauſe for complaint.   Care
ſhall be taken to examine minutely into the particulars, as
well as to afford you all the redreſs in our power.   To this
end, we have ſent you this day the contents of your laſt order, ſelećted under the immediate inſpećtion of one of the
partners, and you will be convinced, it is preſumed, from
the bill of parcels, of our deſign to indemnify you for loſſes
ſuſtained from the cauſes you mention.   As we are ſenſible
of the value of your correſpondence, we hope the means
we have adopted will effećtually ſecure it, and only wiſh to
preſerve it ſo long as we appear to merit it.   We are, Sir,
   Your moſt obliged humble ſervants,

       SURFACE and Co.

LETTER XXXIV.—*Letter of reproof from a Wholeſale Dealer to a Shop-keeper, who had been backward in his remittance.*

Mr. Slowman,

NOTHING can be more irkſome to me than a neceſſity
for writing on the diſagreeable ſubjećt before me;
but the ſtate of my affairs, which I always ſettle at this ſeaſon of the year, renders it indiſpenſible for me not only to
reprove you for former breaches of promiſe, but peremptorily to inſiſt on an immediate adjuſtment of accounts.   Frequent repetitions of your diſappointments have wrought me
to long forbearance; but ſuch are my connećtions, I cannot
longer admit them as apologies for the neglećt of that on
which my intereſt eſſentially depends.   In a word, I expećt
a draught or order for a conſiderable ſum by return, and
muſt aſſure you, that though I am naturally averſe to rigorous
             meaſures,

40. FAMILIAR, USEFUL, INSTRUCTIVE,

meafures, the duty I owe myfelf, family, and creditors, in in cafe of neglect, will compel me to have recourfe to the law to obtain my right; but fhall be happy in being pre-vented from the fame by your compliance. I am, Sir,

Your's, &c.

PETER PUNCTUAL.

LETTER XXXV.—*The Anfwer.*

S I R,

THE lenity you have fhewn me calls for my warmeft acknowledgment, as the neglect of the fulfilment of my promifes gives me the utmoft concern. However, I muft take the liberty of affuring you again moft folemnly, that my remiffnefs has been wholly owing to the remiffnefs of others in the payment of fums due to me; for though the major part of thofe with whom I have dealings feldom fail, the times of their payment are precarious and uncertain. I fhall urge them from the weightieft motives, and at all events, to convince you of the integrity of my defigns, fend you by to-morrow's poft a draught for fixty pounds. I hope in the courfe of a week or two to remit a much larger fum, and in about a month to adjuft the whole account. Let me therefore intreat your further forbearance, as feve-rity would anfwer no other purpofe than that of defeating my intentions of doing what would afford me the greateft happinefs. I remain, Your obliged humble fervant,

SIMON SORROWFUL.

LETTER XXXVI.—*From one Tradefman to Another, re-quefting the payment of a fum of money.*

S I R,

I SHOULD not have requefted the balance of accounts between us at this time, were I not under immediate ne-ceffity of anfwering a very unexpected, though confidera-ble demand. At prefent I have only to affure you, that as my credit is at ftake, if you cannot fend me the whole ba-lance, what part of it you can raife will at this critical juncture be highly acceptable, and of material fervice to

Your humble fervant,

NICHOLAS NEEDY.

LET-

AND ENTERTAINING LETTERS.   4I

LETTER XXXVII.—*The Answer.*

S I R,

I AM very happy in having it now in my power, by means of an unexpected remittance, of sending the whole balance of accounts between us : it amounts, I find, upon revisal, to £ 132 10*s.* for which sum I send you inclosed an order, payable at sight. In future, I hope my remittances will be attended with that punctuality, as to prevent your writing again on the like subject to,

Your very humble servant,   CHA. CANDOUR.

LETTER XXXVIII.—*From a Young Man to a distant relation, requesting the loan of a sum of money to enable him to set up in business.*

Dear Sir,

THE many favours I have already received from your hands, encourages me to solicit one more, which, if I obtain, will probably be the foundation of my future welfare. I have then to acquaint you, that Mr. Steady, with whom I served as apprentice the usual term, and as journeyman two years, died yesterday. The wages I received were for the most part applied to the relief of a necessitous aged parent, therefore of course could not make any reserve. My master, however, as a most satisfactory testimony to me of his approbation of my conduct, has left me in his will 100*l.* But as I find this will not be sufficient to compleat the purchase, presume to apply to you for the loan of 150*l.* which will enable me to begin the world with a reasonable prospect of success. I will give you bond, or any other security you may require. I hope this solicitation will not give you offence ; and should you be so kind as to comply with my request, the obligation shall ever be gratefully acknowledged by, Sir, Your very humble servant,

SAMUEL STRIVEWELL.

LETTER XXXIX.—*The Answer.*

Cousin Samuel,

I HAVE entertained a good opinion of your principles, and am confirmed in the same from the plain manner of your address on the present occasion. Finding myself much inclined to contribute towards putting you in a capacity of doing for yourself, I will call on you in a day or two, when you may introduce me to your master's executors,

when

4ş FAMILIAR, USEFUL, INSTRUCTIVE,

whèn, if I find no juſt obſtacle, ſhall comply with your requeſt. I am your well-wiſher,

BENJAMIN BLUNT.

LETTER XL.—*From a Country Tradeſman to a Dealer
in London, excuſing remiſſneſs in payment.*

SIR,

I FIND from the ſtate of my accounts. that the note I
gave you becomes due in the couſe of a few days, and
have therefore taken the liberty of requeſting your indulgence for about a fortnight, before which time I cannot expect to receive any conſiderable ſums. My general punc-
uality, I preſume, will induce you to grant me this favour,
which, as it is the firſt, ſo it will be, I hope, the laſt of
the kind I ſhall have occaſion to aſk. As ſome degree of
ſecurity, you will hold the two incloſed notes, indorſed by
perſons with whom you have been connected in buſineſs,
on condition of return when mine is taken up. This being
a matter that gives me much anxiety, I beg you would let
me know your pleaſure concerning it by return of poſt, and
you will much oblige,

Your humble ſervant, MATTHEW MEANWELL.

LETTER XLI.—*The Anſwer.*

SIR,

THOUGH I am not averſe to compliance with your
requeſt, I muſt take upon me to cenſure your neglect
of acquainting me with the ſtate of your affairs ſooner.
Indeed, had you deferred writing to me on the matter but
two days longer, your note would have been paid away,
and your credit might have been greatly affected by default. When you offered me the note, I deſired you (as I
do in general thoſe of whoſe integrity I have a good opinion) to take your own time, at the ſame time enjoining
you alſo to obſerve it ſtrictly. I will not be harſh in my
reprimand; but as you are a young man lately entered upon life, I could wiſh you to look upon it in a
friendly light. Your notes I return encloſed, as a proof
that I entertain no doubt of your honeſty, and am,

Your's, &c. FREDERICK FIG.

LET-

AND ENTERTAINING LETTERS.   43

LETTER XLII.—*From a tradesman to a Wholesale Dealer, who had made a demand on him for cash before the usual time for payment.*

S I R,

YOUR drawing upon me, and that for a considerable sum, at least two months before the usual time of credit, gives me much surprize, nor can I possibly answer your demand, as, having no apprehension of it, I made no preparation. You cannot censure me with neglect, or charge me with default in any instance during the whole course of our connection. Conscious of the truth of what I advance, I confess I am anxious to know the cause of a proceeding, which gives me uneasy suspicions, and affords in particular ground to suppose you doubt my integrity. Be explicit on this matter in your answer, and you will oblige,

Your's, &c.   FRANCIS FIREBRAND.

LETTER XLIII.—*The Answer.*

S I R,

I MAKE no doubt of your surprize at the receipt of my last. In conformity to your desire that I would be explicit, I must plainly tell you, that I have very weighty reasons for urging my demand, though I admit it to be out of the common line of transacting business. In a word, I am given to understand, from respectable authority, that you dabble in the stock exchange, and in other matters of uncertainty, which is too frequently the destruction of tradesmen : hence I infer, from such injurious conduct, the expediency of securing my own property, and must insist on my demand being complied with.   Yours, &c.

SIMON SAFEGUARD.

LETTER XLIV.—*From an Embarrassed Tradesman to one of his Creditors, requesting his concurrence in a letter of licence.*

S I R,

I AM extremely concerned in being under a necessity of representing to you, that through a variety of crosses and disappointments, my affairs are in so embarrassed a state, as to put it wholly out of my power to satisfy the demands of my creditors, unless they grant me a letter of licence for eighteen months. You must acknowledge, that during the six years I have dealt with you, my payments have been regular : hence I am encouraged to hope you will

44 FAMILIAR, USEFUL, INSTRUCTIVE,

will be induced to come into the proposal. In short, if this indulgence is refused me, I cannot retrieve my affairs, and my ruin will prevent my doing that justice, which, I trust, my general conduct has proved to be my sincere desire. Your pleasure is impatiently expected by, Sir,

Your most humble servant, LUKE LUCKLESS.

LETTER XLV.—*The Answer.*

SIR,

I MUST frankly acknowledge, that your general punctuality leaves no cause to doubt of your integrity; and am therefore disposed to comply with your request. If I can be of any service with respect to the compliance of others with whom I may have influence, I shall exert it with the greatest pleasure. That the issue may be a happy accommodation, attended with a series of future success, is the wish of   Your's sincerely,

HENRY HUMAN.

LETTER XLVI.—*From a Tradesman to a Principal Creditor, requesting his acceptance of a composition.*

SIR,

I AM under the necessity of informing you, that I am in the number of the unfortunate involved in the common ruin, occasioned by some late capital failures. To you, as my principal creditor, I therefore, first address myself. My books shall be submitted to the inspection of such persons as may be appointed on the occasion. Permit me therefore to request you will be pleased to call a meeting of my creditors, represent my case, and my remaining effects shall be surrendered without reserve. When an estimate is taken, I hope they will accept of such composition as it will admit of, and not deprive me of that liberty which is essential to my future support. Your benevolent compliance will be a prevailing example with the rest of my creditors, and lay under infinite obligation, Sir,

Your most obedient humble servant,

HARRY HAPLESS.

L E T-

AND ENTERTAINING LETTERS. 45

LETTER XLVII.—*The Answer.*

S I R,

THE purport of your laſt gives me much pain, as nothing can be more affecting to an honeſt tradeſman
than unavoidable loſſes ſuſtained in buſineſs. Your propoſal meets my hearty approbation, and I ſhall endeavour to
carry it into execution : at the meeting of your creditors I
ſhall exert myſelf in your behalf, being ſatisfied with your
conduct, ſince our connection in buſineſs. I am, with
ſincerity, your friend, CHRISTOPHER KINDLY.

LETTER XLVIII.—*Offering aſſiſtance to a friend in diſtreſs.*

S I R,

SYMPATHIZING with you for the loſs you ſuſtained
through the failure of Mr. Squander, you will ſuffer
me, as I take a part in your ſorrows, to take a part in ad-
miniſtering to your conſolation. I truſt you bear this in-
cidental evil of life with becoming fortitude, to which
nothing can more effectually conduce than conſcious integrity. To compliment known merit is ſuperfluous, I
ſhall therefore wave all ceremony of that kind, and frankly
authorize you to draw upon me to the amount of 200 l.
which you may uſe for ſuch time as the ſtate of your
affairs ſhall require. I only add, that your acceptance
of the ſervice will afford me equal pleaſure with the offer.
I remain your ſincere friend, PETER PLAINLY.

LETTER XLIX.—*The Anſwer.*

My dear Friend,

THE additional inſtance of your liberality in the generous offer made in your laſt, exalts your character, if poſſible, in my opinion, binds me to you by every
tie of reſpect and gratitude, and enjoins me to a moſt
cordial acceptance of it. I am happy in the approbation
of a man of ſenſe and humanity, who wiſhes to alleviate
my misfortunes, not meerly by word, but his deed; and
therefore with as little ceremony as uſed on your part,
ſhall draw upon you at a twelvemonth for the ſum propoſed. It will fully anſwer my preſent occaſion, and I
hope enable me to adopt ſome method for retrieving my
affairs. I am, Sir, your much obliged humble ſervant,
GREGORY GRATEFUL.

L E T-

46 FAMILIAR, USEFUL, INSTRUCTIVE,

LETTER L.—*From a Merchant's Clerk in town to his Master in the country.*

S I R,

AS bufinefs, it is prefumed, has detained you from home longer than was expected at your departure, my duty directs me to enquire concerning your health, and at the fame time to acquaint you, that the utmoft care and attention have been paid to the tranfaction of your commercial concerns in your abfence. Your return, however, as foon as affairs will permit, is ardently wifhed, on fome affairs which you only can adjuft. You will permit me to affure you, that it is with the greateft pleafure I embrace this opportunity of teftifying with what profound regard, I am, Sir, your moft faithful fervant,

CHARLES CLEARACCOUNT.

LETTER LI.—*The Anfwer.*

Mr. Clearaccount,

YOUR's came duly to hand, and met my approbation as a token of duty in you. With fatisfaction I hear that the profecution of my bufinefs is not interrupted by my abfence, which has been protracted by unforefeen events, longer than I expected. Hope, however, fo to arrange matters, as to be able to fet off for town in a few days. I am, your's, &c.

ROBERT REGULAR.

LETTER LII.—*From a Tradefman in the country to a Friend in London, requefting him to purchafe fome commodities for him.*

Dear Sir, *Derby, Dec.* 23.

AS in this inland fituation it is almoft impoffible to obtain genuine liquor, I fhall efteem it a favour, if you would purchafe for me a pipe of port wine, another of fherry, a puncheon of Jamaica rum, and a piece of Coniac brandy. I fhall divide the contents amongft the circle of my acquaintance, who will be much obliged by being admitted to a fhare. You will be pleafed to fend them by our carrier, with an account of the charge, which fhall be immediately defrayed, with true acknowledgment of the obligation by, Your's moft fincerely,

2

TIMOTHY TUNBELLY.

AND ENTERTAINING LETTERS. 47
LETTER LIII.—*The Answer.*

Dear Friend, London, 26.

AGREEABLE to your request I have purchased, with the advice of a friend, who is a competent judge of liquors, the several articles therein specified. They were sent to the Derby waggon, which set out yesterday morning, with a proper permit, and I hope will arrive safe, to your satisfaction, and that of your acquaintance concerned. I shall ever be happy in executing your commands, and presume I need make no ceremony in assuring you, that a hare, or any game, than can be consequently obtained, will be acceptable at this season. Observe, I prefer my request, not as a requital for services done, but that I may have an opportunity of acknowledging the obligation, as I would be known by my friends in general, to be as capable of conferring as of receiving a favour. I remain your friend, &c.

TITUS TURNABOUT.

LETTER LIV.—*From a Tenant to a Landlord, in excuse of delay in the payment of rent.*

SIR,

UNFORESEEN events constrain me to request your indulgence with respect to the payment of the half year's rent, due at Christmas last, till the ensuing quarter, at the expiration of which time, you may rest assured it being paid up in full, by
Your much obliged humble servant,
PAUL PROMISE-KEEP.

LETTER LV.—*The Answer.*

SIR,—

YOUR general punctuality calls for my indulgence, so that I have only to assure you of my ready compliance with your request, not entertaining a doubt of the fulfillment of your promise. I remain, Sir,
Your's, &c.

MATTHEW MANY-ACRE.

LET-

48. FAMILIAR, USEFUL, INSTRUCTIVE,

LETTER LVI.—*From a tenant in the country on the same occasion.*

Honoured Sir,

SO many misfortunes have come upon me together, that I muſt take the liberty of entreating your indulgence for one quarter longer. Laſt ſeaſon turned out very bad, which added to loſs of cattle, and the expences of a ſick family, has greatly diſtreſſed me. I have at preſent a good proſpect of the enſuing ſeaſon, and ground to hope, both the hay and corn harveſt will prove very favourable, which will enable me to anſwer your juſt demands, and by that means give the higheſt ſatisfaction to, Sir,

Your much obliged and moſt obedient humble ſervant,

PHILIP PLOUGHSHARE.

LETTER LVII.—*From a merchant at Hamburg to a correſpondent in London.*

SIR,

PURSUANT to contract at the laſt interview we had, previous to my departure from England, I have ſhipped on board the Succeſs, Captain Fairweather, 24 bales of linen, of various ſorts, marked T. T. They have ſeparately paſſed my own examination, ſo that I can warrant them all good of their kind. By the next ſhip that ſails for our port, you will ſend me the ſeveral articles ſpecified in the order incloſed. As from our long connexion, I am perſuaded you have a due ſenſe of the duties of commercial life, I cannot doubt of your attention to the quality of the goods, or your care in diſpatching them. I am Sir, your moſt humble ſervant,

DAVID DILIGENT.

LETTER LVIII.—*The Anſwer.*

SIR,

YOUR advice of the goods ſhipped on board the Succeſs, Captain Fairweather, came duly to hand, and I have the pleaſure to inform you of their arrival, a ſhort time after the packet. I ſhall ſhip on board the Speedwell, Captain Bluffman, the ſeveral articles ſpecified in your order, and act, I hope, upon the principles you mention, from a due conviction of their importance in the

the mercantile line. The continuance of our correspondence will be highly acceptable to me, and I doubt not of
its being productive of our mutual benefit.

I remain, Sir, your humble servant,

THOMAS TREATFAIR.

LETTER LIX.—*From a young Man bred to the sea,
requesting of a distant Relation the loan of a small sum of
money, to enable him to proceed on a voyage.*

Dear Sir,

I SHOULD not presume to trouble you on the present occasion, did I not bear in remembrance the
esteem you testified for my late father. His generous and
unsuspicious temper, you well know, laid him open to the
designs of the crafty and overbearing, by which means he
was reduced to indigent circumstances some time before
his death. I am now shipped as second mate on board a
large vessel bound to the island of Jamaica, out destitute
of money to procure not only a venture, but necessaries
for the voyage, which I must of course decline, if not
assisted by some benevolent hand. This is the true state
of my case, which I take the liberty to lay before you, as
a plea for my entreating of you the favour to advance me,
on the best security I can give, the sum of 30l. This
assistance, in all probability, will be the occasion of my
future welfare in life, and will be ever remembered and
acknowledged with that gratitude, which will be always
due from,   Your most humble servant,

HENRY HAZARD.

LETTER LX.—*The Answer.*

Dear Harry,   *Dec.* 29.

THE manner of your address upon an occasion which
much affects me, confirms the opinion I have long
entertained of your modesty and candour, and while it brings
to mind the remembrance of a worthy, though unfortunate relative, it disposes me not only to pity, but succour
his hapless son. I receive that request with a sensible
pleasure, which you preferred with a becoming diffidence,
and rejoice in an opportunity of serving a worthy young
man. Let me know your situation more particularly,
point out any reasonable views that may present, and you

C   then

5ɔ   FAMILIAR, USEFUL, INSTRUCTIVE,

then shall find in me a friend, not merely in word. I expect you to dine with me on Thursday next, and am,

Your's most sincerely,   WALTER WORTHY.

LETTER LXI.—*To a Friend, limiting the re-payment of a sum of money to a certain time.*

SIR,

I RECEIVED your's, stating your present situation, and requesting of me the loan of 40l. to answer an immediate purpose, which you positively affirm it will be in your power to re-pay in three months. As I am disposed to oblige you, though it will be attended with some inconvenience, I have inclosed you a bank-note to the amount specified; but am under a necessity of conjuring you, by all the ties of friendship, to make a point, at all events, of keeping the time of re-payment most precisely, as a failure therein would be attended to me with very injurious consequences. To enforce this injunction, I must assure you, that what I now do to serve you but little suits the state of my finances, and is the sole effect of a friendly regard. I am, your's,

SAMUEL STRAIN-A-POINT.

LETTER LXII.—*To a Friend, who had postponed fulfilling his promise of lending a sum of money on an exigence.*

Dear Friend,

AS I presumed the kind promise you made me twelve days ago, of lending me 50l. upon my bond, arose from a friendly motive of serving me, in a point no less essential than that of preserving my credit, I must assure you that I feel the disappointment more sensibly than I can express. Not doubting your word, I looked no farther, and am thereby involved in the utmost perplexity, as the day set for answering an indispensable demand approaches, and I still remain in an uncertainty of possessing the means. I hope no prejudice on your part, nor misrepresentation on that of any other, has induced you to swerve from your purpose, as the time will not admit of applying elsewhere, and my credit is wholly at stake. I shall wait on you the day after to-morrow, to know your pleasure, and am, Sir,

Your most obliged humble servant,

LET-

AND ENTERTAINING LETTERS. 5r

LETTER LXIII.—*Apology to a perſon deſirous of borrowing Money.*

SIR,

IN matters of moment it is my wiſh to be as brief, though explicit, as poſſible : ſuffer me, therefore, in replying to your requeſt, to aſſure you, that the ſtate of my finances is not adequate to anſwer the demands made upon me, and therefore, to wave excuſe for non-compliance,

I am, your's, &c.

LAURENCE LACONIC.

LETTER LXIV.—*To the ſame purport.*

SIR,

I Am ſorry to inform you, that my caſe is ſo ſimilar to your's, as to require the ſame kind office of ſome other, for which you apply to me. Remember the old adage—"A word to the wiſe." Your's, &c.

BOB SHORT.

LETTER LXV.—*Recommending a Man Servant.*

SIR,

IN reply to your polite addreſs, deſiring a character of the bearer, who has been employed in my ſervice during a ſeries of ſix years, I can aſſure you, upon my honour, that his knowledge and diligence in the buſineſs he profeſſes to undertake, entitle him to a recommendation worthy of your notice. To theſe qualifications are added, honeſty and ſobriety, which I preſume, taken together, form the eſſentials of the character of a ſervant. I am, your's, &c.

LEWIS LOVEMERIT.

LETTER LXVI.—*Requeſting the Character of a Houſekeeper.*

MADAM,

MRS. KEYS, who lately lived with you in the capacity of a houſekeeper, in conſequence of intelligence of a vacancy in my family, has applied to me for employ in the ſame line. As you are doubtleſs as conſcious as myſelf of the importance of the truſt and qualifications neceſſary for the due diſcharge of it, her engagement in my ſervice, will depend on the character ſhe has ſuſtained in your's ; for which I rely on your honour and veracity. Your anſwer by the bearer will greatly oblige,

Madam, your obedient ſervant,

DINAH DAINTY.

C 2

LET-

LETTER LXVII.—*The Anſwer.*

MADAM,

MRS. KEYS, our late houſekeeper, waited on me with your's, reſpecting her character; in reply to which I can take upon me to recommend her as a perſon fully competent to the ſeveral departments in her line; and poſſeſſing a ſhare of good-nature, as well as being ſoberly and honeſtly inclined. I am, Madam,

　　　　Your humble ſervant,

　　　　　　　CATHARINE CANDOUR.

LETTER LXVIII.—*Enquiring the Character of a Cook-Maid.*

MADAM,

A Woman, who calls herſelf Dorothy Dripping, applying to me to be hired as cook, and informing me ſhe laſt lived in your family, you will excuſe the trouble I give you, in deſiring the favour of a line reſpecting her character, according to the cuſtom neceſſarily followed upon ſuch occaſions. I am, Madam, your's, &c.

　　　　　　　DEBORAH DECENT.

LETTER LXIX.—*The Anſwer.*

MADAM,

D ISAGREEMENT amongſt ſervants, than which nothing is more common or more diſguſtful to heads of families, rendered it expedient for me to part with Dorothy our cook. This I can aſſure you was the ſole cauſe, as I muſt ſay ſhe is very expert and cleanly in her buſineſs; nor did I ever find her addicted to any bad habits or cuſtoms. I am, Madam, your's, &c.

　　　　　　　LOUISA LOVEPEACE.

LETTER LXX.—*To a Friend on breach of promiſe, in the neglect of repaying a Sum lent.*

SIR,

Y OU muſt recollect, that when you applied to me, requeſting the loan of 40l. with poſitive declaration of repaying me in three months, I complied with your deſire, and at the ſame time repreſented to you the very injurious conſequences with which your failure would be attended to me. Six months are now elapſed, and have paſſed unnoticed by you. What can I infer from ſuch treatment, but
　　　　　　　　　　　　　　　　　　that

AND ENTERTAINING LETTERS. 53

that I was deceived in my opinion of your principle? I thought you a man of probity, and as such strained a point to serve you, for the sole motive, as I observed, of a friendly regard.. I can hardly refrain still from thinking you one of those I admitted into the number of my friends from a persuasion of your title to social regard; convince me that you are so, and obviate the disagreeable necessity of reproaching you with ingratitude, and myself with folly.

I am, your's, &c.

SAMUEL STRAINAPOINT.

LETTER LXXI.— *From a Merchant in London to a young Man going to the West-Indies.*

Dear Tom,

YOUR's, dated from Liverpool, came duly to hand. I have sent you what I thought necessary for the prosecution of your voyage to Barbadoes, with recommendations to my correspondents on the island. I make no doubt of your obtaining a situation in a capital counting-house, and as it is common for clerks in that country to trade a little for themselves, would offer a word of advice on that subject. Purchase only the natural productions of the island; you are well acquainted with them from being so long in my counting-house. What you buy consign to me, and I will dispose of them to the best advantage, and in return I will send you such goods as I shall deem most saleable, by which means you will always be turning your money. Let diligence and integrity be your guides, and then fear not of success. I am, your sincere friend,

ROBERT RUMBO.

LETTER LXXII.—*The young Man's Answer after his Arrival at Barbadoes.*

Honoured Sir,

I Hope my letter of acknowledgment of the receipt of your's at Liverpool, with your other favours, came duly to hand, and shall now take the liberty of communicating to you the particulars of my situation since my arrival on this island. I am settled with Mr. Candour, a merchant of probity and property, and upon terms adequate to my most sanguine wishes. The conversation here is engrossed by the subject of the slave-trade, which some time ago engaged the attention of the British parliament.

C 3   The

54	FAMILIAR, USEFUL, INSTRUCTIVE,

The grand plea of the advocates in its favour is indispensable necessity, whilst those on the opposite side contend
that no necessity can justify inhumanity. My master stre-
nuously asserts the common rights of mankind of every
climate and complexion, as the creatures of the universally
benevolent parent of nature, whose goodness is extended
to all his works. I have ever been of his opinion, and
cannot be an eye-witness of the cruelties exercised on my
fellow-creatures without horror. But waving the melancholy theme, I take the liberty of informing you, that I
shall shortly trouble you with the confignment of some
commodities, the natural productions of the island, which
I have purchased, according to your instructions, and defire you to use your difcretion with respect to the disposal
of them, and the choice of the articles in return. Present
my respects to whom due; and believe me to be, honoured
Sir,	Your most grateful servant,

QUINTIN QUILL.

LETTER LXXIII.—*From a Gentleman to his Nephew, a
young man going to the East-Indies.*

Dear Dick,

I Am happy to find that the Interest I have exerted in
your favour has produced the desired effect, having
through my interest with some of the directors of the East-
India company, procured you an eligible situation abroad.
There are some things, however, of which I must remind
you respecting the regulation of your conduct. The advantage to be derived from your situation will greatly depend
on yourself. Many circumstances will occur, of which
you never thought. Your health must be one grand object
of your care, in a climate not congenial with your constitution. To this nothing will so effectually conduce as sobriety, to preserve which you must reject the solicitations of
young men of volatile passions, who would lead you to
spend your time in idleness and dissipation. In a country
where you will have frequent opportunity of taking advantage at the expence of honour, justice, and humanity, I
must beg of you never to avail yourself of that circumstance. Bear constantly in your mind, that a penny acquired with honesty is of more intrinsic value than pounds
procured by fraud and barbarity. Peace of mind is superior to all the blandishments of this world, and an approving

conscience

AND ENTERTAINING LETTERS.   55

confcience is a continual feaft. I have fent you every thing neceffary for the voyage, and commending you to the care and protection of an all-wife providence, remain,

Your's moft affectionately,

BENJAMIN BENEVOLENT.

LETTER LXXIV.—*The Anfwer.*

Honoured Sir,

I Am at a lofs in what manner to exprefs my grateful fenfe of the favours you have heaped upon me. My education, on the demife of my father, became the firft object of your care, and now you appear as folicitous for my advancement in life, as you were for my preparation for it. The laft inftance of your friendly, I may fay paternal regard, calls for my warmeft acknowledgment, and I fhould be guilty of the fouleft of crimes, were I remifs in my attention to your falutary advice. I fhall be attentive to your injunction with refpect to availing myfelf of certain advantages, at the expence of thofe principles which alone conftitute refpectability of character, ever remembering, that it is much more noble to be a good than a great man. I return you my fincereft thanks for your favours in general, and fhall be happy in proving with what profound refpect I am, honoured Sir,

Your moft devoted nephew,

GREGORY GRATEFUL.

LETTER LXXV.—*From a young Man going to fettle at Oporto to an Uncle, who had retired from bufinefs.*

Kind Sir,

F ROM the experience I have had of your care and indulgence, fince the death of my worthy parents, I am convinced it is both my duty and intereft to open my mind to my beft friend and benefactor. I fhall therefore wave apology, and frankly acquaint you that I am difpofed to try my fortune abroad, as an opportunity now offers for fo doing. Mr. Pipe, the wine merchant, whom you well know, has declined bufinefs, and made it over to his fon. The young gentleman, who is going to fettle at Oporto, has offered to make me his principal clerk, and to allow me an extraordinary falary, befides confiderable perquifites. The propofal to me appears advantageous; indeed it is my humble opinion, that by accepting it I

C 4   fhall

56   FAMILIAR, USEFUL, INSTRUCTIVE,

shall have an opportunity of becoming more acquainted with the world, and of acquiring, in a reasonable time, as much as will enable me to set up business. I submit the matter, however, to your better judgement, by which I desire ever to be guided; and am, your dutiful nephew,

GEORGE LEDGER.

LETTER LXXVI.—*The Answer.*

Dear Nephew,

YOUR dutiful attachment to me, and regular conduct in life, afford me the greatest pleasure. I have duely considered the matter you submit to my judgement; and am of opinion, that the proposal made by Mr. Pipe is very eligible. I have, however, something to communicate, which I think worthy of your attention.

You are now going to a strange country, where you will find opinions, modes, and customs, different from those which prevail in that of your nativity. I recommend you, therefore, to remember, that notwithstanding this difference in trifling matters, human nature is the same in all ages, and in all nations. Upon this principle I offer you my advice: let your behaviour, not only to those with whom you are immediately connected, but to the natives in general, be obliging and complaisant. Be very careful to avoid any sarcasm or raillery on their religion. They are great bigots, and would not hesitate to resent what you might think a jest at the expence of your life. Avoid gallantry as carefully, they are jealous to madness, which has impelled them frequently to acts of desperation. Lastly, be just in all your dealings with them, that your country may never be dishonoured by any part of your conduct. You will accept of the enclosed for the uses required on the present occasion, and as attended with the best wishes of your affectionate uncle,

SAMUEL LEDGER.

LETTER LXXVII.—*From a Rider, in the Country, to his Employer, in London.*

SIR,   *Lincoln.*

WHEN I wrote to you last from Boston, in this county, I transmitted you a minute account of debts collected, and orders received. I doubt not but you will judge from thence that matters go on favourably hitherto.

therto. Having waited on our three principal correspondents in this city, I am to inform you, that two of them have discharged their bills, and given fresh orders to a considerable amount; but the other still continues tardy. You will readily perceive that I mean Mr. Slowman, whose affairs I am given to understand are in a very embarrassed situation. Some people here are of opinion that a statute of bankruptcy will be taken out against him, whilst others talk of a compromise. I have been advised to arrest him in your name for the debt that is owing, but as this is a tender point, I dare not proceed in it, without your authority; nor does it become me to dictate to you, but to receive and act according to your instructions. I shall, therefore, not take any measure till I know your pleasure, with which I hope to be favoured by return of post; and, remain, Sir, your devoted servant,

HENRY HORSEMAN.

LETTER LXXVIII.—*The Answer.*

Dear Harry, London.

YOUR's from Lincoln came duly to hand, and gave me a mixture of pleasure and pain. Before you transmitted me an account of the state of Mr. Slowman's affairs, I had information of the same from a neighbour, whose rider had just left Lincoln. I highly approve of your conduct with respect to him. If matters can be brought to a compromise, I will accede to such terms as may be proposed. Proceed with the like prudence and diligence you have hitherto done, and rest assured you shall not fail of reward, from your's, &c.

MOSES MARKMERIT.

LETTER LXXIX.— *From a Tradesman in London, to a Correspondent in Liverpool.*

SIR, London.

HAVING written to you thrice on business of importance, and without your taking the least notice, I must now decline all ceremony, and demand of you an explicit reason for such extraordinary conduct. You know the indispensable necessity of money for carrying on trade, which must be attended to with a sort of laborious permanency, or no good consequences can be reasonably expected. No man has a right to gratify his inclination at the expence of

C 5 his

58. FAMILIAR, USEFUL, INSTRUCTIVE,

his neighbour. Your filence upon fuch material bufinefs, after fo often writing to you, gives me no fmall uneafinefs. I therefore beg to hear from you by return of poft, other-wife I fhall charge you with bafenefs, and want of genero-fity, and treat you accordingly. I am, your's, &c.

PAUL PLAINTRUTH.

LETTER LXXX.—*The Anfwer.*

SIR,
Liverpools

THOUGH your letter conveys expreffions that cannot but appear to me harfh and difagreeable, I muft, upon deliberate reflection, exempt you from cenfure. I flatter myfelf, however, with being able to affign fuch rea-fons for the neglect with which I am charged, as will give you entire fatisfaction, and reftore me to your good opi-nion. Know then, fir, that when your letters came (which they did in the courfe of three fucceeding pofts) I was on a journey to Manchefter, and my fhopman, daily expecting my return, thought it moft expedient to fubmit them to my infpection, without undertaking to anfwer them, a bufi-nefs I ordered him always to leave to me, I am as fenfible of the neceffity of money for carrying on trade as you can be, and from that conviction happy in being able to fend you the enclofed order, payable at fight.

The articles you fent me are unexceptionable in their quality, and the prices feverally affixed muft be admitted highly reafonable, confiderations which certainly entitle you to attention and punctuality. I remain, your's,

FRANCIS FUSTIAN.

LETTER LXXXI.—*From a Merchant at Lifbon, to his Correfpondent in London.*

SIR,

YOU would have received your order moft probably before now, had not the packet which brought your letter, by fome accident been detained a confiderable time at Corke, where it had been driven by contrary winds. However, as we expected to hear from you, moft of the articles you want were packed before the order arrived, which of courfe will obviate delay. The wine I am con-fident will prove of excellent quality: but the lemons, I fear, will not give fo much fatisfaction. However, if complaints fhould be made by any of your cuftomers, you

may

may be affured that no better can be procured at this feafon of the year. Your remittance was very acceptable at
the time it arrived, as I was difappointed in my expectation of receiving a confiderable fum from Briftol. You are
requefted to forward the linen ordered in my laft, becaufe
we have great demands for that article. As for the affort-
ment in the ironmongery branch, it muft be left to you,
without fpecifying particulars. Some of the laft articles
received had been damaged, but that I am ready to fuppofe was unknown to you, otherwife you would by no
means have fent them. I fhall rely on your perfonal
care and infpection refpecting every article contained in
my orders, as you muft be convinced of the neceffity of
fuch caution. I am, your's, &c.

GILES GRAPEJUICE.

LETTER LXXXII.—*The Anfwer.*

SIR,

I Received the wines and fruit which arrived in the
fhip Goodwill, and find them correfpond with your
defcription; but am concerned that you fhould have caufe
to complain of any commodity I tranfmitted to you. To
be plain with you, I trufted to my broker, who I find
has deceived me, which I fhall take care he fhall not do a
fecond time, as from henceforward all dealing between him
and me fhall ceafe. The different articles of hardware
have been felected under my immediate fuperintendance,
fo that I doubt not of your finding them anfwer your expectation. I remain, your's, &c.

VINCENT VARIOUS.

LETTER LXXXIII.—*From a Clerk at Bengal, to his Father in London.*

Honoured Sir,

CONSCIOUS of the duty I owe you, I cannot let an
opportunity pafs that affords me the means of expreffing the fenfe I fhall ever retain of it. I have the pleafure to inform you, by the fhip Ofterly, which is juft ready
to fail with the fleet for England, that fince my arrival
here, my fuccefs has exceeded my expectations. You will
find, from what I have fent on board the Ofterly, that I
have not mifapplied my time, though I can affure you I
have ufed no illegal methods, ever remembering the maxim,
that ill-gotten wealth is a curfe inftead of a bleffing. I am

C 6 determined

determined upon the whole, that your advice fhall be the rule of my conduct. You are to me the beft of fathers, I am therefore bound to abide by your directions. You will ufe your own difcretion in the difpofal of the goods I have fent; and next feafon I fhould be glad to have a return of fhoes and hardware, as thofe articles commonly enfure fuccefs. I am with refpectful compliments where due,.

Honoured Sir, your moft dutiful fon,
MICHAEL MUSLIN.

LETTER LXXXIV.—*The Anfwer.*

Dear Son,

WITH infinite pleafure I received an additional tef-timony of your dutiful regard, in your letter by the Ofterly, and rejoice to hear that your fuccefs has exceeded your expectations. The goods came fafe to hand, and I have endeavoured to difpofe of them to the beft advantage. The articles which you think moft commonly fuccefsful I have particularly attended to, and thofe, with others, I have fent by the Edgecote Eaft-Indiaman, hoping you will receive them all fafe. May profperity attend all your laudable undertakings; may you never fwerve from the rule of equity, but perfevere in well doing, as the fureft foundation of your real happinefs, is the ardent wifh of,

Your affectionate father,
M. MUSLIN.

LETTER LXXXV.—*From a Wholefale Dealer in London, to a Correfpondent at Birmingham.*

SIR,

YOUR order came duly to hand, and the articles fpe-cified in it fhall be fent by the Birmingham waggon the latter end of the week. It is with pleafure I inform you, that trade is not fo bad in London as fome have weakly imagined, and others induftrioufly infinuated. There have been capital failures indeed of late, but I cannot apprehend they will much affect the general run of trade. The goods I have fent you are equal to any that can be procured in London, and I fincerely wifh you fuccefs in all your undertakings.

Your's, &c.
TIMOTHY SURECARD.

LET-

LETTER LXXXVI.—*The Answer.*

Dear Sir.

I Received your parcels by the waggon, and though I have not had time to examine them, doubt not but that they will be found fully to answer the description you have given. I am glad to hear that trade in London is not so much on the decline as some have reported. I have only to observe that we have lately had several good orders from correspondents of undoubted credit, and am,

Your's, &c.   FRANCIS FORGE.

LETTER LXXXVII.—*From a young Man who had failed in business to a Gentleman of fortune.*

Honoured Sir,

I Apply to you in my present situation, from the exalted character you bear, of being ever disposed to acts of humanity. It was my misfortune to enter upon a business, with the nature of which I was in a great measure unacquainted. After having been about two years in business, to avoid the miseries of a prison, I took shelter in London, where I have derived all my support from a brother, who is in but very indifferent circumstances. In this melancholy state I was informed that a relation of your's at Manchester wanted a clerk, in the room of one who is going abroad, and therefore embrace this early opportunity of writing to you, to solicit your recommendation. I have yet some friends who will give security for any trust reposed in me, and I hope that no part of my conduct will ever give offence. Though I have been unfortunate, I trust I shall never be dishonest. If you ever did a generous action (and I know of many) the grant of the favour now requested will add to the number, as well as lay me under the most lasting obligations. Waiting your pleasure, if you will deign to let me hear from you, I am, Sir, in the most respectful manner,   Your's, &c.

HUGH HOPELESS.

LETTER LXXXVIII.—*The Answer.*

Friend Hopeless,

Y OUR's I received, and am much concerned for your misfortunes, to alleviate which I have chearfully complied with your request, and my relation has consented to receive you. Go immediately to Manchester, as no time is to be lost; this is a necessary consideration, because you

should

62   FAMILIAR, USEFUL, INSTRUCTIVE,

should have some knowledge of the business before the clerk goes away. I have done all in my power to serve you, and sent something enclosed to defray your expences.

I am, your well-wisher,

GEORGE GRACEFUL.

LETTER LXXXIX.—*From a Tradesman desirous of retiring from business to his Friend in the country.*

Dear Friend,

I Have now been, as you well know, near thirty years in trade, nor have I spent the whole of that in vain.—God has been pleased to bless my honest endeavours, insomuch, that I possess what I think a competence to retire from the noise and bustle of life. I have settled all my accounts to the general satisfaction of those with whom I was concerned. My wife and only son died about two years ago of an epidemical distemper, within a short space of time from each other, and it may be justly said, that I have been in a state of mourning ever since : I therefore beg that you would look out for a snug convenient spot, where I may end my days in solitude—and you will confer a lasting obligation on, your's sincerely,

ROBERT RICHENOUGH.

LETTER XC.—*The Answer.*

My dear Friend,

I Rejoice that success has crowned your honest endeavours, and that you have formed a resolution of ending your days in tranquillity, as I have done, and find no reason to repent. I have looked out for a proper place, where you will be well accommodated. The house is situated near the church, so that you will have frequent opportunities of attending divine worship. The prospect is agreeable, and there are many pleasing walks, calculated to bring the mind into a solid frame of thinking. Every thing shall be ready for your reception, therefore let me beg to hear from you as soon as possible.

I am, your's sincerely,

OLIVER OLDFRIEND.

L E T-

AND ENTERTAINING LETTERS. 63

LETTER XCI.—*To a Merchant in London, giving orders for the shipping of goods.*

   SIR,   *Plymouth, March* 15.

I Received your's, acknowledging the receipt of my last with the enclosed draft on Mr. Peter Punctual, to the amount of your demand. You will be pleased to ship for me, on board the first vessel bound for this port, six hogsheads of Jamaica sugar, six puncheons of molasses, and six barrels of Malaga raisins. For quality and charge I rely upon your integrity and moderation; and remain,

         Sir, your's, &c.

                 SAMUEL STRIVEWELL.

LETTER XCII.—*Answer to the foregoing, written under the bill of parcels.*

   Mr. Strivewell,

PURSUANT to your's of the 15th instant, I have sent the articles therein ordered, as per bill of parcels above, which I hope you will receive safe, and to your satisfaction, by the ship Coaster, Simon Starboard, Master, for Plymouth. Assuring you that your commands shall, at all times, be punctually executed, I remain,

         Your most humble servant,

             MICHAEL MANYMEANS.

LETTER XCIII.—*From a Wholesale Dealer in London to a country shopkeeper, who had left him for another.*

   Mr. Truepenny,

I Am concerned, that the correspondence maintained between us, for several years, has been discontinued, as I am not conscious of having been, in any one instance, the cause of it, and still retain a great esteem for you. You may rest assured, that none will be more ready to give you every opportunity of advantage than myself. Let me, therefore propose to renew our former dealings, and doubt not but whatever goods your commissions may direct in my way, shall be charged on the most reasonable terms.

        I am, Sir, your's, &c.

London.   DONALD DEALFAIR.

                       LET-

64 FAMILIAR, USEFUL, INSTRUCTIVE,

LETTER CXIV.—*From a Shopkeeper in the Country to a Merchant in London, defiring to be informed of the current prices of feveral commodities.*

SIR,

YOU will permit me to requeft as a favour, that you will advife me, by return of poft, of the current prices of the feveral goods undermentioned, for which if they fhould prove agreeable, and admit of a living profit, I may fpeedily tranfmit a confiderable order from myfelf and correfpondents. Waiting your immediate anfwer, I remain, refpecfully, Sir, Your's, &c.

VALENTINE VARIOUS.

LETTER CXV.—*The Anfwer.*

Mr. Various,

PURSUANT to requeft in your laft, this ferves to inform you, that the commodities, concerning the prices of which you want information, are, in general, much cheaper than they were during the war. I would recommend this as a proper time for you and your friends to purchafe, affuring you that you may rely on our beft endeavours to promote our mutual advantage in trade.

I remain, your's, &c.

OLIVER OPULENT.

LETTER XCVI.—*Accompanying a Bill of Exchange remitted to London.*

Meffrs. Brine and Pickle,

PURSUANT to promife in my laft, I here fubjoin my draft for ninety-five pounds ten fhillings on Sir Henry Hoardman and Co. in your favour. Pleafe to advife the receipt of the fame by return of poft, and if any material variation has happened in any of the articles of trade between us, inform me of the particulars, for my future conduct. I remain, in the mean time, moft refpectfully,

Your humble fervant,

NATHANIEL NEVERFAIL.

LETTER XCVII.—*The Anfwer.*

SIR,

WE acknowledge the receipt of your laft favour, with your draft enclofed on Sir Henry Hoardman and Co. value ninety-five pounds, ten fhillings, for which we return you our hearty thanks. There is no material alterations

AND ENTERTAINING LETTERS.   85

tion in the prices of goods, except in that of Spanish indigo, which is confiderably reduced. When any thing further is wanted, you may depend on the punctual execution of your commands. We beg leave refpectfully to fubfcribe ourfelves, Sir, your moft obliged,

And moft humble fervants,

BRINE and PICKLE.

[Anon.], *The American Letter-Writer: Containing a Variety of Letters on the Most Common Occasions in Life* (Philadelphia, PA: John M'Culloch, 1793), title page, pp. 3–8, 13–111. American Antiquarian Society, Dated Books.

Printed by John McCulloch in Philadelphia, *The American Letter-Writer* used Tait's version of Dilworth's *Complete Letter Writer* as its basic framework. It also used Dilworth's Introduction. The compiler excised a large number of Dilworth letters, and supplied their place with letters culled from *The Complete Letter-Writer; or Polite English Secretary*. He also reordered the letters he selected to introduce an implied narrativization based on the ages of man and woman, after the manner of the Bradfords (see Volume 2). This compiler also introduces issues of social class by clustering together letters for different generic types – school children, apprentices and maidservants for instance. This has the effect of emphasizing how different were the virtues and conduct demanded of men and women at different ranks, and distinguishes this manual from those compiled in America before Independence.

Over a third of this *American Letter-Writer* consists of letters of business, an exceptionally large proportion of the letters overall, and one large enough to encompass both the letters needed by thriving businesses, and letters to be written in the course of bankruptcies. The compiler has also included letters of business from Hill's *Young Secretary's Guide*, which had been indited over a century before (see Volume 2). The last third of the collection addresses issues of gentility, and contains letters of courtship, letters of ceremony and letters of advice. The target audience therefore once again appears to be an urban trading and mercantile class of people, who seek to embellish their social lives with genteel forms of conduct and address.

Though combining his directions for letter writing by adding back to back extracts from various manuals, the American compiler replaces the usual list of styles of address offered in British manuals and long reprinted in American ones with the following remarks:

The style of address for those persons who may be entrusted with the administration of the federal government, has been agitated in Congress; but no titles have been allowed them but that of their office, viz. *The President of the United States – The Secretary of the Treasury etc*. And it seems fit that it should be so; as best suited to the nature of a republican government. – The title of Majesty, Royal Highness, Excellency, Worshipful, and down to the humble title of Esquire, given to public officers in royal governments, seems only to beget pride or tyranny in the officers and servility and dependence among the people. But in America, where all men are declared to be equal, those and the like titles ought to be discontinued, of which Congress have set us an example, in their communications with the public officers. (below, p. 361)

T H E
American Letter-Writer:

CONTAINING,

A VARIETY OF LETTERS

O N

The moſt common Occaſions in Life,

viz.

FRIENDSHIP,	§	AMUSEMENT,
DUTY,	§	LOVE,
ADVICE,	§	MARRIAGE,
BUSINESS,	§	COURTSHIP, *&c.*

WITH

FORMS OF MESSAGE CARDS.

To which are Prefixed,

DIRECTIONS for WRITING LETTERS, and
the PROPER FORMS of ADDRESS.

PHILADELPHIA,

Printed and ſold by JOHN M'CULLOCH, No. 1,
North Third-ſtreet.
M·DCC·XCIII

INTRODUCTION.

Directions for writing Letters, and the proper Forms of Addreſs.

THERE is nothing more commendable, and at the ſame time more uſeful in life, than to be able to write letters on all occaſions with elegance and propriety. When you write to a friend, your letter ſhould be a true picture of your heart; the ſtile looſe and irregular; the thoughts themſelves ſhould appear naked, and not dreſſed in the borrowed robes of rhetoric; for a friend will be more pleaſed with that part of a letter which flows from the heart, than with that which is the product of the mind. I would not, however, be underſtood to mean, that the paſſions themſelves may not be dreſſed in wit, provided it ſits eaſy and natural, and ſeems rather expreſſive of the thoughts, than placed there for any beauty of its own.

When you write merely out of compliment, it is done more to pleaſe your correſpondent than yourſelf; and therefore you ſhould endeavour to hit his taſte; but, at the ſame time, never forget to make choice of that ſubject, if poſſible, you are the greateſt maſter of. When

the

4 INTRODUCTION.

the fubject is determined, you muft be careful to fix your eyes on the brighteft part of it, that when you have taken all the pains in your power to adorn it, you may have the fatisfaction to fee it appear pleafing and graceful.

In writing to a ftranger, the firft thing neceffary to be obferved is your correfpondent's ftation in life, and the ceremonies proper to be obferved, that every thing may be conducted accordingly. But, be his condition what it will, you fhould be very careful to let an air of good breeding and humanity appear in every expreffion, which will give a pleafing beauty to the whole.

When you write letters on the common concerns of life, elegance is not required ; eafe and perfpicuity are the only beauties you fhould ftudy. Write freely, but not haftily ; let your words drop from your pen, as they would from your tongue, when fpeaking deliberately on a fubject of which you are mafter, and to a perfon with whom you are intimate.

But be fure to think clofely on the fubject of your letter before you fit down to write. This is a caution which may, perhaps, appear unneceffary; but I will venture to fay, that hundreds appear ridiculous on paper, through hurry and want of thought, for one that is really fo for want of underftanding.

Before you begin any fentence, ponder the whole in your mind, and make ufe of the firft words that offer themfelves to exprefs the mean-

ing ;

INTRODUCTION.   5

ing; for they are the moſt natural, and will, in general, beſt anſwer your purpoſe. Forced expreſſions will ſpoil the eaſy flow of your diction, and render the whole ſtiff and aukward. But above all things, learn to write correct, and never fail to give your letter a careful peruſal before you ſend it. Nor ever be aſhamed to amend any thing you find amiſs, even when you have not time to tranſcribe your letter; for a blot in the writing is, by no means, ſo bad as a blunder in the ſenſe.

With regard to letters of buſineſs, they ſhould be plain, conciſe, and to the purpoſe, but, at the ſame time, full and ſufficient to expreſs your meaning; for it is a moſt ridiculous piece of vanity to write in ſo conciſe a manner as to render your letter doubtful, and perhaps unintelligible. In ſhort, your language in all letters of buſineſs, ſhould be ſo natural, that the thoughts may ſeem to have been conceived in the very words they are expreſſed in, and your ſentiments to have ſprung up naturally like the lilies of the field, whoſe natural beauty excels all the dreſs of human art.

In directing your letters to perſons who are well known, it is beſt not to be too particular; becauſe it is leſſening the perſon you direct to, by ſuppoſing him to be obſcure, and not eaſily found.

If your letter conſiſts of ſeveral paragraphs, begin every freſh, or new one, at the ſame diſtance from the left hand margin of the paper,

as

6 INTRODUCTION.

as when you began the fubject of your letter; always remembering, as you write on, to make your proper ftops, otherwife no perfon will be able to come at the fenfe or meaning of your letter; which neglect often makes *miftakes and misunderftandings;* and be careful to put a period or full ftop at the end of every paragraph, thus .

When the fubject of your letter is finifhed, conclude it with the fame addrefs as at firft ; as, *Sir, Madam,* &c. &c. and always fubfcribe your name in a larger hand than the body part of your letter.

Letters fhould be wrote on fine gilt poft paper to perfons of diftinction ; if to your equals or inferiors, you are at your own option to ufe what fort or fize you pleafe; but take care never to feal your letter with a wafer, unlefs to the latter.

When your letter is fealed, you muft write the fuperfcription, thus :

Mr.

James Juftice,

No. 34, *Broad-Way,*

New-York.

Or, if you write to a perfon in a country town, as there are feveral places of the fame name in America, be more particular in your
direc-.

INTRODUCTION. 7

direction, that your letter may not be miscarried ; as for instance :

Mr.

William Collins,

Merchant,

York-Town,

Pennsylvania.

The style of address for those persons who may be entrusted with the administration of the federal government, has been agitated in Congress; but no title have been allowed them but that of their office, viz. *The President of the United States—The Secretary of the Treasury,* &c. And it seems fit that it should be so; as best suited to the nature of a republican government.—The title of Majesty, Royal Highness, Excellency, Worshipful, and down to the humble title of Esquire, given to public officers in royal governments, seems only to beget pride or tyranny in the officers, and servility and dependence among the people. But in America, where all men are declared to be equal, those and the like titles ought to be discontinued, of which Congress have set us an example, in their communications with the public officers. The proper style of address, then, to public bodies, or officers of government, is as follows:

G. W.

8 INTRODUCTION.

G. W. Prefident of the United States.
A. H. Secretary of the Treafury.
T. J. Secretary of State.
T. M. Governor of Pennfylvania.
T. M. Chief Juftice of Pennfylvania.
W. H. Juftice of the Peace.
The Houfe of Reprefentatives of the United States.
The Houfe of Reprefentatives of the State of Pennfylvania,
And fo on; according to the perfon or body addreffed.

Some neceffary Directions *for writing correctly, and when to ufe* Capital Letters, *and when not.*

Let proper names of perfons, places, fhips, rivers, things perfonified, &c begin with a capital letter; alfo all names of profeffions, &c.

None but fubftantives, whether common, proper, or perfonal, may begin with a capital, except in the beginning, or immediately after a full ftop.

If any notable faying, or paffage of an author, be quoted in his own words, it begins with a capital, though not immediately after a period.

Let not a capital be written in the middle of a word among fmall letters.

The pronoun I, and the exclamative O, muft be written with a capital.

The long ſ muft never be inferted immediately after the fhort s, nor at the end of a word.

‿

THE

American Letter-Writer.

LETTER I.

A Son's Letter at School to his Father.

Honoured Sir,

I AM greatly obliged to you for all your favours; all I have to hope is, that the progress I make in my learning will be no disagreeable return for the same. Gratitude, duty, and a view of future advantages, all conspire to make me thoroughly fensible how much I ought to labour for my own improvement, and your satisfaction, and to shew myself, upon all occasions,

Your most obedient,

and ever dutiful Son,

ROBERT REID.

A   LETTER

14 *The complete*

LETTER II.

A Letter of Excuse to Father or Mother.

Honoured Sir, or Madam,

I AM informed, and it gives me a great concern, that you have heard an ill report of me, which I suppose, was raised by some of my school-fellows, who either envy my happiness, or by aggravating my faults, would be thought to seem less criminal themselves; though I must own I have been a little too remiss in my school-business, and am now sensible I have lost, in some measure, my time and credit thereby; but, by my future diligence, I hope soon to recover both: and to convince you that I pay a strict regard to all your commands, which I am bound to, as well in gratitude as duty, and hope I shall ever have leave, with great truth, to subscribe myself,

Your most dutiful son,
WILLIAM COLLINS.

LETTER III.

Letter from a Youth at School to his Parents.

Honoured Father and Mother.

YOUR kind letter of the 24th instant, I received in due time, and, soon after, the things you therein mentioned, by the stage, for which I return you my sincere thanks. They
came

## Letter-Writer.		15

came very opportunely for my occasions. I hope
soon to improve myself at school, though I own
it seems a little hard and irksome to me as yet ;
but my master gives me great encouragement,
and assures me, I will soon get the better of the
little difficulties that almost every boy meets
with at first, and then it will be a perfect pleasure instead of a task, and altogether as pleasant
and easy as it is now irksome and hard.

My humble duty to yourselves : and I beg the
favour of you to give my kind love to my brothers and sisters, and remember me to all my
friends and acquaintances: which is at present
all from,

Your very dutiful and obedient son,
CHARLES GOODENOUGH.

LETTER IV.

Letter from an Apprentice in Town, to his Friends in
the Country.

Honoured Father and Mother,

THE bearer, Harry Jones, came to see
me last night, and told me he should set out for
home the next morning. I was not willing to
let slip the opportunity of sending you a letter
by him, to let you know I am very well, and
like both my master and mistress, and, by what
I can yet see of it, the business extremely well,
and do intend (please God) to use my utmost
endeavours to make myself master of every
thing

thing that belongs to it, in which I ſhall have
treble ſatisfaction; firſt, in pleaſing my maſter;
ſecondly, in pleaſing my friends; and, thirdly,
in benefiting myſelf. I have but little leiſure,
nor do I want a great deal, but will take every
opportunity to let you know how I go on, and
that I am, with great gratitude,

> Your very dutiful and obedient Son,
> T. R.

LETTER V.

*From an elder Brother in the Country, to his younger
Brother put Apprentice in Philadelphia.*

I AM very glad to hear you are pleaſed
with the new ſituation into which the care of
your friends has put you; but I would have you
pleaſed not with the novelty of it, but with the
real advantage. It is natural for you to be glad
that you are under leſs reſtraint than you were;
for a maſter neither has occaſion nor inclination
to watch over a youth ſo much as his parents:
But, if you are not careful, this, although it now
gives you a childiſh ſatisfaction, may, in the
end, betray you into miſchief; nay, to your
ruin. Though your father is not in ſight, dear
brother, act always as if you were in his preſence; and, be aſſured, that what would not
offend him, will never diſpleaſe any body.

You have more ſenſe, I have often told you
ſo, than moſt perſons at your time. Now is
the opportunity of making a good uſe of it: and
take

Letter-Writer. 17

take this for certain, every right ftep you enter upon now, will be a comfort to you for life. I would have your reafon, as well as your fancy, pleafed with your new fituation, and then you will act as becomes you. Confider, brother, that the ftate of life which charms you fo at this time, will bring you into independence and affluence, and that you will, by behaving as you ought now, be at one time mafter of a houfe and family; have every thing about you at your command, and have apprentices, as well as fervants, to wait upon you. The mafter with whom you are placed was fome years ago in your fituation; and what fhould hinder you from being hereafter in his? All that is required, is patience and induftry; and thefe, brother, are a very cheap price at which to purchafe fo comfortable a condition.

Your mafter, I am told, had nothing to begin the world withal: in that he was worfe than you; for, if you behave well, there are thofe who will fet you up in a handfome manner. So you have a fufficient inducement to be good, and a reward always follows it. Brother, farewel. Obey your mafter, and be civil to all perfons; keep out of company, for boys have no occafion for it, and moft thai you will meet with is very bad. Be careful and honeft, and God will blefs you. If ever you commit a fault, confefs it at once; for the lie, in denying it, is worfe than the thing itfelf. I think I need not

fey

fay more to fo good a lad as you, to induce you to continue fo.

Your affectionate brother.

LETTER VI.

Advice from a Father to a young Beginner, what Company to chufe, and how to behave in it.

Dear Robin,

AS you are now entering into the world, and will probably have confiderable dealings in your bufinefs, the frequent occafion you will have for advice from others, will make you defirous of fingling out, among your moft intimate acquaintance, one or two, whom you would view in the light of friends.

In the choice of thefe, your utmoft care and caution will be neceffary; for, by a miftake here, you can fcarcely conceive the fatal effects you may hereafter experience. Wherefore it will be proper for you to make a judgment of thofe who are fit to be your advifers, by the conduct they have obferved in their own affairs, and the reputation they bear in the world. For he who has by his own indifcretion undone himfelf, is much fitter to be fet up as a land mark for a prudent mariner to fhun his courfes, than an example to follow.

Old age is generally flow and heavy, youth head-ftrong and precipitate: but there are old men who are full of vivacity, and young men replete

Letter-Writer.   19

plete with difcretion; which makes me rather point out the conduct than the age of the perfons with whom you fhould chufe to affociate; tho', after all, it is a never-failing good fign to me of prudence and virtue in a young man, when his feniors chufe his company; and he delights in theirs.

Let your endeavours therefore be, by all means, to confort yourfelf with men of fobriety, good fenfe, and virtue; for the proverb is an unerring one that fays, *A man is known by the company he keeps.* If fuch men you can fingle out, while you improve by their converfation, you will benefit by their advice: And be fure remember one thing, that tho' you muft be frank and unreferved in delivering your fentiments, when occafions offer; yet that you be much readier to hear than to fpeak; for to this purpofe it has been fignificantly obferved, That nature has given a man two ears, and but one tongue. Lay in therefore, by obfervation and modeft filence, fuch a ftore of ideas, that you may, at their time of life, make no worfe figure than they do; and endeavour to benefit yourfelf rather by other people's ills than your own. How muft thofe young men expofe themfelves to the contempt and ridicule of their feniors, who, having feen little or nothing of the world, are continually fhutting out, by open mouths and clofed ears, all poffibility of inftruction; and making vain the principal end of converfation, which is improvement? A filent young man makes, generally, a wife old one,

and

and never fails of being refpected by the beft and moft prudent men ; when, therefore, you come among ftrangers, hear every one fpeak before you deliver your own fentiments; by this means you will judge of the merit and capacities of your company, and avoid expofing yourfelf, as I have known many do, by fhooting out hafty and inconfiderate bolts which they would have been glad to recal, when perhaps, a filent genius in company has burft out upon them with fuch obfervations, as have ftruck confcioufnefs and fhame into the forward fpeaker, if he has not been quite infenfible of inward reproach.

I have thrown together, as they occurred, a few thoughts which may fuffice for the prefent, to fhew my care and concern for your welfare. I hope you will conftantly, from time to time, communicate to me whatever you fhall think worthy of my notice, or in which my advice may be of ufe to you ; for I have no pleafure in this life equal to that which the happinefs of my children gives me. And of this, you may be affured ; for I am, and ever muft be,

Your affectionate Father.

LETTER VII.

A young Gentleman's Letter to his Father.

Dear Father,

ACCORDING to your commands, when you left me at fchool, I hereby obey them ; and,

not

Letter-Writer.   21

not only inform you, that I am well; but also that I am happy in being placed under the tuition of so good a master, who is the best-natured man in the world; and, I am sure, was I inclinable to be an idle boy, his goodness to me would prompt me to be diligent at my study, that I might please him; besides, I see a great difference made between those that are idle and those that are diligent; idle boys being punished as they deserve, and diligent boys being encouraged: but you know, father, that I always loved my book, for you have often told me, if I intended ever to be a great man, I must learn to be a good scholar, left, when I am grown up, I should be a laughing-stock or make-game to others, for my ignorance: but I am resolved to be a scholar.

Pray give my duty to my mother, and my love to my sister.   I am, dear father,

Your most dutiful son.

L E T T E R VIII.

Another on the same Subject,

Dear Father,

AS I know you will be glad to hear from your little boy, I should be very naughty if I did not acquaint you, that I am in good health, and that I am very well pleased with my master; for he is very kind to me, and tells me, that he will always love young gentlemen that

A 2   mind

mind their learning: therefore, I am fure he
will ftill love me; becaufe you have told me,
that boys who do not mind their learning, will
never become gentlemen, and will be laughed
at for their ignorance, though they have ever
fo much money; as I am fure you always
fpeak truth, and I would willingly be a gentleman, like you, I am refolved to be a good fcholar, which, I know, will be a pleafure to you
and my mother, and gain me the love of every
body.

Pray give my duty to my mother, my uncle,
and my aunt, and my love to my fifter and
coufins.

I am, dear father,
Your moft dutiful fon.

LETTER IX.

A letter from a Nephew to an Uncle, who wrote to him
a letter of rebuke.

Honoured Sir,

I Received your kind advice, and by the
contents of your letter perceive I have been reprefented to you as one of immoral principles.
I dare not write you any excufe for the follies
and frailties of youth, becaufe, in fome meafure
I own I have been guilty of them, but not to
that degree which you have had them reprefented: however, your rebuke is not unfeafon-
able, and it fhall have the defired effect, as well

to

to fruftrate the defigns of my enemies (who aim to prejudice you againft me,) as to pleafe you, and obey all your commands and advice; which I now fincerely thank you for giving me; and promife for the future, I will make it my ftudy to reform, and regain, by adhering ftrictly to your inftructions, the good opinion you was once fo kind to entertain of me, I beg my duty to my aunt, and am,

Your moft obliged, and ever dutiful nephew.

H———M————.

L E T T E R X.

From a young Lady to her Mother, requefting a Favour.

Dear Mother,

THE many inftances you have given me of your affection, leave me no room to believe that the favour I prefume to afk will be difpleafing. Was I in the leaft doubtful of it, I hope my dear mother has too good an opinion of my conduct, to imagine I would ever advance any thing that might give her the leaft diffatisfaction.

The holidays are nigh at hand, when all of us young ladies are to pay our feveral perfonal refpects and duties to our parents, except one; whofe friends (her parents being dead,) refide at too great a diftance for her to expect their indulgence in fending for her: befides, were they to do fo, the expence attending her journey

24 *The complete*

ney would be placed to her account, and deducted out of the small fortune left her by her
parents.

This young lady's affability, sense, and good
nature, have gained her the friendship and efteem of the whole school; each of us contending to render her retirement (as I may juftly call it) from her native home and friends,
as comfortable and agreeable as we poffibly can.

How happy should I think myself above the
reft of our young ladies, if you will give me
leave to engage her to spend the holidays with
me at home! And I doubt not but her addrefs
and behaviour will attract your efteem, among
the reft of thofe she has already acquired.

Your compliance with this requeft will greatly add to the happiness I already enjoy from the
repeated indulgences and favours conferred on
her, who will always perfevere to merit the
continuance of them.   I am, with my duty to
my father,

Dear mother,

Your moft dutiful daughter.

L E T T E R XI.

To a young Lady, cautioning her againft keeping Company with a Gentleman of a bad Character.

Dear Niece,

THE fincere love and affection which I
now have for your indulgent father, and ever
had

Letter-Writer. 25

had for your virtuous mother, not long fince deceafed, together with the tender regard I have
for your future happinefs and welfare, have
prevailed on me to inform you, rather by letter
than by word of mouth, that the town rings of
your unguarded conduct, and the too great freedoms that you take with Mr. Freelove. You
have been feen with him, (if fame lies not) in
the fide boxes at the theatre; in the State-houfe
walks on Sunday nights, and afterwards at a certain tavern, not a mile from thence, which is a
houfe (as I have been credibly informed) of no
good repute. You have both, alfo, been feen at
Gray's gardens; and at Harrowgate concert.
Don't imagine, niece, that I am in the leaft prejudiced, or fpeak out of any private pique; but
let me tell you, your familiarity with him gives
me no fmall concern, as his character is none of
the beft; and as he has acted in the moft ungenerous manner by two or three very virtuous
young ladies of my acquaintance, who entertained too favourable an opinion of his honour. 'Tis
poffible, as you have no great expectations from
your relations, and as he has an income, as 'tis
reported, of 500*l.* a-year, left him by his uncle,
that you may be tempted to imagine his addrefs
an offer to your advantage. It is much to be
queftioned, however, whether, his intentions are
fincere; for, notwithftanding all the fair promifes he may poffibly make you, I have heard it
whifpered, that he is privately engaged to a rich
old doating lady not far from Frankfort. Befides,

fides, admitting it to be true, that he is really entitled to the annuity above mentioned; yet it is
too well known, that he is deep in debt; that he
lives beyond his income, and has very little, if
any regard for his reputation. In short, not to
mince the matter, he is a perfect libertine, and
is ever boafting 'of favours from our weak fex,
whofe fondnefs and frailty are the conftant topics of his railiery and ridicule.

All things therefore duly confidered, let me
prevail on you, dear niece, to avoid his company as you would a madman: for notwithftanding I ftill think you ftrictly, virtuous, yet
your good name may be irreparably loft by fuch
open acts of imprudence. As I have no other
motive but an unaffected zeal for your intereft,
and welfare, I flatter myfelf you'll put a favourable conftruction on the liberty here taken by,

Your fincere friend, and affectionate aunt,

J——N——

LETTER XII.

Letter of Thanks.

Sir,

I Received the favour of yours, with a
very kind prefent; and know not indeed, at
this time, any other way to fhew my gratitude,
than by my hearty thanks for the fame. Every
thing you do carries a charm with it; your
manner of doing it is as agreeable as the thing
done. In fhort, Sir, my heart is full, and
would

Letter-Writer. 27

would overflow with gratitude, did I not ftop, and fubfcribe myfelf, your moft obliged, and
Obedient humble fervant.

LETTER XIII.

Letter from a Niece to her Aunt.

Madam,

THE trouble I have already given you really concerns me when I think of ir, and yet I can't help intruding again upon your goodnefs ; for neceffity, that mother of invention, forces us to act contrary to our inclinations ; therefore, pray, dear aunt, excufe me, if I once more intreat your affiftance in this affair, in any manner that you fhall think proper ; and I hope, at leaft one time in my life, to be able to convince you that I have a thorough fenfe of the many obligations your goodnefs has conferred upon,
Your moft dutiful and truly obliged niece,
And very humble fervant,
J——P——

LETTER XIV.

A Letter from a Lady to her Niece, on her expreffing great uneafinefs at the lofs of her Beauty by the Small-pox.

My dear Maria,

WE muft diftinguifh thofe evils which are impofed by Providence, from thofe to which we
ourfelves

28 *The complete*

ourfelves give the power of hurting us. A fmall
part of your calamity is the infliction of heaven;
the reft is little more than the fretting of idle
difcontent. You have, indeed, loft that which
may fometimes contribute to happinefs, but to
which happinefs is by no means infeparably an-
nexed. You have loft what the greater number of the human race never have poffeffed;
what thofe on whom it is beftowed, for the
moft part, poffeffed in vain; and what you,
while it was yours, knew not how to ufe. You
have only loft early, what the laws of Nature
forbid you to keep long; and have loft it while
your mind is yet flexible, and while you have
time to fubftitute more valuable and durable ex-
cellencies. Confider yourfelf, Maria, as a being born to know, to reafon, and to act: rife
at once from your dream of melancholy, to wifdom, and to piety: you will find that there are
other charms than thofe of beauty, and other
joys than the praife of fools.

I am your affectionate aunt,

A——V——

LETTER XV.

From Mifs R. at Wilmington, to her Sifter at Carlifle.

I Have often, I may fay very often, pro-
pofed writing a long epiftle to my deareft
Sukey, and have as often been prevented. Mifs
P. was to have been the bearer of one; but,

to my great furprife fhe left me without taking leave; nay, without giving notice of her going, and I never fo much as faw her fince yefterday fe'enight, when I very agreeably fpent at M——. My uncle, whom I alfo intended to have wrote by, went away, (as you know he always does) in fuch a hurry, that I had no time to fet about writing a long letter, and a fhort one I knew would by no means atone for fuch a long filence. You complain in your laft of my writing with too much referve; for my own part I think I write with too little, when I reflect on fome particulars that my uncle ral-lied me upon before he went hence; which he never could have known, had he not feen my letters, or been acquainted with the contents of them. What fay you to that, my dear? But I forgive.——Well, but what news? fay you: I'll tell you. Laft Monday morning, a very a-greeable party, among whom was Aunt R——, met us at a fweet pleafant cottage of content near Chriftiana bridge, they brought with them a little elegant repaft, exactly fuited to the fize of the cottage, which, though but juft big enough for us to fit down in, was capable of holding a world of happinefs, as we proved; for the weather was extremely pleafant, the company perfectly harmonious, and we were all exceffively agreeble to each other; but in an inftant, for fuch a day of pleafure feemed but a moment, the ftill evening came on, and all our joys were hufhed. In fhort, about eight

o'clock

o'clock we broke up from this fweet little rural retreat, which, believe me, dear Sukey, afforded high entertainment for a day to us all. I wifhed greatly that you could have been a partaker; but, however, at your return we well attempt the like again. By the help of your company, 'tis poffible we may fucceed as well a fecond time; though I muft own that an expectation of this fort is feldom the cafe. Well, for the prefent, I will take my leave of the cote; and now for the news of the town. The firft that occurs to me is the marriage of our old miftrefs, who thought it better late than never, and laft Friday fhook hands for life with Mr. S. the draper. He is a little advanced as well as fhe, but no matter; why may there not be pleafure at the latter time of life, as well as at the beginning? Though, for my own part, I muft confefs I am not for putting happinefs off till tomorrow, if it may be as well had to-day.

But to be ferious, my dear, there is no other news all over the town worth mentioning; 'tis all as infipid as the laft difh of an old batchelor's tea. But when are we to fee you? You have long, very long, talked of returning home; pray talk no more of it, nay write no more, but inftead of your agreeable letters, let us nave your more agreeable company, and you'll moft truly oblige, 　　Your affectionate filter,

E. R.

Letter-Writer.   3¹

L E T T E R XVI.

From a Mother in the Country, to her Daughter at a Boarding-school in Town, recommending the Practice of Virtue.

Dear Child,

ALTHOUGH we are separated in person, yet you are never absent from my thoughts, and it is my continual practice to recommend you to the care of that Being. whose eyes are on all his creatures, and to whom the secrets of all hearts are open ; but I have been lately somewhat alarmed, because your two last letters did not run in that strain of unaffected piety as formerly. What, my dear, is this owing to? Does virtue appear to you unpleasant? Is your beneficent Creator a hard master, or are you resolved to embark in the fashionable follies of a gay unthinking world? Excuse me, my dear, I am a mother, and a concern for your happiness is inseparably connected with my own. Perhaps I am mistaken, and, what I have considered as a fault, may be only the effusions of youthful gaiety.—I shall consider it in that light, and be extremely glad, yea happy, to find it so. Useful instructions are never too often inculcated, and, therefore, give me leave again to put you in mind of that duty, the performance of which alone can make you happy, both in time and in eternity.

Religion,

Religion, my dear, is a dedication of the whole man to the will of God, and virtue is the actual operation of that truth, which diffuses itself through every part of our conduct: its consequences are equally beneficial as its promises: " Her ways are the ways of pleasantness, and " all her paths are peace."

Whilst the gay unthinking part of youth are devoting the whole of their time to fashionable pleasures, how happy should I be to hear, that my child was religious without hypocritical austerity, and even gay with innocence. Let me beg that you will spend at least one hour each day in perusing your Bible, and some of our best English writers, and don't imagine that religion is such a gloomy thing as some enthusiasts have represented ; no, it indulges you in every rational amusement, so far as it is consistant. with morality ;——it forbids nothing but what is hurtful.

Let me beg you will consider attentively what I have written, and send me an answer as soon as you can.

I am your affectionate mother.

LETTER XVII.

The Answer.

Honoured Madam,

I AM so much affected by the perusal of your really parental advice, that I can scarcely hold the pen to write an answer; but duty to

the

Letter-Writer. 33

the best of parents, obliges me to make you easy in your mind before I take any rest to myself. That levity so conspicuous in my former letters is too true to be denied, nor do I desire to draw a veil over my own folly. No, madam, I freely confess it; but with the greatest sincerity, I must, at the same time declare, that they were written in a careless manner, without considering the character of the person to whom they were addressed: I am fully sensible of my error, and on all future occasions, shall endeavour to avoid giving the least offence. The advice you sent me in your valuable letter, wants no encomium; all that I desire is, to have it engraven on my heart. My dear madam, I love virtue, and I hope no consideration will ever lead me from those duties, in which alone I expect future happiness. Let me beg to hear from you often, and I hope that my whole future conduct will convince the best of parents, that I am what she wishes me to be.

I am, honoured madam, your dutiful daughter.

LETTER XVIII.

From a maid Servant in Philadelphia, acquainting her Father and Mother in the Country with a proposal of Marriage, and asking their Consent.

Honoured Father and Mother,

I Think it my duty to acquaint you, that I am addressed to for change of condition, by

one

one Mr. John Brittle, who is a joiner, and lives in the neighbourhood by us. He is a young man of a sober character, and has been set up about two years: has good business for his time, and is well beloved, and spoken well of by every one. My friends here think well of it, particularly my master and mistress; and he says, he doubts not, by God's blessing on his industry, to maintain a family very prettily: and I have fairly told him, how little he has to expect with me. But I would not conclude on any thing, however, till I had acquainted you with his proposals, and asked your blessing and consent; for I am, and ever will be,

Your dutiful daughter,
ANNE LOVEGLASS.

LETTER XIX.

From the Parents, in Answer to the preceding.

Dear Nanny,

WE have received your dutiful letter. We can only pray to God to bless and direct you in all your engagements. Our distance from you must make us leave every thing to your own discretion; as you are so well satisfied in Mr. Brittle's character, as well as all friends, and your master and mistress, we give our blessing and consent with all our hearts. We are only sorry we can do no more for you. But let us know when it is done, and we will

do

Letter-Writer.　　35

do fome little matter, as far as we are able, towards houfe-keeping. Our refpects to Mr. Brittle. Every body joins with us in our wifhes for your happinefs; and God blefs you, is all that can be faid by,

　　　　Your truly loving father and mother.

LETTER XX.

From the fame, informing her Parents of her Marriage.

Honoured Father and Mother,

　　I Write to acquaint you, that laft Thurf-day I was married to Mr. Brittle, and am to go home to him in a fortnight. My mafter and miftrefs have been very kind, and have made one a prefent towards houfe-keeping, of three guineas. I had faved twenty pounds in fervice, and that is all. I told him the naked truth of every thing, and indeed, did not intend to marry fo foon; but when I had your letter, and fhewed it him, he would not let me reft till it was done. Pray do not ftraiten yourfelf out of Love to me. He joins with me in faying fo, and bids me prefent his duty to you, and tell you, that he fears not to maintain me very well. I have no reafon to doubt of being very happy. And your prayers for a bleffing on our in-duftry, will, I hope, be a means to make us more fo. We are, and ever fhall be, with ref-pects to all friends,

　　　Your moft dutiful fon and daughter.

　　　　　　LETTER

LETTER XXI.

From a young Woman, juſt gone to Service in Boſton, to
her Mother in the Country.

Dear Mother,

    I T is now a month that I have been at
Mr. Wilſon's, and thank God, that I like my
place ſo well. My maſter and miſtreſs are both
worthy people, and greatly reſpected by all
their neighbours. At my firſt coming there I
thought every thing ſtrange, and wondered to
ſee ſuch multitudes of people in the ſtreets; but
what I ſuffer moſt from is the remembrance of
your's and my father's kindneſs, but I begin to
be more reconciled to my ſtate, as I know you
were not able to ſupport me at home. I return
you a thouſand thanks for the kind advices you
were ſo good to give me at parting, and I ſhall
endeavour to practiſe them as long as I live:
let me hear from you as often as you have opportunity ; ſo, with my duty to you and my father, and kind love to all friends, I remain ever
          Your moſt dutiful daughter.

LETTER XXII.

The Mother's Anſwer.

My dear Child,

    I A M glad to hear you have got into ſo
worthy a family. You know that we never
ſhould have parted with you had it not been for
                                      your

Letter-Writer. 37

your good. If you continue virtuous and obliging, all the family will love and esteem you.
Keep yourself employed as much as you can,
and be always ready to assist your fellow-servants. Never speak ill of any body, but when
you hear a bad story, try to soften it as much
as you can; don't repeat it again, but let it
slip out of your mind as soon as possible. I am
in great hopes that all the family are kind to
you, from the good character that I have heard
of them. If you have any time to spare from
your business, I hope you will spend some part
of it in reading your Bible, and other books of
instruction. I pray for you daily, and there is
nothing I desire more than my dear child's happiness. Remember that the more faithful you
are in the discharge of your duty as a servant,
the better to you will prosper if you live to have
a family of your own. Your father desires his
blessing, and your brothers and sisters their kind
love to you. Heaven bless you my dear child!
And continue you to be a comfort to us all, and
particularly to   Your affectionate Mother.

LETTER XXIII.

*From a young Tradesman lately entered into Business, to
his Father, asking his Consent to Marry.*

Honoured Sir,

YOU know that it is now above a year
since I entered into business for myself, and find-

B   ing

38 *The complete*

ing it daily increasing, I am obliged to look out for an agreeble partner, I mean a wife: there is a very worthy family in the neighbourhood, with whom I have been some time acquainted. They are in good circumstances, and have a daughter, an amiable young woman, greatly esteemed by all who know her: I have paid my addresses to her, and likewise obtained the parents consent, on condition that it is agreeable to you. I would not do any thing of that nature without your consent; but I hope that upon the strictest enquiry you will find her such a person, that you will not have any objection to a match so advantageous. I, on every occasion, endeavour to act with the greatest prudence, consistent with the rules you were pleased to prescribe for my conduct. The parents are to pay me five hundred pounds on the day of marriage, if the event shall happen to take place; and as they have no other children, the whole of their property becomes ours at their death. In whatever light you are pleased to consider this, I shall abide by your direction, and your answer in the mean time is impatiently expected,

> By your dutiful son.

LETTER

Letter-Writer. 39

LETTER XXIV.

From a Brother to a Sister in the Country, upbraiding
her for being negligent in Writing.

My dear Sister,

I Write to you to acquaint you how un-
kindly we all take it here, that you do not write
oftener to us, in relation to your health, diversions, and employment in the country. You cannot be insensible how much you are beloved by
us all ; judge then if you do well to omit giving
us the satisfaction absence affords to true friends,
which is, often to hear from one another. My
mother is highly disobliged with you, and says
you are a very idle girl ; my aunt is of the same
opinion ; and I would fain, like a loving brother, excuse you if I could. Pray for the future, take care to deserve a better character,
and by writing soon and often, put it in my
power to say what a good sister I have : for you
shall always find me

Your most affectionate brother.

P. S. Due respects of every one here to my
aunt, and all friends in the country.

LETTER

40   *The complete*

LETTER XXV.

From the Daughter to her Mother, in Excuse for her
Neglect.

Honoured Madam,

I AM afhamed I ftaid to be reminded of
my duty by my brother's kind letter. I will
offer no excufe for myfelf; for not writing oftener, though I have been ftrangely taken up
by the kindnefs and favour of your good friends
here, particularly my aunt Windus: for well
do I know, that my duty to my honoured mother ought to take place of all other confiderations. All I beg therefore is, that you will be
fo good as to forgive me, on premife of amendment, and to procure forgivenefs alfo of my
aunt Rutledge, and all friends. Believe me
madam, when I fay that no diverfions here or
elfewhere fhall, make me forget the duty I owe
to fo good a mother, and fuch kind relations;
and that I fhall ever be

Your gratefully dutiful daughter.

P. S. My aunt and coufins defire their kind
love to you, and due refpects to all friends.
Brother John has great reputation with every
one for his kind letter to me.

LETTER

Letter-Writer. 41

L E T T E R XXVI.

To a young Trader generally in a Hurry in Bufinefs, advifing Method as well as Diligence.

Dear Nephew,

    T H E affection I have always borne you,
as well for your own fake, as for your late father's and mother's makes me give you the trouble of thefe lines, which I hope you will receive
as kindly as I intend them.

    I have lately called upon you feveral times,
and have as often found you in an extraordinary hurry; which I well know cannot be fometimes avoided ; but, methinks, need not be always the cafe, if your time were difpofed in
regular and proper proportions to your bufinefs.
I have frequently had reafon to believe, that
more than half the flutter which appears among
traders in general, is rather the effect of their
indolence, that their induftry ; however willing they are to have it thought otherwife ; and
I will give you one inftance, in confirmation of
this opinion, in a neighbour of mine.

    This gentleman carried on, for fome years,
a profitable bufinefs; but indulging himfelf every evening in a tavern fociety, or club, which
the promotion of bufinefs (as is ufually the cafe)
give the firft pretence for, he looked upon thofe
engagements as the natural confequence of the
approach of night : and drove on his bufinefs in

B 2   the

the day with precipitation, that he might get thither with the earlieſt. He ſeldom kept very late hours, though he never came home ſoon. The night being gone, and his bottle emptied, the morning was always wanted to diſpel the fumes of the wine. Whoever therefore came to him before nine, was deſired to call again; and when he roſe, ſo many matters waited for him, as directly threw him into a flutter; ſo that from his riſing till dinner-time he ſeemed in one continued ferment. A long dinner-time he always allowed himſelf, in order to recover the fatigues he had undergone; and all his ta-ble-talk was, how heavy his buſineſs lay upon him! and what pains he took in it! The hear-ty meal and the time he indulged himſelf at ta-ble, begot an unfitneſs for any more buſineſs for that ſhort afternoon; ſo all that could be de-ferred, was put off to the next morning; and the longed for evening approaching, he flies to his uſual ſolace: empties his bottle by eleven; comes home; gets to bed; and is inviſible till next morning, at nine; and then riſing, enters upon his uſual hurry and confuſion.

Thus did his life ſeem to thoſe who ſaw him in his buſineſs, one conſtant ſcene of fatigue, though he ſcarce ever applied to it four regular hours in any one day. Whereas, had he riſen only at ſeven in the morning, he would have got all his buſineſs under by noon; and thoſe two hours, from ſeven to nine, being before many people go abroad, he would have met

with

Letter-Writer.   43

with no interruption in his affairs; but might have improved his servants by his own example, directed them in the business of the day, have inspected his books, written to his dealers, and put every thing in so regular a train, for the rest of the day, that whatever had occured afterwards, would rather have served to divert than fatigue him.

And what, to cut my story short, was the upshot of the matter? Why meeting with some disappointments and losses (as all traders must expect, and ought to provide for) and his customers not seeing him in his shop so much as they expected, and when there, always in a disobliging petulent hurry; and moreover, mistakes frequently happening through the flurry into which he put himself and every one about him; by these means his business dwindled away insensibly, and not being able to go out of his usual course, which helped to impair both his capacity and ardour for his business, his creditors began to look about them, and he was compelled to enter into the state of his affairs; and then had the mortification to find the balance of 1000l. against him.

This was a shocking case to himself; but more to his family; for his wife had lived, and his children had been educated, in such a manner, as induced them to hope their fortunes would be sufficient to place them in a state of independence.

In short, being obliged to quit a business, he
had

44 *The complete*

had managed with fo little prudence, his friends
got him upon a charitable foundation, which afforded him bare fubfiftence for himfelf; his
children were difperfed fome one way and fome
another, into low fcenes of life; and his wife
went home to her friends, to be fnubbed and
reflected on by her own family, for faults not
her own.

This example will afford feveral good hints
to a young tradefman, which are too obvious to
need expatiating upon. And as I dare fay,
your prudence will keep you from the like fault,
you will never have reafon to reproach yourfelf on this fcore. But yet, as I always found
you in a hurry, when I called upon you, I
could not but give you this hint, for fear you
fhould not rightly proportion your time to your
bufinefs, and left you fhould fufpend to the next
hour, what you could and ought to do in the prefent, and fo did not keep your bufinefs properly
under. Method is every thing in bufinefs, next
to diligence. And you will, by falling into a
regular one, always be calm and unruffled, and
have time to beftow in your fhop with your cuftomers; the female ones efpecially; who always love to make a great many words in their
bargainings, and expect to be humoured and
perfuaded; and how can any man find time for
this, if he prefers the tavern to his fhop, and
his bed to his bufinefs? I know you will take in
good part what I have written, becaufe you are
fenfible how much I am

           Your truly affectionate, &c.

Letter-Writer.   45

LETTER XXVII.

To a Friend, on his Recovery from a dangerous Illness,

Dear Sir.

GIVE me leave to mingle my joy with that of all your friends and relations, in the recovery of your health, and to join with them to bless God for continuing to your numerous well wishers the benefit of your useful and valuable life. May God Almighty long preserve you in health, and prosper all your undertakings, for the good of your worthy family, and the pleasure of all your friends and acquaintance, is the hearty prayer of, sir,

Your faithful friend, and humble servant,

LETTER XXVIII,

On the same Occasion.

Good Sir,

I Have received, with great delight, the good news of your recovery from the dangerous illness with which it pleased God to afflict you. I most heartily congratulate you and your good lady and family upon it; and make it my prayer, that your late indisposition may be succeeded by such a renewal of health and strength, both of body and mind, as may make your life equally happy to yourself, as it must be to all

who

46 *The complete*

who have the pleafure to know you. I could not avoid giving you this trouble, to teftify the joy that affected my heart on the occafion: and to affure you, that I am, with the greateft affection and refpect, fir,

Your faithful humble fervant.

LETTER XXIX.

In Anfwer to the preceding.

Dear Sir,

I Give you many thinks for your kind congratulations. My return of health will be greater pleafure to me, if I can contribute in any meafure to the happinefs of my many good friends; and, particularly, to that of you and yours; for I affure you, fir, that no body can be more than I am,

Your obliged humble fervant.

LETTER XXX.

From a Father to a Son, on his Negligence in his Affairs.

Dear Jemmy,

Y O U cannot imagine what a concern your careleffnefs and indifferent management of your affairs give me. Remiffnefs is inexcufable in all men, but in none fo much as in a man of bufinefs, the of foul which is induftry, diligence, and punctuality.

Let

Letter-Writer. 47

Let me beg of you to ſhake off the idle habits you have contracted; quite unprofitable company, and unſeaſonable recreations, and apply to your compting-houſe with diligence. It may not yet be too late to retrieve your affairs. Inſpect therefore your gains and caſt up what proportion they bear to your expences; and then ſee which of the latter you can, and which you cannot contract. Conſider, that when once a man ſuffers himſelf to go backward in the world, it muſt be an uncommon ſpirit of induſtry that retrieves him, and puts him forward again.

Reflect, I beſeech you, before it be too late, upon the inconveniencies which an impoveriſhed trader is put to, for the ramainder of his life ; which, too, may happen to be the prime part of it ; the indignities he is likely to ſuffer from thoſe whoſe money he has unthinkingly ſquandered ; the contempt he will meet with from all, not excepting the idle companions of his folly ; the injuſtice he does his family, in depriving his children, not only of the power of raiſing themſelves, but of living tolerably; and how, on the contrary, from being born to a creditable expectation, he ſinks them into the loweſt claſs of mankind, and expoſes them to the moſt dangerous temptations. What has not ſuch a father to anſwer. for ! and all this for the ſake of indulging himſelf in an idle, a careleſs, a thoughtleſs habit, that cannot afford the leaſt ſatisfaction, beyond the preſent hour, if in that ;

and

and which muft be attended with deep remorfe, when he comes to reflect. Think ferioufly of thefe things, in time refolve on fuch a courfe as may bring credit to yourfelf, juftice to all you deal with, peace and pleafure to your own mind, comfort to your family; and which will give at the fame time the higheft fatisfaction to
Your careful and loving father.

LETTER XXXI.

The Son's grateful Anfwer.

I Return you my fincere thanks for your feafonable reproof and advice. I have indeed too much indulged myfelf in an idle carelefs habit, and had already begun to feel the evil confequences of it, when I received your letter; in the infults of a creditor or two, from whom I expected kinder treatment. But indeed they wanted but their own, fo I could only blame myfelf, who had brought their rough ufage upon me. Your letter came fo feafonably upon this, that I hope it will not want the defired effect; and as, I thank God, it is not yet too late, I am refolved to take another courfe with myfelf and my affairs, that I may avoid the ill confequences you fo judicioufly forewarn me of, and give to my family and friends the pleafure they fo well deferve at my hands; and particularly that fatisfaction to fo good a father, which is owing to him by His moft dutiful fon.

LETTER

Letter-Writer. **49**

LETTER XXXII.

From a Country Merchant beginning Trade, to a City
Dealer, offering his Correspondence.

Sir,

  THE time of my apprenticeship with Mr.
Walker of this town being expired, I am just
going to begin for myself, in Chambersburg;
having taken a shop there for that purpose. And
as I know the satisfaction you always gave to
my master in your dealings, I make an offer to
you of my correspondence, in expectation that
you will use me as well as you have done him,
in whatever I may write to you for. Walker
will not be offended by it, because of the distance
I shall be from him; and I shall endeavour to
give you equal content with regard to my payments, &c. Your speedy answer, whether or
not you are disposed to accept of my offer, will
oblige   Your humble servant.

LETTER XXXIII.

In Answer to the foregoing.

Sir,

  I Have received yours of October 20th,
and very chearfully accept the favour you offer
me. I will take care to serve you in the best
manner I am able, and on the same footing

      C   with

with Mr. Walker, not doubting you will make
as punctual returns as he does; which entitles
him to a more favourable usage than could o-
therwise be afforded.   I wish you success with
all my heart, and am,

Your obliged servant.

LETTER XXXIV.

A pressing and angry Letter from a City Dealer, to his
Correspondent in the Country.

Mr. Thompson,

   I AM sorry your ill usage constrains me to
write to you in the most pressing manner. Can
you think it is possible to carry on business after
the manner you act by me? You know what
promises you have made me, and how, from
time to time, you have broken them; and can
I depend upon any new ones you make? If you
use others as you do me, how can you think of
carrying on business? if you do not, what must
I think of a man, who deals worse with me
than he does with any body else? if you think
you may trespass more upon me, than you can
upon others, that is a very bad compliment to
my prudence, or your own gratitude; for surely good usage should be entitled to good usage.
I know how to allow for disappointments as
well as any man; but, can a man be disappointed for ever? trade is so dependent a thing, you
know, that it cannot be carried on without mutual

Letter-Writer.   5t

tual punctuality. Does not the merchant expect
it from me, for thofe very goods I fend you?
And can I make a return to him without receiving it from you? what end can it anfwer to give
you two years credit, and then be at an uncertainty, for goods, which I fell at a fmall profit,
and have not fix months credit for myfelf? indeed, Sir, this will never do; I muft be more
punctually ufed by you, or elfe muft deal with as
little punctuallity with others; and what then
muft be the confequence? In fhort, Sir, I expect
a handfome payment by the next return, and fecurity for the remainder; and fhall be very loath
to take any harfh methods to procure this juftice
to myfelf, my family, and my own creditors.
For I am, if it be not your own fault,

Your faithful friend and fervant.

L E T T E R   XXXV.

In Anfwer to the preceding.

Sir,

I Muft acknowledge I have not ufed you
well, and can give no better anfwer to your juft
expoftulations, than to fend you the inclofed
draught for fifty pounds, which you will be
pleafed to carry to my credit; and to affure you
of more punctual treatment for the future. Your
letter is no bad leffon to me; I have conned it
often, and hope I fhall improve by it. I am ready to give you my bond for the remainder,

which

which I will keep paying every month something till all is difcharged; and what I write to you for in the interim, fhall be paid for on receipt of the goods. This, I hope, Sir, will fatisfy you for the prefent. If I could do better, I would, but fhall be ftraitened to do this: but, I think, in return for your patience, I cannot do lefs, to convince you that I am now, at laft, in earneft. I beg you will continue to me the fame good ufage and fervice I have met with from you hitherto; and that you will believe me to be, unfeignedly,

Your obliged humble fervant.

LETTER XXXVI.

From an Infolvent Debtor, to defire the Acceptance of a Compofition.

Sir,

IT is with the greateft concern I now inform you, that fome loffes I have lately fuffered ender it impoffible for me to carry on bufinefs ny longer. I am forry, Sir, that your debt is o large, and the compofition I am able to make) fmall; for I am able to pay but five fhillings 1 the pound. I have, however, the comfort f being confcious that my intentions were always honeft, and that it would have given the igheft pleafure to me, fully to have difcharged very debt I have contracted. If, upon the ifpection of my books, you will accept of fuch

a

Letter-Writer.   53

a dividend as I am able to make, my other creditors, I have reafon to hope; will follow your
example. They are to have a meeting next
Tuefday at the Bunch of Grapes, and a favourable line from you, who is my principal creditor, will have much weight with them, and lay
me under the greateft obligation; and I fhall
think myfelf bound in honour and confcience, if
ever Providence fhould place me in a profperous fituation, to make good what you and my
other creditors will lofe by accepting the compofition.   I am, Sir,
Your moft unhappy, and moft humble fervant.

L E T T E R XXXVII.

The Anfwer.

Sir,

    I A M really concerned for your unhappy
fituation, and readily confent to accept of the
compofition you mention. I have appointed
Mr. Lawfon, a very honeft attorney of your
town, to act for me in your affairs, and have
wrote to him accordingly. I always thought
you a very honeft man, and have defired him
to exert himfelf in your behalf with your other
creditors, in order to bring them to amicable
terms. He is alfo to examine your books, and
to make fuch enquiries as he fhall judge necefla-
ry; and if every thing turns out as I wifh, I
                       shall

54 *The complete*

fhall readily give you frefh credit. I heartily wifh you better days, and am,

Your real friend,
WILLIAM LEWIS.

LETTER XXXVIII.

An offer of Affiftance to a Friend, who had received great Lofs by a Perfon's Failure.

Dear Sir,

I AM exceedingly concerned at the great lofs you have lately fuftained by the failure of Mr. Potts, I hope you behave under it like the man of prudence you have always fhown your-felf, and as one who knows how liable all men are to misfortunes. As I am really defirous of giving you confolation, I chearfully offer my fervice to anfwer any prefent demand, and you are at liberty to draw upon me to the amount of 200l. which you may have the ufe of for a twelvemonth or more, if your affairs require in. In accepting of which you will give great plea-fure to   Your fincere friend.

LETTER XXXIX.

The Friend's Anfwer, on accepting the generous Offer

My dear Friend,

I AM at a lofs to find words to exprefs the grateful fenfe I have of this inftance of true ge nerou

Letter-Writer. 55

ıerous friendſhip. My loſs indeed is heavy; but
find that ſo kind a friend is capable of making
t light. I thankfully accept of a part of your
generous offer, and am ready to give you my
ɔond for 100l. payable in a year. This ſum is
ıll I ſhall have occaſion for; and if I did not
ſnow I could then return it, I would not accept
ɔf your favour. I am, dear ſir,

Your moſt faithful,

and obliged humble ſervant.

LETTER XL.

The ſame Offer being alſo made to another Friend, who
had no occaſion for the Money, he returned the following Anſwer.

Sir,

I Return you a thouſand thanks for you
generous offer. I have, indeed, been much affected at the unexpected failure of a man, whom
I thought in very happy circumſtances; but at
preſent have no occaſion for your friendly aſſiſtance. If I ſhould, I know no one in the world
to whom I would ſooner chooſe to be obliged.
I am, ſir, with the warmeſt gratitude,

Your moſt obliged,

and moſt humble ſervant.

LETTER

56 *The complete*

LETTER XLI.

Upon the Death of a near Friend, from a Relation.

Dear Madam,

THOUGH I am fenfible that to a real grief nothing can be fo impertinent as the ceremony of condolence, yet I think from relations and friends fo ftrictly united as we have been, fomething may be allowed, becaufe a great deal is required of them. When I judge by myfelf, I confider with what diftafte and averfion I fhould view the ceremony of condolance from thofe who neither knew the deceafed enough, nor cared enough for me, to be concerned about it; yet, when I confider how true a fatisfaction any notice from you would be in that melancholy fituation; nay, when I recollect (for it affuredly would be fo) that this would be one of the greateft comforts of which I was capable, I cannot deny myfelf the mournful indulgence of writing to you.

I am not about to blame that forrow which fhuts you from the day-light, and from the company even of your neareft friends; the caufe is worthy of it; and you owe no lefs to his memory, who would have paid no lefs to yours. Do to his remembrance this juftice; but remember, when you have paid the tribute, that fomething is alfo due to yourfelf; or could you fuppofe that you might neglect that, to your children.

You

Letter-Writer.   57

You have no right to impair your own health; and in a constitution so tender as yours, this is easily done; nor had you, could you answer it to those who want a guide and guardian, and who can have none so interested in their good, or so able to promote it as you, if you neglect any care of yourself.

I know to reason with you, would be to engage with an antagonist too powerful for me on any occasion; but I also know, that when I press this on you as a duty, and assuredly I have a right so to do, you will be convinced and yield to the superiority of the cause. Dear cousin, we are all interested in this, and therefore you must give me leave to press the consideration upon you. Discharge your duty to the dead, but remember you owe it also to the living; and that these little ones have a claim to your care of your own health. I shall say no more: perhaps, less would have become me better; but you will excuse a fault, if it be one, which has so honest a motive. Give me leave to assure you, that none is more solicitous of your welfare than,

Dear madam,

Your most obedient and humble servant.

58 *The complete*

LETTER XLII.

To a Friend, whofe Indifcretion had engaged him in a Difpute likely to end in Law.

Dear Charles,

I Take the liberty of writing to you, though I know beforehand my letter muft be difagreeable ; but it is to ferve, and not humour, you in a thing where you are wrong. You know I was prefent when there happened to pafs fome words between you and Mr. Nicholas, and I hear fince that he has been confulting an attorney, to know if what you faid was not actionable. You never have been at law, elfe you would be in more care than you feem about it. Take it for granted, trying a caufe is like boxing out a difpute ; which ever gets the better, both are heartily beaten.

As to the words you faid, they certainly reflected upon his character, and, therefore, you may depend upon it, he will have his remedy, I grant you it was all true you fpoke ; but that is the reafon why he feels fo much. People are always nicelt about their characters who have no characters at all.

I fay all this to you firft, dear Charles, that you may take my advice about your conduct. I would have you make it up by any means in the world, before it goes farther. Afk his pardon at the Club where you fpoke it, own you

was

Letter-Writer.　　59

was in liquor, or you would not have faid it: and if this will not do, offer him ten pounds to drop it; for he is a dirty fellow, and will take it. It is more, perhaps, than he would get by a verdict, but then it would coft you an hundred.

I know, dear Charles, you are of a paffionate temper, and you will not be ready to give up a point, efpecially when you are in the right; but, it is better to do that, than be plagued with a law-fuit that will take up all your time, and coft you heaven knows what into the bargain. Do be advifed, and get the better of yourfelf, though you are in the right; for, it is much better to do fo, than to be ruined by one's obftinacy. I beg you will do as I defire you, for your family's fake, for, if you once get into the lawyer's hands, you know not what will be the end of it.

> I am,
> 　Dear Charles,
> 　　Your friend and fervant.

LETTER XLIII.

The Anfwer.

My dear Friend,

I Received your letter, and am convinced you are in the right. It is the moft unfortunate thing in the world to have to do with bad people

60. *The complete*

ple in any refpect, and nothing is worfe than to quarrel with them. I am fure all I faid was true, and I can bring proof of it: but, notwith-ftanding that, I am fenfible of the prudence of your advice, and am refolved to follow it. I am willing to do any thing that is neceffary to make up the matter; and will give more mo-ney than you mention, if that be neceffary; but I do not know how to fpeak to the fellow my-felf. As you have been fo kind in your advice, I beg you will talk to him. Whatever your fettle with him I will agree to; and fhall al-ways remember how much I am obliged to your friendfhip. I am, dear fir,

Your moft humble fervant.

LETTER XLIV.

From a Perfon in Trade to his late Mafter, on Account of a bad Debt.

Honoured Sir,

THERE is but one thing in the manage-ment of my bufinefs, in which I find myfelf now at a lofs for your inftruction; but there is no one to whom I can fo properly apply for ad-vice. The only part of your conduct, of which you left me uninformed, was that with refpect to the getting in of your bills; and this I am fenfible the fecrecy that is due to thofe who are indebted is a fufficient reafon never to divulge. I beg you, however, now, fir, to inftruct me

in

Letter-Writer.   61

in my own affairs, although I had no right to enquire into yours. I am in great uneasiness about a debt that is due to me, and I will relate the circumstances. The person I have trusted so deeply is a physician; he seems to be considerably in business, and is very much respected by every body; but I have heard some whispers that he has answered some demands but very indifferently. A part of my debt is money lent out of pocket. This I can less afford to lose than the money due in trade; and the time of payment is elapsed a considerable time ago. I have asked him more than once, and he has put me off for a certain time, and when that time is expired, I am not at all nearer than I was. I must confess that it would be a very difficult thing for me to spare the money, and I beg you'll tell me what step I should take. I hope you will not, sir, take amiss this application, for I believe there is no person who wishes me better than you do. I return you my humble thanks for your many favours, and am,

Sir, your most obedient,

and humble servant.

LETTER XLV.

The Answer,

Dear William,

THERE is one very good rule I shall give you about what you ask, and that is, to

take

62 *The complete*

take care never to make bad debts. I affure
you, this has been the great fecret of my conduct, and I owe what fuccefs I have had in the
world more to this than to any thing elfe whatever. Nobody in trade ever refufed fo many
cuftomers as I have done; but, William, one
bad debt runs away with the profit of many
good ones; for this reafon, I have lefs experience than you think in thefe matters, but I fhall
give you my advice as well as I can.

I am not of opinion you fhould arreft the gentleman by any means. It is a very good method where people have money and will not
pay: but there are two reafons againft it in
fuch a cafe as you fpeak of; it is cruel, and it
anfwers no purpofe. Inftead of getting the
money now, it will prevent his ever being a-
ble to pay you at all; for a man that has nothing but his bufinefs, will never make much of
that in the walls of a prifon. Never lend money to your cuftomers for the future; for it is a
common maxim, and it is too true, that thofe
who borrow money feldom pay it.

I would have you depend in this matter upon frequent afking for your money; and tell
the gentleman that you are diftreffed in your
own circumftances. I have known fome people, who, when they were uneafy about a large
debt, have infifted upon the debtor's finding
fome perfons to be fecurity that he would pay
them; this is getting bail without going to law;
but, I believe, it is very feldom that they are

able

Letter-Writer. 63

able to obtain this. A man would sooner bid them do their worst, and give in bail to an action, because he can then pretend some dispute about the demand, and it is an excuse for delay, and the law will give him as much time as the creditor is generally inclined to allow ; for, if you arrest the gentleman to-morrow, you would not be able to recover your money this twelve-month ; nay, most likely, you would never get it at all, for the law allows all that delay ; and then the debtor, if he cannot pay, may take the benefit of the bankrupt act.

Take, care, William, how you have any dealings, for the future, with people that are at all dubious ; if you get them into your books, never let them get far ; and, whatever you do, never lend money to those who are in your debt already. These are the best rules I can give for your future conduct ; as for the present, it is my opinion, the best way is to dun continually. Plead the necessity of your own affairs ; and take any thing if it be ever so little at a time : he will find that he is obliged to you not to distress him farther ; and, as you never design to do it, never threaten ; this is the greatest folly of all in a creditor ; if he designs to proceed to law, he never should tell the person of it beforehand, for it is bidding him keep out of the way ; and if he does not intend to do it, it is only making him hate him as well as fear him, and never answers any purpose. By civil behaviour and constant application, you
will

64 *The complete*

will get in your money by degrees, as faft as he can pay it, and, in the mean while, you will have him for a cuftomer with ready money.

I have wrote you a long letter; but, as you afked my advice, I was willing to give you my reafons for it: befides, I think, you have a right to know every thing that I do, relating to trade; and, if you had not, I have a refpect for you that would make me comply with any fuch requeft, or readily do any thing to ferve you.   I am, your faithful friend.

LETTER XLVI.

A Letter from a man Servant in New-York, to his Mafter in the Country.

Sir,

AS I find you are detained longer in the country than you expected, I thought it my duty to acquaint you that we are all well at home; and to affure you that your bufinefs fhall be carried on with the fame care and fidelity as if you were perfonally prefent. We all wifh for your return as foon as your affairs will permit; and it is with pleafure that I take this opportunity of fubfcribing myfelf, fir,

Your moft obedient and faithful fervant.

LETTER

Letter-Writer.   65

L E T T E R ᵼXLVII.

To an Acquaintance to borrow a Sum of Money for a little Time.

Dear Sir,

IF it be quite convenient and agreeable to you, I will beg the favour of you to lend me fifty pounds for the space of three months precisely; any security that you shall require, and I can give, you may freely ask. A less time would not suit me; a longer, you may depend on it, I shall not desire. Your answer will oblige, sir,

Your very humble servant,

J——R——.

L E T T E R XLVIII.

An Answer to the foregoing.

Dear Sir,

ANY thing in my power is always very much at your service; the sum you mention I have now by me, and can very conveniently spare it for the time you fix, and you are most heartily welcome to it. Any hour that you shall appoint to-morrow I will be ready: and am with the greatest sincerity, your affectionate friend and humble servant,

R——M——.

L E T T E R

66 *The complete*

LETTER XLIX.

From a Tradesman to a Correspondent, requesting the Payment of a Sum of Money.

Sir,

A Very unexpected demand that has been made on me for money, which I was in hopes of keeping longer in my trade, obliges me to apply for your affiftance of the balance of the account between us, or as much of it as you can fpare. When I have an opportunity to inform you of the nature of this demand, and the neceffity of my difcharging it, you will readily excufe the freedom I now take with you ; and as it is an affair of fuch confequence to my family, I know the friendfhip you bear me will induce you to ferve me effectually.

I am, fir, your moft obedient fervant,

TIMOTHY JONES.

LETTER L.

The Anfwer.

Sir,

IT gives me fingular fatisfaction that I have it in my power to anfwer your demand, and am able to ferve a man I fo much efteem. The balance of the account is two hundred pounds; for half of which I have procured a

bank

bank note, and for fecurity divided it, and fent one half by the carrier, as you defired, and have here inclofed the other. I wifh you may furmount this and every other difficulty that lies in the road to happinefs; and am,

Sir, Yours, &c.

LETTER LI.

To an intimate Acquaintance to borrow Money.

PRAY favour me, Charles, with twenty guineas, by the bearer, who is my fervant. I have immediate occafion; but will repay it again whenever you pleafe to make a demand. This letter will anfwer all the purpofes of a note; from your obliged humble fervant,

W——D——.

LETTER LII.

From a young Perfon in Trade to a Wholefale-dealer, who had fuddenly made a Demand on him.

Sir,

YOUR demand coming very unexpectedly, I muft confefs I am not prepared to anfwer it. I know the ftated credit of this article ufed to be only four months; but as it has been a cuftom to allow a moderate time beyond this, and as this is only the day of the old time, I had not yet prepared myfelf. Sir, I beg you will

will not suppose it is any deficiency more than
for the present, that occasions my desiring a little more time of you; and I shall not ask any
more than is usual among the trade. If you will
pleased to let your servant call for one half of
the sum this day three weeks, and the remainder a fortnight afterwards, it shall be ready.
However, in the mean time, I beg of you not
to let any word slip of this because a very little
hurts a young beginner. Sir, you may take the
greatest safety, that I will pay you as I have
mentioned; and if you have any particular
cause for insisting on it sooner, be pleased to let
me know that I must pay it, and I will endeavour to borrow the money; for if I want credit with you, I cannot suppose that I have lost
it with all the world, not knowing what it is
that can have given you these distrustful thoughts
concerning   Your humble servant.

LETTER LIII.

The Wholesale-dealer's Answer.

Sir,

  I Am very sorry to press you; but if I
had not reason, I should not have called upon
you. It is not of any disrespect to you that I
have made the demand, but we have so many
losses, that it is fit we should take care. However, there is so much seeming frankness and
sincerity in your letter, that I shall desire leave
           first

Letter-Writer.   69

First to afk you, whether you any have dealings with an ufurer in High-ftreet; and, if you pleafe, what is his name? until you have given me the fatisfaction on this head, I fhall not any farther urge the demand I have made upon you; but, as this may be done at once, I defire your anfwer by the bearer, whom you well know; for he lwas, as he informs me, very lately your fervant.

I affure you, fir, it is in confideration of the great opinion I have for your honour, that I refer the demand I have made, to this queftion: for it is not cuftomary, and is fuppofed not to be fair or prudent, to mention our reafons on thefe occafions. If this is cleared up to me, fir, as I wifh, but I fear it cannot be, I fhall make no fcruple of the time you mention. I beg your anfwer without delay, and am fincerely,

Your friend and well-wifher.

LETTER LIV.

Letter of Advice to a Perfon in Trade, from his Mafter to whom he ferved his Apprenticefhip.

Dear William,

YOU will forgive me that I addrefs you by a name which calls up my remembrance of your good qualities, though Mr. Aylworth might feem a title of more refpect; I mean this as a name of friendfhip: befides, I defign

to

70   *The complete*

to advise you, and therefore, may be supposed still to keep up something of the matter.

I meet with you at the Coffee-house every day, and you seem to be the busiest men at the place; I know your affairs cannot be so very numerous there; nor, indeed, are they who have the most numerous, those who one sees in the greatest bustle in transacting them. I am afraid you confuse yourself in all this bustle; and fearing that I have, in this article, omitted to give you the due instruction while you was with me, I hold it an act of duty, as well as friendship, to do it now. I believe you have seldom seen me perplexed and hurried by my business; and yet nobody knows better than you how considerable a share I have had of it; and you know also that I have gone through it well. The method I used was always to set down in the morning what was to be done in the day, and the order in which it was to be done; and he that does this will never have any trouble, because he will always be doing only one thing at a time, and he will know what to do next.

If you only remember, in a general manner, that you have such and such things to do, you will be confused which to set about next, and leave half of them undone; but, if you bestow one quarter of an hour thus in the morning, you will never be hurried in the rest of the day. You will know three things that contain all the secrets of business; first, what you have to do that day; secondly, how much of it you can do

and

Letter-Writer. 71

and, thirdly, what time to fet about each part of it.

I am under fome concern to fee you pufhing every body about at the Coffee-houfe, and all in a heat and hurry the whole time ; when you fee **Mr.** Gordon, who has a hundred times your bufinefs, walking about as leifurely as if he was in his compting-houfe, and yet doing it all ; while yours is left undone, though there is fo little of it.

I hope you will take this friendly, as it was meant, and as you ufed to obferve me when it was a duty, that you will now do it by choice.

I am, your fincere friend.

LETTER LV.

Fom a Perfon in Trade to his late Mafter, thanking him for friendly Advice.   In Anfwer to the former.

Sir,

I Would be wanting in civility, as well as gratitude, if I did not take the firft opportunity of returning you my thanks, for your kind advice; Sir, I look upon it as the greateft obligation, and fhall obey it ftrictly. I have been ufed to hear perfons fay, that when the doctor knows the difeafe, he is half way towards the cure of it ; and this, I affure you, is fairly the cafe between you and me. I am fenfible that what you fay is exactly the cafe with me, and

I fhall

I fhall begin to morrow to purfue the courfe which you prefcribe for the cure.

I do not wonder you have taken notice of my hurry; I have been many times afhamed of it, but I never knew to what it was owing till you told me. I fhall fhew my gratitude in the beft manner by avoiding it for the future, and I am with the greateft fincerity,

Sir, your moft obliged fervant.

LETTER LVI.

Recommending a man Servant.

Sir,

THE bearer has ferved me with integrity and fidelity thefe three years, but having a defire to fettle in Philadelphia, he left my houfe about a week ago, and by a letter received from him this day, I find you are willing to employ him on my recommendation; and it is with the greateft pleafure that I comply with his requeft, His behaviour while with me was ftrictly honeft, fober, and diligent, and I doubt not but it will be the fame with you. I have fent this inclofed in one to himfelf, and if you employ him I hope he will give fatisfaction.

I am, fir, your humble fervant.

LETTER

LETTER LVII.

The Answer.

Sir,

I Received your obliging letter in recommendation of the young man; and in consequence of that have taken him into my family. I doubt not, from what you say, of his giving satisfaction, and you may be assured of his being treated with humanity, and rewarded according to his merit.

I am, Your humble servant.

LETTER LVIII.

From a Tenant to his Landlord in Excuse of Delay of Payment.

Sir,

I Have been a tenant above ten years in the house where I now live, and you know that I have never failed to pay my rent quarterly when due. At present I am extremely sorry to inform you, that from a variety of losses and disappointments I am under the necessity of begging that you will indulge me one quarter longer. By that time I hope to have it in my power to answer your just demand, and the favour shall be very gratefully acknowledged by your Obedient humble servant.

D LETTE

74 *The complete*

LETTER LIX.

From a Tradeſman in diſtreſſed Circumſtances deſiring a Letter of Licence.

Sir,

IT is now about ten years ſince I firſt had
dealings with you, and during that time you
well know that I always paid you regularly;
but at preſent I am ſorry that my affairs are ſo
perplexed, that it is not in my power to comply with the juſt demands of my creditors, nor
even to pay them any thing, until my affairs are
ſettled: for that reaſon, ſir, I have ſent to you,
deſiring a letter of licence only for twelve
months, in which time I hope to be able to ſettle my affairs to their ſatisfaction; but if they
will not comply with this, I am utterly ruined.
Your anſwer is impatiently expected by

Your obedient humble ſervant.

LETTER LX.

Adviſing a Friend againſt going to Law.

Dear Sir,

I Am ſorry to hear, that the difference
between you and Mr. Archer is at laſt likely to
be brought to a law-ſuit. I wiſh you would
take it into your ſerious conſideration before
you begin, becauſe it will hardly be in your
power

Letter-Writer. 75

power to end it when you pleafe. For you immediately put the matter out of your own hands, into the hands of thofe whofe intereft it is to protract the fuit from term to term, and who will as abfolutely prefcribe to you in it, as your phyfician in a dangerous illnefs.

The law, my good friend, I look upon, more than any one thing, as the proper punifhment of an over-hafty and perverfe fpirit, as it is a punifhment that follows an act of a man's own feeking and choofing. You will not confent, perhaps, now to fubmit the matter in difpute to reference; but let me tell you, that after having expended large fums of money, and fquandered away a deal of time in attendance on your lawyers, and preparations for hearing, one term after another, you will probably be of another mind, and be glad five years hence to leave it to that arbitration which you now refufe. He is happy who is wife by other men's misfortunes, fays the common adage: and why, when you have heard from all your acquaintance, who have tried the experiment, what a grievous thing the law is, will you, notwithftanding, pay for that wifdom, which you may have at the coft of others?

The reprefentation that was once hung up as a fign, for a tavern, on one fide, a man all in rags, wringing his hands, with a lable, importing that he had loft his fuit; and on the other, a man that had not a rag left, but ftark naked, capering and triumphing, that he had
carried

76 ***The complete***

carried his cause, was a fine emblem of going to law, and the infatuating madness of a litigious spirit.

How excellent to this purpose is the advice of our blessed Saviour, rather than seek this redress against any who would take one's coat, to give him his cloak also? For, besides, the Christian doctrine inculcated by this precept, it will be found, as the law is managed, and the uncertainty that attends, even in the best grounded litigations, that such a pacific spirit may be deemed the only way to preserve the rest of one's garments, and to prevent being stripped to the skin.

Moreover, what wise man would rush upon a proceeding, where the principal men of the profession are not ashamed, under the specious, but scandalous notion, of doing the best they can for their client, to undertake, for the sake of a paltry fee, to whiten over the blackest cause, and to defeat the justest? where your property may depend altogether upon the impudence of an eloquent pleader asserting any thing, a perjured evidence swearing whatever will do for his suborner's purpose? where the tricks and mistakes of practisers, and want of trifling forms, may nonsuit you? where deaths of persons made parties to the suit, may cause all to begin again? What wise man, I say, would subject himself to these vexations and common incidents in the law, if he could any way avoid it; together with the intolerable expences and

attend-

attendances confequent on a law-fuit? befides, the fears, the cares, the anxieties, that revolve with every term, and engrofs all a man's thoughts? As to the law part only, obferve the procefs; firft, comes the declaration; 2dly, a plea; 3dly, a demurrer to the plea; 4thly, a joinder in demurrer; 5thly, a rejoinder; 6thly, a fur-rejoinder; which fometimes is conclufive, fometimes to begin all over again. Then may fucceed trials upon the law part, and trials upon the equity part; oftentimes new trials, or re-hearings; and thefe followed by writs of error. What wife man, permit me to repeat, would enter himfelf into this confounding circle of the the law?

I hope, dear fir, you will think of this mat-ter moft deliberately, before you proceed in your prefent angry purpofe; and if you fhall judge it proper to take my advice, and avoid a law-fuit, I am am fure you will have reafon to thank me for it, and for the zeal wherewith I am   Your fincere friend and fervant.

LETTER LXI.

To a Father, on the Neglect of his Children's Education.

Dear Sir,

I AM under a concern to fee fuch a re-miffnefs, as every body takes notice of, in the education of your children. They are brought up, it is true, to little offices in your bufinefs, which keeps them active, and may make them

in

in some degree of present, though poor, use to you; but, I am sorry to say, of none to themselves with regard to their future prospects, which is what a worthy parent always has in view.

There is a proper time for every thing; and, if children are not early initiated into their duty, and those parts of learning which are proper to their particular years, they must necessarily be discouraged and set behind every one of their school-fellows though much younger than themselves; and you know not, sir, what a laudable emulation you by this means destroy, than which nothing is of greater force to children to induce them to attend to their books; nor what disgrace you involve them in with respect to children among children, for the biggest and oldest to be so much outdone by the least and youngest.

Nor is the consequence of this defect confined to the school-age, as I may call it; for, as they grow up, they will be looked upon, in an equally discouraging disadvantageous light, by all who converse with them; which must of course throw them into the company of the dregs of mankind; for, how will they be able to converse or correspond with those whose acquaintance it is most worth their while to cultivate; and, indeed, they will probably be so conscious of their unfitness to bear a part in worthy conversation, that, to keep themselves in countenance, they will, of their own accord, shun the better company,

Letter-Writer.   **79**

pany, and affociate with the worſt ; and what may be the conſequence of this, a wiſe man, and a good father, would tremble to think of, eſpecially when he has to reflect upon himſelf as the cauſe of it, let it be what it will.

And with regard more immediately to your-ſelf, how can you expect, when they know you could do better for them, but that their behaviour to you will be of a piece with the reſt ? for, if they are not poliſhed by learning, but are left to a kind of inſtinct rather, is it to be expected that they ſhould behave to you, and their mother, with that ſenſe of their obligations which learning inculcates? Nor, indeed, will they have thoſe obligations to you, which other children have to their parents, who take care to give them opportunities of improvement, which are denied to yours. Conſider, dear ſir, what a contemptible character, even among the ſordid vulgar, that of an illiterate fellow is ; and what reſpect, on the contrary, a man of letters is treated with, by his equals, as well as inferiors. And when you lay all theſe plain reaſons and obſervations together, I make no doubt but you will endeavour to retrieve loſt time, and be adviſed in this material point (which I can have no intereſt in) by,

   Your ſincere friend and ſervant.

LETTER

8p *The complete*

L E T T E R LXII.

To a Lady, inviting her to a Party of Pleasure.

Dear Madam,

PEOPLE are interested who invite you to be of their parties, because you are sure to make them happy. This is the reason why you will not perhaps always comply when you are asked to be of them ; but, it is certainly a cause of your being solicited oftener than any woman in the world. After you were gone yesterday, Mr. Bohun proposed an expedition to German-town for to-morrow, and he requested me (for he thought he had no title to such liberty him-self) to tell you that we all understood you to be of the party, though you happened to be out of the way when it was proposed.

I hope you are not engaged ; the weather promises to be favourable, and your company you know how we value, I need not tell you that we shall suppose it a matter of form, if you are absent. What we shall think of it if you go with us, you will know when you remember what every body thinks, who has the pleasure of your company. I beg you will not invent an excuse, but go with us. I am, with the greatest sincerity, dear madam,

Your most obedient humble servant.

LETTER

Letter-Writer. 81

LETTER LXIII.

From a Youth to his Sister.

Most loving Sister,

OUR absence so long from each other has occasioned my writing to you, that I might be informed of your health and welfare, of which I am as solicitous and tender, as of my own; not forgetting you in my prayers, nor neglecting to do you all the good offices I can with our parents, friends, and acquaintance. In requital of which, let it be your part to return me an answer, that so I may be satisfied in what I have required, which will render me no small contentment of mind : in expectation whereof, I rest,   Your ever loving brother.

LETTER LXIV.

The Answer.

Dear Brother,

YOUR letter had luckily found me, though I am removed from the place you directed it to; and am not a little glad that I have the happiness to hear from you, considering we are so far distant one from another. As for my health, thanks be to heaven, it continues as heretofore ; and, of my welfare, I have no cause to complain, as being in an honest family, where nothing

thing convenient is wanting; that enjoying health, plenty, freedom, and content, I may juſtly account myſelf happy; and ſo wiſhing you and every one of my relations and friends the like, with a continuance of my hearty pray-ers to that end, I am,

Your moſt loving and obliged ſiſter,
A. P.

LETTER LXV.

From a Lady to her Niece, on the Subject of Dreſs.

Dear Bibby,

I Am much of your opinion, that the make of a woman's mind, greatly contributes to the ornament of her body. Behold Mrs. Vicars! ſhe has the largeſt ſhare of ſimplicity of man-ners, perhaps, in her whole ſex. This makes every thing look native about her; and her clothes are ſo exactly fitted, that they appear, as it were, part of her perſon. Every one that ſees her, knows her to be a lady; but her diſ-tinction is owing to her manner, and not to her habit. Her beauty is full of attraction, but not of allurement. There is ſuch a compoſure in her looks, and propriety in her dreſs, that you would think it impoſſible ſhe could change the garb you one day ſee her in, for any thing ſo becoming, till the next day you ſee her in another. There is no myſtery in this, but that however ſhe is apparalled, ſhe is herſelf the

ſame;

Letter-Writer.   83

same ; for there is fo immediate a relation between our thoughts and geftures, that a woman
muft think well to look well : this I have no
doubt of your endeavouring to do, my dear ;
which will give the utmoft fatitfaction to

Your affectionate and tender aunt,
                    LETITIA.

LETTER LXVI.

Letter from Bifhop Atterbury to his Son Obadiah,
at Chrift Church College, in Oxford.

Containing fome ufeful Hints in regard to writing Letters.)

Dear Obby,

   I Thank you for your letter, becaufe there
are manifeft figns in it of your endeavouring to
excel yourfelf, and of confequence to pleafe
me. You have fucceeded in both refpects,
and will always fuceeed, if you think it worth
your while to confider what you write, and to
whom, and let nothing, though of a trifling nature, pafs through your pen negligently ; get
but the way of writing correctly and juftly, time
and ufe will teach you to write readily afterwards ; not but that too much care may give a
ftiffnefs to your ftyle, which ought in all letters,
by all means to be avoided. The turn of them
would be always natural and eafy, for they are
an image of private and familiar converfation.
I mention this with refpect to the four or five
laft lines of yours, which have an air of poetry,

                       and

84 *The complete*

and do therefore naturally refolve themfelves
into blank verfe. I fend you your letter again,
that yourfelf may now make the fame obfervation. But you took the hint of that thought
from a poem, and it is no wonder, therefore,
that you heightened the phrafe a little when you
were expreffing it. The reft is as it fhould be;
and particularly there is an air of duty and fincerity, which, if it comes from your heart, is
the moft acceptable prefent you can make me.
With thefe good qualities an incorrect letter
would pleafe me, and without them the fineft
thoughts and language will make no lafting impreffion on me. The great Being fays, you
know, ' My fon give me thy heart,' implying,
that without it, all other gifts fignify nothing.
Let me conjure you, therefore, never to fay a-
ny thing, either in a letter, or common converfation, that you do not think of; but always to
let your mind and words go together on the
moft trivial occafions. Shelter not the leaft degree of infincerity under the notion of a compliment, which, as far as it deferves to be practif-
ed by a man of probity, is only the moft civil
and obliging way of faying what you really
mean; and whoever employs it otherwife,
throws away truth for breeding: I need not
tell you how little his character gets by fuch an
exchange.

I fay not this, as if I fufpected that in any part
of your letter you intended to write what was
proper, without any regard to what was true;
and

Letter-Writer. 85

for I am refolved to believe that you were in
earneft from the beginning to the end of it, as
much as I am, when I tell you that I am,

Your loving father, &c.

LETTER LXVII.

Thanks for proffered kindnefs.

Sir,

LET me firft beg your pardon, before I
tell you that at prefent I do not ftand in need of
your kindnefs, and, I dare fay, unfeigned prof-
fer of love and affiftance. Indeed may neceffities, not many days fince, did require it ; but,
I fuppofe, before they reached your ear, I was
fupplied by another hand ; yet, fhould not I pay
you the fame acknowledgement for the care
you exprefs of my welfare, as if I had really accepted the kindnefs, I might, with good reafon,
be termed ungrateful, and not worthy to be
numbered in the lift of your real friends : wherefore, I refolve whilft I live, not only to confefs
your kindnefs, but remain,

Yours to ferve you in what I may.

LETTER LXVIII.

Notice to a Friend.

Sir,

THE caufe of my writing (though the
news, perhaps, may be unwelcome to your ears)

E   is

is to let you know, that T. B. of D. with whom I underſtand you had conſiderable deal- ings, is dead ; and has left, as I hear and fear, his eſtate and effects much incumbered and em- barraſſed, to the no ſmall admiration of his neigh- bours, who all along imagined it fared with him far otherwiſe; though, indeed, it is a com- mon ſaying, " That few know what a man is worth until he dies." This, though unrequir- ed, I thought fit to advertiſe you of; and, ſo leaving the further proſecution to your diſcre- tion, whom it mainly concerns, I remain,

Your frend and ſervant.

LETTER LXIX.

From a young Tradeſman to a Lady he had ſeen in Public.

Madam,

PERHAPS you will not be ſurprized to receive a letter from a perſon who is unknown to you, when you reflect how likely ſo charm- ing a face may be to create impertinence; and I perſuade myſelf, that when you remember where you ſat laſt night at the play-houſe, you will not need to be told this comes from the per- ſon who was juſt before you.

In the firſt place, madam, I aſk pardon for the liberty I then took of looking at you, and for the greater liberty I now take in writing this letter: But after this, I beg leave to tell

you,

Letter-Writer.   87

you, that my thoughts are honourable, and to inform you who I am: I shall not pretend to be any better. I keep a shop, madam, in Second-street, and though but two years in trade, I have tolerable custom: I do not doubt but it will increase, and I shall be able to do something for a family. If your inclinations are not engaged, I should be very proud of the honour of waiting on you, and, in the mean time, if you please to desire any friend to ask my character in the neighbourhood, I believe it will not prejudice you against,

Madam,

Your most humble servant.

LETTER LXX.

From a Relation of the Lady, in Answer to the last.

Sir,

THERE has come into my hands a letter which you wrote to Miss Maria Stebbing: she is a relation of mine, and is a very good girl; and, I dare say, you will not think the worse of her for consulting her friends in such an affair as that you wrote about. Besides, a woman could not well answer such a letter herself, unless it was with a full refusal, and that she knew would have been wrong; and, until she knew something of the person that wrote it, as wrong as to have encouraged him.

You seem very sincere and open in your designs;

figns: and as you gave permiffion to enquire a-
bout you among your neighbours, I, being her
neareft friend, did that for her. I have heard
very good accounts of you; and from all that I
fee, you may be very fuitable for one another.
She has fome fortune; and I fhall tell you further, that fhe took notice of you at the play,
and does not feem at all difinclined to think favourably of you.

I am, with refpect, fir,

Your friend and fervant.

L E T T E R LXXI.

From a refpectful Lover to his Miftrefs.

Dear Madam,

    I Have long ftruggled with the moft ho-
nourable and refpectful paffion that ever filled
the heart of man; I have often tried to reveal
it perfonally; as often in this way; but never,
till now, could prevail upon my fears and doubts.
But I cannot longer ftruggle with a fecret that
has given me fo much torture to keep, and yet,
hitherto, more when I have endeavoured to reveal it. I never entertain the hope to fee you,
without rapture; but, when I have that pleafure, inftead of being animated, as I ought, I am
utterly confounded. What can this be owing
to, but a diffidence in myfelf, and an exalted o-
pinion of your worthinefs? And is not this one
ftrong token of ardent love? Yet if it be, how

various

various is the tormenting paſſion in its operations? Since ſome it inſpires with courage,
while others it deprives of all neceſſary confidence. I can only aſſure you, madam, that the
heart of man never conceived a ſtronger, or
ſincerer, paſſion than mine for you. If my reverence for you is my crime, I am ſure it has
been my ſufficient puniſhment. I need not ſay
my deſigns and motives are honourable: who
dare approach ſo much virtuous excellence,
with a ſuppoſition that ſuch an aſſurance is neceſſary? What my fortune is, is well known;
and I am ready to ſtand the teſt of the ſtricteſt
enquiry. Condeſcend, madam, to embolden
my reſpectful paſſion, with one favourable line;
that if what I here profeſs, and hope further to
have an opportunity to aſſure you of, be found
to be unqueſtionably true, then I hope my humble addreſſes will not quite be unacceptable to
you; and thus you will for ever oblige, dear
madam,   Your affectionate admirer,
and devoted ſervant,

J——R——.

LETTER LXXII.

The Anſwer.

Sir,

    IF modeſty be the greateſt glory of our
ſex, ſurely it cannot be blame worthy in yours.
For my own part, I muſt think it the moſt a-
miable quality either man or woman can poſſeſs.
Nor

Nor can there be, in my opinion, a true ref-pect, where there is not a diffidence of one's own merit, and an high opinion of the perfons we efteem.

To fay more on this occafion, would little become me : to fay lefs, would look as if I knew not how to pay that regard to modeft merit, which modeft merit only deferves.

You, Sir, beft know your own heart ; and, if you are fincere and generous, will receive as you ought this franknefs from, fir,

Your humble fervant.

LETTER LXXIII.

From a young Lady to her Father, acquainting him with a Propofal of Marriage made to her.

Honoured Sir,

AS young Mr. Lovewell, whofe father, I am fenfible, is one of your intimate acquaintance, has, during your abfence in the country, made an open declaration of his paffion for me, and preffed me clofely to comply with his overtures of marriage, I thought it my duty to decline all offers of that nature, however advantageous they may feem to be, till I had your thoughts on fo important an affair; and I am abfolutely determined either to difcourage his addreffes, or keep him at leaft in fufpenfe, till your return, as I fhall be directed by your fuperior judgment. I beg leave, however, with

due

Letter-Writer.   9 1

due fubmiffion, to acquaint you of the idea I have entertained of him, and hope I am not too blind, or partial in his favour. He feems to me to be perfectly honourable in his intentions, and to be in no wife, inferior to any gentleman of my acquaintance hitherto, in regard to good fenfe or good manners.—I frankly own, fir, I could admit of his addreffes with pleafure, were they attended with your confent and approbation. Be affured, however, that I am not fo far engaged, as to act with precipitation, or comply with any offers inconfiftent with that filial duty, which, in gratitude to your paternal indulgence, I fhall ever owe you. Your fpeedy inftruction, therefore, in fo momentous an article, will prove the greateft fatisfaction to,

Honoured fir, your moft dutiful daughter.

LETTER LXXIV.

From an Aunt to her Nephew, who had complained of ill Succefs in his Addreffes.

Dear Nephew,

I Received your doleful ditty, in regard to your ill fuccefs in your late love-adventure with Mifs Snow. No marble monument was ever half fo cold, or veftal virgin half fo coy! She turns a deaf ear, it feems, to your moft ardent vows! And what of all that? By your own account it appears, fhe has given you no flat denial; neither has fhe peremptorily forbid

your

your vifits. Really, nephew, I thought a young gentleman of your good fenfe and penetration, would be better verfed in the arts of love, than to be caft down all at once, and quit the field at the firft repulfe. You fhould confider, that fhe is not only a beauty, but a very accomplifh- ed lady. You muft furely be very vain to ima- gine, that one of her education, good fenfe, and real merit, fhould fall an eafy victim into your arms. Her affections muft be gradually engaged; fhe looks upon matrimony as a very ferious affair, and will never give way, I am fully perfuaded, to the violence of an ill-ground- ed paffion. For fhame, nephew, fhake off that unbecoming bafhfulnefs, and fhew yourfelf a man. Lovers, like foldiers, fhould endure fa- tigues. Be advifed: Renew the attack with double vigour; for fhe is a lady worth your con- queft. The revolution of a day (as the ingeni- ous Mrs. Rowe has it) may bring fuch turns as Heaven itfelf could fcarce have promifed. Cheer up, dear nephew, under that thought. When I hear from you again, a few weeks hence, I am not without hopes, if you will follow my advice, of your carrying the fiege, and making her comply with your own terms of accommo- dation. In the mean time, depend upon it, no ftone fhall be left unturned on my part, that may any wife contribute towards your good fuc- cefs, as I cannot, without injuftice to the lady, but approve of your choice.

> I am, your loving aunt.

L E T T E R

Letter-Writer.   93

L E T T E R LXXV.

A Gentleman to a Lady, profeffing an averfion to the tedious Formality in Courtfhip.

Dear Madam,

I Remember that one of the ancients, in
defcribing a youth in love, fays, he has neither
wifdom enough to fpeak, nor to hold his tongue.
If this be a juft defcription, the fincerity of my
paffion will admit of no difpute: and, whenever, in your company, I behave like a fool,
forget not that you are anfwerable for my incapacity. Having made bold to declare thus
much, I muft prefume to fay, that the favourable reception of this, will, I am, certain, make
me more worthy of your notice: but your difdain would be what I believe myfelf incapable
ever to furmount.

To try by idle fallacies, and airy compliments, to prevail on your judgment, is a folly
for any man who knows you to attempt. No,
madam, your good fenfe and endowments have
raifed you far above the neceffity of practifing
the mean artifices which prevail upon the lefs
deferving of your fex: you are not to be fo
lightly deceived; and if you were, give me
leave to fay, I fhould not think you deferving
of the trouble that would attend fuch an attempt.

This, I muft own, is no fafhionable letter

from one who, I am fure, loves up to the
greateft hero of romance; but, as I would hope
that the happinefs I fue for would be lafting, it
is certainly moft eligible to take no ftep to procure it but what will bear reflection; for I
would be happy to fee you mine, when we have
both outlived the tafte for every thing that has
not virtue and reafon to fupport it. I am, madam, notwithftanding this unpolifhed addrefs,

Your moft refpectful admirer,
and obedient humble fervant,

LETTER LXXVI.

The Lady's Anfwer, encouraging a farther Declaration.

Sir,

 I AM very little in love with the fafhionable methods of courtfhip: fincerity with me is
preferable to compliments; yet, I fee no reafon
why common decency fhould be difcarded.
There is fomething fo odd in your ftile, that
when I know whether you are in jeft or earneft, I fhall be lefs at a lofs to anfwer you.
Mean time, as there is abundant room for rifing, rather than finking, in your complaifance,
you may poffibly have chofen wifely to begin
firft at the loweft end. If this be the cafe, I
know not what your fucceeding addrefles may
produce: but, I tell you fairly, that your prefent one makes no great impreffion, yet, perhaps, as much as you intended, on

Your humble fervant.

Letter-Writer.   95

LETTER LXXVII.

The Gentleman's Reply, more openly declaring his Paffion.

Deareft Madam,

NOW I have the hope of being not more defpifed for my acknowledged affection. I declare to you with all the fincerity of a man of honour, that I have long had a moft fincere paffion for you; but, I have feen gentlemen led fuch dances, when they have given up their affections to the lovely tyrants of their hearts, and could not help themfelves, that I had no courage to begin my addrefs in the ufual forms, even to you, of whofe good fenfe and generofity I had neverthelefs a great opinion. You have favoured me with a few lines, which I moft humbly thank you for. And I do affure you, madam, if you will be pleafed to encourage my humble fuit, you fhall have fo juft an account of my circumftances and pretenfions, as, I hope, will entitle me to your favour in the honourable light in which I profefs myfelf, dear madam,   Your moft obliged,
          and faithful admirer.

P. S. Be fo good as to favour me with one line more to encourage my perfonal attendance, if not difagreeable.

LETTER

96   *The complete*

LETTER LXXVIII.

The Lady's anfwer to his Reply, putting the Matter on a fudden Iffue.

Sir,

     A S we are both fo well inclined to avoid unneceffary trouble, as well as unneceffary compliments, I think proper to acquaint you, that Mr. Richardfon of Winchefter, has the management of all my affairs; and is a man of fuch probity and honour, that I do nothing in any matters without him. I have no diflike to your perfon; and if you approve of what Mr. Richardfon can acquaint you with, in re-lation to me, and I approve of his report in your favour, I fhall be far from fhewing any gentleman, that I have either an infolent or a fordid fpirit, efpecially to fuch as do me the honour of their good opinion.

I am, fir,

Your humble fervant,

LETTER LXXIX.

A modeft Lover defiring an Aunt's Favour to him for her Niece.

Good Madam,

     I Have feveral times, when I have been happy in the company of your good niece, thought to have fpoken my mind, and to de-
clare

Letter-Writer.   97

clare to her the true value and affection I have
for her; but juſt as I have been about to ſpeak,
my fears have vanquiſhed my hopes, and I have
been obliged to ſuſpend my deſign. I have
thrown out ſeveral hints, that I thought would
have led the way to a fuller diſcloſing of the ſecret that is too big for my breaſt; and yet,
when I am near her, it is too important for utterance. Will you be ſo good, Madam, to
break the way for me, if I am not wholly diſ-
approved of by you, and prepare her dear mind
for a declaration that I muſt make, and yet I
know not how to begin.——My fortune and expectations make me hope that I may not on
thoſe accounts be deemed unworthy. And could
I, by half a line from your hand, hope that
there is no other bar, I ſhould be enabled to
build on ſo deſirable a foundation, and to let your
niece know how much my happineſs depends
upon her favour. Excuſe, good Madam, I beſeech you this trouble, and this preſumptuous
requeſt, from

> Your obliged humble ſervant.

LETTER LXXX.

The Aunt's Anſwer, ſuppoſing the gentleman deſerves
Encouragement.

Sir,

I Cannot ſay I have any diſlike, as to my
own part, to your propoſal, or your manner of
mak-

making it, whatever my niece may have; because diffidence is generally the companion of
merit, and a token of refpect. She is a perfon
of prudence, and all her friends are fo thoroughly convinced of it, that her choice will have
the weight it deferves with us all; fo I cannot
fay what will be the event of your declaration
to her; yet fo far as I may take upon myfelf to
do, I will not deny your requeft, but on her
return to-morrow will break the ice, as you defire, not doubting your honour, and the fincerity of your profeffions. And I fhall tell her,
moreover, what I think of the advances you
make. I believe fhe has had the prudence to
keep her heart entirely difengaged, becaufe fhe
would otherwife have told me; and is not fo
mean fpirited as to be able to return tyranny
and infult for true value, when fhe is properly
convinced of it. Whoever has the happinefs
(permit me, though her relation, to call it fo)
to meet with her favour, will find this her character; and it is not owing to the fond partiality of, Sir, Your friend and fervant.

LETTER LXXXI.

From a young Perfon in Bufinefs, to a Gentleman, defiring Leave to wait on his Daughter.

Sir,

I Hope the juftnefs of my intentions will
excufe the freedom of this letter, wherein I
am

Letter-Writer. 99

am to acquaint you of the affection and esteem
I have for your daughter. I would not, fir,
offer any indirect addrefs, that fhould have the
leaft appearance of inconfiftency with her duty
to you, and my honourable views to her; chu-
fing, by your influence, if I may approve myfelf to you worthy of that honour, to commend
myfelf to her approbation. You are not infenfible, fir, by the credit I have hitherto preferved in the world, of my ability, by God's bleffing, to make her happy: and this the rather
emboldens me to requeft the favour of an evening's converfation with you at your firft convenience; when I will more fully explain myfelf,
as I earneftly hope, to your fatisfaction, and
take my encouragement, or difcouragement,
from your own mouth. I am fir, in the mean
time, with great refpect,

Your moft obedient humble fervant,

R———M———.

LETTER LXXXII.

*From a Gentleman to his Miftrefs, who, feeing no
hopes of Succefs, refpectfully withdraws his Suit.*

Madam,

I Make no doubt but this will be the wel-
comeft letter that ever you received from me:
for it comes to affure you, that it is the laft
trouble you will ever have from me. Nor
fhould I have fo long withheld from you this fatisfaction,

tisfaction, had not the hope your brother gave me, that in time I might meet with a happier fate, made me willing to try every way to ob-tain your favour. But I see, all the hopes giv-en by his kind confideration for me, and thofe that my own prefumption have made me entertain, are all in vain, and I will, there-fore, rid you of fo troublefome an importuner, having nothing to offer now, but my ardent wifhes for your happinefs; and thefe, madam, I will purfue you with to my life's lateft date.

May you, whenever you fhall change your condition, meet with a heart as paffionately, and as fincerely, devoted to you as mine! and may you be happy for many, very many years, in the man you can honour with your love! For, give me leave to fay, madam, that, in this, my end will be, in part, anfwered, be-caufe it was moft fincerely your happinefs I had in view, as well as my own, when I prefump-tuoufly hoped, by contributing to the one, to fecure the other. I am, madam, with the high-eft veneration,

        Your moft obedient humble fervant.

                          LETTER

Letter-Writer.   IOI

LETTER LXXXIII.

From a Lady to a Gentleman, who had obtained all her Friends' Consent, urging him to decline his Suit to her.

Sir,

YOU have often importuned me to return marks of that consideration for you, which you profess for me. As my parents, to whom I owe all duty, encourage your address, I wish I could. I am hardly treated by them, because I cannot. What shall I do? Let me apply to you, sir, for my relief, who have much good sense, and, I hope, generosity. Yes, sir, let me bespeak your humanity to me, and justice to yourself, in this point; and that shall be all I will ask in my favour. I own you deserve a much better wife than I shall ever make: but yet, as love is not in one's own power, if I have the misfortune to know I cannot love you, will not justice to yourself, if not pity to me, oblige you to abandon your present purpose?

Cease then, I beseech you, this hopeless, this cruel pursuit! make some worthier person happy in your addresses, that can be happy in them!—by this means, you will restore me (if you decline as of your own motion) to the condition you found me in, the love of my parents and the esteem of my friends. If you really love me, this will be a hard task, but, it will be a most generous one—and there is some rea-

son

fon to expect it; for who that truly loves,
wifhes to make the object of his love miferable?
This muft I be, if you perfift in your addreffes;
and I fhall know, by your conduct, on occafion of this uncommon requeft, how to confider
it, and in what light to place you, either as the
moft generous, or the moft ungenerous of men.
Mean time, I am, fir, moft heartily, though I
cannot be what you would have me,

     Your well-wifher, and humble fervant.

LETTER LXXXIV.

A Sailor to his Sweetheart.

My dear Peggy,

    IF you think of me half fo often as I do of
you, it will be every hour; for you are never
out of my thoughts; and when I am afleep, I conftantly dream of my dear Peggy. I wear my
half bit of gold always at my heart, tied to a blue
ribbon round my neck; for true blue, my deareft love, is a colour of colours to me. Where,
my dearest, do you put yours? I hope you are
careful of it; for it would be a bad omen to lofe it.

    Our captain talks of failing foon for England;
and then, and then, my deareft Peggy!—O
how I rejoice, how my heart beats with delight
that makes me I cannot tell how, when I think
of arriving in England, and joining hands with
my Peggy! as we have our hearts before, I
hope! I am fure I fpeak for one.

     Your faithful lover till death.

Letter-Writer.   103

LETTER LXXXV.

From a Lady, newly married, to an Intimate.

Dear Bid,

DO not stare at a strange name at the bottom of this letter. It was Miss Newell that writes to you, but the barbarous man has overturned all that. What cannot these men do when they persuade us out of our very names. My servant brings you a dozen of French gloves: you will remember that you, and the poor girl I have just been talking of, entered into a bargain, that which ever married first should send this present to the other: If you are married too, send it back again; if not, take a friend's advice, dear Biddy, and marry as soon as you can. I believe you will find it has not taken away my spirits yet; and by what I see of it, I do not think it ever will. One may have occasion to be grave sometimes, but I do not see that that need make them unhappy. My dear, you will excuse me for not writing a longer letter: You will guess that a woman, who has not been married above twelve hours, has enough to do with herself. I have only told Mr. Williams I must have a moment to write to the only person in the world I love next himself. My dear, good bye. I suppose I shall see you. Your most affectionate humble servant.

LETTER

104   *The complete*

LETTER LXXXVI.

To a new married Lady.—In Anſwer.

My dear Charlotte,

THERE is not one among all your ac-quaintance that congratulates you with more pleaſure or ſincerity than I do on the preſent oc-caſion. I hope you will write to me twenty years hence to confirm all your happy expectations; for I ſhall preſerve your letter to compare with it. My dear, God ſend you may be long as hap-py as you ſeem to be this moment. But take a friend's advice : do not ſay ſo much about it to any body elſe. Your friends will banter you a-bout it; and thoſe that are not ſo, will compare it with your gravity, by and bye ; and ſuſpect that becauſe you do not laugh ſo much, you are not ſo happy ; for depend upon it, though you may be much happier a twelvemonth hence, you will not be ſo merry.

I expected the gloves, ſo your new name did not ſurpriſe me. You could not imagine all the people in the town did not know your match. The day alone was a ſecret. I thank you for your friendly advice ; but my dear, I ſhall ſtay and hear what you ſay of the married life, when you are a little better acquainted with it, before I am at all in the more haſte to enter up-on it for your recommendation : but I do not doubt you will always continue in the ſame opi-nion.

Letter-Writer. 105

nion. That you may be fo as long as you live,
is, my dear Charlotte, the moft fincere wifh
of   Your very faithful fervant.

L E T T E R LXXXVII.

*From a fenfible Lady, with a never-failing Receipt
for a Beauty-wafh.*

AS you feem fo intent on improving the
perfonal charms of your already amiable daughter, I can no longer delay anfwering your letter.—You would be glad, you fay, of a receipt
to make a wafh; but it muft be perfectly innocent. What I recommend, madam, is truly
fo, and will greatly illuftrate and preferve her
complexion.

Pray let her obferve the following rules :

In the morning, fair water is to be taken
preparatory; after which fhe muft abftain from
all fudden gufts of paffion, particularly envy, as
that gives the fkin a fallow palenefs. It may
feem trifling to talk of temperance; yet muft
this be attended to both in eating and drinking,
if fhe would avoid thofe pimples, for which the
advertifed wafhes are a boafted cure. Inftead
of paint, let her ufe moderate exercife, which
will excite a natural bloom in her cheeks, not
to be imitated by art. Ingenuous candour, and
unaffected good humour will give an opennefs
to her countenance that will make her univer-
ally agreeable. A defire of pleafing will add
fire

106   *The complete*

fire to her eyes, and breathing the morning air
at fun rife, will give her lips a vermillion hue.
That amiable vivacity, which fhe now poffeffes;
may be happily heightened and preferved, if
fhe avoids late hours and card-playing, but not
otherwife: for the firft, gives the face a drow-
fy difagreeable afpect; and the laft is the
mother of wrinkles.—A white hand is a very
defirable ornament; and a hand can never be
white unlefs it be kept clean: Nor is this all;
for if the young lady will excel her companions
in this refpect, fhe muft keep her hands in conftant motion, which will occafion the blood to
circulate freely, and have a wonderful effect.
The motion I would recommend is working at
her needle, brufhing up the houfe, or twirling
the diftaff. It was this in our grandmothers
which gave Kneller an opportunity of gratify-
ing pofterity with the view of fo many fine
hands and arms in his incomparable portraits—
A few words more and I have done.—Let her
preferve an unaffected neatnefs in her apparel;
her fortune will permit her to drefs elegantly
but her good fenfe fhould always prevent her
from defcending to gaudinefs, which ftrikes the
eyes of the ignorant, but difgufts thofe of true
tafte and difcernment; befides, madam, your
daughter has fo many natural charms, that fhe
can have no occafion to wear cloaths that will
attract the attention of the multitude. She poffeffes more beauties than fhe is acquainted with,
which is no fmall addition to her merit; but
how

Letter-Writer. 107

how can it be otherwife, when fhe is your daughter, and has you for an example?

I am, &c.

LETTER LXXXVIII.

To a Lady with a Looking-glafs, after having broke hers.

Madam,

ACCEPT this as a reftitution, not a prefent; which, though it may feem of a trifling value, yet if you look attentively upon it, it will fhew you one of the moft charming objects in the world. To keep you no longer in fufpenfe, you will fee there the picture of my miftrefs. I fhould not care to make th's difcovery to another perfon, but I think I may venture to confide in you without being thought indifcreet. I muft tell you that you will fee there two charming eyes, fuch eyes as are worth a thoufand others; but then I muft confefs they are very mifchievous. I know you have an abfolute power over them, and that they are entirely at your difpofal. Wherefore I take the liberty of befeeching you to order the matter fo, that I may be no longer a fufferer by them; which will infinitely oblige, madam, your moft humble, and obedient fervant, &c.

LETTER

108　　　　*The complete*

LETTER LXXXIX.

The following Letter, written by Mr. Gay, giving an Account of two Lovers who were struck dead by the same flash of Lightning, is reckoned a Master-piece in epistolary descriptive Writing.

　　　　　　Stanton-Harcourt, Aug. 9, 1718.

THE only news you can expect to have from me here, is news from heaven; for I am quite out of the world, and there is scarce any thing can reach me, except the noise of thunder, which undoubtedly you have heard too. We have read in old authors, of high towers levelled by it to the ground, while the humble vallies have escaped. The only thing that is proof against it is the laurel, which however I take to be no great security to the brains of modern authors. But to let you see that the contrary to this often happens, I must acquaint you, that the highest and most extravagant heap of towers in the universe, which is in this neighbourhood, stands still undefaced, while a cock of barley in our next field has been consumed to ashes. Would to God that this heap of barley had been all that had perished! but unhappily beneath this little shelter sat two much more constant lovers than ever were found in romance, under the shade of a beech tree. John Hewit was a well-set man, of about five and twenty. Sarah Drew might rather be called comely than beautiful, and was about the same age.

Letter-Writer. 109

age. They had paſſed thro' the various labours of the year together, with the greateſt ſatisfaction; if ſhe milked, it was his morning and evening care to bring the cows to her hand. It was but laſt fair that he bought her a preſent of green ſilk for her ſtraw hat, and the poſey on her ſilver ring was of his chuſing. Their love was the talk of the whole neighbourhood; for ſcandal never affirmed that they had any other views than the lawful poſſeſſion of each other in marriage. It was that very morning that he had obtained the conſent of her parents, and it was but till the next week that they were to wait to be happy. Perhaps, in the interval of their work, they were now talking of their wedding cloaths, and John was ſuiting ſeveral ſorts of poppies and field flowers to her complexion, to chuſe her a knot for the wedding day. While they were thus buſied, (it was on the laſt of July, between two and three in the afternoon,) the clouds grew black; and ſuch a ſtorm of lightening and thunder enſued, that all the labourers made the beſt of their way to the beſt ſhelter the trees and hedges afforded. Sarah was frightened, and fell down in a ſwoon on a heap of barley. John, who never ſeparated from her, ſat down by her ſide, having raked together two or three heaps, the better to ſecure her from the ſtorm. Immediately there was heard ſo loud a crack, as if heaven had ſplit aſunder. Every one was ſolicitous for the ſafety of his neighbour, and called to one

F   ano-

another throughout the field. No anſwer being returned to thoſe who called to our lovers, they ſtepped to the place where they lay. They perceived the barley all in a ſmoke, and then eſpied this faithful pair. John with one arm a-bout Sarah's neck, and the other held over her, as if to ſcreen her from the lightening. They were both ſtruck in this tender poſture. Sarah's left eye-brow was ſinged, and there appeared a black ſpot on her breaſt. Her lover was all over black, but not the leaſt ſigns of life were found in either. Attended by their melancholy companions, they were conveyed to the town, and the next day interred in Stanton-Harcourt church yard. My Lord Harcourt, at Mr. Pope's and my requeſt, has cauſed a ſtone to be placed over them, upon condition that we ſhould fur-niſh the epitaph, which is as follows:

When eaſtern lovers feed the funeral fire,
On the ſame pile the faithful pair expire;
Here pitying heaven, that virtue mutual found,
And blaſted both, that it might neither wound.
Hearts ſo ſincere, th' Almighty ſaw well pleas'd,
Sent his own light'ning, and the victims ſeiz'd.

But my Lord is apprehenſive the country-people will not underſtand this, and Mr. Pope ſays he will make one with ſomething of Scrip-ture in it, and with as little poetry as Hopkins and Sternhold.   I am, &c.

XC. A

Letter-Writer.   III

XC. A Letter from Judge Hale, Chief Juftice of England, to his Children, on the ferious obfervance of
the Lord's day, (commonly called Sunday,) when he
was on a Journey; which well deferves our Attention,

I AM now come well to ——, from
whence I intend to write fomething to you on
the obfervance of the Lord's day, and this I do
for thefe reafons: 1ft, Becaufe it has pleafed
God to caft my lot fo, that I am at reft at this
place on that day, and the confideration therefore of that duty is proper for me and you, viz.
the work fit for that day. 2dly, Becaufe I
have, by long and found experience, found,
that the due obfervance of that day, and the duties of it, has been of fingular comfort and advantage to me; and I doubt not but it will prove
fo to you. God Almighty is the Lord of our
time, and lends it us; and it is but juft we
fhould confecrate this part of that time to him;
for I have found, by a ftrict and diligent obfervation, that a due obfervance of the duties of
this day, has ever had joined to it a bleffing on
the reft of my time; and the week that hath
been fo begun, has been bleffed and profperous
to me. On the other fide, when I have been
negligent of the duty of this day, the reft of the
week has been unfuccefsful, and unhappy to my
own fecular employment; fo that I could eafily
make an eftimate of my fucceffes the week following, by the manner of my paffing this day;
and this I do not write lightly or inconfiderately, but upon a long and found obfervation and
experience.

EDITORIAL NOTES

A Gentleman of Fortune, *The New Art of Letter Writing, Divided into Two Parts*

p. 3, l. 10: *indite*: compose, put into words.

p. 3, l. 16: *Friends*: kin, relatives, patrons and helpers as well as friend in the modern sense.

p. 4, l. 4: *the Commerce of Life*: any kind of exchange, communication or dealings that may occur in life, not just trade.

p. 4, l. 6: *except*: exclude. The author is underlining the difference between this *Letter-Writer* and *Academies of Complement*, which modelled conversation as well as correspondence. See Volume 1.

p. 4, l. 8: *Entertaining*: receiving or engaging with others, with connotation of filling time.

p. 4, ll. 10–11: *Ease and Propriety*: Ease consisted of doing what propriety required without awkwardness, in an unconstrained manner, and without drawing attention to the artifice involved. Ease also suggested that one had seen something of the world, and learned to conduct oneself by mixing in society rather than merely by reading a how-to book. Ease and Propriety were key terms for the characterization of politeness during this period.

p. 5, ll. 1–2: *agreeable Emotions*: By the second half of the century, Scottish rhetoricians had redirected rhetoric from its traditional emphasis on invention, narration and argument – and thus from a primarily rational mode of persuasion – to an emphasis on delivery and on evoking emotion in hearers or readers and therefore to a more sensibility- and reception-oriented mode of persuasion.

p. 5, ll. 2–3: *Pronunciation*: delivery – at this time, primarily the art of reading aloud with the emphases and cadences of the normal speaking voice.

p. 5, ll. 4–5: *the good Presence of him that speaks*: demeanour, ability to project one's personality.

p. 5, l. 10: *ill polished*: to be polished was to be refined, cultured, elegant and to perform one's social role with ease and propriety. Ill-polished means that one has not the ability to perform in this way.

p. 5, l. 14: *Inconveniences*: disadvantages.

p. 5, l. 30: *Dispositions*: natural aptitudes.

p. 5, l. 33: *transcribe*: the first stage in imitation. See the General Introduction in Volume 1.

p. 7, l. 24: *more Sentiments than Thoughts*: here sentiments mean feelings or emotions.

p. 8, ll. 2–3: *to support the character that has been made Choice of*: to sustain the qualities, characteristics or personality one has chosen, thus to play a part.

p. 8, ll. 21–2: *Fustian*: gibberish, rant.

p. 9, l. 3: *The Sallies of the Imagination*: flights of imagination.

p. 9, l. 14: *Eclaircissement*: (French) clarification.

p. 9, ll. 15–16: *that of a Compliment*: in the complemental style. The author has been contrasting the style he is describing with this 'former style' throughout. This chapter therefore very conveniently characterizes both complemental and 'perspicuous' styles.

p. 9, l. 24: *equal*: uniform.

p. 9, l. 27: *Periods*: sentences.

p. 9, l. 30: *Strokes of Genius*: striking ideas or images.

p. 9, l. 37: *servile Complaisance*: Complaisance was that part of politeness which consisted of pleasing others by deferring to their wishes or agreeing with their ideas. The author is suggesting that to take this too far is to be servile, i.e. to conduct oneself ignobly as if one were a slave.

p. 10, l. 36: *Consonance*: assonance.

p. 10, l. 37: *copious*: rich abundance of words, synonyms and repetitions, with a profusion of images, producing a diffuse style. This was a style favoured by Erasmus and other Elizabethan humanists, as well as the style of complemental letters.

p. 12, l. 1: *banish from it all Common places*: This manual goes on to describe all the commonplaces that each class of letter is expected to repeat, much as John Hill did in Volume 1. The author also insists that letter writers should follow Horace's advice to say common things in a new way. What he must mean here, therefore, is: 'banish the common formulae and clichéd expressions' rather than banish the conventional ideas or sentiments they represent.

p. 12, ll. 32–3: *the four Parts*: Letters were constructed on the model of orations, which had six parts: *exordium, narratio, divisio, confirmatio, refutatio* and *peroratio*. The writer is reducing these to four to suggest a more informal and flowing rendering of one's point or argument. It was a commonplace to say that a letter must be more informal than an oration.

Samuel Richardson, *Letters Written to and for Particular Friends, on the Most Important Occasions*

p. 19, ll. 2–3: *Chapman ... Dealer*: country shopkeeper, corresponding with a middleman, who dealt in and distributed merchandise.

p. 19, l. 3: *offering his Correspondence*: offering to have business relations – and by letter.

p. 19, l. 12: *use me*: treat me.

p. 20, ll. 9–10: *more favourable Usage*: In the eighteenth century, credit usually had to be extended for extremely long periods of time, and payment for goods and services was all too often hard to obtain. These two letters are promoting better business practices, by recommending punctual or prompt payment on the one hand, and more favourable terms in exchange on the other.

p. 21, l. 11: *Engagements*: undertakings.

p. 21, ll. 19–20: *Housekeeping*: provisions for household use.

p. 22, l. 3: *I had saved Twenty Pounds in Service*: It was common for live-in maidservants who got bed and board to save their earnings to create a sort of dowry, which would enable them to marry a tradesman; or, alternatively, for a maidservant and footman, both of whom had saved their earnings, to marry and set up in trade together in or around London. This young maidservant has not done the saving that others had.

Charles Hallifax, *Familiar Letters on Various Subjects of Business and Amusement*

p. 26, l. 22: *tedious*: disagreeable, tormenting.

p. 27, l. 18: *Transport*: ecstasy, being carried out of oneself.

p. 31, l. 3: *abroad*: out of the house.

p. 34, ll. 27–8: *the Straightness of my Circumstances*: straightened circumstances, poverty.

p. 35, ll. 10–11: *less than Thirty Pounds a Year*: for what constituted a 'competence' (i.e. enough money to live on) see Peter Earle, *The Making of the English Middle Class: Business, Society and Family Life in London, 1660–1730* (Berkeley: University of California Press, 1989); and Edward Copeland, *Women Writing about Money, 1790–1820* (Cambridge: Cambridge University Press, 1995).

p. 36, ll. 9–10: *an Interest to keep up*: personal connections enabling one to exert influence on a person or body of people. This was also a precondition for acting as a patron, and here, for being considered a power in the neighbourhood. There is some irony in offering this as an excuse for refusing his patronage.

p. 37, l. 37: *Industry:* productive labour.

p. 38, ll. 27–8: *with my own Hand*: At certain ranks, it was still a mark of distinction and/or particular friendship to pen a letter oneself rather than leave that to a secretary.

p. 40, l. 4: *Marshalsea*: a debtor's prison in Southwark, London, abolished only in 1842.

George Fisher, *The Instructor: Or, Young Man's Best Companion*

p. 43, l. 10: *chine of bacon*: a joint consisting of the backbone with adjoining flesh.

p. 43, ll. 10–11: *a good Stomach*: good appetite, relish.

p. 43, l. 14: *in our level*: in our stretch of country.

p. 44, l. 27: *suddenly*: immediately.

p. 45, l. 21: *my quondam* playfellows: my erstwhile school fellows.

[Anon.], *The Complete Letter-Writer; or Polite English Secretary*

p. 50, ll. 20–1: *here supplied*: Some of the imperfections of other letter manuals have been corrected by supplying what was wanting. However, the grammar and list of modes of address which the writer goes on to represent as examples of such additions appeared in *Secretaries* too.

p. 51, l. 18: *a Pattern*: a model.

p. 60, l. 18: *sensible*: aware.

p. 61, l. 35: *Make-Game*: synonym for laughing-stock, butt of humour or ridicule.

p. 65, l. 2: *Bustos*: busts.

p. 66, l. 31: *Address*: adroit and courteous manner of behaving and conversing.

p. 67, l. 8: *the Employment your purpose*: It was widely held that a child's education should be strictly fitted to his or her intended place, post or position in society.

p. 67, l. 27: *more essential than dancing a Minuet*: Dancing masters taught these other skills – how to walk well, bow appropriately etc – as well as the steps to dances such as the minuet.

p. 72, l. 6: *mine is come again*: my appetite (good stomach) has returned.

p. 76, ll. 29–30: *Hazard ... Quadrille*: a game of dice and a game of cards.

p. 81, l. 9: *unmerciful Jaunt*: a taxing and troublesome journey.

p. 85, l. 5: *his Address*: his courtship.

p. 88, l. 8: *Occasions*: needs, requirements.

p. 93, l. 7: *a Note*: legal record, promissory note.

p. 95, l. 19: *Mr. Wycherley*: William Wycherley (1651–1716), one of the principal comic play-wrights of the Restoration, whose letters frequently appeared in letter manuals.

p. 95, l. 20: *Mr. Pope*: Alexander Pope (1688–1744), well known poet, whose poems included 'Windsor Forest' and 'Essay on Man', and whose published letters were at one time much admired and included in letter manuals.

p. 96, l. 3: *Windsor*: a royal palace near London, and the village near which it is located.

p. 96, ll. 4–5: *Elysian Groves*: heavenly groves.

p. 96, l. 32: *Maidenhead*: village by the Thames, where the fashionable had houses flanking the river.

p. 97, l. 7: *the Itch*: contagious disease produced by a mite; scabies.

p. 97, l. 28: *Madam Roland*: Madame Roland (1754–93) held a famous salon in Paris. A Girondist during the French Revolution, she was guillotined in 1793 and came to be viewed as a champion of liberty.

p. 97, ll. 36–7: *Fern Hill, Brook-Street*: Fern Hill was a fashionable area near Windsor Castle, Brooke St. a fashionable street in London .

p. 97, l. 38: *Mr. Locke's Associations*: John Locke argued in an *Essay Concerning Human Under-standing* that we learn, think and remember by associating ideas.

p. 99, ll. 33–4: *tie up that Knocker*: a conventional way of signalling that the family was out of town.

p. 100, l. 16: *St. Swithin*: Anglo Saxon saint, associated with the weather.

p. 101, l. 8: *divided it*: tore it in half. Tearing a bank note in half and sending each half by a separate route was a way of ensuring that the note would be useless to anyone but the designated recipient. It was thus a way of preventing theft.

p. 102, l. 15: *made a Demand*: demanded payment.

p. 102, l. 32: *hurts a young Beginner*: If suspicion were aroused that he lacked the money to pay his bills, credit would be withdrawn, everyone would ask for payment at once, and he would be bankrupted.

p. 103, l. 7: *Losses*: from others who had not paid what they owed him.

p. 103, l. 11: *Usurer in Bread-Street*: The wholesaler has heard that the young tradesman has been borrowing money to keep going; he therefore fears that the will not get his money if he does not ask for it before this becomes more widely known and the tradesman is bankrupted (see note to p. 102, l. 32).

p. 103, l. 37: *in putting me out*: in getting me apprenticed.

p. 105, l. 10: *Freedom*: frankness, boldness, undue familiarity.

p. 107, l. 36: *Exceptions*: objections.

p. 109, l. 30: *Vestal Virgin*: The vestal virgins were priestesses of the goddess Vesta at Rome, who had to remain chaste, virginal and pure.

p. 110, l. 12: *the ingenious Mr. Rowe*: Nicholas Rowe (1674–1718), popular playwright and poet laureate under George I.

p. 111, l. 11: *grand Climacterick*: a critical or fatal time of life, when a person is liable to a marked change in health (between forty-five and sixty!).

p. 111, l. 22: *like my Lady Grace in the Play*: Lady Grace is a pattern of perfection in the popu-lar play, *The Provok'd Husband*.

p. 114, ll. 30–1: *Coxcomb*: fool, from the name of the cap worn by professional fools.

p. 130, ll. 17–18: *Citron Water*: brandy flavoured with lemon peel.

p. 131, l. 16: *tro'*: an obscure expletive, possibly on the lines of 'Fancy!' or 'Would you believe it!'

p. 135, l. 34: *how fallen, how changed*: Echoes here from Satan's speech in Milton's *Paradise Lost* playfully suggest that marriage can be equated with a fall from single bliss into hell.

p. 136, l. 3: *Grogram*: coarse, stiff fabric, made of mohair, wool and silk.

p. 136, ll. 26–7: *the Ring at Hyde Park*: The fashionable would drive around Hyde Park in their carriages every afternoon to see and be seen. The ring was (and remains) a road within Hyde Park which runs around its periphery.

p. 136, ll. 40–1: *Porcia, Sabine &c. Roman Wives*: Porcia, daughter of Cato and wife of Brutus, wounded herself in the thigh to see if she could withstand torture. Sabine refers to the Sabine women who were forcibly carried off by the first Romans, who needed wives; when the Sabine men came after them, the women interposed themselves between the two armies and made peace between Rome and the Sabines. The Sabine women are also therefore Roman wives. This mixed catalogue – a woman's name, the name of a people, a general noun – suggests that the writer is merely showing off, pretending to learning that she does not really have.

p. 137, ll. 3–4: *Mrs. Modish's Tea-Table*: Lady Betty Modish is a character in Colley Cibber's popular play, *The Careless Husband* (1704). As her name suggests (*la mode* (French): fashion), Lady Modish is the epitome of the fashionable lady.

p. 138, ll. 18–22: our Poet *Waller* ... Lord *Spencer*: Edmund Waller (1606–87) was a court poet and panegyrist who was very friendly with the Sidneys, and often visited their country estate, Penshurst. This longstanding home of the Sidneys was celebrated by Jonson in his poem 'To Penshurst' as an ideal estate characterized by natural abundance, social order and good government. Waller was thought by some to have been in love with Lady Dorothy Sidney (1617–1684); certainly he wrote many poems to and about her under the poetic name of 'Sacharissa'. Lady Dorothy married Henry, Lord Spencer in 1639; in sad contrast to the sentiments in this letter, he was killed in battle in 1643 at the age of twenty-three.

p. 139, ll. 25–6: Lady *Mary Wortley Montague*: Lady Mary (1678–1761) eloped to marry Edward Wortley Montague, and accompanied him on his embassy to Constantinople, capital of the Ottoman empire, in 1716. The marriage did not prove as happy as she had expected. Lady Mary introduced smallpox inoculation to Britain, which she had seen in Turkey. A prolific letter writer, as well as a poet, she is perhaps best known today for her *Letters Written during her Travels*, 3 vols, published posthumously in 1763.

p. 139, ll. 29–30: the Collection lately published: *An Additional Volume to the Letters of Hon. Lady Mary Wortley Montague* (London, 1767). This volume contains several letters of doubtful attribution, including perhaps, this one. This manual contains what is in fact an abbreviation of the letter published there, which alters its meaning.

p. 139, l. 34: *Mons. Rochefoucault's*: Francois, Duc de la Rochefoucauld (1613–80) was a cynical epigrammist, whose *Reflections and Moral Maxims*, published anonymously in 1665, were widely read.

p. 146, l. 7: Judge *Hale*: Sir Mathew Hale (1609–1676) was Lord Chief Justice of England from 1671 to 1676. His *Historia placitorum coronae* was an authority on criminal law for more than a century.

p. 147, l. 10: Earl of *Stafford*: ambiguously Thomas Wentworth, first Earl of Strafford (1593–1641) or William Howard, Viscount Stafford (1593–1641). Both men were impeached for treason, shut up in the Tower, and beheaded; both were also probably innocent of the charges against them. The Earl had two wives, but no children by the first; the Viscount had a wife and six children.

p. 150, l. 10: *Ring of Gyges*: a story told in *Tully's Offices*, Book III. Gyges goes down into a pit, and finds – inside a brass horse – a corpse with a ring of gold on his finger. Having discovered that turning the ring towards his palm made him invisible, Gyges uses it in evil ways (murder and mayhem) to further his own ambitions.

p. 150, l. 11: *Cap of Fortunatus*: a wishing hat. See *The Famous and Delightful History of Fortunatus and His Two Sons*, 6th edn (1712). There were reprints throughout the century.

p. 150, l. 21: *her Brussels*: possibly her bustle.

p. 154, l. 9: *Demetrius*: It was fashionable for friends to adopt classical pseudonyms and to address each other by them in poems and letters.

p. 155, l. 4: *Adam*: Milton, *Paradise Lost*, Book V, ll. 153–9.

p. 157, l. 26–p. 158, l. 2: *With thee Conversing ... sweet: Paradise Lost*, Book IV. Adam says this to Eve before the Fall.

p. 161, l. 5: Bishop *Atterbury*: Francis Atterbury (1663–1732), Bishop of Rochester, was a Jacobite conspirator who was ultimately banished from England. Pope's letter to him in the Tower and his reply were also favourites in letter manuals.

p. 166, l. 31: *talking in Buskins*: in a tragic style.

p. 167, l. 36: Mrs. *Rowe*: Elizabeth Rowe (1674–1737) was a popular devotional writer. Her *Friendship in Death: in Twenty Letters from the Dead to the Living* (1728) went through sixty editions in the eighteenth century.

p. 168, l. 34: Mr. *Locke*: John Locke (1632–1704), secretary to Anthony Ashley Cooper, first Earl of Shaftsbury, tutor to his grandson, secretary to the Board of Trade and Plantations, and a philosopher whose works include *Essay on Toleration, Essay Concerning Human Understanding, Two Treatises on Government* and *Thoughts on Education*.

p. 168, l. 35: *Anthony Collins*: Anthony Collins (1676–1729) met Locke in 1703. Locke saw him as his intellectual successor and a close friendship developed between them. Collins was a freethinker whose *Discourse on Free Thinking* (1713) and *Essay Concerning the use of Reason in Propositions* (1707) argued that free rational thought was a universal right and a duty in religion. He arranged for some of Locke's unpublished writings to be published posthumously.

p. 169, l. 23: Earl of *Rochester*: John Wilmot (1647–1680), second Earl of Rochester, was a libertine, a poet, and a prominent courtier in Charles II's licentious court.

p. 169, l. 23: Honourable *Henry Saville*: Henry Savile (1642–87) was a close friend of Rochester's, who joined him in debauchery and scandalous escapades. He was also Groom of the Bedchamber to Charles II, and a fairly accomplished diplomat and envoy-extraordinaire.

H. W. Dilworth, *The Complete Letter Writer; or Young Secretary's Instructor* (1783)

p. 182, ll. 15–16: *by divers ships*: Writing from overseas, people numbered their letters, told their correspondents how many letters they had sent, or sent the same letter by several different ships, to ensure that letters got through and/or that both parties knew whether they had got through or not – despite ships captured or sunk by privateers, enemy ships, and storms, the Post Office's secret office which intercepted mail, and other hazards of the route.

p. 197, ll. 3–4: *the blue-coat hospital*: a charity school. Blue was the colour of the uniform children at charity schools wore.

p. 197, l. 25: *Hackney*: a village near London, with a possible play on hackney, a woman who prostitutes herself, a bawd.

p. 202, ll. 23–4: *compting house*: office; place in a business where book-keeping, correspondence, etc is done.

p. 202, ll. 36–7: *those whose money ... squandered*: The suggestion here is that the son is on the road to bankruptcy.

p. 215, l. 7: *harsh methods*: euphemism, for: he will bankrupt him to get his money if he has to.

p. 215, l. 20, *conned it*: perused, studied.

p. 216, l. 3: *a Composition*: a settling of claims and debts by a mutually agreed arrangement. This usually involved all an insolvent tradesman's creditors consulting together, and was recommended in letter manuals as the best way of preventing the domino effect of one bankruptcy causing a series of others, in a system where everyone lived on credit and was therefore indebted to ('dependent' on) everyone. There was also the hope that, by being allowed to carry on his business, the insolvent tradesman would become solvent again, and able to pay his debts. The usual method of dealing with debtors who could not pay their debts at this time was to incarcerate them in debtors' prisons.

p. 220, l. 15: *a Person's Failure*: bankruptcy. This letter and the next are about the way the bankruptcy of one tradesman puts another, to whom he owes a considerable amount of money, at risk of going bankrupt too (the domino effect discussed in the previous note). The letters show how a friend can help get the latter past the crisis, and thus prevent both his bankruptcy and others that his bankruptcy would cause.

p. 226, ll. 3–4: *Madam de Pompadour*: Jeanne Antoinette Poisson Pompadour (1721–64) was mistress to Louis XV of France from 1745 to her death. She had great influence over government and foreign policy, and turned a blind eye to Louis's peccadilloes. Hence, perhaps, the allusion to his sleeping in the arms of the daughter of an Irish shoemaker. Pompadour's successor, Madame du Barry (1743–93), was the illegitimate daughter of a French dressmaker.

p. 226, l. 21: *Prior's thief*: The scene is a hanging: 'Now fitted the halter, now travers'd the Cart/And often took leave; but was loth to depart'. From Matthew Prior, 'The Thief and the Cordelier, a Ballad' in Prior, *Poems on Several Occasions*, 2 vols (Glasgow: Robert and Andrew Foulis, 1759), vol. 2, p. 14.

p. 240, l. 17, *Letter LIII*: This and the next letters on elections were often omitted from American versions.

p. 241, l. 19: *to put up*: to offer yourself for election.

p. 253, l. 8: *rules of a prison*: areas around certain prisons where prisoners, such as debtors, were permitted to live and work without being locked up.

p. 265, l. 6: *the vapours he had put me into*: here, depression.

H. W. Dilworth, *The Complete Letter Writer, or Young Secretary's Instructor* (1793)

p. 278, l. 7: *most generous*: should read most ungenerous.

p. 278, l. 20: *prepossession*: literally, a previous possession, so the word implies that her heart is already possessed by some other man.

p. 281, l. 13: *Vauxhall*: Vauxhall Gardens at Lambeth, on the south bank of the Thames, was a favorite resort for Londoners from the seventeenth to the nineteenth centuries. Its gardens were notable for a long gravel walk hedged on either side with imposing trees, for the Lovers' Walk, and for spectacular lights, pavilions and musical entertainments.

p. 281, ll. 14–15: *Ranelagh*: another favourite resort, this time by the Thames in Kensington-Chelsea. Opened to the public in 1745, its major attractions consisted of an ornamental lake and a large Rotunda, which included an orchestra stand and booths around the walls for drinking and smoking. It was closed down in 1805.

p. 282, l. 22: *Richmond*: an area of royal palaces and parks near London. In 1731, Frederick, Prince of Wales, acquired what is now Kew (botanical) Gardens; in 1769 it had more than 3,400 plant species. Horace Walpole built his famous Gothic home, Strawberry Hill, at Richmond.

David Fordyce, *The New and Complete British Letter-Writer; or Young Secretary's Instructor in Polite Modern Letter-Writing*

p. 311, l. 3: Academy: a name used primarily by the newer 'English' schools which prepared students for commerce, trade, manufacture, surveying, estate business and such by teaching grammar and letter writing in the vernacular, arithmetic, book keeping, drawing, history and geography.

p. 311, l. 16 & l. 27: *candour*: a complex word meaning integrity, innocence, fairness, justice and frankness. It is used in the sense of justice in l. 16 and in the sense of frankness and integrity in l. 27.

p. 312, l. 29: *the Spectators*: Addison and Steele's early eighteenth-century periodical, the *Spectator*, was widely read throughout the century on both sides of the Atlantic. Half its papers consisted of letters, which were regularly recommended as models in letter manuals, and used in schools. See Eve Tavor Bannet, '"Epistolary Commerce" in *The Spectator*', in Don Newman (ed.), *Emerging Discourses in The Spectator* (Delaware: University of Delaware Press, 2005), pp. 220–47.

p. 318, l. 14, *a reserve*: capital kept on hand by a banker to meet probable demand.

p. 325, l. 7: *vend*: sell.

p. 329, l. 32: letter of licence: a document negotiated and drawn up by a bankrupt's creditors, at once determining how they are to be repaid and leaving the bankrupt at liberty to continue his business in hopes that he will earn the wherewithal to repay them in full.

p. 330, ll. 32–3: *not deprive me of that Liberty ... support*: By imprisoning him, as was their right, they would remove from him all possibility of getting back on his financial feet.

p. 331, l. 5: *unavoidable losses*: His losses were unavoidable because he was bankrupted by the bankruptcy of others. Failed and broke are euphemisms for bankrupt; 'embarrassed' suggests a person is well on his way to bankruptcy.

p. 332, ll. 32–4: *pipe ... brandy*: A pipe was a cask containing about two hogsheads or sixty-three gallons of wine; a puncheon was also a large cask – the quantity of liquor it contained varied according to the liquor; a piece suggests a smaller standard container.

p. 335, ll. 1–2: *correspondence*: commerce.

p. 335, l. 18: *a venture*: a commercial enterprise involving risk. Mariners were permitted to trade a little for themselves by buying goods at one port and selling them at another. However, this obviously required some initial capital.

p. 336, l. 23: on an exigence: in an emergency.

p. 342, l. 38: *Boston*: Boston, on the River Witham in Lincolnshire, was a small port which traded in wool and wine from the thirteenth century on. Many of the Puritans set out from there for the new world.

p. 344, l. 23: *payable at sight*: without the waiting period on bills which only became due on a particular date.

p. 345, l. 22: *broker*: factor or agent.

p. 349, l. 5: *draft on Mr. Peter Punctual*: merchants also served as bankers.

[Anon.], *The American Letter-Writer: Containing a Variety of Letters on the Most Common Occasions in Life*

p. 375, l. 9: *the State-house*: American locations replace the English ones in the copy text.

p. 375, l. 14: *Gray's gardens ... Harrowgate Concert*: not identified.

p. 380, l. 10: *the cote*: an animal shed or cottage occupied by the very poor.

p. 397, l. 3: *apply to*: devote yourself to.

p. 399, l. 7: *Chambersburg*: Chambersburg in Franklin County, Southern Pennsylvania, settled in 1730.

p. 425, l. 13: *to reference*: to arbitration.

p. 426, l. 27: *nonsuit you*: stoppage of the suit by the judge when a plaintiff fails to make his case properly.

p. 427, l. 6: *a demurrer to the plea*: A demurrer admits the facts stated by the opponent, but denies he is legally entitled to redress; so it stops the proceedings until this point is decided.

p. 427, ll. 6–7: *a joinder*: coupling of two in a suite or action.

p. 427, l. 7: *rejoinder*: the defendant's answer to the plaintiff.

p. 430, ll. 11–12: *Germantown*: Incorporated in 1689, Germantown (now part of Philadelphia) was first settled by German Pietists in 1683.

p. 432, l. 17: *look native about her*: look as though they are a natural part of her.

p. 458, l. 2: *Mr. Gay*: John Gay (1685–1732) was a playwright, poet, and friend of Swift, Pope and Steele. He is best remembered now for *The Beggar's Opera* (1728).

p. 458, l. 15: *the laurel*: emblem of victory or of distinction in poetry, worn as a crown or wreath around the head.

p. 459, l. 18: *knot*: ornament for the dress or hair.

p. 460, ll. 28–9: *Hopkins and Sternhold*: Charles Hopkins (1671?–1700) was the author of *Epistolary Poems on Several Occasions* (1694) and Thomas Sternold or Sternall (d. 1549) wrote metrical psalm paraphrases.

For Product Safety Concerns and Information please contact our EU
representative GPSR@taylorandfrancis.com
Taylor & Francis Verlag GmbH, Kaufingerstraße 24, 80331 München, Germany

www.ingramcontent.com/pod-product-compliance
Lightning Source LLC
Chambersburg PA
CBHW070928100726
47908CB00001B/137